THE POLITICAL ECONOMY
OF RESOURCE REGULATION

THE POLITICAL ECONOMY OF RESOURCE REGULATION

AN INTERNATIONAL AND COMPARATIVE HISTORY, 1850–2015

Edited by Andreas R.D. Sanders,
Pål Thonstad Sandvik, and Espen Storli

UBCPress · Vancouver · Toronto

© UBC Press 2019

All rights reserved. No part of this publication may be reproduced, stored in a retrieval system, or transmitted, in any form or by any means, without prior written permission of the publisher, or, in Canada, in the case of photocopying or other reprographic copying, a licence from Access Copyright, www.accesscopyright.ca.

27 26 25 24 23 22 21 20 19   5 4 3 2 1

Printed in Canada on FSC-certified ancient-forest-free paper (100% post-consumer recycled) that is processed chlorine- and acid-free.

ISBN 978-07748-6060-4 (hardcover)
ISBN 978-07748-6062-8 (pdf)
ISBN 978-07748-6063-5 (epub)
ISBN 978-07748-6064-2 (Kindle)

Cataloguing data is available from Library and Archives Canada.

Canadä

Printed and bound in Canada by Friesens
Set in Segoe and Warnock by Artegraphica Design Co. Ltd.
Copy editor: Joanne Richardson
Proofreader: Judith Earnshaw
Indexer: Cheryl Lemmens
Cartographer: Eric Leinberger

UBC Press
The University of British Columbia
2029 West Mall
Vancouver, BC V6T 1Z2
www.ubcpress.ca

Contents

Introduction: Natural Resource Regulations and the
Global Economy / 3

ANDREAS R.D. SANDERS, PÅL T. SANDVIK, AND ESPEN STORLI

**Part 1 Evolution of the Domestic Regulation of Natural
Resources**

1 The Australian Gold Rushes, 1850–1900:
Elites, Mineral Ownership, and Democracy / 23

ZDRAVKA BRUNKOVA AND MARTIN SHANAHAN

2 Regulation of Natural Resources in the Nordic Countries,
1880–1940 / 45

ANDREAS R.D. SANDERS, PÅL T. SANDVIK, AND ESPEN STORLI

3 Regulating Natural Resources in Canada:
A Brief Historical Survey / 67

ROBIN S. GENDRON AND ANDREAS R.D. SANDERS

4 National Oil Companies and Political Coalitions:
Venezuela and Colombia, 1910–76 / 96

MARCELO BUCHELI

5 Managing Russia's Resource Wealth: Coalitions and
Capacity / 118

STEPHEN FORTESCUE

6 Regulatory Regimes for Petroleum Production in Brazil / 139
GAIL D. TRINER

Part 2 Impact of Imperialism on Resource Policy

7 Regulating Oil Concessions in British West Africa: The Case of Nigeria and the Gold Coast during the Colonial Period / 165
JON OLAV HOVE AND JOHN KWADWO OSEI-TUTU

8 Regulating Oil in Iran and India: The Anglo-Iranian Oil Company and Burmah Oil, 1886–1953 / 186
NEVEEN ABDELREHIM AND SHRADDHA VERMA

9 "In the National Interest": Regulating New Caledonia's Mining Industry in the Late Twentieth Century / 210
ROBIN S. GENDRON

Part 3 Growing Internationalization of Resource Policy

10 Regulating the Regulators: The League of Nations and the Problem of Raw Materials / 231
MATS INGULSTAD

11 Regulating the Natural Resources in the Antarctic Region: A Historical Review / 259
BJØRN L. BASBERG

12 The Rights of Indigenous Peoples to Land and Natural Resources: The Sami in Norway / 277
HANNE HAGTVEDT VIK

13 "Europe Cannot Engage in Autarchical Policies": European Raw Materials Strategy from 1945 to the Present / 302
HANS OTTO FRØLAND AND MATS INGULSTAD

14 Mitigating Import Dependency: Japan's Energy and Mining Policies / 327
TAKEO KIKKAWA

Conclusion / 342
ANDREAS R.D. SANDERS, PÅL T. SANDVIK, AND ESPEN STORLI

Contributors / 354

Index / 356

THE POLITICAL ECONOMY
OF RESOURCE REGULATION

Introduction

Natural Resource Regulations and the Global Economy

ANDREAS R.D. SANDERS, PÅL T. SANDVIK, and ESPEN STORLI

The meek shall inherit the earth, but not its mineral rights.

– JOHN PAUL GETTY

Natural resources are the raw materials or natural assets that occur in nature and that can be used for economic production or consumption.[1] Throughout history, natural resources have always been a foundation for power and wealth. Important in war and peace alike, access to and control over natural resources is therefore a key issue for all societies. The question of access is intimately linked to the nature of these resources. As they are unevenly scattered across the globe, no state contains all the natural resources it needs within its own boundaries. Consequently, since prehistoric times, these different natural endowments have provided a key incentive for trade between and among societies. At the same time, this situation also means that the question of control is far more than a local issue. The question of who gets to exploit natural resources and under what terms has wide-ranging implications not only for the society in which the resources are found but also for all the other societies that depend on having access to those resources. Although cross-border dependence on natural resources has always existed, this became particularly significant during the nineteenth century. As industrialization and population growth generated an ever-increasing demand for raw materials, new innovations and investments in transportation and communication laid the foundations for a truly global exchange of natural resources. The scale and scope of this trade reached a new and unprecedented intensity after the breakthrough of the Second Industrial Revolution towards the end of the nineteenth century. Accordingly, the question of who should have the right to access, control, and profit from natural resources became a vital political issue.

Natural resources are natural objects for political regulation due not least to some peculiarities of raw materials in economic activity. First, just as the availability, quantity, and quality of natural resources vary greatly from place to place, so the extent to which they can be profitably exploited will also vary. Thus, if all other input factors are equal, richer natural resources will yield a higher return than will less rich natural resources. This specific profit is often referred to as scarcity rent, or *resource rent*.[2]

Second, the exploitation of natural resources is not simply a source of wealth: it can also have considerable negative externalities in terms of environmental and social impact. Many sources for raw materials are nonrenewable, which means that they are finite by their very nature. Yet, even when they are not, the exploitation of natural resources can easily be a matter of trading short-term windfalls for long-term deprivations if they are not managed in a sustainable manner. Even when exploited in a way that can be continued in perpetuity, such exploitation can still be detrimental to biodiversity and to affected populations and their way of life.

According to regulation theory,[3] as natural resources are the source not only of "market failures" (i.e., a situation in which the allocation of goods and services in a market is not efficient) such as *resource rents* but also of considerable *externalities*, they are natural subjects for political regulation. Exerting political regulation over natural resources has been a historical process, and it has been shaped by a third important feature of natural resources: over the course of the nineteenth century they have come to epitomize the interdependence of a global economy. During this time industrial economies increasingly depended on a continued supply of a complex array of natural resources from outside their own territories, without which they would have suffered and possibly ground to a halt. Thus, the regulation of natural resources both determined – and was determined by – the relationship between nations.

The primary objective of this book is to give an international historical account of the different ways natural resources have been politically regulated since the Second Industrial Revolution and how this has evolved. With

Introduction

regard to governments, since the mid-nineteenth century, both the goals and the means of regulating the exploitation of natural resources have changed substantially, as have economic realities and the demands of interest groups as well as the broader public. Moreover, the international rules and norms for what is considered to be legitimate government action have also evolved, crucially shaping the framework within which governments operate.

We believe that natural resource regulation has played a decisive role in shaping both the political economy of resource-dependent nations and the international political economy. Through a series of historical case studies, mainly of resource-rich countries but also of have-not countries, spanning all seven continents, we discuss how, over time, different ideas, interest groups, international institutions, and political configurations have created different regulatory regimes in different countries. Our aim is to provide an international and comparative history of natural resource politics, something that has too often been confined to more narrow national perspectives or that is simply missing from current discussions on natural resource regulations.

Resource Nationalism and Democracy: A Short History of Resource Regulation

Both for their strategic and their economic value, control over the gifts of nature has been of key political importance. Throughout history, minerals, rivers, and often land itself have frequently been the legal domain of kings and nobles. In the liberal era of the mid-nineteenth century, or what Eric Hobsbawm dubbed the "Age of Capital," private ownership and control over natural resources was to a large extent recognized. The retreat from the idea of a state prerogative over natural resources was never total, yet most states either had adopted, or were forced to adopt, liberal principles or practice regarding natural resource ownership. Taxation and royalties were usually light and private investors – both foreign and domestic – were in most cases free to exploit resources as they pleased and retain any profits they might gain from the venture. This brief apex of laissez-faire forms the starting point of this book.

From this point on, this consensus of economic liberalism in dealing with natural resources would be challenged primarily from the rising force of three partially related developments. The first was the general tendency of increasing state power. State capacity – and ambitions – for intervention in the economy and regulation increased. However, one should note that this development took place at very different points of time and in varying ways around the world. In some countries, as in Scandinavia, the rise of the modern regulatory or interventionist state was well under way by 1900; in other parts of the world it happened in the wake of the world wars, the depression, or decolonization; in quite a few countries, an efficient state apparatus is yet to be developed.

Rising state interventionism in the economy was often intertwined with the emergence of protectionist economic nationalism, which appeared – or reappeared – in the latter part of the nineteenth century. As many states saw fit to break with free trade and protect their own industrial and agricultural production, the liberal policy on natural resources was also questioned. Within several raw material-exporting countries, economic nationalists spoke in favour of rent-capture policies that would secure a greater share of the profits generated by natural resource extraction. These policies included reserving valuable natural resources for domestically owned companies, or introducing export duties or other limitations, to capture downstream processing within the country's borders. Economic development was not the only issue at stake: policy makers also feared that foreign political dominance could follow in the wake of foreign investments in resource industries.

The third major force challenging a laissez-faire world order and attitude towards natural resources was the rise of democracy. As suffrage spread to the middle and lower strata of society, the justice of private individuals and companies reaping monopoly rents from natural resources, which were provided as much by providence as by human toil, came into question. For governments, retaining a share of profits from natural resources was not only a question of principle but also of practicality as public expenditure rose to provide an increasing level of welfare to its citizens. In the interwar years, economic liberalism was also challenged by the rise of fascist and communist governments in various parts of the world.

The rise of the interventionist state, resource nationalism, and democratization were all prevalent in the decolonization process in the decades after the Second World War. Millions of formerly colonized people gained new political rights. At the same time, newly independent resource-exporting states had to prove both their sovereignty and their viability. This meant that the existing political economy was increasingly challenged. As it had been for many resource-rich countries before them, the regulation of natural resources became a central political issue, and a vital feature of state building.

The rise of state power, resource nationalism, and democracy in raw material-dependent countries did not unfold in a vacuum but, rather, was

Introduction

played out against and shaped by the interests of the raw material consumers. Nor was this a stable relationship: it was determined both by the changes in the international political economy and by the fluctuating prices of raw materials. Several resource-importing states also at times introduced autarkic policies to substitute cheaper foreign-produced raw materials for domestic-produced ones, thus reducing demand for internationally traded raw materials.

The price fluctuations were often increased by Malthusian assumptions that natural resources were likely to increase in value as their extraction passed its "peak" level, only to have prices plummet when demand subsided or when supply proved to be more elastic than the market had anticipated. Technological change also played a key role in altering the value of natural resources as some key resources were rendered almost worthless while previously worthless resources became economically viable.

All these forces were decisive in shaping the regulatory institutions of natural resource-rich countries. While also altering the regulatory regimes within countries, the conflicts and deal-making over natural resources also helped to shape international law and the norms for what were considered legitimate actions on the part of governments of resource-rich countries. In the liberal and imperial era before the First World War, private concessions and/or ownership of natural resources were almost universally protected, and few governments attempted to force through renegotiations of concessions or the nationalization of resources.[4] However, following the nationalization of privately owned resources in the Soviet Union during the First World War, and in Mexico and Bolivia in the late 1930s, the decolonization process after the Second World War led to the passing of UN resolution 1803 in 1962, which established "permanent sovereignty over natural resources."[5] This controversial resolution gave all states the right to fully control all natural wealth on their territory, including the right to nationalize existing private operations, with "appropriate compensation in accordance with the rules in force in the State taking such measures."[6] Building on this principle, special rights over natural resources were not only extended to states but also, increasingly, to Indigenous peoples within states, culminating with the UN General Assembly passing the Declaration on the Rights of Indigenous Peoples in 2007.[7]

With a bird's-eye view of the development of natural resource regulations since the mid-nineteenth century, we can divide this history into four distinct periods. First, the era before the First World War was characterized by a liberal practice in most independent states as well as by a forced liberalism in the European empires. However, some independent resource-rich countries moved towards a more interventionist policy before the outbreak of the Great War. The second period, between the outbreak of the First World War and the end of the Second World War (1914–45), was characterized by increased resource nationalism in raw material-exporting countries as well as by a stark realization among resource-importing states that they were dependent on foreign supplies, which led to different degrees of autarky or imperial preference systems. The third period (c. 1945–c. 1980) was dominated by the great wave of decolonization and the subsequent nationalization and other rent-capture measures carried out by these new states in the natural resource sectors. Restrictions on international capital movements also reduced the flow of foreign direct investments into resource extraction.

After 1980, a more libertarian international regime developed. The commodity markets collapsed in the early 1980s and several developing countries experienced severe debt problems. As state-led policies lost much of their former political support, private and multinational companies gained more important roles in the raw materials industry. However, this reliberalization was fundamentally different from what occurred in the period before the First World War in that there was a broad consensus that high resource rents belonged to the host country and that taxation of natural resources was overall much higher than it had been in the first two periods. The first decade of the twenty-first century also saw a resurgence of resource nationalism, most notably in Venezuela, Argentina, and Bolivia.

Institutions and the "Resource Curse": Theories of Resource Regulation

The economic and societal impact of natural resources has long been a key issue in economics, especially since the birth of modern development economics. In the 1950s, mainstream development economists suggested that natural resource abundance in underdeveloped countries was a major boon as raw material-exporting states were better situated to overcome the shortage of capital required for economic development.[8] However, this position was heavily criticized, particularly by structuralist and Marxist economists. This critique formed the foundation of the so-called *dependencia* school, popularized in the 1960s and 1970s,[9] as well as the Canadian "staple trap" thesis and,[10] later, "world-systems theory."[11]

The main source of criticism was that raw material exports did not bring enough revenue, particularly in the long run, and that they did not induce the development of manufacturing. In other words, liberal structuralists,

Introduction 9

most prominently Albert O. Hirschman, suggested that the mainstream development theory's idea of raw material exports as a source of capital would be undermined if foreign companies were allowed to repatriate profits from raw material enclaves, creating few forward and backward linkages in the economy. Thus, a government needed to establish a system that captured rents from natural resources in order to increase the economic ripple effects of these industries.[12] The more radical structuralists claimed that increasing linkages was not enough to break dependency and, instead, favoured the complete nationalization of natural resource industries. Furthermore, Raúl Prebisch and Hans Singer famously formulated a hypothesis that the price of raw materials declined in relation to industrial goods in the long run and that raw material exports for world markets was an inferior path to economic development.[13] Thus, developing countries would be better off by attempting to industrialize through import-substitution. However, these ideas were not simply a product of the postwar era; rather, they resonated with concerns frequently voiced within independent raw material-exporting countries since the end of the nineteenth century.[14]

Despite the fact that many producer countries took a greater share of revenue from raw material exports, the economic performance of resource-abundant countries remained at best mixed. Some resource-rich countries (such as Canada, Australia, and Norway) can now be found among the most affluent, while other resource-rich countries have failed to build on their natural wealth and have remained poorer than their less resource-rich neighbours. Towards the latter quarter of the twentieth century, the theories that raw material exports were a poor strategy due to their low long-term return fell out of favour and were replaced by new theories that natural resources were actually a curse to development rather than a blessing. This debate on a "resource curse" was particularly invigorated by a highly influential econometric study by Jeffrey Sachs and Andrew Warner,[15] which showed that, between 1971 and 1989, countries with high raw material exports had overall experienced slower economic growth than had countries without these exports.[16] A common denominator of these new hypotheses of a resource curse was that the lack of resource rent flowing into the host economy was no longer the problem. On the contrary, instead of natural resources acting as a source of much needed capital, the large income stemming from them was blamed for causing "Dutch disease"[17] – irresponsible pro-cyclical government overspending and the bankrolling of inefficient import-substitution schemes. More dramatically, the existence of valuable resources and large resource rent income was claimed to increase political corruption, rent seeking, and the likelihood of political instability and armed conflict.[18]

While the existence of a resource curse is sometimes treated as an undisputed fact, some scholars question it, pointing both to historical examples and to alternative interpretations of data.[19] In recent years, a number of scholars have tempered the idea of an outright resource curse and instead adopted the idea that natural resource riches are a mixed blessing, the problems of which can be overcome if they are properly handled, and especially highlighting the importance to the quality of institutions within resource-rich states.[20]

Several scholars have, however, suggested that institutions within resource-rich countries were particularly corroded by resource nationalist policies.[21] In other words, interventionist policies meant to alleviate the "low-income" concerns of natural resource-dependent development might have helped fuel the resource curse. Several states that introduced rent-capture policies did so through nationalization or forced contract negotiations, thus sidelining liberal conceptions of property and contract rights – the very institutions often highlighted as prerequisites for sustained economic growth.[22] It has been suggested that the negative effects of this manifest themselves in several ways. First, the lack of respect for property rights in the natural resource sectors will lead to lack of respect for property rights in the rest of the economy, thus undermining effective checks on the executive.[23] Second, anticipation of future expropriation might lead extractive industries to increase their output of non-renewable resources in order to secure a return on their investments.[24] Third, expropriation or forced contract renegotiations may scare future investors away from the resource sector, possibly leaving the resource-rich state without the capital or knowledge necessary to utilize its resources in the most efficient way and thus, in the long run, leading to a decline in all sectors.[25]

How to strike a balance between property rights and resource nationalist and redistributive policies has been a recurring dilemma for resource-rich countries throughout modern history. The frequent swings between resource nationalism and investor friendly policies in raw material-exporting countries have led some analysts to describe it as an almost inevitably cyclical phenomenon.[26] By bringing the historical experiences of less successful regulatory regimes together with more successful ones, we explore how some resource-rich countries managed to combine stability and predictability in the resource sector with popular legitimacy. Ultimately, in order to be stable

Introduction 11

and successful, a regulatory regime needs to obtain legitimacy, which again is based on its ability to provide what the public thinks it ought to provide in terms of economic growth, employment, accountability, environmental protection, national control, and wealth redistribution.

The focus of our book is not on measuring the economic performance of regulatory regimes and institutions but, rather, on investigating their origins and transformation. Through a historical approach, we seek to bring forth the multitude of actors who moulded the various regulatory regimes and to examine how they handled political processes and pre-existing legal principles in order to shape the political economy of nations. In doing so, we are able not only to highlight new aspects of institutional development but also to paint a broader account of how the politics of natural resources have evolved in the modern world.

The Political Economy of Resource Regulation: A Global History, 1850–2015

This text is divided into three main parts: the first part explores the evolution of the domestic regulation of natural resources. Three chapters analyze the development in Australia, the Nordic countries, and Canada, respectively. All these countries were able to generate substantial economic growth and were among the world's most affluent countries in the early twentieth century. The chapters show that there were some notable differences between these countries with regard to how they managed their resource endowments, but they were generally able to find ways of exploiting their natural resources that fostered growth and benefitted large parts of their populations. The next three chapters discuss the regulatory policies in countries in which outcomes were more mixed. Venezuela, Colombia, Russia, and Brazil were less able to convert their resource endowments into lasting economic advantage. The explanations for this are highly context-specific, but they typically involve limited state capacity, regulatory capture, flawed policies, and/or a dependence on foreign markets and companies that was so strong that it thwarted effective domestic regulation.

The second part of the anthology examines the impact of imperialism on resource policy. These chapters investigate the resource policies in Nigeria and the Gold Coast, Iran and India, and New Caledonia. They all show that resource policies were potentially very contentious. Policy formation and outcomes were strikingly different, depending on metropolitan strategic and economic interests, local political cultures, and the level of resource rent.

The third part of the anthology charts the growing internationalization of resource regulation. This happened in a multitude of ways. The first three chapters in this section explore the League of Nations' attempts to establish an international framework for resource policies, the evolution of the Antarctic Treaties, and how international treaties influenced Norwegian legislation on Sami customary rights to natural resources. The last two chapters explore the internationalization of resource policy from a different perspective – namely, how resource-poor Japan and the EEC/EU have tried to limit the disadvantages caused by their import dependency and how they have endeavoured to influence the global political economy of natural resources.

Chapter 1, by Zdravka Brunkova and Martin Shanahan, explores the regulation of the goldfields in Australia during the gold rushes between 1850 and 1900. Initially, access to the goldfields was controlled by pastoral elites; however, faced with intense pressure from gold diggers, authorities developed more open and inclusive resource policies and embarked on democratic reforms. Brunkova and Shanahan state that democratic processes were an outcome of the gold rushes, not a precursor to them. Australia thus provides an intriguing antithesis to the old current in Western thought that idealizes pastoral harmony in contrast to the vices and social degradation that often follow in the wake of the discovery of gold.

In Chapter 2, Sanders, Sandvik, and Storli chart the development of resource regulation in the Nordic countries between 1890 and 1940. Natural resources played an important role in the Nordic economies. State regulation enjoyed high legitimacy, and the public had a strong belief in the benevolent potential of state intervention, probably more so than was the case in North America. While interest groups certainly tried to influence resource policies, there were few outright examples of regulatory capture. Sanders, Sandvik, and Storli identify four main objectives of Nordic resource policies: (1) domestic ownership of natural resources; (2) the establishment of regulations that would generate economic growth; (3) ensuring that natural resources benefited or would be accessible to large parts of the population; and, last but not least, (4) respect for private property rights.

In Chapter 3, Gendron and Sanders give a brief historical survey of another Western country whose economy has been and, to a large extent, still is dependent on natural resources. Throughout Canada's history, resource policies have always been a contentious issue, dominated by the recurring question of resource-rich states – namely, how the benefits and drawbacks of natural resources industries should best be shared. In Canada, these questions have been shaped by competing visions of how best to deal with the

Introduction 13

nation's role as a natural resource exporter to its powerful southern neighbour. Views on this have often differed between and among Canada's provinces and its federal government. In recent years, the most ambitious strains of Canadian resource nationalism have declined as the country has entered into new comprehensive multinational trade agreements. Yet past controversies have given way to new as both environmentalism and First Nations rights have become increasingly prominent in Canadian resource policy.

In Chapter 4, Marcelo Bucheli compares oil policies in Venezuela and Colombia. He links the development of oil policy and, more specifically, the distribution of rents to the political basis of the countries' governments. If the regime's survival depended on the loyalty of a small coalition, the rents were distributed as a private good among the members of that coalition. Conversely, regimes whose survival depended on large coalitions tended to distribute the oil rents as a public good. He also explains the decision to create national oil companies by referring to the strategies followed by a regime to ensure the loyalty of its supporting coalition. Regulatory capture was, in other words, not an unfortunate by-product but, rather, the main aim of the governments' resource policies.

In Chapter 5, Stephen Fortescue discusses Russia's petroleum policies in the Yeltsin and Putin eras. He charts the development from the privatization of the oil industries and the rise of the so-called oligarchs in the 1990s to the re-emergence of effective state control in the early 2000s. The government has tried to strike a balance between what can be called a small coalition- and a large coalition-strategy. Most of the oligarchs have been allowed to continue their operations, but the state has secured more of the resource rents. Fortescue analyzes the debates on how to alter the tax system in order to increase state revenue and to attract new investments. The latter has been especially important as most of Russia's production comes from mature fields. Fortescue maintains that the technocratic element in Russian decision making and resource management is stronger than is often acknowledged in the West.

In Chapter 6, Gail Triner describes how Brazil has moved from strong resource nationalism in the mid-twentieth century to a more open and market-based system. She focuses on the regulation of access and activities in the petroleum industry. The scope for international investments and ownership has increased significantly, but preferences for domestic and, especially, state ownership remain. Triner concludes that recent governance reforms have changed the actors and permissible actions without mitigating the deeply entrenched ambitions that originally governed the structure of the sector: energy security, sophisticated industrialization, national control of the industry, and public-sector financial gains.

The second part of the book explores the colonial/imperial legacies of resource policies. In Chapter 7, Jon Olav Hove and John Kwadwo Osei-Tutu analyze the concession policies in the colonial era in Nigeria and the Gold Coast. They show that colonial authorities sought to adapt the exploration policies to local socio-political and economic conditions. In the Gold Coast, the government was unwilling to revise existing regulations because of fears of local unrest. In Nigeria, the regulations were to some extent tailored to local interests, but the end result came to favour the interests of the oil companies. Hove and Osei-Tutu state that it is misleading to generalize about a monolithic colonial experience – something that is inherent in many accounts of imperial development policy. Whereas the British Empire may be seen as an imposing unit, the reality was that its component parts exercised large degrees of autonomy. This was also the case in the oil sector.

Regulation of oil was never a purely domestic issue. This general point is clearly demonstrated in Chapter 8 by Neveen Abdelrehim and Shraddha Verma in their discussion of oil policy in Iran and India in the first half of the twentieth century. The two countries were very differently situated with regard to oil: Iran was one of the largest producers in the world while India had limited oil resources. Politically, both were firmly placed within the British sphere of influence. In addition, in both countries the oil industry was dominated by British companies. In Iran an acrimonious conflict developed between the British-owned Anglo-Iranian Oil Company and the country's government, leading to nationalization, a coup, and reprivatization between 1951 and 1953. India avoided these violent ruptures: the post-independence government recognized that it had a weak negotiating hand and only cautiously sought to push foreign-owned oil companies to invest in refining capacity. The trajectories caused by oil and imperialism were thus very different in these two countries, as they were in Nigeria and the Gold Coast/Ghana.

Nickel is the key natural resource in French-ruled New Caledonia in the Southwest Pacific. Most of the nickel was originally controlled by a single French firm, the Société Le Nickel (SLN). In Chapter 9, Robin Gendron examines how the company's dominance and the question of foreign access became a burning political issue in the 1950s and 1960s. He states that many Caledonians viewed foreign investment as a potentially liberating force. It could help diversify and modernize the territory's economy, break SLN's power, and increase local self-government. Caledonians differed in this

Introduction

respect from the general pattern established after the Second World War, when peoples and governments in the Global South resisted the incursions of multinational companies into their national economies. Yet New Caledonia also differed from most other colonial territories and developing countries in that, instead of gaining regulatory powers, its degree of self-governance was actually reduced as France sought to maintain its grip on the archipelago's nickel reserves.

The third part of the book discusses the different ways in which resource regulation has been internationalized. In Chapter 10, Mats Ingulstad investigates the interwar attempts to develop an international regime for raw materials through the League of Nations. The League's efforts marked a new departure in international regulation. It embodied a new set of norms and rules for the behaviour of states in international relations, and it had an internationalized civil service to monitor and encourage developments. While the League ultimately proved unsuccessful in its attempts to solve the international raw materials problem, Ingulstad emphasizes that many of the ideas resurfaced in the postwar world in the UN system. The main difference between the League's and the UN's approaches to natural resources was related to the Third World. The UN system became the vehicle for a new and radical idea: the Principle of Permanent Sovereignty over Natural Resources. This principle, which was adopted by the UN in 1962, vested the regulatory power over natural resources in the territorial states that had the resources within their borders.

In Chapter 11, Bjørn Basberg charts the development of resource regulation in the Antarctic. The regulatory history of the Antarctic started with British attempts at regulating whaling before the First World War, followed by an international agreement under the auspices of the League of Nations in 1931 and the establishment of the International Whaling Commission in 1946. However, the regulations proved insufficient, failing to protect large stocks of whales from extermination. The international agreements, beginning with the Antarctic Treaty in 1959, are more successful examples of international regulation. A series of international treaties are now in force covering mining, fishing, bioprospecting, and other activities in the Antarctic.

In Chapter 12, Hanne Hagtvedt Vik examines the development of an international normative regime concerning the rights of Indigenous peoples and its impact on the Sami in Norway. She argues that internationalization was crucial to Norway's recognition of Sami collective rights to land and natural resources. Norway's Sami policies started to change in the 1940s and 1950s when human rights norms were being formulated on European and indeed global levels. In the 1980s, the UN and the International Labour Organization developed modern norms for the rights of Indigenous peoples. Vik documents that, since then, international norms have directly affected the negotiations over Sami rights to land and natural resources.

Chapter 13, on European raw materials diplomacy, investigates the internationalization of resource policy from a different angle – namely, from the perspective of import-dependent countries. Hans Otto Frøland and Mats Ingulstad show that, after 1945, there is a long history of collective European action to deal with challenges to the supply of natural resources, especially in times of scarcity and supply risks. They point out that, when the sun set on the European empires, a new set of relationships had to be forged with the Global South to keep the raw materials flowing. The Western European states embraced what they call resource intraregionalism through the formation of the European Coal and Steel Community, then entered a long phase of resource interregionalism embedded in the European Economic Community's relations with former colonies, before transitioning to a post-Uruguay strategy of resource multilateralism to ensure that European industries receive access to necessary input factors from around the world.

Japan has been even more dependent on imports of raw materials than Western Europe. It has therefore been a key Japanese aim to reduce the country's import dependency on vital raw materials and to increase its supply security. In Chapter 14, Takeo Kikkawa shows that Japan's policies include exploration for new resources, development of alternative sources of energy, conservation, stockpiling and foreign policy programs, as well as government support for Japanese investments in overseas resource industries. As in the case of the Western European countries, Japan's efforts have had both a domestic and an international impact. It has affected not just the demand for natural resources but also the development of the countries exporting raw materials.

The Conclusion draws on empirical case studies to highlight several of their most important lessons. It indicates where further research is needed.

Notes

1 Definition taken from OECD, "Glossary of Statistical Terms," at https://stats.oecd.org/glossary/detail.asp?ID=1740 (OECD website).
2 This concept of scarcity rent was first formulated in David Ricardo, *On the Principles of Political Economy and Taxation*, 3rd ed. (London: John Murray, 1821), at http://www.econlib.org/library/Ricardo/ricP.html (Library of Economics and Liberty website).

Introduction 17

3 Lars Magnusson and Jan Ottosson, "Private Actors, Policy Regulation and the Role of History: An Introduction," in *The State, Regulation and the Economy: An Historical Perspective*, ed. Lars Magnusson and Jan Ottosson (Cheltenham and Northampton, MA: Edward Elgar, 2001), 1–4.

4 Charles Lipson, *Standing Guard: Protecting Foreign Capital in the Nineteenth and Twentieth Century* (Berkeley: University of California Press, 1985), 37–64.

5 Nico Schrijver, *Sovereignty over Natural Resources: Balancing Rights and Duties* (Cambridge and New York: Cambridge University Press, 1997).

6 UN, General Assembly resolution 1803, Permanent Sovereignty over Natural Resources, 1962, §4.

7 UN, General Assembly resolution 61/295, UN Declaration on the Rights of Indigenous Peoples, 2007.

8 See, for instance: Jacob Viner, *International Trade and Economic Development* (Glencoe, IL: Free Press, 1952); W. Arthur Lewis, *The Theory of Economic Growth* (London: Allen and Unwin, 1955); W.W. Rostow, *The Stages of Economic Growth: A Non-Communist Manifesto* (Cambridge: Cambridge University Press, 1960).

9 The most influential English language books are Andre Gunder Frank, *Capitalism and Underdevelopment in Latin America: Historical Studies of Chile and Brazil* (New York: Monthly Review Press, 1969); and Fernando Henrique Cardoso and Enzo Faletto, *Dependency and Development in Latin America* (Berkeley: University of California Press, 1979). For an overview, see Tulio Halperin-Donghi, "'Dependency Theory' and Latin American Historiography," *Latin American Research Review* 17, 1 (1982): 115–30.

10 The "staple-trap" thesis is a more pessimistic version of the "staple thesis," first developed by Harold Innis and W.A. Mackintosh. The "staple trap" was a particularly popular subject in the 1970s and 1980s. Some important works include Gary Teeple, *Capitalism and the National Question in Canada* (Toronto: University of Toronto Press, 1972); Mel Watkins, "The Staple Theory Revisited," *Journal of Canadian Studies* 12 (1977): 83–94; Glen Williams, *Not for Export: Toward a Political Economy of Canada's Arrested Development* (Toronto: McClelland and Stewart, 1983).

11 World-systems theory was originally devised in the works of Immanuel Wallerstein. See Immanuel Wallerstein, *The Modern World-System*, vol. 1, *Capitalist Agriculture and the Origins of the European World-Economy in the Sixteenth Century* (New York and London: Academic Press, 1974).

12 Albert O. Hirschman, *The Strategy of Economic Development* (New Haven: Yale University Press, 1958).

13 Raúl Prebisch, *The Economic Development of Latin America and Its Principal Problems*, United Nations Document (Lake Success, NY: UN Deptartment of Economic Affairs, 1950); H.W. Singer, "The Distribution of Gains between Investing and Borrowing Countries," *American Economic Review* 40, 2 (1950): 473–85.

14 See, for example, the debates on natural resources and development in Sweden, Norway, and Canada: Bo Jonsson, *Staten och malmfälten: En studie i svensk malmfältspolitik omkring sekelskiftet* (Stockholm: Almqvist and Wiksell, 1969); Andreas R.D. Sanders and Pål T. Sandvik, "Avoiding the Resource Curse? Democracy and

Natural Resources in Norway since 1900," in *Natural Resources and Economic Growth: Learning from History*, ed. Marc Badia-Miró, Vincente Pinilla, and Henry Willebald (London and New York: Routledge, 2015), 313–38; H.V. Nelles, *The Politics of Development: Forests, Mines and Hydro-electric Power in Ontario, 1849–1941*, 2nd ed. (Montreal and Kingston: McGill-Queen's University Press, 2005).

15 The term was originally coined in Richard M. Auty, *Sustaining Development in Mineral Economies: The Resource Curse Thesis* (London and New York: Routledge, 1993).

16 Jeffrey D. Sachs and Andrew M. Warner, "Natural Resource Abundance and Economic Growth," *NBER Working Paper*, No. 5398 (Cambridge, MA: National Bureau of Economic Research, 1995).

17 The term "Dutch disease" was coined by the *Economist* in 1977 when describing the negative effects of the exploitation of the Groningen gas field upon the Dutch manufacturing industry. This theory stipulated that commodity booms hurt other export-oriented sectors of the economy, both by outcompeting them for labour and investments and through an appreciation of the currency that was likely to follow from a commodity boom.

18 For an overview of the debate on the resource curse, see Jeffrey Frankel, "The Natural Resource Curse: A Survey," in *Beyond the Resource Curse*, ed. Brenda Shaffer and Taleh Ziyadov (Philadelphia: University of Pennsylvania Press, 2012), 17–57; Michael L. Ross, "What Have We Learned about the Resource Curse?" (Los Angeles: UCLA Political Science, 2014); Erika Weinthal and Pauline Jones Luong, "Combating the Resource Curse: An Alternative Solution to Managing Mineral Wealth," *Perspectives on Politics* 4, 1 (2006): 35–53.

19 Galvin Wright and Jesse Czelusta, "The Myth of the Resource Curse," *Challenge* 47, 2 (2004): 6–38; Daniel Lederman and William F. Maloney, "Trade Structure and Growth," in *Natural Resources: Neither Curse nor Destiny*, ed. Daniel Lederman and William F. Maloney (Palo Alto and Washington, DC: Stanford University Press and The World Bank, 2007), 15–40; Galvin Wright and Jesse Czelusta, "Resource-Based Growth Past and Present," in Lederman and Maloney, *Natural Resources*, 183–212.

20 See James A. Robinson, Ragnar Torvik, and Thierry Verdier, "Political Foundations of the Resource Curse," *Journal of Development Economics* 79, 2 (2006): 447–68; Halvor Mehlum, Karl Moene, and Ragnar Torvik, "Institutions and the Resource Curse," *Economic Journal* 116 (2006): 1–20; Anne D. Boschini, Jan Pettersson, and Jesper Roine, "Resource Curse or Not: A Question of Appropriability," *Scandinavian Journal of Economics* 109, 3 (2007): 593–617; Henry Willebald, Marc Badia-Miró, and Vincente Pinilla, "Natural Resources and Economic Development: What Can We Learn from History?," in *Natural Resources and Economic Growth: Learning from History*, ed. Marc Badia-Miró, Vincente Pinilla, and Henry Willebald (London and New York: Routledge, 2015), 1–25. A more all-encompassing deliberation on the crucial role of institutions for economic and political development has been popularized in Daron Acemoglu and James A. Robinson, *Why Nations Fail: The Origins of Power, Prosperity, and Poverty* (New York: Crown Publishers, 2012).

Introduction 19

21 Nathan M. Jensen and Noel P. Johnston, "Political Risk, Reputation, and the Resource Curse," *Comparative Political Studies* 44, 6 (2011): 662–88; Michael L. Ross, *The Oil Curse: How Petroleum Wealth Shapes the Development of Nations* (Princeton and Oxford: Princeton Univesity Press, 2012).

22 Dani Rodrik, "Institutions for High Quality Growth: What They Are and How to Acquire Them," *NBER Working Paper,* No. 7540 (Cambridge, MA: National Bureau of Economic Research, 2000); Daron Acemoglu, Simon Johnson, and James A. Robinson, "The Colonial Origins of Comparative Development: An Empirical Investigation," *American Economic Review* 91, 5 (2001): 1369–401.

23 Jensen and Johnston, "Political Risk, Reputation, and the Resource Curse."

24 Henning Bohn and Robert Deacon, "Ownership Risk, Investment, and the Use of Natural Resources," *American Economic Review* 90 (2000): 526–49.

25 George Joffé, Paul Stevens, Tony George, Jonathan Lux, and Carol Searle, "Expropriation of Oil and Gas Investments: Historical, Legal and Economic Perspectives in an Age of Resource Nationalism," *Journal of World Energy Law and Business* 2, 1 (2009): 3–23; Jensen and Johnston, "Political Risk, Reputation, and the Resource Curse."

26 Paul Stevens, "National Oil Companies and International Oil Companies in the Middle East: Under the Shadow of Government and the Resource Nationalism Cycle," *Journal of World Energy Law and Business* 1, 1 (2008): 5–30.

PART 1

EVOLUTION OF THE DOMESTIC REGULATION OF NATURAL RESOURCES

1
The Australian Gold Rushes, 1850–1900

Elites, Mineral Ownership, and Democracy

ZDRAVKA BRUNKOVA and MARTIN SHANAHAN

The discovery of gold in Australia in 1851 transformed the nation.[1] The rush that followed saw the population treble in less than a decade. This provided the critical mass of people necessary to establish a sustainable economy. Gold was also one of a range of natural resources that helped establish, and maintain, the country's standard of living.

The regulations controlling resource exploitation are critical to the development of an economy. A New World country has the advantage that these regulations may be determined as much by need and practical imperatives as by vested interest groups or centuries of tradition. In the case of Australia, the regulations that arose to control the gold rushes of the 1850s proved to be critical to the subsequent decades of mineral regulation and development as well as providing the economic basis for universal male suffrage. They thus serve as an important case study for this volume, the purpose of which is to explore the implications of resource regulations in the global economy.

Acemoglu and Robinson have argued that the quality of political institutions is critical in explaining why some countries are cursed by their resource endowments: those with high-quality institutions will benefit most from their resources. They suggest that even small differences in institutions may explain divergent growth paths. Australia, with six separate colonies, provides the basis for making a natural experiment of this idea.[2]

For the first fifty years of gold's discovery and exploitation, Australia, as a nation, did not exist. It was a collection of six independently founded colonies with separate administrations, governed by British-appointed administrators and local pastoral elites who dominated law making and administration. It was not until 1901 that these colonies joined into a single federation of states under a national government. Differences in the responses of political elites to rapid change in their local populace, and variation in their efforts to control rights to gold, provide insights into Acemoglu and Robinson's argument and the link between rent-seeking, resource access, and democratic institutions.[3]

In this chapter six case studies examine whether democratic institutions preceded more equally distributed rights to mineral ownership and facilitated more diverse exploitation of resources. It also addresses the effect of small social variations on subsequent resource regulation. The experiences of each colony reveal that the rate of population change and the dominance of pastoral interests were important in shaping their responses. Democratic processes were an outcome of the gold rushes, not a precursor. Mineral regulations that were conceded under the tide of gold-seeking immigrants were embedded once democratic processes had been achieved.

Gold in Nineteenth-Century Australia

Gold was a critical factor that, by 1870, had helped propel Australia to the highest living standards in the world. While the reasons for Australian prosperity were more complex than this, the discovery of gold had a profound effect on the economy.[4]

After the Californian discoveries in 1848, the 1851 announcement of gold in New South Wales (NSW) sparked a wave of prospectors. Within weeks, much larger discoveries were made in Victoria (Vic). Not only did several of the finds sustain years of development, additional discoveries around the country continued the "rush to be rich" over decades.[5] After the discoveries in the early 1850s, significant discoveries were made in Queensland (Qld) in the 1860s and 1870s, and in Western Australia (WA) in the 1890s. There were finds of other minerals in the other colonies. The export of gold was sustained. After the initial rush saw a high of 3 million fine ounces per annum exported in the 1850s, by the 1860s it was still at 2.5 million ounces and in the 1890s it was again at 3 million per annum.[6]

Besides gold, the significant change was people. The impact of gold on the population is shown in Figure 1.1. From a penal colony of 350 people in NSW in 1788, the population grew to 375,000 Europeans in Australia by

FIGURE 1.1
Colonial populations in Australia, 1825–1900

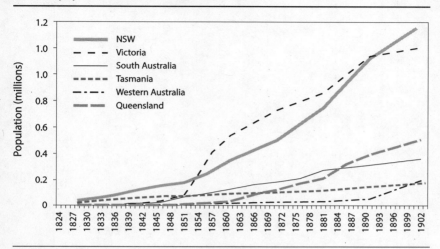

Source: W. Vamplew, ed., *Australians, Historical Statistics* (Broadway, NSW: Farifax, Syme & Weldon Associates, 1987), Chapter 3.

1850 to 1.1 million by 1861. By 1900 it was 3.7 million.[7] This massive increase in population and subsequent economic development was not equally shared by the colonies, nor were their historical circumstances identical. While each colony had similar legal and political structures and English heritages, the political elites formed in different circumstances and held different attitudes towards controlling resources (especially land), allocating opportunities, and governance. NSW, for example, saw itself as the jurisdictional hub, while Tasmania (Tas) and Qld began as penal "outposts." Victoria was created by free settlers from NSW while South Australia (SA) and Western Australia (WA) were freely settled.

Each colony faced different challenges as a result of the gold rushes. Access to gold and the rules around mineral exploitation were largely determined by the existing dominant rural interests, and, as a result, the regulatory outcomes varied between the colonies. Each colony is briefly reviewed in what follows.

The Colonies

New South Wales
New South Wales was the first colony with significant gold discoveries, and

TABLE 1.1

Selected Australian colonial mineral discoveries, exports, and legislation, 1849–1900

Colony	Gold	Other significant minerals	Decades pertaining to exports*	Minerals as % of exports	Wool as % of exports	Government leasehold adopted	Land selector bill	Tax
NSW	1849	Copper (1844); tin (1872); silver, lead zinc (1882)	1861–71 1871–81 1881–91 1891–1901	36 23 20 15	28 31 45 38	1851	1861	Gold royalty 3%; licence fee
VIC	1851		1861–71 1871–81 1881–91 1891–1901	56 29 21 25	23 30 33 26	1851	1862	Lease fee; export duty; royalty on non-gold minerals
QLD	1858	Tin (1872); copper (1879)	1861–71 1871–81 1881–91 1891–1901	31 39 34 28	72 39 41 35	1860 and 1872	1868	Leasing rent; royalty on coal
TAS	1852	Tin (1871); silver, lead (1885); copper, zinc (1893)	1861–71 1871–81 1881–91 1891–1901	1 27 34 46	42 38 26 18	1852 and 1859	1858	Royalty on coal

SA	1846	Lead (1841); copper (1842); iron ore (1900–)	1861–71	25	36	1877	1869 and 1872	Royalty of 6.3% dropped in 1851; returned at 2.5% in 1890s
			1871–81	13	37			
			1881–91	6	26			
			1891–1901	4	16			
WA	1882	Tin (1888)	1861–71	7	51	1887	1896	No royalty or licence fee
			1871–81	6	47			
			1881–91	13	45			
			1891–1901	59	18			

* Mineral and wool shares are ten-year average.

Sources: For policies and years related to mining, mineral resources, and years of discovery, see Arthur Veatch, *Mining Laws of Australia and New Zealand* (Washington, DC: Government Printing Office, 1911). Export shares calculated from British House of Commons Parliamentary Papers (various issues).

it was the first to exploit a range of minerals. As Table 1.1 shows, mineral resources earned between 36 percent (in the 1860s) and 15 percent (in the 1890s) of NSW's export income. Gold was but one, and not the most significant, of its non-renewable resources. For much of the nineteenth century wool was the mainstay. Yet wool's unrivalled primacy before 1851 was permanently unsettled with the discoveries of gold. Gold constituted a high percentage of New South Wales' exports in the 1850s, 1860s and 1870s, after which it declined to less than 10 percent.[8]

The discovery of gold meant that NSW was the first colony to face pressure to determine the rules around access to mineral resources. Prior to 1851, the colony treated land with mineral deposits similarly to agricultural land; the rights of land-holders extended to all subsoil resources. In 1847, the British government had given the colonial governors permission to reserve rights to royal metals, yet that right was not consistently exercised.

On the discovery of gold the government geologist was dispatched to assess the situation. He found four hundred people at the site digging and recommended immediate action to maintain order. There were already too many people for a government with limited police capacity to evict them and start auctioning the land. Governor FitzRoy adopted the strategy used with the illegal land squatting earlier in the nineteenth century; he instituted a licence system. The government reserved the ownership of gold on Crown lands, but anyone could obtain a licence to prospect and mine an exclusive area for thirty shillings per month (roughly equal to one week's wages for a labourer).[9] For optimistic diggers, the amount was not considered too high, but when many did not find gold, the fee was reduced and the range of minerals covered increased. These arrangements were later referred to as a "democratic form of mining." In combination with small individual plots, the result was "small-man's mining," which offered "one of the country's richest resources equally to all men."[10]

Apart from raising revenue, the fee was also designed to thwart a rush to the goldfields. The fee had to be paid in advance and only by persons not "improperly absent from hired service." The licence was non-transferable. What was more democratic but produced more dissatisfaction was the small lot size. At first the aim was to accommodate as many people as possible. After three and a half years, precipitated by unrest, the licence fee was reduced, and decisions about plot size decentralized to local mining boards.

Alluvial minerals are often regarded as "democratic" because they are hard to enclose. The government could have auctioned land to syndicates, or set larger plot sizes and higher fees, to encourage pooled capital and companies. It did not, perhaps because of a perceived lack of local capital or the need to decide policy quickly. The government's approach followed that of the UK, which, before the NSW discoveries, had expressed the view that it was best not to hinder exploration or to block land sales.

The sovereign's right to gold was extended to all minerals in 1855, and leasing became the standard approach to mineral exploration.[11] The reduced licence fee meant the system was open to most individuals. From the beginning mineral titles were granted and kept only on the condition they were developed. If a deposit was not worked, the licence was forfeit and the deposit reopened, thus discouraging speculative investment.

To increase revenues the NSW government introduced a royalty. While the fee taxed any person, the royalty taxed only the successful diggers. Although NSW was the only colony to impose a royalty, it taxed lightly. Mineral-based revenues were at their highest in the period between 1858 and 1865, at around 3 percent of the total revenues. In all years customs duties contributed about a third of the revenues and land revenues about a fifth.

Gold discoveries preceded the creation and expansion of an expanded adult franchise. Up to 1824, NSW was governed by a single military officer appointed from the UK. While the Westminster Parliament was the ultimate authority, time and distance meant that the governor effectively had all control. From 1824 seven appointed colonists helped form a legislative council; this increased to thirty-six in 1842. One-third were appointed, and two-thirds were elected by males meeting minimum property qualifications.

Convict transportation ended in 1840, and in 1850 the Australian Colonies Government Act was passed in the UK. This permitted NSW, Victoria, Tasmania, and SA to form parliaments (with ultimate authority remaining in the UK). They all followed British institutions and adopted a bi-cameral structure. The equivalent of the House of Commons was the Legislative Assembly. The electoral franchise included a property restriction, as in the UK, but because of differences in price levels, it was more inclusive. The upper house (the Legislative Council) included members who were nominated for life by the governor. It was established as an undemocratic house of judicial review to ensure the Legislative Assembly's legislation was neither populist nor impulsive, and it remained undemocratic well into the twentieth century.

Rapidly increasing property prices, due to the gold discoveries, saw the eligible franchise in Sydney leap to 48 percent in 1851. It continued to expand with property prices; the percentage of adult males possessing the vote in Sydney was 95 percent in 1856, and in the whole of NSW it was 55 percent.[12] This threatened the wealthy elite. who tried to introduce malapportionment and maintain plural voting (the right to vote in any district in which a person owned property). By the time of the second election in 1858, when the Liberals won the majority and universal male suffrage and the secret ballot were adopted, the issue hardly mattered – so extensive was the suffrage enabled by inflation. Elimination of plural voting followed in the 1890s, female suffrage in 1902. By the standards of the time, NSW political institutions were more inclusive than those in Britain, although the Legislative Council remained undemocratic longer than in some other countries.

The connection between resources and democratic institutions in NSW was almost symbiotic. The demand for self-governance and representative institutions had started earlier than the gold discoveries, but the biggest threat to democratic expansion was the local elite of land-owning pastoralist squatters. They had exclusive control over the main resources and sought to perpetuate this through the Legislative Council.

The gold rushes created pro-democratic pressure in two additional ways. Pressure to eliminate the squatters' hold over land in NSW had been resisted prior to 1851. The wool industry was the mainspring of prosperity, and gold production contested this. The gold rushes also helped the development of other industries, unsettling the pastoralists' dominant role. Second, after the exhaustion of the initial alluvial gold, the ranks of people demanding access to land increased, and "un-locking" pastoral runs became important. Robertson's 1861 Land Act, which was also followed in the other colonies, removed the pastoralists' hold over land and opened it for selection. These laws ultimately saw NSW Democrats break the political power of the wealthy squattocracy. Faced with a potential swamping of the Legislative Council, the wealthy elite passed the land selector laws. This was a critical and lasting achievement that widened access to resources.

Victoria

If NSW saw the first dramas caused by gold, Victoria was the true centre of conflict. Prior to gold discoveries pastoralists had virtually complete hold over the land, and Victoria had the most conservative Upper House. The gold rush in Victoria dwarfed that in NSW and caused a massive influx of people. For three decades after 1851, gold exports dominated. Tens of thousands of men arrived on the Australian coast in just a few years, pouring over the land, clearing regions where gold was suspected, and disrupting pastures, townships, and existing hierarchies. The new and the old sectors clashed. Due to the size of the discoveries, and the number of diggers, it was in Victoria that the undemocratic licence fee and the plot sizes copied from NSW led to social crisis. It was in Victoria that gold diggers had more claims and directly contributed to the expansion of democratic institutions.

The colony had begun as a pastoral outpost, and by 1844 pastoralists occupied 75 percent of the land.[13] Wool was the key product. By 1852, Victorian exports of wool surpassed those of NSW. The population of Victoria doubled in the five years between 1846 and 1851. As two-thirds of the land was claimed for pastoral occupation, it was inevitable that any large influx of people would create tensions.

The rush began in Ballarat in August 1851. Between 1851 and 1900 Victoria produced over 60 million fine ounces, or two-thirds of all the gold produced in Australia.[14] It produced 90 percent of Australia's gold in the 1850s and 80 percent in the 1860s. Up to 1900 Victoria had exported almost £91 million worth of gold, with exports amounting to 76 percent of all exports in the 1850s and, as indicated in Table 1.1, 56 percent of exports in the 1860s.

Gold fundamentally transformed Victoria. Even with the population growth, per capita income in Victoria grew. In 1849 total imports amounted to £400,000; by 1853 a dozen imported items each exceeded this. Apart from the gold licences, a large part of the government's revenue came from tariffs and land sales. Victoria did not, however, have other substantial mineral resources to exploit. What increased was the population. In 1851, Victoria had seventy-seven thousand people; ten years later it had just over half a million. The economy diversified more than in the other colonies, in part due to protective tariffs. Gold transformed the city of Melbourne into one of the wealthiest and most prosperous places in the world at the end of the nineteenth century. It became the financial and banking centre of the colonies.

As in NSW, Governor La Trobe proclaimed government ownership of gold resources. It was illegal to work deposits without a licence or trespass on Crown lands. The monthly fee was increased from thirty to sixty shillings – over two weeks' wages for a labourer.[15] This was perceived as exorbitant and thousands of men protested. Resentment intensified when NSW reduced its fee to ten shillings. The monitoring of licences was frequently corrupt as police fined "illegal" diggers and retained half the fine. The plots were small, and after the early surface gold was found, only deeper riches, which sometimes took months to dig out – or not – remained. The discontent burst out in a violent and lethal rebellion in 1854. A subsequent Royal Commission recommended lower fees, free entry to Crown lands, and protecting the exclusive right of the first entrant. Local mining courts were established to settle disputes and determine plot size. These were unprecedented and democratic changes, and they ended the disturbances.

Pastoralists initially blocked access and acquired freehold ownership over extensive areas because of potential gold rents. The Victorian government drew around 10 percent of its revenues from gold (with a peak of 30 percent in 1852). There was a strong developmental bias in the mineral regulations, the government encouraging development with financial and technical "support. From the 1860s, the Assembly sought tariff protection to develop local industries.

NSW governed the area of Victoria until 1851. The new Victorian Constitution of 1853 established the most restrictive upper house in all the colonies. It had no processes for the resolution of deadlocks. The lower house only recognized men earning salaries of £100 (more than double the average annual wage at this time) and those paying ten pounds of annual rent as eligible voters. Miners who had taken annual licences were eligible, however, thus greatly expanding, perhaps unintentionally, the electorate. By the first Legislative Assembly election, the system approximated universal male suffrage, which it immediately adopted along with the secret ballot.

The constitution-makers preserved plural voting and malapportionment for the upper house. The composition and rules of the upper house could not be altered without its own approval, and members had to own £5000 worth of property (equivalent to around one hundred years of average wages) to be elected. To be eligible to vote, a man had to hold property worth £1000 or pay annual rent of £100. The upper house could block any measure and was dominated by pastoralists until 1881.[16] It blocked bills to open the pastoral lands for agricultural use five times before 1864. It only agreed to universal male suffrage for the lower house in 1857 because it did not include the Legislative Council. The abolition of plural voting was accepted only in 1899, and it rejected female suffrage on eleven occasions.[17]

The squatters in Victoria, faced with huge increases in population, were insecure about their tenure, and they created a conservative, independent, and indissoluble Legislative Council. They sought to control future laws by building a bastion of power for the wealthy.[18] Democratic processes in Victoria were much more hard won than was the case in NSW, with open mineral rights requiring bloodshed to be achieved.

Queensland
From 1824, Moreton Bay in Queensland was a penal settlement under NSW. In 1859 it separated from NSW, when it also held 3.5 million sheep and half

The Australian Gold Rushes

a million cattle.[19] With squatters contributing 70 percent of the revenue and over 90 percent of the exports, pastoralism was Queensland's only viable industry.

The first ministry had promised not to legislate on land without a public inquiry, but its first bills included four that advantaged the squatters and enabled pastoralists to aggregate their holdings. Unlike the other colonies, Queensland granted additional protection to its squatters. Unsurprisingly, the 1860 Parliament was dominated by pastoral interests.[20]

Several non-renewable resources played a role in the Queensland economy. Gold was discovered in 1867 and rushes followed. Multiple later discoveries meant that, by 1900, Queensland produced around 13 percent of Australia's gold.[21] The peak export years were 1875–77 and 1889–90, when gold contributed close to 40 percent of all exports by value. Copper, tin, and silver were also discovered and mined in the 1860s and 1880s, contributing 5 to 10 percent of exports.

In other colonies gold had contributed to the diversification of the economy, but this happened less in Queensland. The gold rushes created booms around small alluvial deposits but they left virtual ghost towns once the gold was exhausted. Government revenues from gold only ever reached 1 to 2 percent of total revenue.

At the time of separation Queensland inherited the annual miner's fee of ten shillings. While the government could have exercised sovereign ownership over gold, it did not enforce reservation rights for gold and silver until 1885, and not for other minerals until after 1909. As in Victoria, the right to mine in pastoral and agricultural lands was a point of friction. The capital needed for deep-reef mining required security of tenure for capital, and this became more important than individual access. Alienating land without allowing individual miners entry and exploration rights angered the diggers as the government protected pastoral interests. Given Queensland's land area, the density of settlement was less but the miners' demands for access were a threat to the tenure of agricultural settlers.[22] While smaller agricultural settlers felt powerless against the miners' demands, pastoralists and squatters did have the necessary power to block access.

At separation, the act directed the Legislative Council to create the new colony with a bi-cameral legislature as nominated by the Legislative Council, universal manhood suffrage for the Legislative Assembly, and simple majorities. This did not happen. After much controversy, a restricted electoral franchise was initiated with an expectation that the new Parliament would immediately instigate universal manhood suffrage. The disenfranchisement remained until 1872. Thus, Queensland's representative institutions re-gressed after separation from NSW, assisting the squatters' interests. In 1872, and after the initial gold rushes, universal manhood suffrage with a residential requirement was enacted but with preserved property privileges and the need for an "elector's right." Malapportionment and plural voting remained.

All progressive changes were blocked by the upper house – a Legislative Council where the members were appointed for life. The Queensland Council was initially more recalcitrant than that in NSW, and as obstructionist as that in Victoria. This radicalized the labour movement, which succeeded in abolishing the Legislative Council in 1922. With the exception of the secret ballot, Queensland achieved all the other democratic milestones later than any other colony except Western Australia. With the exception of the miner's right, every other change that removed barriers to entry was only adopted after the expansion of suffrage. Again, it was the weight of population that forced democratic change and accessible mining rights, the delay in Queensland reflecting the initial dominance of the pastoralists.

Tasmania
Van Diemen's Land (later Tasmania) was created as a convict settlement in 1803 and separated from NSW in 1825. By the mid-1830s, Tasmania was sufficiently prosperous to hope to surpass NSW politically and economically. Convict transportation ceased in 1852, but the loss of cheap labour meant Tasmanian agriculture lost its competitive edge. English investment plummeted. The gold rushes on the mainland attracted over half the adult males from Tasmania. Prices, wages, and land values fell, while revenue and exports shrank to half of their pre-1856 values. The only industry that did not decline was pastoralism, which had steady external demand.

Wool was the backbone of the Tasmanian economy with 1.7 million sheep in 1860, contributing almost half the exports by value in the 1860s. Graziers controlled the majority of alienated land and the one hundred largest properties occupied over 40 percent of the freehold land. Alarmed by the exodus of people in 1851, Governor Denison introduced a more liberal land policy. Tasmanian pastoralists had more secure property rights than their counterparts in Victoria and, as in Queensland, the pastoralists were never really challenged.[23]

The Tasmanians were desperately hoping for their own mineral boom; this did not occur until the 1870s. Gold was not plentiful but Tasmania became one of the world's biggest tin exporters. By 1900, Tasmania produced

The Australian Gold Rushes

barely 1 percent of total Australian gold but 14 percent of its copper and 18 percent of the world's tin.[24] After these discoveries, the economy prospered. Mineral exports rose to 60 percent of exports by value, dethroning wool in 1879 and attracting capital and thousands of wage miners and creating new towns.

After the first small gold findings in 1852, government ownership was proclaimed, and in 1859 alienated land could be "withdrawn" if it was suspected to contain gold (and later, any mineral). Alluvial gold belonged to the individual miner, and this was codified in 1859. As late as the 1890s miners were demanding the size of the claim be increased. Individual miners could not participate in developing alluvial tin without licences that covered large areas and required high payments. Governments resisted small-scale tin mining, while individuals complained that large leases were mostly speculative and remained unworked. The government did not strictly enforce forfeiture for fear of dampening investment.

The Tasmanian governments did not provide development assistance, dispense bounties, or directly assist deep mining. They were slow to build infrastructure. This lack of attention came from conservative legislatures dominated by landed gentry. It was after the mid-1880s, when their districts received better representation, that the miners' interests began to be addressed.

At the time of the mineral discoveries Tasmania had self-governance but undemocratic institutions.[25] Outside WA, Tasmania had the most restrictive electoral franchise for its Legislative Assembly and Legislative Council. Its upper house could not be dissolved, and without any procedures for resolving deadlocks, its landed elites dominated. The first Constitution contained a property-restricted franchise. While gold-induced inflation expanded the franchise on the mainland, the depression in Tasmania had the reverse effect. In Tasmania there was no pressure for male adult suffrage until the mid-1880s.

As is evident in Table 1.2, apart from the secret ballot, Tasmania was a laggard in expanding all other democratic institutions. It was only after the mining discoveries of the 1870s that stronger voices and pressure for expanding the electorate merged. In this decade the landed elite's hold over the Legislative Assembly was broken. Property qualifications were reduced and the percentage of voters to adult males rose to 76 percent in 1891. It was only with Australian Federation in 1901 that Tasmanian Legislative Council members finally adopted universal suffrage, equal districts, and eliminated plural voting. In the absence of mineral discoveries, pastoralists dominated, and the political system retreated to non-democratic institutions until Federation. Pressure for democratic institutions only appeared after the mineral boom of the 1870s. Tasmanian mineral policies favoured big capital and speculation rather than development as these aligned closest to the interests of the landed elite.

South Australia

South Australia was planned and populated as a settlement colony, created through legislation. Its early self-governing institutions were more democratic than those in the other Australian colonies as there was no fear of ex-convicts voting. Pastoralists never dominated as agriculture was envisioned to be the main activity from first settlement.

The first mineral boom occurred with the discoveries of copper in 1842, boosting immigration at a critical juncture. By 1850, SA was producing 10 percent of the world's copper and by 1900 it had produced 60 percent of all Australia's copper.[26] Production peaked in the 1870s and slowly declined thereafter. Copper reinvigorated immigration and was a major export earner. Although the mines were owned by former pastoralists, their success helped prevent the graziers' political domination by encouraging faster land surveys, which advanced land sales and agricultural development.

The copper discoveries caused immigration to grow from 15,000 in 1841 to 66,000 by 1851.[27] The discoveries encouraged new towns as well as the expansion of agriculture and pastoralism. A significant benefit from copper was its balancing effect on the economy. The pastoralist industry had established faster than agriculture, and it began to lead exports. By 1845, wool constituted 55 percent of all exports, but by 1846 copper constituted half of SA's exports. The Victorian gold rushes than changed exports again. After initially losing population to the goldfields, South Australia became the largest exporter of wheat in the country, both to Victoria and overseas. The pressure to open new land strongly affected pastoralists' interests.

The property rights of the pastoralists were never prioritized as elsewhere. From settlement, SA had encouraged land sales as opposed to leasing. The Legislative Council, a pastoralist citadel in all the other colonies, was only dominated by pastoralists between 1857 and 1865, after which time their number declined. Nor were the pastoralists exclusively defined by grazing; they were often involved in mining operations or represented their interests in the city.[28] The Strangways Act of 1869 allowed for credit sales,

TABLE 1.2

Democratic milestones of the political institutions of the Australian colonies/states

Milestone	NSW	Years elapsed	VIC	Years elapsed	QLD	Years elapsed	TAS	Years elapsed	SA	Years elapsed	WA	Years elapsed
First year of European settlement	1788		1835		1824		1804		1836		1827	
First year of autonomous governance	1823	35	1851	16	1859	35	1825	21	1836		1827	
Partly elected Legislative Council	1842	19	1850	15	1859	35	1850	25	1850	14	1870	43
Lower house universal male suffrage	1858	35	1857	22	1872	48	1901	76	1856	20	1893	66
Secret ballot	1858	35	1856	21	1859	35	1858	33	1856	20	1877	50
Plural voting eliminated*	1893	70	1899	64	1905	81	1901	76	1856	20	1907	80
Payment of members	1899	76	1870	35	1886	62	1890	65	1887	51	1901	74
Lower house universal female suffrage	1902	79	1909	74	1905	81	1903	78	1894	58	1899	72
Elected upper house universal suffrage	1978		1950		NA[†]		1968		1973		1964	

* Initially voters were allowed to vote in each district in which they had a property – plural voting.
† Queensland eliminated its Legislative Council (upper house) in 1921.
Sources: John Hirst, *Australia's Democracy: A Short History* (Sydney: Allen and Unwin, 2002); Ian McAllister, Malcolm Mackerras, and Carolyn Boldiston, *Australian Political Facts* (Melbourne: Macmillan, 1997).

allowing small farmers to gain access to land. The land under cultivation expanded rapidly.

It was not until the 1880s that minerals were accepted as a public, as opposed to a private, resource. While SA started without sovereign reservations over minerals, by 1843, Governor Robe placed reservations on mineral lands and imposed a royalty on ores.[29] This provoked an outcry. The law was revoked in 1849. South Australian mineral access institutions were neither inclusive nor development oriented. South Australia sold land with full subsoil private property rights via auctions – a system that favoured the wealthy. In 1886, SA claimed sovereign ownership of gold and silver, extending this to all minerals in 1888. Thus, for the first fifty years of its existence, South Australia accepted full private property rights over minerals. Attention to private property was stronger in South Australia than attention to mineral exploration. It took longer in SA than in any other colony to permit and regulate access to private lands.

South Australia did not enforce forfeiture for non-development until 1888. Its other forms of encouraging mineral development involved rewards for finds, subsidies to companies, and technical assistance. After the initial opposition in the 1840s, a 2.5 percent mining royalty on net profits was introduced in 1877. As in the other colonies, customs and land sales provided the biggest source of revenue.

After 1857, SA had the most inclusive and democratic political institutions of all the Australian colonies. The colonists demanded self-governance almost from the beginning. There were no property qualifications for members. The lower house, the Assembly, was elected by universal male suffrage from the beginning, while the electorate of the upper house was restricted to adult males who owned one hundred pounds' worth of property or payed a lease or rent of ten pounds – requirements that enfranchised many working men.[30] The ballot was secret, and plural voting was never instigated. Universal female suffrage for the Legislative Assembly, and property-based female suffrage for the upper house, occurred in 1895. Malapportionment advantaged rural interests and the Legislative Council retained absolute veto powers. Attempts at further democratization were regularly blocked; however, this conservatism was defended not by pastoralists but by wealthy land-owners and merchants.[31]

Population influx was not crucial for introducing democratic institutions, nor did pastoralists ever enjoy the privileged position seen in other colonies, thus lessening their hold on power. Copper discoveries occurred early, offsetting pastoralist interests. Democratic processes developed without the massive population increase of other colonies.

Western Australia

Western Australia was settled in 1829. Its economy languished for most of the nineteenth century until the discovery of gold. An insufficient population, unworkable land, and inadequate capital created a vicious circle that kept the economy stagnant. In 1850 Western Australia petitioned the British for convicts to solve its labour and population problems. This helped the only viable sector at the time – pastoralism. This dominated exports to an extent comparable only to Queensland and Victoria prior to the gold rushes. Wool comprised 86 percent of Western Australian exports in 1843 and over two-thirds in 1851. Yet pastoralists were not in conflict with other agricultural interests as they were not an exclusively defined group, and there was a fusion of interests among the economic and political elite.

WA was the last colony to develop representative and democratic institutions, mostly because of delayed economic development and delayed self-governance from the British. With self-governance, however, WA created property-restricted political participation and a biased system that favoured pastoral and agricultural interests. The political institutions were only made more inclusive and democratic after the influx of gold diggers.

Before the introduction of the Representative Council in 1870, Western Australian policies were proclaimed by the governor. While there had been a legislative council after 1832, the governor had the power to initiate or veto legislation. The Legislative Council consisted of the four official executives and four nominated settlers, but after 1870 these last four were elected on a restrictive franchise basis. Between 1839 and 1870, over half of the twenty-two colonists who sat in the Legislative Council were farmers or pastoralists.[32]

The early land policies favoured pastoral interests. Governor Fitzgerald (1848–55) recognized the need to change the land laws, but a system of perpetual lease renewal gave pastoralists a virtual monopoly. Slightly modified regulations were initially welcomed, but pastoralists and agriculture received protection through import duties on grain, livestock, and imported food.[33]

Western Australian governors offered bonuses for discoveries; local businessmen pooled capital to explore.[34] Finally, a small discovery in the Kimberley in 1885 was followed by Coolgardie in 1892 and Kalgoorlie in

1893. Ultimately, WA had more gold and minerals than any other colony. By 1914, WA gold mines had produced 28 million fine ounces of gold. From non-existent in the early 1880s, gold exports were worth 45 percent of exports by 1893 and 80 percent by around 1901 at £8.5 million per annum. Gold reversed the dominance of wool. The population exploded between 1891 and 1901, tripling to 184,000. Gold also enabled the construction of significant infrastructure previously unaffordable to the colony.

The government did not extract high rents from the mining sector. Following SA's lead, Governor Clarke declared a 6.6 percent royalty, which was changed to an export duty in 1886. Revenue from licences increased, but modestly; customs and railways contributed 30 to 40 percent each to revenues. Indirect taxes were resented by the gold miners, however, as the duties on food meant it was the diggers, not the farmers, who carried the biggest burden.

During the nineteenth century the Western Australian political elite favoured companies with substantial capital. Until the discovery of gold the government treated mineral-bearing land like agricultural land and allowed alienation on the same terms. When the government allowed mineral leases in 1865 it also gave prospecting rights at two shillings per acre per year, and allowed the sale of mineral lands, excluding those with gold and silver, at the fixed price of £3. The 1888 Goldfield Licensing Act allowed for both miner's rights at £1 per year for ten years and, for larger leases, for twenty-one years. WA allowed company mining on goldfields at the same time as it allowed individual diggers.[35]

Serious political agitation was created by the easy exemptions given to labour laws while companies regularly evaded regulations and government officers granted exemptions that were not subject to judicial appeal. The majority of diggers came from the eastern colonies, where they had previously won more inclusive access to minerals. They demanded that the laws be changed and that they be granted political representation. Universal manhood suffrage was introduced in 1894. With larger representation, more inclusive goldfield acts were passed in 1895 and 1904. The 1904 act excluded leases from alluvial fields, reduced fees, enforced stricter labour laws, and moved disputes to the courts. WA miners' regulations became both more inclusive and more developmentally oriented in conjunction with changes to the political system.

In 1850, the colonists elected two-thirds of councillors on a restricted property base. It was not until 1870 that the Legislative Council was fully elected, although the property qualifications for a member were freehold land of £100 or capital of £2000. The electoral franchise required owner-ship of freehold property of £100 (the equivalent of two years' average wages) or an annual lease of £10.[36] Western Australians were granted self-governance in 1890. The fifteen-member Legislative Council was nominated by the governor until the population reached sixty thousand, when it was doubled, although electors were limited to owners of property worth £200 or £30 annual rent. The lower house consisted of thirty members, who were also elected by males meeting a restricted property franchise. No pro-vision for resolving legislative deadlocks was adopted, giving the Legislative Council veto power. The landed and pastoral interests dominated the Legislative Council before self-governance, and both plural voting and mal-apportionment ensured that rural and propertied interests dominated.

Almost three-quarters of the members of the 1890 Legislative Assembly represented pastoral, agricultural, and trading interests. In the Legislative Council, old landed interests constituted two-thirds of the membership. The Western Australian political system was democratized due to the gold diggers, their large number highlighting the unrepresentativeness of the system. In 1890, only 12 percent of the total male population could vote. By 1893, the male population was 136,000, but no one on the goldfields was eligible to vote. No other colonial assembly began with a lower level of rep-resentativeness. Although this was intended by the pastoral and landed in-terests, the 1890s premier was a pragmatist. He sought to give citizens representation sooner rather than "at the point of a bayonet."[37] Universal male suffrage was introduced and extended to women in 1899. Plural voting was retained, however, and the enlargement of the Legislative Assembly and residence requirements ensured that the miners were underrepre-sented. The 1897 election was a turning point as four in ten were newcomers to the assembly. They were mostly not landed men, and this resulted in fur-ther democratization.

The mineral boom provided the spur for the democratization of the Western Australian political system. It was the diggers' numbers that most affected this system. The democratization of the Western Australian polit-ical system as a result of the gold-induced population influx was more deci-sive and faster than in Queensland and was similar to what had occurred in Victoria and NSW.

Conclusion

Australia is a country blessed with multiple abundant resources, the single largest being land. The resources both above and under the soil have proved to be of long-term benefit to the people and economy. This outcome, however, was not guaranteed by the political institutions and processes in place for the first half century of white settlement. Prior to the discovery of gold, the colonial governance structures were not democratic regimes but, rather, institutions designed to oversee Britain's colonial settlements and to advance the economic prosperity of local pastoral and landed interests.

The six case studies reveal different paths to democratic governance. In all colonies but South Australia, gold discoveries and their regulation preceded universal male suffrage. The Australian colonial experience, therefore, raises intriguing questions for the Acemoglu and Robinson hypothesis: How did the Australian colonies overcome the restrictive institutions created by the landed elite and achieve democratic government and relatively open mineral regulations?

The mineral regulations established in NSW certainly influenced the other colonies, although it took a violent uprising before Victorians aligned with NSW. In every colony, the more dominant the pastoral sector, the slower the universal access to minerals and to universal suffrage. Nonetheless, change occurred. The lack of time vested interests had to respond and the absolute size of the population rush appear to be important factors in explaining why institutions changed. The sheer number of new people and relatively rapid spread of wealth produced economically independent individuals who sought more democratic processes, which then helped embed egalitarian mineral regulations. The imperative for each colony to build a viable economic base was also critical. In Australia's pastorally based colonies, gold and the people it attracted offered an opportunity to grow at a rate unimaginable before 1851. While vested interests initially hesitated and slowed open access to minerals and democratic change, they were overwhelmed by the rush of people and wealth before realizing the necessity (and then benefits) of changing institutional structures and processes. The material prosperity derived from the exploitation of gold resources, when combined with more democratic institutions, ultimately became undeniable.

Australia's particular experience is unlikely to be replicated elsewhere. History is too complex for such simple comparisons, and things other than political institutions also influence development.[38] In the case of Australia, the discovery of gold, the people it attracted, and the institutional structures that emerged helped contribute to the development of the nation's economy and political institutions – a double benefit that has proved elusive for too many countries over the past two hundred years.

Notes

1 Geoffrey Blainey, *The Rush That Never Ended: A History of Australian Mining* (Melbourne: Melbourne University Press, 1963).
2 Daron Acemoglu and James A. Robinson, *Why Nations Fail: The Origins of Power, Prosperity, and Poverty* (New York: Crown Publishers, 2012).
3 Sambit Bhattacharyya and Roland Hodler, "Natural Resources, Democracy and Corruption," *European Economic Review* 54, 4 (2010): 608–21; James A. Robinson, Ragnar Torvik, and Thierry Verdier, "Political Foundations of the Resource Curse," *Journal of Development Economics* 79, 2 (2006): 447–68.
4 Ian McLean, *Why Australia Prospered: The Shifting Sources of Economic Growth* (Princeton: Princeton University Press, 2012), 246–56.
5 Blainey, *Rush That Never Ended.*
6 McLean, *Why Australia Prospered.*
7 All official figures at this time excluded the Indigenous population.
8 All statistical information is from various issues of the British House of Commons *Parliamentary Papers,* "Statistical Tables Relating to the Colonial and Other Possessions of the United Kingdom," Pt. I–XXXVII (London: Parliament Papers by Command, 1856–1914), at http://parlipapers.proquest.com/parlipapers (Proquest UK Parliamentary Papers website).
9 All wage equivalences calculated from Dianne Hutchinson and Florian Ploeckel, "Weekly Wages, Average Compensation and Minimum Wage for Australia from 1861–Present," *Measuring Worth,* 2018, http://www.measuringworth.com/auswages/ (Measuring Worth website).
10 Blainey, *Rush That Never Ended,* 129.
11 Mineral regulations throughout the colonies are from Arthur Veatch, *Mining Laws of Australia and New Zealand* (Washington, DC: Government Printing Office, 1911).
12 John Hirst, *The Strange Birth of Colonial Democracy: New South Wales 1848–1884* (Sydney: Allen and Unwin, 1988).
13 All references to colonial land laws are from Stephen Roberts, *History of Australian Land Settlement, 1788–1920* (Melbourne: Macmillan, 1968).
14 Z. Kalix, L. Frazer, and R.I. Rawson, *Australian Mineral Industry: Production and Trade, 1842–1964* (Canberra: Commonwealth of Australia, Bulletin No. 81, 1966).
15 Veatch, *Mining Laws of Australia and New Zealand.*
16 Joy Mills, "The Composition of the Victorian Parliament, 1856–1881," *Historical Studies: Australia and New Zealand* 2, 5 (1942): 25–39.
17 Geoffrey Serle, "The Victorian Legislative Council, 1856–1950," *Historical Studies: Australia and New Zealand* 6, 22 (1954): 186–203.
18 Jim Main, "Making Constitutions in New South Wales and Victoria, 1853–1854," *Historical Studies: Australia and New Zealand* 7, 28 (1957): 369–86.
19 Michael Pearson, Michael Lennon, and Jane Lennon, *Pastoral Australia: Fortunes, Failures, and Hard Yakka – A Historical Overview, 1788–1967* (Melbourne: CSIRO Publishing, 2010).
20 William Johnston, *The Call of the Land: A History of Queensland to the Present Day* (Brisbane: Jacaranda Press, 1982).
21 Kalix, Frazer, and Rawson, *Australian Mineral Industry.*

22 G.P. Taylor, "Political Attitudes and Land Policy in Queensland, 1868–1894," *Pacific Historical Review* 37 (1968): 247–64.

23 Bronwyn Meikle, "Squatters and Selectors: The Waste Lands Acts of Tasmania, 1858–68," *Tasmanian Historical Studies* 16 (2011): 1–23.

24 Glyn Roberts, *Metal Mining in Tasmania, 1804–1914: How Government Helped Shape the Mining Industry* (Launceston: Bokprint, 2007).

25 Hirst, *Strange Birth of Colonial Democracy.*

26 Bernard O'Neil, *Above and Below: The South Australian Department of Mines and Energy, 1944–1994* (Adelaide: South Australian Department of Mines and Energy, 1995).

27 Douglas Pike, *Paradise of Dissent: South Australia, 1829–1857* (Melbourne: Melbourne University Press, 1967).

28 Ron Gibbs, *History of South Australia: From Colonial Days to the Present* (Adelaide: Peacock Publication, 1984).

29 Dean Jaensch, ed., *The Flinders History of South Australia: Political History* (Adelaide: Wakefield Press, 1986).

30 Ibid.

31 Howard Coxon, John Playford, and Robert Reid, *Biographical Register of the South Australian Parliament, 1857–1957* (Adelaide: Wakefield Press, 1985).

32 Brian De Garis, "Political Tutelage, 1829–1879," in *A New History of Western Australia,* ed. Charles Stannage (Perth: University of Western Australia Press, 1981), 297–325.

33 Frank Crowley, *Australia's Western Third* (London: Macmillan, 1960).

34 Ken Spillman, *A Rich Endowment: Government and Mining in Western Australia* (Perth: University of Western Australia Press, 1993).

35 M.A. Mossenson, "Mining Regulations and Alluvial Disputes: 1894–1904," *University Studies in History and Economics* 2, 1 (1955): 5–31.

36 James Battye, *Western Australia: A History from Its Discovery to the Inauguration of the Commonwealth* (Oxford: Clarendon Press, 1924).

37 Charles Stannage, "The Composition of the W.A. Parliament," *University Studies in History and Economics* 4, 4 (1966): 3.

38 Jeffrey Sachs, "Review Essay: Government, Geography, and Growth – The True Drivers of Economic Development," *Foreign Affairs* 91, 5 (2012): 142–50.

2

Regulation of Natural Resources in the Nordic Countries, 1880–1940

ANDREAS R.D. SANDERS, PÅL T. SANDVIK,
and ESPEN STORLI

This chapter investigates how the four Nordic countries of Denmark, Sweden, Norway, and Finland chose to regulate their natural resources. The Nordic countries are usually considered quite similar in character when it comes to political, cultural, legal, and economic institutional factors. However, their economic sophistication and resource endowments differed. The question is whether there was a "Nordic" way of regulating natural resources. By studying the laws regulating resource extraction, as well as their implementation, it becomes clear that the Nordic countries wished to achieve three main aims: (1) to secure domestic ownership over national resources, (2) to use the resources in order to stimulate growth, and (3) to distribute the resource-generated income in ways that would benefit large parts of the population. However, these aims were to some extent contradictory, and the Nordic countries came to follow somewhat different policies. This chapter also shows that the trend towards comprehensive resource regulation started well before 1914. This means that the national regulations were just as much national responses to the expanding global economy of the prewar years as they were reactions to the collapse of the first global economy.

Like most other European states, the Nordic countries liberalized their economies in the late eighteenth and early nineteenth centuries. By the early 1860s, almost nothing was left of the old mercantilist privileges and regulations. The Nordic countries became liberal societies with strong property rights. They adhered to free trade, but they never adopted a radical version of Manchester Liberalism or an ideal type night-watchman state.[1] In a renowned article, Lars G. Sandberg describes Sweden as "the impoverished sophisticate."[2] While lagging far behind Great Britain and the Netherlands in terms of wealth in the mid-nineteenth century, Sweden invested heavily in education. It also had competent and honest state bureaucracy with a high degree of legitimacy. Sandberg's epithet could certainly be extended to Denmark and Norway, and perhaps also to Finland. There was a strong belief in the benevolent potential of state regulation. During the nineteenth century, especially in Sweden and Norway, the state embarked on quite ambitious modernization policies. One could say that the Nordics combined some elements of the Prussian (or German) and the Anglo-Saxon ways of organizing society. They had interventionist states as in Prussia but, at the same time, were liberal, open, and fairly democratic societies.

Dismantling mercantilist regulations on resource ownership and resource exploitation was a drawn out process in the Nordic area. The Swedish Ancien Régime regulations pertaining to the iron and forest industries were abolished step by step from the mid-1830s. The iron works' privileged access to charcoal was terminated between 1846 and 1850, and remaining sawmill privileges were abolished by the early 1860s. This was significant as it created free markets for forestry products, leading to a huge expansion of the forestry industries. Similarly, export restrictions of iron ore were abolished between 1857 and 1864.[3] In Norway, mining enterprises lost their remaining privileges regarding access to charcoal in 1816. The sawmill privileges were curtailed in 1818, and they were abolished altogether between 1854 and 1860.[4] Finland's sawmill privileges were dismantled between 1859 and 1861.[5] Denmark differed from its Scandinavian neighbours as its only significant natural resource was farmland. While the Danes had liquidated most mercantilist regulations (trade, crafts, etc.) by the mid-nineteenth century farm ownership remained strictly regulated. For reasons that are discussed below, a free market for farmland was never introduced. Similarly, the Ancien Régime forestry regulations remained in place until 1935.

In the Nordic countries, laissez faire was not only embedded but also transitory. From the late nineteenth century onwards, state intervention increased significantly, including veterinary and health measures, social insurance, basic regulation of the labour market, as well as more active trade policies. As in many other Western countries, the state assumed increasing responsibility for the health, welfare, and prosperity of its inhabitants. The relationship between state, society, and the economy was thus slowly changed. Given the resource dependence of the Nordic economies one should not be surprised that the question of resource regulation became a burning political issue in the decades around 1900.

Before delving into the details of resource policies, something must be said about economic development in the Nordic countries. Their economies were in many respects strikingly different from one another. According to Angus Maddison, Denmark was Europe's fifth richest country in 1900 measured by GDP per capita.[6] Swedish, Norwegian, and Finnish GDP per capita were 85 percent, 66 percent, and 55 percent, respectively, of Denmark's. However, in the following decades, all Nordic countries, especially the laggards Norway and Finland, grew considerably faster than the European average. By 1939, the Nordic area was one of Europe's most prosperous corners.

Property Rights vs. Equality: Danish Farmland Regulations

Farmland, Denmark's most significant resource base, has always been regulated. The Danish state was much more interventionist with regard to farmland than were the other Nordic states. This regulatory regime had a long prehistory as the Danish state had been engaged in some sort of social engineering (to protect farmers from estate owners) since the late eighteenth century. Danish agriculture was at that time totally dominated by noble estates, but this dominance was increasingly challenged during the nineteenth century as farmers started to claim moral ownership of the land.[7] The Danish Constitution of 1849 (when absolute monarchy was abolished) blocked, as well as stimulated, these claims. The Constitution guaranteed the sanctity of property rights, thus protecting the estates. At the same time, the Constitution introduced universal male suffrage for the lower chamber of Parliament (*Folketinget*). Universal suffrage made land reform a contested, but unresolved, political issue in Danish politics right up to 1919.

The key question was whether farmland was a commodity that could be sold or purchased without any restrictions or whether moral and/or social considerations should limit its marketability. Farmers demanded that estate owners be compelled to sell their tenant farms (of which there were many) to the tenants or their families. However, every attempt to enforce this stalled in Parliament due to respect for established property rights. But neither were estate owners allowed to incorporate tenant farms into their estates. The laws, dating from the Ancien Régime, protecting the tenants were upheld after 1849.[8] In contrast, in the "neighbouring" German province of Mecklenburg, traditional tenant farming was wiped out when the land was incorporated into the estates. The Danish development was much more "Scandinavian" as most estate owners voluntarily sold off most of their tenant farms during the second half of the nineteenth century.[9] By the 1890s, the estates' landholdings were thus reduced to only 15 percent of all Danish farmlands.[10]

The Danish Parliament also upheld eighteenth-century laws prohibiting absentee farming and restricting mergers of independent farms. The aim was to prevent the rise of new large landholdings at the expense of small independent farmers. It was, however, possible to merge small or medium-sized farms in order to create viable farms. The provisions requiring that farmers reside on their farms were rigorously enforced. In a famous ruling in 1871, the Danish Supreme Court compelled a Jutland farmer to sell a newly acquired allotment because he had not complied with the residence clause.[11] These provisions thwarted the creation of new estates or large-scale agriculture (as occurred in parts of the New World) or absentee landowner-ship (as occurred in Ireland). These policies thus sustained the long trad-ition of the role of social engineering in Danish farmland regulation.

In the late nineteenth century the crofters (the traditional rural under-class) gained political strength and demanded the right to own farmland. This was crowned with success in 1899, when crofters were given the right to establish farms on state-owned land and got access to subsidised loans.[12] The democratization of the Danish regulatory regime of farmland reached its zenith in 1919 when Parliament abolished some quite rare types of estates (*len, stamhus,* and *fideikomisser*) and sold the land cheaply to farmers. In addition, a new tenancy law forced the estates to sell remaining tenant farms to the tenants (on advantageous terms for the latter). The Danish Supreme Court accepted the legality of these laws with some doubt as they infringed upon the constitutional guarantees of property rights.[13]

Forestry was also strictly regulated. The Danish Ancien Régime author-ities believed forests to be a limited resource that had to be protected. Danish regulations were therefore stricter and more long-lasting than were those in the other, and much more heavily forested, Nordic countries. The 1805 forest regulations (*Fredsskovforordningen*) aimed at securing rational forest management and preventing deforestation. It was illegal to let cattle and other animals graze in private forests or to cultivate areas designated to forestry.[14] When a forest was sold, in order to limit deforesta-tion, the new owner had to accept restrictions on logging for ten years.[15] The 1805 provisions came under increasing attack after 1849, and several polit-icians called for a liberalization of Danish forestry. However, the parlia-mentary majority blocked all attempts at market-oriented reforms. The laws were only revised in 1935, when environmental protection of forests was in fact strengthened.[16]

It is worth highlighting four important aspects of the Danish regulatory regime. First, there was a widespread notion that the farmers (i.e., the people) had some kind of moral property rights to the farmland. This was – as we shall see – in many ways similar to popular perceptions in other Nordic countries about the ownership of forests, minerals, and hydropower. Second, Danish resource regulations remained in place even when most other mercantilist-era regulations were abolished. Third, the state combined resource regulation and social engineering even during the golden age of laissez faire. There were more restrictions on farmland ownership in Denmark than there were in Sweden and Norway. Fourth, even though Parliament sought to improve the position of ordinary tenant farmers it never trampled on the property rights of the estates (with the above-mentioned exception in 1919).

Swedish Iron Ore and Foreign Ownership

By the turn of the twentieth century, Sweden was the largest economy of the Nordic countries. In comparison to Denmark, land ownership has historically been less concentrated, and estates were rarer.[17] By the middle of the nineteenth century, the percentage of Swedish farmland owned by farmers had risen to 60 percent, after both the Crown and the nobility had voluntarily sold large tracts of land.[18] Regulation of land ownership never became as contested as it was in Denmark.

Sweden's exports were dominated by non-agricultural resources. In the 1890s, the most important Swedish exports were wood-based products, followed by butter and iron goods. Over the following decades, the relative importance of butter and sawn timber declined, overtaken by mineral ores, pulp and paper, and manufactured goods.[19] Both for its strategic and historic importance iron ore, and the iron and steel industry, held a special place in the Swedish economy. It had formed the backbone of much of Sweden's economic and military strength in the seventeenth and eighteenth centuries. In the nineteenth century, mining policies were liberalized and the rich ore deposits attracted considerable foreign investments. By 1899, 27 percent of total iron ore production came from foreign-owned companies.[20]

However, foreign involvement, particularly the British ownership of large iron ore deposits in Gällivare and Kiruna, fostered political controversy. The main organized opposition to foreign investment in iron ore extraction came from Swedish ironworks owners. They feared that increased ore exports to the European steel industry would not only increase competition for the ailing Swedish iron and steel industry but also diminish the ore reserves necessary for its future.[21]

The issue was exacerbated by the fact that the ore was located in northern Sweden. The north was rich in natural resources but was scarcely populated. Big (foreign) companies could – according to those who opposed them – effectively overpower political authorities. There was also the ever-present fear that Russia, Sweden's traditional nemesis, harboured secret designs to gain control over northern Sweden, perhaps by secretly financing the British company. Yet, even without a Russian bugbear in the woodpile, the protectionist-oriented press frequently pointed to examples where British investments had led to negative outcomes for the host country, particularly Transvaal.[22]

In the end, the Swedish state was brought to intervene. The British company owning the Kiruna and Gällivare ore fields filed for bankruptcy in 1889 after cost overruns and increasingly vocal calls for restrictions in Sweden shattered its standing in the international capital markets. The yet unfinished railway linking the mine to the coast was bought by the Swedish state at a fraction of the money invested, and the ore deposits passed into the hands of Swedish investors. Yet, as Swedish successor companies had unstable economic foundations, the possibility of a foreign takeover remained. After years of political wrangling, the Swedish state made a deal with the mining company *Trafik AB Grängesberg-Oxelösund* in 1907. The state obtained half of the Kiruna and Gällivare ore fields, and was given considerable control over the other half – thus ensuring future Swedish ownership and control over the richest ore fields.[23]

While the state had intervened to keep the Norrland ore out of foreign hands, the legislation regulating ownership of mines remained more or less unchanged until the outbreak of the First World War. Ever since 1829 foreign citizens needed a royal licence to obtain property, and from 1872 onwards foreigners also needed a royal licence to engage in mining operations.[24] But there were no restrictions on foreign stock ownership of a Swedish company, and, while it was frequently debated, the Swedish Parliament could not agree on what a law regulating foreign ownership would look like. Sweden was a large importer of foreign capital, and opponents argued that nationalist ownership restrictions would damage Swedish businesses' access to capital. While the majority of both chambers of Parliament were

Regulation of Natural Resources in the Nordic Countries 51

eager to keep the Norrland ore fields in Swedish hands, they were seen as a special case and there was no majority for creating a completely new regulatory system.[25]

The issue of regulating foreign ownership re-emerged in 1912. Once again it was ownership of iron mines that took centre stage in the debate as, over the preceding years, German investors had bought Swedish mining companies totalling nearly one-sixth of output. Furthermore, ore exports from these mines to Germany had increased markedly, which again appeared to threaten the long-term ore reserves of the Swedish iron and steel industry. This led the Swedish Parliament to pass the so-called Restriction Act (Swedish: *inskränkningslagen*) in 1916. The new law required companies to obtain a government licence to acquire property or to engage in mining if more than 20 percent of its shares, or more than 20 percent of the voting power, was in the hands of foreigners. Increasing unease over tighter economic integration, particularly after the outbreak of the First World War, made the potential damage to access foreign capital a risk worth taking. The proponents of the law also noted that stricter regulations on natural resource extraction in neighbouring Norway had not led to capital flight. They emphasized that the new law did not completely bar foreign investors from taking part in mining or other economic activity.[26]

Yet the law was implemented along a strict nationalist line. Companies without a clause that limited foreign share ownership to 20 percent were not allowed to buy new forests, mines, or waterfalls between 1916 and 1930.[27] There were only some minor exceptions to this rule.[28] This confirms Sven Nordlund's observation that the law marked an abrupt end to further foreign acquisitions of Swedish mining companies.[29] However, the law was to some extent circumvented by the use of straw men.

Mining was not the only resource sector in which there were increased calls for state regulation. Sawn timber, pulp, and paper accounted for around 40 percent of Swedish exports before the First World War,[30] and foreign ownership of this industry was a controversial issue. Interestingly, the Swedish timber companies welcomed foreign investments and objected to stricter ownership regulation. In this sense, they differed from the domestic iron and steel industry. In forestry, Swedish smallholders and crofters – backed by urban radicals, socialists, and liberals – demanded state intervention. They wanted to secure access to forest resources for crofters and smallholders and were opposed to large corporate acquisitions of woodlands. This issue also played into the larger Swedish debate on emigration, which was perceived as a major national problem. It was hoped that improvements to the livelihood of smallholders could divert the emigration of young Swedes from emigrating to North America in favour of moving to northern Sweden instead. Foreign companies were singled out as being the most exploitive and the least concerned with the long-term well-being of the Swedes. A Swedish government report from 1901 showed that a number of timber, pulp, and paper companies had foreign shareholders, mostly from Norway and Great Britain. However, only ten of the 192 companies surveyed had a majority of shares in foreign hands.[31]

In 1906, the Swedish Parliament passed a new law that severely restricted further acquisitions of forests in the northern counties for all private companies (including domestic companies). The years 1917 and 1926 saw further extensions to this law, so that eventually it encompassed the whole country. The resulting legislation opened the forests for increased state control and local ownership by farmers. Investments by both foreign and private Swedish forest product companies were halted.[32]

The third major natural resource in Sweden was hydropower. In this sector, state involvement was triggered by the need to revise the old water laws, which were ill-suited to hydropower development. By archaic law, the Swedish Crown owned one-third of navigable rivers, with strong protection of the natural flow of water. As the law placed fewer restrictions on state intervention in natural water flow, in 1909 the Swedish state itself undertook the construction of the large power plant in Trollhättan. The project was carried out in close cooperation with Swedish industrialists and was primarily aimed at providing Swedish industry with cheap electricity. This state-led electrification continued in the following years, partly spurred by coal shortages during the First World War, partly by ambitious (and unfulfilled) plans to develop hydropower-based steel and fertilizer production. In the postwar depression, the economic rationale for the hydropower plants disappeared. While this dampened the enthusiasm for further large-scale state-led hydroelectric developments, these early power plants formed the foundation of the huge – and still state-owned – Swedish energy company *Vattenfall*.

For the most part, the water law of 1918 favoured Swedish industry. The legal framework was made easier and more predictable, and an independent water court was established. It was thought that making regulation and development permissions the purview of an independent court rather than the government would render questions regarding water use safe from the meddling of future left-leaning governments who might regulate and tax development in a way more akin to what was happening in neighbouring Norway (see below).[33]

The main outcomes of the Swedish debates on resource ownership were as follows: (1) the state was given new powers to regulate the economy; (2) the state promoted domestic ownership of its most valuable resources, both for national security reasons and to ensure domestic resource capture; (3) the state cooperated closely with domestic industrialists, both by promoting domestic ownership and by developing hydroelectricity for industrial use; and (4) the cooperation between state and industry had its limits (e.g., forest laws had a strong element of social engineering as they protected smallholders' access to land against large forestry companies).

Norwegian Hydropower and the Concession Laws

Norway was an autonomous part of the Kingdom of Sweden and Norway until it achieved full independence in 1905. Norway had a somewhat different socioeconomic structure than did the other Nordic countries, and this undoubtedly had some implications for its resource policies. Historically, Norway had very few estates. By 1850, the large majority of Norwegian farmers were freeholders. Land ownership was therefore not a contested issue as it was in Denmark and Finland, and there were no calls for any comprehensive land reform. Norway was for a long time the most democratic of the Nordic countries, and the centre of gravity in Norwegian politics tended to be further left than was the case in neighbouring countries.

Norway had followed fairly liberal policies on both trade and resource ownership in the nineteenth century. At the beginning of the century, Norwegian exports were dominated by shipping, fish, and forestry products. Shipping was by far the largest enterprise, constituting about 39 percent of total exports, with wood-based products accounting for 20 percent in 1895.[34] There was significant foreign ownership in the wood processing industry as well as in the mining industry. For most of the nineteenth century, foreign ownership of natural resources was largely uncontroversial.

The major turning point in Norwegian natural resource regulation came with the rise of the energy-intensive electrochemical and electrometallurgical industries. Norway's numerous rivers and streams flowing down from its high mountain plateau suddenly became an economic asset as it provided the country with a huge potential for hydroelectric energy. These new industries required large amounts of capital to be exploited, and the best situated waterfalls were rapidly purchased by speculators and foreign-owned electrochemical companies. By 1906, over three-quarters of all hydroelectric works with a turbine capacity of more than three thousand horsepower (hp) were in foreign hands.[35] The dominant position of foreign owners in this highly valuable natural resource caused alarm in the newly independent country. The same year, the Norwegian Parliament passed a hastily prepared law that made all acquisitions of riparian rights by foreigners or limited companies dependent upon a government concession.

The new laws opened a Pandora's Box of government regulations, and, over the following years, the reach of the so-called Concession Laws was considerably extended. In the summer of 1906, acquisition of forests and mineral claims was also included, and the year after, the law was expanded to cover power lease contracts.

The Norwegian government quickly adopted the practice of adding a number of specific terms to its resource concessions. At first, these terms only covered the number of Norwegian nationals on the company board of directors, but it soon became common to include terms that gave preference to Norwegian-made machinery and materials. Later, concession taxes, clauses requiring power companies to sell power to the local municipality at a low set price, as well as minimum conditions on workers housing and welfare would also become commonplace. These particular developments stand in contrast to what happened in Sweden. They illustrate how Norwegian liberal reformers used the Concession Laws in a somewhat ad hoc way in order to reduce hardships and stifle discontent among the working classes and rural farmers.

Another radical new principle, the Right of Reversion (*Hjemfallsrett*), was introduced in 1907. This clause stated that the waterfall in a concession, with all dams, buildings, turbines, and generators, would pass to the state without compensation when the concession expired (usually after sixty to eighty years). The Right of Reversion became obligatory for all hydropower as well as mining concessions in 1909.[36] Proponents argued that this would prevent long-term monopolization of power by private companies and would ensure that, in the end, the benefits and profits of cheap hydroelectricity would come into Norwegian hands. When challenged over the prospect of a future state monopoly, Prime Minister Knudsen – one of the important architects of the Concession Laws – responded that he did not see that as a problem: "The state is all of us. It is not just a company of a few."[37]

As in Sweden, so in Norway the Concession Laws reflected both a continuation of policy as well as a radical new principle of government domain. The hydropower policy had some resemblance to nineteenth-century railway policy as all trunk lines were state owned. But, as in Sweden, the concession laws also aimed to ensure that the benefits of the country's

Regulation of Natural Resources in the Nordic Countries   55

natural wealth came into Norwegian hands, both through measures to facilitate spillover effects to the rest of the economy and as future public ownership. However, the Norwegian Concession Laws on foreign ownership of natural resources provide an interesting contrast to the Swedish Restriction Act. Whereas the Swedish law was a tool to prevent unwanted foreign ownership of natural resources, the Norwegian policy of applying conditions to concessions created a compromise solution whereby foreign ownership could be accepted but with set conditions designed to prevent perceived negative consequences. Norway opted for such an approach largely due to its lack of strong domestic industrial companies. In Norway, barring foreign-owned companies from investing in natural resources could effectively have meant barring growth in these industries as a whole.

Thus, Concession Laws were not initially used to refuse new foreign investments in hydropower and mining. Rather than an unbreachable barrier, inward foreign direct investment continued on a large scale after the first Concession Law, with the share of foreign ownership increasing rather than decreasing in the years leading up to the Great War. By 1909, foreign share ownership of mining and the electrochemical industries was as high as 80 percent and 85 percent, respectively.[38] Furthermore, the laws only applied to new acquisitions, leaving out mines and hydropower plants that predated them.

To what extent domestic-owned companies' access to natural resources should also be regulated remained a controversial aspect of the Concession Laws debates. Treating all joint stock companies equally regardless of which nation owned them had some key advantages as determining exactly who owned what shares, and ensuring that they remained in the hands of a certain nation after a concession had been given, was notoriously difficult. Extending all aspects of the laws to Norwegian-owned companies – which for the most part did not have the necessary capital to undertake large hydroelectric or mining operations anyway – closed an important loophole. Furthermore, some aspects of the law ensuring workers welfare and safety, and guarding against monopolies, were not only applicable to foreign-owned companies. Thus, the radical Liberal Party opted for equal treatment, which, in 1909, became the guiding principle of the first permanent Concession Laws on hydropower and mining.

The Norwegian government followed a much stricter policy on foreign ownership of forests. In contrast to the electrochemical and mining industries, Norway had a competitive domestic-owned forest industry.[39] After the first Concession Law was introduced in 1906, further acquisitions of forests by foreign-owned companies were practically halted. This policy was then cemented when, in 1909, the first permanent Concession Law on forests categorically banned companies with as much as a single foreign-owned share from buying forests. However, the new legislation was not exclusively aimed at foreigners. The law also contained provisions to protect farmers against industrial interests by, for example, prohibiting the sale of forests owned by farmers (Norwegian: *gårdsskog*) to non-local residents.[40] In this regard, the Norwegian forest law bears some similarity to the Swedish law.

When the final Concession Law on hydropower and mining was passed in 1917, resource nationalism was given a more profound presence. According to the new law, public ownership was strongly favoured, and foreign companies were only allowed to acquire Norwegian hydroelectric plants or riparian resources under "singular circumstances."[41] The First World War had dramatically altered the Norwegian economy as revenue from booming export industries and Norwegian shipping created a vast capital surplus, much of which was used to fund the first significant Norwegian-owned hydroelectric and electrochemical companies or to "repatriate" key foreign-owned companies operating in Norway.[42] Consequently, the Norwegian government shifted towards a stricter concession policy according to which new foreign direct investments in hydropower and energy-intensive industry were discouraged.[43] Repatriations were not carried out only by private investors: during the war, the Norwegian state purchased a large unfinished Swedish-owned hydropower plant in northern Norway as well as rich pyrite claims in central Norway from a French-owned aluminium company as a precondition for a power lease concession to a new aluminium smelter.[44]

The restrictive policy on foreign investments was relaxed in the 1920s. The postwar depression, which began in the autumn of 1920, hit Norway hard and was particularly detrimental to the electrochemical industries. In the following years several Norwegian banks failed and were placed under receivership, and unemployment rose dramatically. The state investments in hydropower and mining turned out to be spectacular economic failures and became a permanent stain on the resource policy of the Liberal wartime government. State investments in resource development or resource-based industries were not repeated until the post 1945-era; instead, the Norwegian governments of the interwar era agreed to give concessions to foreign investors willing to refinance Norwegian resource-based industries.[45]

The Norwegian governments developed an altogether different system of rent capture than did their Swedish neighbours. Through the terms system

Regulation of Natural Resources in the Nordic Countries 57

the government was given the option to compromise between denying and allowing unrestricted foreign ownership in the resource sectors. Another crucial difference between the Norwegian and the Swedish systems was the willingness to strictly regulate domestically owned companies. All in all, the Norwegian regulation system had a stronger pro-public ownership and decentralized rent redistribution element than did the Swedish.

Finland's "Green Gold"

Finland was a part of Sweden until 1809, when it was transferred to Russia as an autonomous grand duchy. The Finns were allowed a relatively large degree of independence in terms of domestic policies. Swedish legislation and institutional settings remained largely intact. Like Norway and Sweden, Finland had both important mineral ores and hydropower resources, yet, just as in Denmark, it was the question of ownership of agricultural land that first became a burning political issue. However, after Finland gained full independence in 1917, the question of foreign ownership of natural resources became as important as the predominantly social question of ownership of land.

Finland was a country of small farms – increasingly so during the nineteenth century. Estate farming was never widespread in Finland.[46] In addition, the country had a large number of crofters – seventy thousand by 1895.[47] The crofters leased land from a landlord and paid rent either in money, in kind, or in labour. The crofters lived on tiny scraps of leased land insufficient to sustain their families, and they made their living through seasonal work in the forests or on the watercourses. The lease conditions for the crofts deteriorated in the second half of the nineteenth century. Yet the increasing number of crofts could not match the general population growth. Since Finland was late to industrialize and had low emigration rates compared with Sweden and Norway, the number of its rural poor increased.[48]

As Finnish exports of wood products increased in the late nineteenth century the forests became more valuable. Landlords therefore became less willing to give the crofters the right to free use of the forests. Many crofters had only verbal lease contracts with their landlords, and the agreements frequently had no set timeframes,[49] meaning that the crofters could be evicted on short notice. At the turn of the twentieth century there were a number of conflicts between landlords and crofters, and there were some cases of large-scale evictions of crofters.[50] In 1909, the Finnish state decided that all crofters should have a minimum tenancy of fifty years, and evictions were temporarily banned.[51]

The crofter question was provided with a more permanent solution in 1918. After the Finns gained full independence in December 1917 following the Russian Revolution, in January 1918 the National Assembly was presented with a proposal concerning crofters' rights. Yet before that proposal could be debated, the country descended into a short, but violent, civil war between the forces of the Social Democrats and socialists (commonly called the reds) and the forces of the non-socialist, conservative-led Senate (commonly called the whites). The whites won the war, but the victors realized that they had to alleviate the widespread rural poverty if they were to minimize the political attraction of the socialists. Many crofters had joined the reds during the civil war. The Leaseholder's Act of October 1918 gave crofters the right to purchase up to ten hectares of farmland and twenty hectares of forest. The state paid compensation to the landowners, and the former crofter, now farmer, reimbursed the state over several years. In 1922, a new law opened up for expropriations. Up until the end of the 1930s more than forty-six thousand crofts were converted into independent farms. More than one-eighth of all agricultural land in the country had changed status from leased land to farmland, mostly through voluntary sales.[52]

Development in Finland has several similarities to development in Denmark; however, whereas the Danish Parliament's attempt to improve the position of ordinary tenant farmers did not lead to widespread challenges to property rights, the Finnish state, with its new legislation (put in place between 1918 and 1922), did not shy away from challenging the sanctity of private property. This must be understood against the backdrop of the Finnish civil war, which made it imperative to do something forceful about widespread rural poverty.

At the same time as the young Finnish state was involved in social engineering, it was also addressing the question of foreign ownership over natural resources. Besides agricultural land, the key resource in Finland has always been its vast forests of "green gold." In 1920, as much as 93.7 percent of Finnish exports were wood-based products.[53] However, before Finnish independence, the forestry industry in Finland was to a large extent dominated by foreign – mostly Norwegian – companies, supported by British and continental capital, that had bought large tracts of forests in the latter decades of the nineteenth century.[54] Forestry's crucial importance to the Finnish economy ensured that foreign ownership of forests would be controversial. Finland had used its licence laws – which required foreign legal subjects (but not foreign-owned Finnish companies) to acquire government permission for land and mineral acquisitions – sparingly in the nineteenth century.[55] However, restrictions were tightened in 1915, when Finland introduced a new law limiting further acquisitions of forests on the part of companies. The new law must be understood in connection with the crofter question. The government wanted to avoid a situation in which large companies purchased all forest areas, thus making it difficult for cottagers and crofters to become independent farmers.

After independence, the Finnish government intervened and bought several of the largest foreign-owned forestry companies, such as *Gutzeit* and *Tornator*.[56] These companies also owned the riparian rights to some of Finland's most important watercourses. Other foreign-owned forestry firms, such as *Salvesen* and *Halla*, were acquired by private Finnish investors.

The state also took an active interest in the ownership of hydropower. Before 1917, the Finnish government had done its best to prevent foreign investors from developing the Imatra Falls, one of the country's largest waterfalls. These foreign ventures were primarily motivated by the prospects of selling electric power to St. Petersburg, which, in the eyes of the Finnish government, would link Karelia uncomfortably tightly to the imperial capital. Moreover, the Imatra Falls could also serve as a vital source of cheap energy for Finland if its electricity were not exported to Russia. After gaining independence, the Finnish government moved to cement this policy. All export of electricity from Finland was banned, and, in 1920, the Finnish government expropriated the remaining, primarily French-owned parts of the falls. Not satisfied with the compensation, the foreign owners tried to improve their position by enlisting support from the British and French governments, but to no avail. With this, foreign direct investments in Finnish hydroelectricity came to an end, with the Finnish government owning all major hydropower resources in southern Finland.[57]

There were two main considerations behind the large state acquisitions. First, the government wanted to increase the state's influence on the country's development. The new-won political independence would be worthless if it were not followed by economic independence. Second, the companies that the state took over owned large tracts of land that could be distributed to crofters and cottagers.[58]

The Finnish state also engaged in copper mining. The Outokumpu Company was established before the First World War as a joint venture between the Finnish state and Finnish capitalists. In 1917, a Norwegian-Finnish company leased the mine, but after it went bankrupt three years later the Finnish state took control by buying a share majority. While the country could use both foreign capital and know-how to develop the copper deposits, nationalist considerations and fear of foreign exploitation of a non-renewable Finnish resource prevailed. Domestic production of copper was also important for defence purposes and was not seen as compatible with foreign ownership. Numerous foreign company bids on Outokumpu were turned down, and instead the state increased its stake, making it fully state-owned from 1925.[59]

Yet Finland eventually came to accept foreign investments in its other great mineral deposit – the nickel of the Petsamo region. Following the discovery of nickel in the early 1920s, the Finnish state first tried to develop the finds through the domestic Outokumpu Company. However, by 1930, the government realized that the undertaking was beyond its capacities and that it needed both foreign know-how and foreign capital. In 1934, the deposits were sold to the world's largest nickel company, the Canadian-American International Nickel Company (INCO).[60]

As the country entered a period of relative high growth in the second half of the 1930s, the Finnish political stance once more shifted against inward foreign investments. With foreign capital less crucial for economic growth, Finland passed new restrictive laws on foreign acquisitions in 1939. Henceforth, foreign citizens and foreign companies would need government permission to obtain, or acquire the long-term lease of, real estate in Finland. The law also applied to Finnish joint stock companies that allowed more than 20 percent foreign share ownership.[61]

Compared to neighbouring Sweden and Norway, Finland initially took a different approach to solving the issue of foreign ownership of natural resources. Rather than introducing laws regulating all ownership of natural resources the Finnish state nationalized key natural resource-owning companies. This also happened on a smaller scale in Norway around the time of the First World War. Yet when raw material prices plummeted after the First World War, Finland did not experience the same political backlash against state ownership as did Norway, and the policy continued for much of the interwar era.

Conclusion

It is possible to identify four main objectives of the Nordic countries' resource policies. The first objective was *to secure domestic ownership of natural resources.*[62] Even Denmark, where hydropower played no significant economic role, introduced strict provisions against foreign ownership for its only major hydropower plant.[63] In a nationalistic era, domestic ownership was perceived as an important goal in itself, especially for natural resources, which were viewed as a collective good for the countries' citizens. However, in some cases ownership issues and national security were intertwined, most notably in the Swedish fear of Russia prior to 1914 and the Finnish fear of the Soviet Union after 1917. In general, policy makers feared foreign *political* domination, which was thought might follow in the wake of economic influence. This was not necessarily so much an immediate fear of hostile neighbours as a caution against the longer-term effects of being too closely integrated into another country's economy.

The second objective was *to exploit natural resources to foster economic growth*. This growth policy could manifest itself in different ways. In Sweden and Finland (and less successfully in Norway) the state initiated hydropower projects. It also manifested itself in rent capture policies aimed at increasing the spillover effects of natural resource extraction. Promoting domestic ownership can also be explained as a policy of rent capture as it was thought that domestic owners were more inclined to plough their profits back into the national economy.

The first and second objectives were at times at odds with one another. This led the three non-agricultural resource-rich countries to choose quite different policies. In Sweden, private Swedish-owned companies were the main "harvesters" of resource rents, with the state acting as a guardian against unwanted foreign ownership through state ownership and/or regulation. Norway solved this issue through a comprehensive and complex system of government concessions with specific terms. Substantial foreign investments were thus allowed. In post-independent Finland the state maintained national rent capture and control through widespread government ownership. However, even the Finns welcomed foreign ownership of its huge nickel deposit, which could not be developed by domestic interests. The Nordics were pragmatists: they were willing to sacrifice some growth in order to achieve domestic ownership over natural resources, but if the costs were too high, foreign ownership was tolerated.

The third objective of the Nordic countries was *to ensure that natural resources would benefit or be accessible to a large part of the population*. This is particularly apparent in Danish and Finnish land policies, but it was also an important aspect of Swedish and Norwegian forest laws. The Norwegian concession laws for hydropower ensured that household consumers in municipalities with private hydropower ownership would have access to electricity at reasonable rates.

The fourth objective of the Nordic resource policies was *respect for private property rights*. Natural resources owned by domestic or foreign companies were not forcefully nationalized or confiscated. The only cases in which property rights were clearly infringed upon involved agricultural land during the social turmoil following the Great War and the Russian Revolution. Furthermore, it is important to note that the comprehensive Norwegian Concession Laws did not apply to mines or hydropower plants built before these laws were passed. The government also did its utmost to appear as a trustworthy and reliable partner when it negotiated natural resource concessions with foreign-owned companies. It is, however, worth mentioning that regulations came at a cost; there were examples in which long processing times and uncertainty over concession terms put potential investors off investing in Norway.[64]

To sum up: Is it possible to find a common Nordic natural resource regulation policy? While the resource endowments and the policy details differed, the countries aimed at achieving fairly similar objectives – namely, domestic ownership, economic growth, economic redistribution, and respect for property rights. In all four countries the state became increasingly interventionist, partly because of comprehensive resource regulations. However, as the regulatory systems were so different from one another, it is perhaps more prudent to talk about a Nordic "approach" than a Nordic "regulatory system."

Notes

1 For detailed analysis of the political economy of the late nineteenth-century Nordic countries, see Bo Stråth, *Union och demokrati: De förenade rikena Sverige och Norge, 1814–1905* (Nora: Nya Doxa, 2005); Niels Kayser Nielsen, *Bonde, stat og hjem: Nordisk demokrati og nationalisme – fra pietismen til 2. verdenskrig* (Århus: Aarhus Universitetsforlag, 2009); and Niels Thomsen, *Industri, stat og samfund, 1870–1939* (Odense: Odense Universitetsforlag, 1991); Niels Thomsen, *Hovedstrømninger, 1870–1914: Idélandskabet under dansk kultur, politik og hverdagsliv* (Odense: Odense Universitetsforlag, 1998).

2 Lars G. Sandberg, "The Case of the Impoverished Sophisticate, Human Capital and Swedish Economic Growth before World War I," *Journal of Economic History* 39, 1 (1979): 225–41.

3 Martin Fritz, *Svensk järnmalmsexport, 1883–1913*, Meddelanden från Ekonomiskhistoriska institutionen vid Göteborgs universitet (Göteborg: Ekonomiskhistoriska institutionen vid Göteborgs universitet, 1967); Artur Attman, *Svenskt järn och stål, 1800–1914* (Stockholm: Jernkontoret, 1986); Fredrik Olsson, *Järnhenteringens dynamik: Produktion, lokalisering och agglomerationer i Bergslagen ock Mellansverige,*

1368–1910 (Umeå: Umeå universitet, 2007); Ernst Söderlund, *Svensk Trävaruexport under hundra år* (Stockholm: Svenska Trävaruexportforeningen, 1951).

4 Francis Sejersted, *Den vanskelige frihet: Norge, 1814–1850* (Oslo: Pax, 2001), 179–80; Fritz Hodne, *Norges økonomiske historie, 1815–1970* (Oslo: Cappelen, 1981); Pål Thonstad Sandvik, "En mer demokratisk kapitalisme? Økonomi og samfunnsutvikling i Trøndelag, 1750–1920," *Historisk Tidsskrift* 86, 1 (2007): 44–45; *Nasjonens velstand: Norges økonomiske historie, 1800–1940* (Bergen: Fagbokforlaget, 2018).

5 D.G. Kirby, *A Concise History of Finland*, Cambridge Concise Histories (Cambridge: Cambridge University Press, 2006), 110.

6 Angus Maddison, *The World Economy: Historical Statistics* (Paris: OECD Publishing, 2003), Table 1c.

7 Hans Jensen, *Dansk Jordpolitik, 1757–1919* (København: Gyldendal, 1945), 97, 275–76, 453–54; Claus Bjørn, Troels Dahlerup, S.P. Jensen, and Erik Helmer Pedersen, eds., *Det Danske landbrugs historie III, 1810–1914* (Odense: Landbohistorisk Selskab, 1988), 121.

8 Jensen, *Dansk Jordpolitik*, 274–350.

9 Ibid.

10 Thomsen, *Hovedstrømninger*, 127.

11 Jensen, *Dansk Jordpolitik*, 94–95, 276–82, 372–77.

12 Ibid., 405–14; Torben W. Smith, *Vi vil rejse nye huse: statshusmandsloven af 1899* (Auning: Landbohistorisk Selskab, 1999).

13 Jensen, *Dansk Jordpolitik*, 415–16.

14 Bo Fritzbøger, *Kulturskoven, Dansk skovbrug fra oldtid til nutid* (København: Gyldendalske Boghandel, 1994), 69–71, 80–81, 132–33, 380–82.

15 Hanne Serup, "Forstordning, skovordning og forstplanlægging, treforsyningen fra de danske skove ordnes," in *Skovhistorie for fremtiden*, ed. Bo Fritzbøger and Petter Friis Møller (Hørsholm: Skovhistorisk Selskab, 2005), 50.

16 Fritzbøger, *Kulturskoven*, 80–81, 95–98, 387–92.

17 Bo Stråth, *1830–1920*, vol. 6, Sveriges historia (Stockholm: Norstedts, 2012), 178.

18 Brynjulf Gjerdåker, *1814–1920: Kontinuitet og modernitet*, vol. 3, Norges landbrukshistorie (Oslo: Samlaget, 2002), 107–8.

19 Lennart Schön, *En modern svensk ekonomisk historia: Tillväxt och omvandling under två sekel*, 2nd ed. (Stockholm: SNS Förlag, 2007), 237–39.

20 Sven Nordlund, *Upptäckten av Sverige: Utländska direktinvesteringar i Sverige 1895–1945*, Umeå Studies in Economic History (Umeå: Umeå universitet, 1989), Table 19.

21 Sweden had a long tradition of iron export, but the advent of the Bessemer process and the low price of coal as opposed to Swedish charcoal had hurt the Swedish iron industry's competitiveness. Sweden could only cover about 6.5 percent of its annual consumption from domestic coal mines (1913). See Schön, *En modern svensk ekonomisk historia*, 175–76; and Timo Myllyntaus and Eerik Tarnaala, "Economic Crisis in Finland and Sweden, 1914–1924," in *Economic Crises and Restructuring in History: Experiences of Small Countries*, ed. Timo Myllyntaus (St. Katharinen, DE: Scripta Mercaturae, 1998), 44.

22 See, for instance, Bo Jonsson, *Staten och malmfälten: En studie i svensk malmfälts-politik omkring sekelskiftet* (Stockholm: Almqvist and Wiskell, 1969), 16, 28, 30–31, 83–85; Nils Meinander, *Gränges: en krönika om svensk järnmalm* (Helsingfors: Tilgmann, 1968), 72–73; Stråth, *1830–1920*, 352.

23 The Swedish state bought the remaining half in 1957, and LKAB remains wholly state owned to this day.

24 Albert Kôersner, *Lag om vissa inskränkningar i rätten att förvärva fast egendom eller gruva eller aktier i vissa bolag given den 30 maj 1916* (Stockholm: Aktiebolaget Nordiska bokhandeln, 1916), 6.

25 Nordlund, *Upptäckten av Sverige*, 44–52.

26 Kôersner, *Lag om vissa inskränkningar i rätten att förvärva fast egendom*; Nordlund, *Upptäckten av Sverige*, 54.

27 This policy is expressly stated in this case: Svenska Riksarkivet (SRA), Justitie-departementet Statsrådsprotokoll 1920, 18.06.1920: Nr. 44.

28 See the case of Skandinavisk Montainindustri, Zinc de la Vieille Montagne and Fagersta Bruk SRA, Justitiedepartementet Statsrådsprotokoll, 29.08.1924: Nr. 26, 29.08.1924: Nr. 24, 22.06.1928: Nr. 56, 07.02.1919: Nr. 26.

29 Nordlund, *Upptäckten av Sverige*, 121.

30 Mats Larsson, *En svensk ekonomisk historia, 1850–1985* (Stockholm: SNS, 1993), 61.

31 Nordlund, *Upptäckten av Sverige*, 49.

32 This paragraph is based on Jan Jörnmark, *Skogen, staten och kapitalisterna: Skapande förstörelse i svensk basindustri 1810–1950* (Lund: Studentlitteratur, 2004), 54; Nordlund, *Upptäckten av Sverige*, 106–14; Sverker Sörlin, *Framtidslandet: Debatten om Norrland och naturresurserna under det industriella genombrottet* (Stockholm: Carlsson, 1988).

33 K.H. Högstedt, *Vattenlagen av den 28. juni 1918 med däri den 19. juni 1919 och den 11. juni 1920 vidtagna förändringar,* suppl. ed. (Stockholm: P.A. Norstedt & Söner 1923), 145–66; Eva Jakobsson, *Industrialisering av älvar: Studier kring svensk vattenkraftutbyggnad 1900–1918,* Avhandlingar från Historiska institutionen i Göteborg (Göteborg: Historiska institutionen, 1996).

34 Hodne, *Norges økonomiske historie*, 160, Table 6.

35 Lars Thue, *Statens kraft 1890–1947: Kraftutbygging og samfunnsutvikling,* 2nd ed. (Oslo: Universitetsforlaget, 2006), 75.

36 Olaf Amundsen, *Lov om erhvervelse av vandfald, bergverk og anden fast eiendom: koncessions-loven av 14 december 1917 – med kommentar* (Kristiania: Aschehoug, 1918).

37 Anders Haaland, *Fra konsesjonslov til "midlertidig trustlov" – norsk konkurransepolitikk, 1905–1926,* SNF-rapport (Bergen: Stiftelsen for samfunns- og næringslivsforskning, 1995), 72.

38 Arthur Stonehill, *Foreign Ownership in Norwegian Enterprises,* Samfunnsøkonomiske studier (Oslo: Statistisk sentralbyrå, 1965), 36.

39 Haaland, *Fra konsesjonslov til "midlertidig trustlov,"* 62.

40 Per Augdahl, *Skogkoncessionsloven: Lov om erhvervelse av skog av 18. september 1909 med ændringslove av 13. august 1915 og 26. juli 1916 – med kommentar* (Kristiania: Cappelen, 1920).

41 Amundsen, *Lov om erhvervelse av vandfaldr*, 93.

42 Stonehill, *Foreign Ownership in Norwegian Enterprises*, 41–43.

43 Andreas R. Dugstad Sanders, "Europe's Northern Resource Frontier: The Political Economy of Resource Nationalism in Sweden and Norway 1888–1936" (PhD thesis, European University Institute, Florence, 2018), 203–75.

44 Espen Storli, "Out of Norway Falls Aluminium: The Norwegian Aluminium Industry in the International Economy, 1908–1940" (PhD diss., Norwegian University of Science and Technology, Trondheim, 2010), 99–102; Sanders, "Europe's Northern Resource Frontier," 233–39.

45 Stonehill, *Foreign Ownership in Norwegian Enterprises*, 45–55; Pål Thonstad Sandvik, *Multinationals, Subsidiaries and National Business Systems: The Nickel Industry and Falconbridge Nikkelverk*, Studies in Business History (London: Pickering and Chatto, 2012), 32–33.

46 Jari Ojala and Ilkka Nummela, "Feeding Economic Growth: Agriculture," in *The Road to Prosperity: An Economic History of Finland*, ed. Jari Ojala, Jari Eloranta, and Jukka Jalava (Helsinki: Suomaleisen Kirjallisuuden Seura, 2006), 76–77.

47 Matti Klinge, *Kejsartiden* (Helsingfors: Schildts, 1996), 97.

48 Kirby, *Concise History of Finland*, 113.

49 "Torpväsen," in *Uppslagsverket Finland*, ed. Henrik Ekberg (Helsinki: Schildts Förlags AB, 2007).

50 Klinge, *Kejsartiden*, 98.

51 Kirby, *Concise History of Finland*, 154–56.

52 Klinge, *Kejsartiden*, 98–99; Ojala and Nummela, "Feeding Economic Growth," 77; "Torpväsen," 182.

53 Karl-Erik Michelsen and Markku Kuisma, "Nationalism and Industrial Development in Finland," *Business and Economic History* 21, 2 (1992): 343–53.

54 Riitta Hjerppe and Jorma Ahvenainen, "Foreign Enterprises and Nationalistic Control: The Case of Finland since the End of the Nineteenth Century," in *Multinational Enterprise in Historical Perspective*, ed. Alice Teichova, Helga Nussbaum, and Maurice Lévy-Leboyer (Cambridge: Cambridge University Press, 1986), 288.

55 Ibid., 286–87; Ojala and Nummela, "Feeding Economic Growth," 16–18.

56 Knut Sogner and Sverre A. Christensen, *Plankeadel: Kiær- og Solberg-familien under den 2. industrielle revolusjon* (Oslo: Andresen and Butenschøn for Handelshøyskolen BI, 2001), 93–95, 134–35.

57 Timo Myllyntaus, *Electrifying Finland: The Transfer of a New Technology into a Late Industrialising Economy*, Series A/ETLA, the Research Institute of the Finnish Economy (Basingstoke: Macmillan in association with ETLA, 1991), 61f; Victor Hoving, *Enso-Gutzeit Osakeyhtiö, 1872–1958*, vol. 1 (Helsinki: Frenckellska Tryckeri Aktiebolaget, 1961), 166–72.

58 Hoving, *Enso-Gutzeit Osakeyhtiö*, 170.

59 Markku Kuisma, *A History of Outokumpu* (Jyväskylä: Gummerus kirjapaino OY, 1989), 3–45.

60 Matt Bray, "INCO's Petsamo Venture, 1933–1945: An Incident in Canadian, British, Finnish and Soviet Relations," *International Journal of Canadian Studies* 9 (1994):

175–77; Jari Eloranta and Ilkka Nummela, "Finnish Nickel as a Strategic Metal, 1920–1944," *Scandinavian Journal of History* 4, 32 (2007): 328–31.

61 Jukka Luukkanen, "How to Deal with the Legislation Concerning the Rights of Foreigners to Own Shares and Real Estate in Finland – Especially Concentrating on Voting Agreements" (LLM thesis, Harvard Law School, 1991), 1–4; Hjerppe and Ahvenainen, "Foreign Enterprises and Nationalistic Control," 290.

62 Andreas R. Dugstad Sanders, Pål Thonstad Sandvik, and Espen Storli, "Dealing with Globalisation: The Nordic Countries and Inward FDI, 1900–1939," *Business History* 58, 8 (2016): 1210–35.

63 *Lov om Udnyttelse af Vandkraften i Gudenaa 1918 (Denmark)* §1 o, https://www.retsinformation.dk/Forms/R0710.aspx?id=12299 (viewed 17 August 2018).

64 Dugstad, "Chasing Waterfalls," 107–9.

3
Regulating Natural Resources in Canada
A Brief Historical Survey
ROBIN S. GENDRON and ANDREAS R.D. SANDERS

Canada is a resource-rich country that historically has depended upon the exploitation of its natural resources for much of its wealth and prosperity. Indeed, an influential argument – the staples thesis – first developed in the 1920s postulated that much of Canada's history, the structure of its economy, its politics, and its society could be explained in relation to the exploitation of a sequence of resources from furs and fish through timber and wheat and, ultimately, minerals and energy products.[1] The staples thesis no longer wields the influence over the study of Canadian history that it once did, yet its eclipse has not diminished the basic truth that the exploitation and thus the regulation of natural resources has played and continues to play a vital role in the Canadian economy and in Canada's societal and political discourse.

The long-term importance of natural resources in Canada provides an interesting opportunity for a long timescale survey of the evolution of Canadian natural resource regulations. And while the Canadian experience is in many ways unique, the broader transformation of Canadian resource policy also corresponds to the global trends identified in this volume. Here we divide the history of Canadian resource regulations into three periods: (1) the transitional period in the early twentieth century when states such as Canada began to impose degrees of resource nationalism on older models of liberalism in the exploitation of resources such as hydro power, forestry products, and minerals; (2) the mid-twentieth century period, which is highlighted by an even greater degree of resource nationalism in the management of resources such as the St. Lawrence River and the oil industry (though still within continental constraints); and (3) the late twentieth century period, which features the resurgence of liberal approaches to the regulation and exploitation of natural resources characterized by the abandonment of the National Energy Program and the completion of major international trade deals such as the Free Trade Agreement and the North American Free Trade Agreement.

Moreover, this brief examination highlights the degree to which, in Canada, political disputes and controversy have been central to the regulation of natural resources and their exploitation since the late nineteenth century. This provides an important historical perspective on present-day debates, which are now marked by a degree of pessimism about the future of resource development in Canada after a number of pipeline and mineral developments have stalled, partly due to societal division over the wisdom of such projects and how to divide the expected benefits among the various stakeholders, including (especially) Indigenous peoples in Canada.[2] This contemporary pessimism, however, forgets that resource development and resource regulation have always been complicated issues subject to intense jurisdictional disputes between different levels of Canadian government, to competing societal visions of what constitutes appropriate resource regulation and development, and to the constraints imposed upon Canadian governments and industry by the continental and global/imperial contexts within which they operate. Consequently, they are not unique to the early twenty-first century.

The Jurisdictional Framework for Resource Regulation in Canada

Canada is a federal state in which political powers and responsibilities are divided or shared between the federal/national government and the ten provincial and three territorial governments. The British North America Act, 1867, Canada's original Constitution, awarded the ownership of land and resources to the provincial governments and reserved to them the management and sale of public land (i.e., Crown lands); the Constitution, however, gave the federal government jurisdiction over the regulation of trade and commerce, fisheries, shipping and navigation, and other powers, including the power to disallow any provincial law, which enabled it to exert influence over the regulation of natural resources after 1867.[3] As a result of this division of powers, in the late nineteenth century the federal and provincial governments – especially Ontario – engaged in extensive jurisdictional disputes over Crown lands and natural resources, the royalties from which represented the largest portion of state revenues at the time.[4] However, as, by 1900, the courts largely decided the jurisdictional issue in favour of the provinces, thereafter the federal government's involvement in the direct regulation of natural resources and its use of the power of disallowance declined significantly.[5] Still, the federal government continued to exercise direct control over Crown lands in the territories acquired as a result of the transfer of Rupert's Land and the North-West Territory to Canada in 1870, only relinquishing this control to the provinces of Alberta, Manitoba, and Saskatchewan in 1930 and to the territories of the Northwest Territories, Nunavut, and Yukon in the late twentieth century.

Even with the gradual diminishment of the federal government's direct involvement in the regulation of natural resources, this continues to be a field of overlapping responsibilities between the federal and the provincial governments. Through its powers over trade and commerce, in particular, as well as its ability to control such things as foreign investment or, increasingly, environmental regulations, the federal government still exercises significant influence over the development and exploitation of Canada's extensive natural resources.[6] In addition, the regulation of natural resources in Canada has also been affected and/or conditioned by international treaties and conventions, from the Boundary Waters Treaty of 1909 between Canada and the United States to the United Nations Convention on the Law of the Sea, the North American Free Trade Agreement (NAFTA), and beyond. Finally, to the above must be added the belated recognition and weight given to the treaty rights and powers of Aboriginal peoples in Canada, particularly after 1982, when reforms entrenched respect for Aboriginal treaty rights within Canada's Constitution. In recent decades, the acknowledgment of Aboriginal title to and rights over their lands has resulted in Canada's First Nations being accorded an increasingly important role in the management of the country's natural resources at both local and regional levels.[7]

Overall, the evolution of Canada's constitutional, legal, and institutional frameworks has resulted in a system wherein the regulation of natural resources is primarily the responsibility of the thirteen provincial and territorial governments, albeit with significant inputs and/or constraints from the federal government, the nation's international commitments, and its treaty obligations to First Nations. It is a patchwork system in which resource regulations can vary widely in different parts of the country, but it is also one that often involves significant intergovernmental and stakeholder collaboration, which is generally geared towards maximizing the economic and other societal benefits of the exploitation of Canada's natural resources.

The "New Staples" and Provincial Resource Nationalism, 1880–1939

One element that makes Canada stand out is the high degree of public ownership of land. Here Canada stands in considerable contrast to its neighbour to the south. Whereas much of what is now the United States was parcelled off to European settlers, much of Canada remained in public hands. Good agricultural land in much of Canada was sparse, and outside these regions it was other resources that attracted European settlers.

Canada not only stands in contrast to the United States, but in many ways it was also shaped by its proximity to its large and populous neighbour. Economically, the rapidly industrializing United States held the potential to act as a source of investments and an important outlet for Canadian products, especially as the British move towards free trade in and after the 1840s sharpened competition for bulky Canadian exports. On the other hand, the growing and increasingly dominant United States was also a source of unease in Canada. One major concern was the United States' consistently protectionist trade policy, which allowed free imports of raw materials but placed heavy tariffs on industrial imports. Critics argued that this could retard Canada's industrialization and turn the country into little more than a dependent raw material provider appended to the United States. This unease laid the foundation for the turn towards the "National Policy" in 1879, which combined protectionist tariffs with the construction of an expensive transcontinental railway, along with increasing settlement of the Prairies, as a means of promoting a more cohesive and industrial Canada.[8] The tension between the possibilities and problems presented by proximity to the United States would also become a defining aspect of Canadian resource regulations in this period.

Whereas tariff policy was set at the federal level, natural resources were managed by the provinces. Support for the Canadian tariff policy was strongest in the most populous and most industrialized provinces of Ontario and Quebec, and was weakest in the Prairie provinces.[9] Some of the same tensions would come to mark the country's natural resource policies as well, with the manufacturing interests in Ontario being the most forceful proponent of a resource policy favouring domestic downstream production.

It was Canada's vast forests that would become the focal point of a new form of protectionist policy, which today is often referred to as resource nationalism. The United States was Canada's most important outlet for timber, and exports had increased rapidly as timber resources in the east and central United States became exhausted. However, the American Dingley Tariff, passed in 1897, heightened tariffs on processed timber but placed none on unprocessed logs. This effectively put Canadian sawmills at a disadvantage compared to those located in the United States, potentially leaving little of the value-added processing in Canada.[10]

As the Dingley Act contained an automatic retaliatory tariff increase on increased Canadian export duties, the federal government in Ottawa was reluctant to start a trade war with its much larger neighbour. However, Ontario lumbermen successfully lobbied the provincial government to use its control over the resources to sidestep both the federal government and the Dingley Act's automatic tariff response. In 1897, the Ontario government introduced a "manufacturing condition" on timber leases, which reserved pine for domestic Canadian industry.[11] While American timbermen were incensed at what they saw as an unwarranted confiscation of their timber leases, the new policy had legal backing in that all leases were subject to annual renewals in case of changes in the Crown Timber Act. Two years later, the policy was also extended to include pulpwood spruce, whose economic importance was fast outgrowing that of the older pine industry in eastern Canada.

The varied economic circumstances of the different provinces made it hard to coordinate a cohesive national natural resources policy. When Ontario introduced the manufacturing condition on pulpwood in 1900, there were high hopes within the province that neighbouring Quebec would follow suit. However, Quebec already had a more developed pulpwood export industry, which the provincial government was reluctant to regulate too strictly. Instead of introducing an export ban, Quebec introduced an increase in the fees for pulpwood cut for export. Quebec did not follow Ontario's "manufacturing condition" until 1910, which was then followed by New Brunswick in 1911 and British Columbia in 1913.[12] Furthermore, even though the Crown lands were extensive, their relative size differed and did not include all forested lands. Exceptions from the "manufacturing condition" were also made for settlers who depended on the sale of spruce to survive as homesteaders in the inhospitable Canadian North. The exploitation of loopholes, and creative interpretations of what counted as "processed," was, according to some historians, fairly widespread, even in protectionist Ontario.[13] The differing economic interests of the forest-dependent Canadian provinces eventually scuttled a relaunched campaign to introduce a complete export ban on pulpwood in the 1920s, which was promoted as a measure to help preserve Canada's dwindling forests.[14]

Yet, while the provinces' individual policies created problems pertaining to coordination, they were somewhat of an advantage in the trade relationship with the United States. As previously mentioned, the provinces' policies circumvented American retaliatory tariffs. When the American government addressed the pulpwood question as part of the US-Canada reciprocity negotiations in 1911, the Canadian federal government found it difficult to accommodate the US request to scrap the "manufacturing condition" in return for lower US import tariffs on newsprint and wood pulp as Crown lands in the provinces were beyond federal jurisdiction. While this jurisdictional impasse put any agreement on hold, the US government eventually decided to unilaterally scrap import duties on wood pulp in 1913 to accommodate domestic newspaper publishers who wanted cheaper paper.[15]

The manufacturing condition was left intact, and the Canadian pulp and paper industry entered a boom that was nearly uninterrupted for two decades. Yet how much of this was due to the manufacturing condition is not clear. At the time, supporters of the resource nationalist policy saw the rapid establishment of pulp and paper companies in Canada as testament that the manufacturing condition had worked. Yet some historians have downplayed this interpretation and have instead put more weight on the role played by market forces.[16]

Attempts to introduce resource nationalist policies to further industrialization were not limited to forests. Sudbury, Ontario, was the home of the richest nickel mine in the world. But while mining and smelting was done in Canada, for the most part the final refining took place in the United States. As the provincial legislature was in the process of introducing the manufacturing condition on sawlogs and pulpwood, the possibility of doing something similar with nickel came to the forefront of the political discourse.

There were, however, some major differences between nickel and forest resources. The mining claims in Sudbury were not leased from the province of Ontario; rather, they had been granted outright. This meant that the Ontario legislature did not have the legal grounds to include a manufacturing condition in the leasing contract.[17] Political intervention to promote domestic downstream production had to come in some other form. Thus, the Ontario provincial legislature passed a further licence law on nickel, in addition to a manufacturing condition on nickel and copper on Crown lands. This law placed prohibitive fees on the extraction of nickel, which, however, would be reimbursed by the provincial government if the nickel were refined in Canada. This act greatly upset the American-owned nickel company, which promptly appealed to the Canadian federal government, where it found sympathetic ears. The federal Liberal government did not want any part of the Ontarian scheme and saw the licensing law – which in effect would constitute an export ban on unrefined nickel – as an overreach of provincial authority into the federal domain of trade policy.[18] Pending a verdict in the courts, the Ontario government agreed to delay proclamation of the law in 1901, and it remained unproclaimed until it was repealed in 1907, pre-empting an expected negative outcome for Ontario.[19] As the act was repealed, the Ontario government decided to switch from the stick to the carrot and introduced a domestic smelting subsidy for nickel, as well as for copper, silver and cobalt, but with little success.[20]

Domestic Canadian nickel refining re-emerged as a hot political topic during the First World War.[21] As nickel was a strategic metal, the issue of domestic refining became not only a question of retaining value-added production in Canada but also of securing political control over a metal of wartime importance. Most of the nickel mined at Sudbury was refined at the International Nickel Company's (INCO) refinery in the neutral United States, which meant that the refined nickel could be sold to the Central Powers. This fear was proved to be justified in 1916, when the Canadian press got wind of a German cargo submarine that was transporting nickel out of Baltimore – nickel that had been bought from INCO through third parties. This further increased popular outrage against INCO, with more calls for an export ban, a government takeover of the mines, and/or government assistance to construct a competing refinery in Canada. After the provincial government in Ontario put together a commission to examine the issue,[22] INCO decided to head off a possible negative outcome by accommodating the Canadian clamour for domestic production by announcing its intention to construct an expensive new refinery in Ontario. This decision went a long way to quiet the anti-INCO campaign. Thus, the threat of political intervention against its raw material supply forced INCO to relocate key value-added production to Canada. However, as with pulpwood, Canadian pressure was not the only reason the American refiners decided to relocate to Canada. Ontario could also provide cheap electricity, which was a key ingredient in electrolytic refining.

FIGURE 3.1
Mineral taxation in Ontario, 1900–35

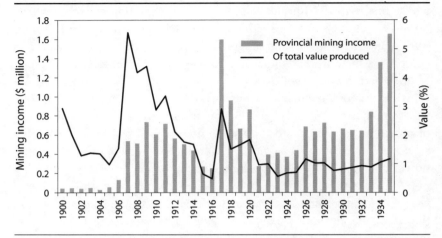

Source: Adapted from Ian A. Drummond, *Progress without Planning: The Economic History of Canada from Confederation to the Second World War* (Toronto: University of Toronto Press, 1987), 382–85, Tables 4.1 and 4.2.

Beyond the fact that resource nationalism in this period was carried out by the provinces, Canadian policy was also remarkable for its relatively positive attitude towards foreign ownership.[23] Foreign direct investments into Canada remained high, and the natural resource sectors were among the main attractions for foreign investors.[24] At the beginning of 1922, 45.7 percent of all stock in Canadian mining was foreign owned, of which over three-quarters was American-held, while the remainder was mostly British-held.[25] Similarly, between 40 and 50 percent of Canadian paper output in the interwar era was produced by American-owned mills, with forest reserves of almost equivalent proportion.[26] But whereas some other resource "late-industrializers" of the period pursued a policy of restricting or regulating foreign ownership of their natural resources,[27] Canada instead followed a policy intended to force inward foreign direct investments by regulating unprocessed exports rather than giving its own citizens and companies preferential access to resource ownership.

In a similar vein, Canadian resource policy in this period generally prioritized increased investments over rent extraction. This policy was most marked in the mining industry.[28] Even though there were significant variations in the taxation system between the provinces, leases and royalties on mineral claims were, for the most part, low, particularly in provinces

FIGURE 3.2
Total mined value of major minerals in Canada, 1895–1939

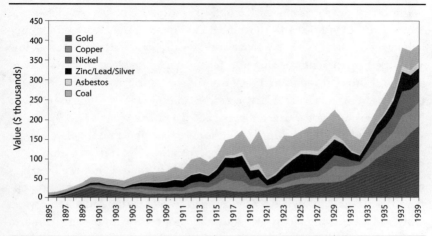

Source: Adapted from F.H. Leacy, M.C. Urquhart, and K.A.H. Buckley, *Historical Statistics of Canada*, 2d ed. (Ottawa: Canadian Government Publishing, 1983), Table Q6-12, P1-26, P82-105.

that were keen to promote mineral exploration and settlement in their large hinterlands. On occasion, mineral taxation was adjusted upwards as high returns in the mining industries improved the bargaining power of the provinces as well as leading to public agitation for higher mining taxes. Yet, given the booming mineral industry of the period, the overall provincial take of total revenue remained fairly light, particularly given the services the state provided to facilitate the industry.[29] Still, even modest taxation could provide a significant income to some provinces. Between about one-fifth and one-half of provincial revenue in Nova Scotia from 1890 to 1925 came from taxes on mining and minerals, predominantly coal.[30]

Private ownership of hydroelectricity and the rents it generated would prove to be more controversial. Here as well it was the province of Ontario that went furthest in introducing an interventionist policy.[31] The enormous potential of Canadian hydroelectricity became increasingly clear around the turn of the twentieth century, helped to no small degree by early development of hydroelectricity from Niagara Falls, which forms part of the border between New York State and Ontario. At the turn of the century, the Canadian side of Niagara Falls was leased to an American company, which had the right to export 50 percent of the power produced to the United States. The company was, however, slow to complete construction and fulfill its obligation to make power available to Canada. Dissatisfaction with the exports of power to the United States, and the fear of a private monopoly of important power resources, led to the creation of a broad "public power" movement in Ontario. This movement championed the creation of a publicly owned power company that would ensure wide distribution at a low price. Led by the enterprising and tenacious Adam Beck, the movement grew and broke through in 1906, when the Ontario legislature approved the creation of the Hydro-Electric Power Commission of Ontario (Ontario Hydro). This new governmental body, headed by the same Adam Beck, distributed power in the province and was given the power to regulate private utility companies and, if need be, to expropriate power infrastructure.

While American ownership had been part of the rallying cry for a different hydro policy, the creation of Ontario Hydro was most bitterly opposed by a Canadian-owned power company. Whereas the American-owned Ontario Power Company (OPC) chose to cooperate with the new Ontario Hydro, the Canadian-owned Electrical Development Company (EDC), which had obtained its own part of Niagara Falls in 1903 and planned to sell to the Canadian market, chose to fight.[32] Unable to agree on the price that it should pay to expropriate EDC's power lines, Ontario Hydro decided to construct a competing transmission line to Toronto. Such public competition with a private company could be construed as confiscatory and thus as a threat to respect for private ownership. This prompted negative reaction in the London financial press, which the EDC's owners did their best to stir up, with calls for the federal government to overturn Ontario's legislation. Yet, despite repeated warnings that Ontario's policy would discredit Canada in the capital markets, this did not come to pass, and without a clear danger to Canada's standing in the international credit markets, the federal government did not dare to risk overturning a popular provincial law. Ontario Hydro continued to expand over the following decades, moving into power generation and eventually buying out both the OPC and the EDC.

Through the creation of Ontario Hydro, the province had developed a form of public rent-capture and a redistributive system. The resource rents generated from Ontario's hydropower did not flow to the state but, instead, were "redistributed" as widely available cheap power, resulting in significantly lower rates for domestic and farm consumers.[33] Yet Ontario's hydro policy also bore many similarities to policy on other resources in that its main goal was to promote investments and industrialization. Cheap energy would benefit a wide range of industries and manufacturers. This point was reflected in the key role played by businesspeople in Ontario's "public power" movement.[34]

Despite the creation and relative success of Ontario Hydro, it remained an anomaly in Canada until the Second World War. A publicly owned power company was established in Winnipeg, Manitoba, in 1906 but lacked the wide provincial support enjoyed by Ontario Hydro. It was not imbued with the same regulatory power as Ontario Hydro and did not come to dominate the province.[35] Quebec, which had a flourishing hydroelectric industry, was dominated by private electricity companies with significant American ownership.[36] Nevertheless, in both Manitoba and Quebec there was a gradual shift towards what Alexander Netherton calls a "rentier-redistributive policy paradigm."[37] Initially, riparian rights in Quebec and Manitoba had been sold outright, often at prices that later proved to be very low. In Quebec this policy was changed in 1907 in favour of long-term leases with annual taxes. However, by this time much of the most accessible riparian rights had been sold off, which came to constitute the majority of Quebec's hydropower before the Second World War. This exempted power companies with full ownership from an annual power tax connected to the lease. This tax could, however, also be imposed on permits to regulate reservoir lakes.[38] The Dominion government, which controlled hydropower in Manitoba until 1928, did not change its policy until the 1920s. In Manitoba, the taxes the province garnered from leasing out riparian rights were in part redistributed as subsidies for rural electrification.

While much of the resource nationalism relating to hydropower was carried out by the provinces, regulation of electricity exports to the US was not left solely to them. As the controversy over Niagara Falls raged, the Canadian Parliament passed an act that made further electricity export contracts subject to a government licence, reviewed every year, with the possibility of adding up to a ten-dollar export duty per horsepower/year. However, after long-term power lease contracts had been entered into and accepted at the federal level, it proved very difficult for the Canadian government to repatriate power to Canada, something that became an urgent problem for Canadian munitions production during the First World War. While the United States eventually agreed to a temporary reduction after its entry into the war, the interwar era saw a more restrictive policy, and exports continued to shrink as a share of total production (see Figure 3.3). Like other natural resources, Canadian hydropower would increasingly be reserved to promote industrialization in Canada.[39] Overall, the federal government

FIGURE 3.3
Canadian electricity exports, 1908–30

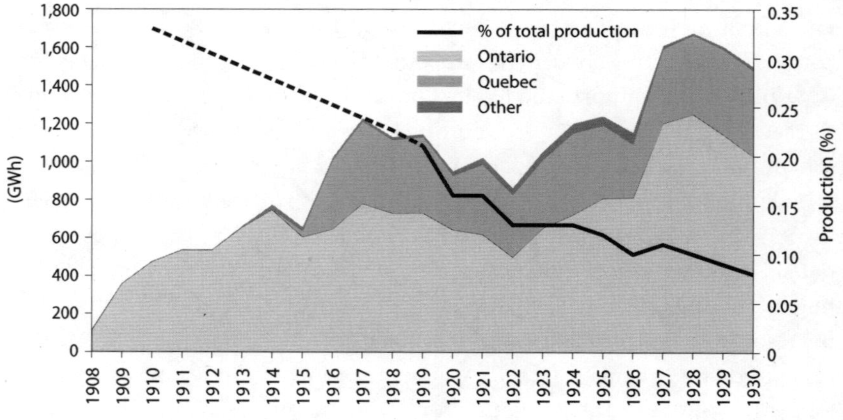

Source: Adapted from A.E. Dal Grauer, "The Export of Electricity from Canada," in *Canadian Issues: Essays in Honour of Henry F. Angus,* ed. Robert M. Clark (Toronto: University of Toronto Press, 1961), 257, 267.

would increasingly take an active role in formulating Canadian nationalist resource policy from the interwar era and on, eventually superseding the provinces as the key initiator and coordinator.

The Nationalist Era, 1930 to the 1980s

When the provinces of Alberta, Manitoba, and Saskatchewan finally gained full control over their natural resources from the federal government in 1930, the pattern of resource development and regulation in Canada had been firmly established. The provinces were responsible for managing and regulating Canada's natural resources, with the federal government playing a more indirect role in their regulation through, for example, its control over the rules governing trade and foreign investment in Canada. Though tensions between the two senior levels of government remained, the federal-provincial resource wars of the late nineteenth and early twentieth centuries were consigned to the past, at least for several decades. Moreover, after 1930 the two levels of government continued to share the belief that Canada's bountiful natural resources remained an asset whose value to the country lay in their exploitation. From the opening of Alberta's oil industry in 1947 to Quebec's asbestos and iron ore, or Ontario's timber, nickel, and gold, Canada's governments were united in their determination to extract the economic potential contained in the nation's resources.

Regulating Natural Resources in Canada   79

This determination contributed greatly to the elaboration of several major "nation-building" resources projects in the years after the Second World War, including the St. Lawrence Seaway, built between 1954 and 1959 to enable ocean-going vessels to navigate the St. Lawrence River to Lake Ontario while expanding the hydroelectric power generated in Ontario and New York; the TransCanada Pipeline, built between 1956 and 1958, that allowed for the export of natural gas from Alberta to the industrial and consumer markets of Ontario and Quebec; and the Columbia River Treaty, signed by Canada and the United States in 1964, that provided flood control and expanded hydroelectric capacity along the Columbia River in British Columbia and in the northwest United States. Vastly expensive and jurisdictionally complicated, these types of projects had previously languished until the postwar period when their economic importance became too manifest to ignore. And, in contrast to the earlier period studied in this chapter, in the postwar period Canada's federal government played a leading role in these kinds of projects; indeed, it was only Prime Minister Louis St. Laurent's stated intention to "go it alone" in building the St. Lawrence Seaway that finally persuaded the American government, and subsequently the governments of Ontario and New York, to come to an agreement vis-à-vis that project.[40] Yet the enthusiasm for large-scale resource projects as a catalyst for economic development was felt by most Canadian governments in this period, whether in Ottawa; British Columbia, which created BC Hydro in 1961; Quebec, where the building of massive dams at Manicouagan and in the James Bay region in the 1960s and 1970s played a vital role in the "modernization" of the province; or elsewhere.

These projects notwithstanding, Canadian governments generally continued to prioritize the development of natural resources through private capital and interests from the 1930s to the 1970s. The federal government did operate a uranium mine in the Northwest Territories as a Crown corporation from 1942, and the government of Saskatchewan similarly took control of Potash Corp., a major fertilizer mining company in the province, in 1975, yet these and other examples of direct government ownership of resource companies remain the exception rather than the rule.[41] For the most part, Canadian governments continued to restrict their role vis-à-vis the exploitation of natural resources to the support, encouragement, and regulation/management of the various industries and their privately owned participants. The government of Alberta's financial support and scientific research in the 1940s and 1950s helped lay the foundations for the economic viability of the province's oil sands industry in the 1960s, for example, while government subsidies also underlay the development of Saskatchewan's fertilizer industry in the 1950s.[42] Even the federal government began subsidising resource development through such vehicles as the Canada Forestry Act, 1949, by which it provided grants to the forestry sector and, later, through grants provided to resource industries by its expanding network of regional development programs and agencies.[43]

Arguably, however, it was through enhanced and expanded regulatory structures that the state had its biggest effect on resource industries in the postwar period. In particular, growing awareness of and research into the environmental and societal effects of industrial pollution and environmental degradation catalyzed the enactment of a series of regulatory measures and agencies aimed at minimizing or mitigating the negative effects of resource development on the Canadian environment. British Columbia, for example, enacted its Pollution Control Act and established a pollution control board in 1967, while Ontario established its Water Resources Commission in 1956.[44] By the 1980s, Canada's provinces had introduced a growing array of environmental regulations and licensing systems, had introduced environmental impact assessments, and had established government ministries of the environment.[45] Though the provinces led the way in expanding the environmental regulatory framework in Canada, the federal government also established its own Department of the Environment in 1971 as well as other more specific agencies such as the Environmental Protection Service. As a whole, this collection of environmental legislation, regulations, and agencies did not directly affect the management of Canada's natural resources or specifically target resource industries, but it did represent one of the two most significant regulatory/policy developments facing these industries in this period. It did not alter the overarching belief within Canada's government circles that natural resources existed to contribute to the economic progress of the country, but it did represent an increasingly more important set of questions that needed to be addressed before a resource company acquired the governmental and community support – or social licence – needed to exploit those resources.

From the 1950s to the 1970s, resource industries also faced an evolving political environment that called into question their existing corporate and investment frameworks. Resource rich but small in population, relatively poor in sources of available capital, and a follower in terms of technological innovation and adoption, Canada as a country had always depended upon foreign investment for the capital needed to develop its resource base economically.[46] As such, foreign ownership in resource industries had typically

Regulating Natural Resources in Canada 81

been welcomed. Even when complaints were raised about foreign ownership – as, for instance, during Ontario's prolonged debate about the Nickel Question in the early twentieth century – the issue was not foreign ownership per se but, rather, the perceived reluctance of foreign companies to invest more fully in higher-value manufacturing of their Canadian resources. Yet, in the postwar years, attitudes towards foreign direct investment began to change; slowly at first, but with gathering fervour by the late 1960s and 1970s. One of the first real hints of this change occurred during the debate about the building of the TransCanada Pipeline in 1956.

Perceived by the Liberal federal government of the day as exactly the type of big development project that Canada needed to sustain its postwar prosperity, the TransCanada Pipeline was designed to transport natural gas from the production fields of Alberta to Ontario and points east. Anxious for construction to begin in 1956 for political reasons – the Liberals wanted to ensure that they stood to benefit from it during the national election in 1957 – the government not only gave financial assistance to the company building the pipeline, half-owned by American interests, but also forced approval for the pipeline through Parliament by limiting debate. While most of the outrage that resulted focused upon the government's muzzling of opposition to the pipeline, the genesis of the problem lay in questions about American ownership of such an important piece of Canadian energy infrastructure and the use of Canadian public monies to underwrite an American investment.[47] In short, while American investment had fuelled Canada's economic development throughout the twentieth century, especially after 1945, by the mid-1950s many Canadians were growing uneasy over the extent of their country's dependence upon American capital and the tightening bonds of the continental relationship. Given this dependence, individuals such as Walter Gordon, a prominent businessman as well as a future federal Liberal minister of finance, feared for Canada's economic independence and ultimately its political autonomy. Appointed to lead a Royal Commission examining Canada's economic prospects in 1955, Gordon's report on the subject criticized the federal government for allowing Canada's natural resource industries to be dominated by foreign companies.[48]

For those like Walter Gordon, the problem was manifestly clear. American investments of CDN$6.5 billion represented three-quarters (76 percent) of all foreign investment in Canada in 1950; five years later those investments had grown to $10.3 billion, with the increases largely taking place in the energy, mining, and mineral sectors.[49] By 1970, American capital controlled 61 percent of Canada's oil and gas industry and 59 percent of its other mining and smelting industries.[50] Unless this situation changed and Canada reclaimed control over its own economy and industry, many feared, the country was doomed to economic and indeed political dependence upon the United States. Initial attempts to address this problem proved unsuccessful, however. Most famously, when he became minister of finance in the new Liberal government in 1963, Walter Gordon introduced a federal budget that contained several measures designed to discourage foreign takeovers of Canadian companies, including a 30 percent tax on shares in Canadian companies sold to non-residents and measures to penalize dividends paid by non-Canadian-owned companies. The furious reaction from the American government as well as important segments of the Canadian business community forced Gordon to withdraw these measures, yet economic nationalism was becoming a force to be reckoned with in Canada.[51]

The reckoning came in the 1970s. In 1971, the government established the Canada Development Corporation to foster investment in Canadian companies and enterprises, an idea first raised by Walter Gordon a decade before. Then the release of a report by Herb Gray, the minister of national revenue in the Liberal government, critical of the extent of foreign investment in Canada led to the creation of the Foreign Investment Review Agency in 1973. Through its Third Option policy, the Trudeau government announced in 1973 that its foreign policy as a whole would shift in an attempt to decrease Canada's economic dependence on the American market. The government also enacted measures to protect Canadian cultural industries from American dominance by introducing, for example, Canadian content rules for radio and television broadcasting.[52] By the early 1970s, therefore, the Canadian government had well and truly embraced an agenda of economic nationalism through a series of measures designed to promote Canadian control of Canada's economy.

Other countries felt the pull of economic nationalism as well, and when Saudi Arabia, Libya, Iraq, and the other oil-producing members of the Organization of the Petroleum Exporting Countries (OPEC) embargoed sales of oil to the United States and other industrialized countries during the Arab-Israeli War in October 1973 while simultaneously quadrupling the price of oil the resultant oil crisis had dramatic effects on Canada's oil industry.[53] This industry had developed within a continental context, with heavy investment by the big American oil companies, and was geared towards exporting surplus production to the United States. By the early 1970s, though, the Canadian government worried about the extent of American control of the industry and Canada's own energy security. Canadian ownership in the oil industry was promoted by the creation in 1973 of Petro Canada, a Crown corporation, while Canadian energy security in an era of market volatility was to be secured by freezing the domestic price of oil at four dollars a barrel and, to pay for the freeze, adding a surtax to every barrel exported to the United States.[54] A pipeline to bring western oil to eastern Canada was also planned as a way to reduce the dependence of Quebec and the Atlantic provinces on imported oil.

Though these measures did not all last – it proved impossible in the end to maintain the freeze on domestic prices as the world price of oil kept rising and the proposed pipeline remained a pipedream – the Canadian government's intervention in the oil industry infuriated both the American government and the government of Alberta. While the former objected to higher taxes being imposed on American consumers of Canadian oil and worried about the possibility of Canadian exports ultimately ending altogether, the latter, led by Conservative premier Peter Lougheed, bitterly resented the federal government's regulation of the industry through export and pricing policies while also taking a greater share of the profits for itself through the export surtax. For the United States as well as for Alberta, however, worse was yet to come. In the fall of 1980, the Trudeau government, newly returned to office after a brief electoral hiatus, announced its National Energy Program (NEP). A renewed attempt to ensure comprehensive energy security for Canada in a volatile global oil market deeply affected by the Iranian Revolution and the outbreak of war between Iran and Iraq, NEP stabilized the domestic price of oil in Canada below the world price; renewed plans for a pipeline bringing western oil to Canada's east; introduced a controversial new federal tax on the gross revenues of oil and gas companies, taking the federal government's share of the oil industry's profits from 10 to 24 percent while simultaneously reducing the provincial share of the profits from 45 to 43 percent; created an incentive program to encourage Canadian companies to explore for oil in Canada's North; and introduced legislation mandating a 25 percent share for Petro Canada of all existing as well as all future projects on federally owned lands.[55]

Intended to provide Canada with energy security in a volatile world while Canadianizing the ownership and control of the domestic oil industry, NEP failed miserably. Its ideals and policies, though popular with many Canadians, were viscerally rejected by the American and Albertan governments as well as by Albertans more generally.[56] More problematically, NEP's implementation coincided with a period of weakness in the world price of oil, thereby undermining the program's entire logic and structure.

The subsequent crisis in Alberta's oil industry was blamed squarely on the Trudeau government's ill-advised taxes, rules, and regulations, all of which, it was felt in that province ineptly interfered with the principles of the free market and provincial control over natural resources. Even though a subsequent agreement between the federal government and its provincial counterparts in Alberta, British Columbia, and Saskatchewan on revenue sharing eased some of the intergovernmental acrimony, NEP as a whole was doomed.[57] In 1984, in one of its first acts, the newly elected Progressive Conservative government led by Brian Mulroney cancelled NEP.

The Neoliberal Era, 1984 to the Present
The cancellation of NEP largely brought to an end the era in which the federal government attempted to promote Canadian national interests through government-led large-scale resource projects or policy and regulatory intervention. The Progressive Conservative government not only killed NEP but it also dismantled the Foreign Investment Review Agency and privatized Crown corporations such as Petro Canada. Realistically, the measures introduced in the Trudeau years had never been quite as nationalistic, anti-American, or anti-capital as many critics alleged – the Foreign Investment Review Agency, for example, approved the overwhelming majority of applications it reviewed for foreign takeovers of Canadian companies[58] – yet, by 1984, the dominant ethos in Canadian public policy had changed. The confidence that government intervention could alter the nature and structure of economic activity had ebbed, replaced by renewed expressions of confidence in the wisdom and efficiency of freer markets.

By the end of its mandate even the Trudeau government was flirting with the idea of more unrestricted economic activity and had initiated limited trade talks with the United States. It was the Mulroney government, however, that expanded upon these discussions and negotiated a comprehensive trade deal with the United States. Signed in 1988, the Canada-US Free Trade Agreement (FTA) dramatically reduced or removed tariffs on a wide array of goods and products traded between the two countries over a ten-year period. Significantly, the FTA also incorporated a variety of protections for investors and capital designed in large part, according to Peter Lougheed, the premier of Alberta, to "preclude a federal government from bringing in a National Energy Program ever again."[59] In reality, as pointed out by political scientist André Plourde, the FTA did not prohibit the Canadian government from introducing new measures to regulate Canada's resource industries; instead, it simply dictated that the Canadian government could not discriminate against American-owned companies in doing so.[60] As long as it treated Canadian and American companies equally, the Canadian government retained the ability to regulate natural resources in the national interest. Nonetheless, politically the tide had turned against the type of government intervention in the economy represented by NEP and its manipulation/regulation of Canada's oil and gas industry.

By 1994, Canada had joined an expanded FTA, the North American Free Trade Agreement (NAFTA), which included Mexico, and, in the years thereafter, the Canadian government ardently pursued broad-based trade agreements both multilaterally and bilaterally. By early 2017, the Canadian government had concluded fifteen separate free trade agreements with countries such as Korea, Chile, Columbia, and Israel as well as the Comprehensive Economic and Trade Agreement (CETA) with the European Union and the Trans-Pacific Partnership (TPP) agreement with eleven Pacific Rim partners, including Australia, Japan, and Vietnam. In addition, Canada has concluded a total of forty-two Foreign Investment Promotion and Protection agreements with various other countries.[61] Though the election of Donald Trump to the presidency of the United States called into question the future of NAFTA and the TPP in particular, to date the trade and investment agreements have all contributed to the liberalization of Canada's trade and investment regimes and have helped further entrench the neoliberal ideal that tariff, regulatory, and other barriers to trade and investment need to be minimized as far as possible to maximize Canada's prosperity and economic growth. The FTA and NAFTA in particular necessitated some difficult economic adjustments and have not shielded Canada from punitive trade measures – witness the long-running softwood lumber dispute with the United States from the 1980s to the present[62] – yet Canada has generally prospered under the impetus of freer trade, with its trade with the United States in particular expanding dramatically after 1988. As a whole, however, the commitments Canada has entered into through its free trade agreements have at least somewhat narrowed the options available to Canadian governments when it comes to regulating the country's resources and resource industries. This is evidenced, for example, by the $130 million in compensation the federal government paid to AbitibiBowater Inc. (a large American forest-products company) after the government of Newfoundland and Labrador was deemed to have illegally expropriated Abitibi's assets and properties in the province in 2008, and by contemporary anxiety in Canada over NAFTA's implications regarding the commodification of the country's water resources.[63]

In contrast to resource regulation, environmental policy as a field of governmental activity has not been overly impinged upon by the number of free trade or investment protection agreements into which Canada has entered. Indeed, this is one area in which government regulations have proliferated during the neoliberal era.[64] Yet, even so, there have at times been attempts to rein in environmental regulations due to concerns that they have become so onerous as to inhibit economic development and resource projects. Most notably, in 2012 the federal Conservative government under Prime Minister Stephen Harper introduced legislation – Bill C-38 – that, among other things, eliminated the need for environmental assessment of projects such as oil pipelines regulated by the federal government; streamlined the process for the approval of resource projects; decreased the species of fish and the number of bodies of water subject to federal environmental protections; and vested the final authority over the approval of federally regulated resource projects in the federal cabinet rather than in the responsible government ministry.[65] The current federal government, a Liberal government elected in October 2015, is more progressive than its predecessor and has promised to restore many of the environmental regulations weakened or repealed by Bill C-38, yet even this government is faced with the seemingly intractable dilemma of reconciling environmental concerns with the fact that much of Canada's national economic prosperity depends, at least in part, on the exploitation of its natural resources.

In the contemporary political climate in Canada, any government's ability to reconcile these often seemingly contradictory economic and environmental imperatives has been further complicated by the growth in the number of actors seeking a voice in the debate over resource projects. In the 1950s, the construction of the St. Lawrence Seaway and associated hydroelectric facilities resulted in the submergence of all or parts of eleven communities and the relocation of some sixty-five hundred people in eastern Ontario. Controversial even at the time, the Canadian and Ontario governments nonetheless successfully subordinated the fate of these "Lost Villages" to the larger provincial and national economic interests at stake in the Seaway project.[66] It is difficult to conceive that they would so easily prevail on a similar issue today, at least in part because, from the 1950s to the 1970s, the St. Lawrence Seaway project, the construction of the James Bay dams, and the Superstack at the INCO nickel refinery in Copper Cliff, Ontario, for example, all helped mobilize local, regional, national, and international networks of environmental and other activists who were concerned about the broader societal effects of such resource projects. The growth of the environmental movement in the second half of the twentieth century is a familiar story, in Canada and elsewhere; by the early twenty-first century this movement has succeeded, at the very least, in inserting environmental concerns into the heart of discussions about resource development in Canada.

At the same time, other actors have become equally prominent and important in discussions of resource development and regulation in Canada. In some cases, this has been mandated by legal and constitutional developments, as with the series of Supreme Court decisions from *Guerin* (1984) through *Marshall* (1999) to *Tsilhqot'in* (2014) and others that, cumulatively, have recognized both Aboriginal rights over resources in Canada and the constitutional requirement that governments and businesses consult with Aboriginal peoples over the exploitation of resources on their lands.[67] Though the Aboriginal rights identified by the Supreme Court are not absolute – the Court has articulated that they can still be subordinated to compelling national or provincial interests – in recent years the need to secure the agreement of Aboriginal peoples vis-à-vis resource development, a concept defined as "social licence," has become a defining element of resource projects across much of Canada, including the currently stalled negotiations over the development of the chromite deposits in northwestern Ontario known as the "Ring of Fire." Moreover, the concept of "social licence" has broadened to include other community members, actors, and governments, even those without the legally defined status and rights of First Nations.

One of the more intriguing developments of the debates over the various pipeline proposals under consideration by the Canadian government (Northern Gateway, Energy East, Keystone XL, Mackenzie Valley, and the Kinder Morgan/Trans Mountain expansion) between roughly 2010 and 2017 is the degree to which provincial and municipal governments across the country have weighed in on these debates and even gone so far as to make demands of the federal government in return for their support of these projects. In July 2012, for example, Premier Christy Clark of British Columbia issued five demands that would need to be met in order for her government to support the construction of the Northern Gateway pipeline across her province. Despite having no legal authority over the approval of the pipeline, which is a responsibility of the federal government, Clark demanded not only strengthened federal and corporate capacities to respond to oil spills in British Columbia and its coasts but also a "fair share" of the fiscal and economic benefits from the project itself in return for her province bearing the project's associated environmental risks.[68] In April 2014, the inhabitants of Kitimat, BC, the proposed terminus for the Northern Gateway pipeline, voted 58 percent to 42 percent against the pipeline in a non-binding referendum that nonetheless increased the difficulties faced by the troubled project.[69] Following the example of their BC counterpart, both the governments of Ontario and Quebec highlighted what they called an imbalance in the economic benefits versus environmental risks for their provinces in relation to the Energy East pipeline, while communities along the pipeline's proposed route have studied the issue and voiced their position, most notably in January 2016 when Mayor Denis Coderre and his city council in the metropolitan region of Montreal announced their rejection of it.[70] In contrast, mayors from the region of Quebec City as well as the city of Calgary in Alberta have spoken in favour of Energy East. It was at least in part this opposition to its plan that compelled TransCanada to cancel its Energy East pipeline in October 2017, while the election of a Green Party-supported New Democratic Party minority government in British Columbia in May 2017 has raised even more doubts that the Trans Mountain Pipeline will ever get built. As of spring 2018, the provinces of BC and Alberta and the federal government are engaged in a full-fledged political and constitutional struggle for and against the Trans Mountain Pipeline. At a time when the dominant economic and governmental ethos is geared towards removing or minimizing the regulatory and other barriers to economic development, it is the need to secure a broad-based social licence that is proving to be one of the most significant obstacles to the successful pursuit, by both governments and business, of new resource projects in Canada.[71]

Conclusion

The history of Canadian resource regulations thus in many ways mirrors the larger international trends in resource regulations of the past century and a half. Beginning around the turn of the twentieth century, Canadian provinces began to break with the liberal system and to use their ownership and regulatory power over natural resources for protectionist ends. This system of resource nationalism was expanded over time and was embraced by the federal government, reaching its peak in the postwar era, before eventually being abandoned in the 1980s. These resource nationalist policies were at times controversial, but Canada never opted for the radical nationalizations favoured in some other countries. While Canadian protectionist ambitions have declined, environmental and societal concerns as well as the rights of

Regulating Natural Resources in Canada   89

First Nations in Canada have become increasingly important in the regulation of resource developments.

A key feature that stands out in an international historical comparison of the Canadian case is the importance of the Canadian provinces. It was the provinces, most prominently Ontario, that first actively began to use the regulation of natural resources to facilitate domestic downstream production in place of raw material exports. Yet the provinces ultimately also set the limits for Canadian resource nationalist ambitions. In the first period, the effect of Canadian regulations depended on coordination between the provinces and, after the initiative for resource nationalist policies was assumed by the federal government, NEP failed in part because it was rejected by the province of Alberta.

Thus, as this brief historical survey of some key eras in the history of resource development and regulation in Canada attempts to illustrate, the exploitation and regulation of Canada's natural resources has typically involved the need to balance local, regional, provincial, and national interests as well as economic, societal, environmental, and other concerns. Consequently, the pessimism expressed by many Canadians about the future of resource development in Canada seems overblown. Although the number of voices clamouring to influence or benefit from resource developments expanded significantly over the course of a century and a half, the fundamental need for resource companies as well as governments to secure some form of social licence from a variety of communities and actors has been a fundamental component of resource projects since the early twentieth century if not earlier.

Notes

1 On the staples thesis, see, for example, Mel Watkins, "A Staple Theory of Economic Growth," in *Approaches to Canadian Economic History*, ed. W.T. Easterbrook and M.H. Watkins (Toronto: McClelland and Stewart, 1967), 49–73; R.T. Naylor, "Trends in the Business History of Canada, 1867–1914," *Canadian Historical Association Historical Papers* 11 (1976): 255–67.

2 Numerous planned resource projects – notably at least four pipelines for western oil and the Ring of Fire mineral/chromite development in northwestern Ontario, among others – are currently stalled due at least in part to societal divisions over the wisdom of such projects, how to go about them most responsibly, or how to divide the expected benefits among the various stakeholders, including especially Indigenous peoples. As a result, several commentators have wondered recently whether the obstacles that seemingly impede major resource development projects in contemporary Canada are too great to be overcome. See, for example, Jeffrey

Simpson, "Confusion Reigns on Aboriginal Rights When Court Rulings Meet Reality," *Globe and Mail*, 11 July 2015.

3 The British North America Act, 1867, at http://www.justice.gc.ca/eng/rp-pr/csj -sjc/constitution/lawreg-loireg/p1t13.html (viewed 14 October 2015) (Government of Canada, Department of Justice website).

4 Melody Hessing, Michael Howlett, and Tracy Summerville, *Canadian Natural Resource and Environmental Policy: Political Economy and Public Policy*, 2nd ed. (Vancouver: UBC Press, 2005), 55.

5 See Christopher Armstrong, *The Politics of Federalism: Ontario's Relations with the Federal Government, 1867–1942* (Toronto: University of Toronto Press, 1981).

6 In 2010, for example, the federal government blocked a bid by the Anglo-Australian company BHP Billiton to acquire Saskatchewan-based Potash Corp on the grounds that allowing this important Canadian resource company to fall under foreign ownership would not provide a "net benefit" to Canada.

7 Notably, in June 2014 the Supreme Court of Canada ruled that the Tsilhqot'in First Nation owned clear title to seventeen hundred square kilometres of land in British Columbia and therefore had "not merely a right of first refusal with respect to Crown land management or usage plans. Rather it is a right to proactively use and manage the land." This decision has been hailed – or decried – as a "game changer" for First Nations in British Columbia and across Canada, with particular resonance for the future of resource development. See *Tsilhqot'in Nation v. British Columbia*, 2014 SCC 44; and Amber Hildebrandt, "Supreme Court's Tsilhqot'in First Nation Ruling a Game-Changer for All," *CBC News*, 27 June 2014, http://www.cbc.ca/news/ aboriginal/supreme-court-s-tsilhqot-in-first-nation-ruling-a-game-changer-for -all-1.2689140 (viewed 12 August 2015).

8 A good overview of the "National Policies" can be found in: William L. Marr and Donald G. Paterson, *Canada, an Economic History* (Toronto: Macmillan of Canada, 1980), chap. 12; Kenneth Norrie and Douglas Owram, *A History of the Canadian Economy* (Toronto: Harcourt Brace Jovanovich, Canada, 1991), chap. 11.

9 Marr and Paterson, *Canada*, 386.

10 H.V. Nelles, *The Politics of Development: Forests, Mines and Hydro-Electric Power in Ontario, 1849–1941,* 2nd ed. (Montreal and Kingston: McGill-Queen's University Press, 2005), 63–67.

11 Armstrong, *Politics of Federalism*, 34–42; Nelles, *Politics of Development*, 68–79.

12 Robert Armstrong, *Structure and Change: An Economic History of Quebec* (Agincourt: Gage, 1984), 241–42; Bill Parenteau and L. Anders Sandberg, "Conservation and the Gospel of Economic Nationalism: The Canadian Pulpwood Question in Nova Scotia and New Brunswick, 1918–1925," *Environmental History Review* 19, 2 (1995): 57; Nelles, *Politics of Development*, 336–38; Herbert Marshall, Frank A. Southard, and Kenneth W. Taylor, *Canadian-American Industry: A Study in International Investment* (New Haven: Yale University Press, 1936), 36–37.

13 This is particularly forcefully argued in Mark Kuhlberg, "'Pulpwood Is the Only Thing We Do Export': The Myth of Provincial Protectionism in Ontario's Forest Industry, 1890–1930," in *Smart Globalization: The Canadian Business and Economic History Experience*, ed. Andrew Smith and Dimitry Anastakis (Toronto: University of Toronto Press, 2014), 59–91. But widespread circumvention is also mentioned in

Nelles, *Politics of Development*, 375–82. For the low criteria for Nova Scotia pulpwood to be considered "processed," see L. Anders Sandberg, "Forest Policy in Nova Scotia: The Big Lease, Cape Breton Island, 1899–1960," *Acadiensis* 20, 2 (1991): 105–28.

14 Parenteau and Sandberg, "Conservation and the Gospel of Economic Nationalism."

15 Ibid., 57; Nelles, *Politics of Development*, 340–45.

16 Trevor J.O. Dick, "Canadian Newsprint, 1913–1930: National Policies and the North American Economy," *Journal of Economic History* 42, 3 (1982): 659–87.

17 A similar issue scuttled Quebec's plans to force domestic downstream production of asbestos in the 1920s. See Armstrong, *Structure and Change*, 278–79.

18 Armstrong, *Politics of Federalism*, 42–48.

19 Nelles, *Politics of Development*, 96–102.

20 Ibid., 132.

21 This paragraph is based on: Daryl White, "Managing a War Metal: The International Nickel Company's First World War," in *Smart Globalization: The Canadian Business and Economic History Experience*, ed. Andrew Smith and Dimitry Anastakis (Toronto: University of Toronto Press, 2014), 92–107; Philip Smith, *Harvest from the Rock: A History of Mining in Ontario* (Toronto: Macmillan of Canada, 1986), 204–13; Nelles, *Politics of Development*, 349–61.

22 Royal Ontario Nickel Commission, *Report of the Royal Ontario Nickel Commission* (Toronto: A.T. Wilgress, 1917).

23 See Gordon Laxer, *Open for Business: The Roots of Foreign Ownership in Canada* (Toronto: Oxford University Press, 1989), esp. chap. 6; and Peter Karl Kresl, "Before the Deluge: Canadians on Foreign Ownership, 1920–1955," *American Review of Canadian Studies* 6, 1 (1976): 86–125. The issue is also discussed in Nelles, *Politics of Development*, 149–53, 308–10.

24 Mining, land, and timber constituted 52.2 percent and 53.1 percent of US (1909) and British (1910) foreign direct investments, respectively. See D.G. Paterson, *British Direct Investment in Canada, 1890–1914* (Toronto: University of Toronto Press, 1976), 50, 55.

25 Elwood S. Moore, *American Influence in Canadian Mining* (New York: Arno Press, 1980), 84, Table 1.

26 Marshall, Southard, and Taylor, *Canadian-American Industry*, 39.

27 See Chapter 2 on the Nordic countries. The same point is highlighted in Laxer, *Open for Business*. Besides Scandinavia, Laxer draws some comparisons to Japan and Russia.

28 Armstrong, *Structure and Change*; Ian M. Drummond, *Progress without Planning: The Economic History of Ontario from Confederation to the Second World War* (Toronto: University of Toronto Press, 1987); Marr and Paterson, *Canada*; Nelles, *Politics of Development*.

29 In comparison, mining taxation and royalties in the BC gold industry between 1898 and 1915 was 2.685 percent of total value extracted. See Commission, *Report of the Royal Ontario Nickel Commission*, 507.

30 William C. Wicken, *The Colonization of Mi'kmaw Memory and History, 1794–1928: The King v. Gabriel Sylliboy* (Toronto: University of Toronto Press, 2012), 370, Table 7.1.

31 Nelles, *Politics of Development*, 215–324; Merrill Denison, *The People's Power: The History of Ontario Hydro* (Toronto: McClelland and Stewart, 1960); Drummond, *Progress without Planning*, 134–47; Andrew Dilley, "Politics, Power, and the First Age of Globalization: Ontario's Hydroelectric Policy, Canada, and the City of London, 1905–10," in *Smart Globalization: The Canadian Business and Economic History Experience*, ed. Andrew Smith and Dimitry Anastakis (Toronto: University of Toronto Press, 2014), 31–58.

32 Nelles, *Politics of Development*; Dilley, "Politics, Power, and the First Age of Globalization."

33 John H. Dales, *Hydroelectricity and Industrial Development: Quebec, 1898–1940* (Cambridge, MA: Harvard University Press, 1957), 47, Table 4.

34 Nelles, *Politics of Development*, 237–49.

35 H.V. Nelles, "Public Ownership of Electrical Utilities in Manitoba and Ontario, 1906–30," *Canadian Historical Review* 57, 4 (1976); Alexander J. Netherton, "From Rentiership to Continental Modernization: Shifting Policy Paradigms of State Intervention in Hydro in Manitoba, 1922–1977" (PhD thesis, Carleton University, 1993).

36 For more information, see Marshall, Southard, and Taylor, *Canadian-American Industry*, 139–52; Dales, *Hydroelectricity and Industrial Development*. Marshall estimates that 34 percent of all electric power generated in Canada (around the time of publication in 1936) stems from American-owned companies. For a comparison between Ontario and Quebec, see Christopher Armstrong and H.V. Nelles, "Contrasting Development of the Hydro-Electric Industry in the Montreal and Toronto Regions, 1900–1930," *Journal of Canadian Studies* 18, 1 (1983): 527.

37 Netherton, "From Rentiership to Continental Modernization."

38 Conflicts over such a tax was a central factor in delaying the Saguenay development. See David Perera Massell, *Amassing Power: J.B. Duke and the Saguenay River, 1897–1927* (Montreal and Kingston: McGill-Queen's University Press, 2000).

39 A.E. Dal Grauer, "The Export of Electricity from Canada," in *Canadian Issues: Essays in Honour of Henry F. Angus*, ed. Robert M. Clark (Toronto: University of Toronto Press, 1961), 248–85.

40 For an analysis of the complicated history of the St. Lawrence Seaway, see Daniel Macfarlane, *Negotiating a River: Canada, the United States, and the Creation of the St. Lawrence Seaway* (Vancouver: UBC Press, 2014). On the Columbia River Treaty, see Neil Swainson, *Conflict over the Columbia: Canadian Background to an Historic Treaty* (Montreal and Kingston: McGill-Queen's University Press, 1979).

41 In 1980, for example, twenty-three of Canada's top four hundred industrial companies by assets were wholly owned either by the federal government or by a provincial government. These companies included, however, both Hydro-Quebec and Ontario Hydro and similar Crown corporations. See Jeanne Kirk Laux, "Expanding the State: The International Relations of State-Owned Enterprises in Canada," *Polity* 15, 3 (1983): 333.

42 Paul Chastko describes the extent of governmental support for the oil sands industry in *Developing Alberta's Oil Sands: From Karl Clark to Kyoto* (Calgary: University of Calgary Press, 2004), chaps. 3–4.

43 Hessing, Howlett, and Summerville, *Canadian Natural Resource and Environmental Policy*, 57.
44 Ontario Water Resources Commission, *Water Saga: A Story of Water Management in Ontario, 1956–1968* (Ottawa: Queen's Printer for Ontario, 1969).
45 Hessing, Howlett, and Summerville, *Canadian Natural Resource and Environmental Policy*, 58–59. For a sense of the explosion in environmental regulations and initiatives undertaken by Canadian provinces from the 1950s to the 1970s, see Mark Winfield, *Blue-Green Province: The Environment and the Political Economy of Ontario* (Vancouver: UBC Press, 2012), chaps. 2–3.
46 Jeremy Mouat, *Metal Mining in Canada, 1840–1950* (Ottawa: National Museum of Science and Technology, 2000).
47 Norman Hillmer and J.L. Granatstein, *For Better or for Worse: Canada and the United States into the Twenty-First Century* (Toronto: Nelson, 2007), 188.
48 See Stephen Azzi, *Walter Gordon and the Rise of Canadian Nationalism* (Montreal and Kingston: McGill-Queen's University Press, 1999), 34–65.
49 Hillmer and Granatstein, *For Better or For Worse*, 188.
50 Statistics Canada, *Canada's International Investment Position*, Table G249-290a, "Ownership and Control of Capital Employed in Selected Canadian Industries, Selected Year Ends, 1926 to 1973," http://www.statcan.gc.ca/pub/11-516-x/sectiong/G249_290a-eng.csv (viewed 20 January 2016); and Statistics Canada, *Canada's International Investment Position*, Table G291-302, "Foreign Control of Selected Canadian Industries, Selected Year Ends, 1926 to 1973," http://www.statcan.gc.ca/pub/11-516-x/sectiong/G291_302-eng.csv (accessed 20 January 2016).
51 Hillmer and Granatstein, *For Better or For Worse*, 217–18; Azzi, *Walter Gordon and the Rise of Canadian Nationalism*, 95–110.
52 For further information about these measures, see, for example, J.L. Granatstein and Robert Bothwell, *Pirouette: Pierre Trudeau and Canadian Foreign Policy* (Toronto: University of Toronto Press, 1990), 61–75.
53 Hillmer and Granatstein, *For Better or For Worse*, 248.
54 Jorge Niosi and Michel Duquette, "La loi et les nombres: Le Programme énergétique national et la canadianisation de l'industrie pétrolière," *Canadian Journal of Political Science* 20, 2 (1987): 321.
55 See G.B. Doern and G. Toner, *The Politics of Energy: The Development and Implementation of the NEP* (Toronto: Methuen, 1985).
56 Edward Wonder, "The US Government Response to the Canadian National Energy Program," *Canadian Public Policy* 8, supplement (October 1982): 483–93.
57 John Helliwell and Robert N. McRae, "Resolving the Energy Conflict: From the National Energy Program to the Energy Agreements," *Canadian Public Policy* 8, 1 (1982): 14–23.
58 Between 1974 and 1984, FIRA received 7,947 applications, of which it reviewed 7,132. Of those, it only rejected 435. See Canada, *Foreign Investment Review Act: Final Annual Report, 1984–85* (Ottawa: Supply and Services Canada, 1985), Table 1.
59 Statement by Peter Lougheed to the Standing Committee on External Affairs and International Trade, as cited in André Plourde, "The NEP Meets the FTA," *Canadian Public Policy* 17, 1 (1991): 1.

60 Plourde, "NEP Meets the FTA," 14–24.

61 For complete lists of Canada's in force and concluded free trade agreements and foreign investment promotion and protection agreements, see Global Affairs Canada, *Opening New Markets: Trade Negotiations and Agreements*, http://www.international.gc.ca/trade-agreements-accords-commerciaux/index.aspx?lang=eng (Global Affairs Canada website, viewed 18 February 2016).

62 The heart of the dispute lay in the fact that American producers of softwood objected to the stumpage fees paid by Canadian producers for trees cut on Crown land in Canada, which they considered excessively low compared to the cost of purchasing timber rights in the United States. In response, the American government repeatedly imposed countervailing duties on Canadian softwood exported to the United States of up to 27 percent, despite the fact that the American claims were repeatedly dismissed by various NAFTA and WTO dispute adjudication panels. See Granatstein and Bothwell, *Pirouette*, 307.

63 On the Abitibi case against Newfoundland and Canada, see Peter Bowal and Christopher Tang, "When Free Trade Is Not Free: The Abitibi Case," posted 9 March 2015 on *LawNow*, http://www.lawnow.org/when-free-trade-is-not-free-the-abitibi-case/ (website for the Centre for Public Legal Education Alberta, viewed 19 February 2016). On the vulnerability of Canadian water resources to international trade agreements, see Maude Barlow and Tony Clarke, *Blue Gold: The Fight to Stop the Corporate Theft of the World's Water* (New York: New Press, 2005).

64 For a discussion of governmental approaches to environmental policy in Canada since the mid-twentieth century, see Winfield, *Blue-Green Province*.

65 *Jobs, Growth, and Long-Term Prosperity Act, Statutes of Canada*, 2012, chap. 19. See http://www.parl.gc.ca/HousePublications/Publication.aspx?Docid=5697420&file=4 (Parliament of Canada website, viewed 19 February 2016).

66 For a discussion of the fate of these "Lost Villages," see Macfarlane, *Negotiating a River*, 139–78.

67 On the Supreme Court of Canada and Aboriginal rights to natural resources in Canada see, for example, Ken Coates, *The Marshall Decision and Native Rights* (Montreal and Kingston: McGill-Queen's University Press, 2000).

68 See, "BC Seeks 'Fair Share' in New Gateway Pipeline Deal," *CBC News*, 23 July 2012, http://www.cbc.ca/news/canada/british-columbia/b-c-seeks-fair-share-in-new-gateway-pipeline-deal-1.1205829 (viewed 28 February 2016).

69 Robin Rowland, "Kitimat Residents Vote 'No' in Pipeline Plebiscite," *Globe and Mail*, 12 April 2014, http://www.theglobeandmail.com/news/british-columbia/kitimat-residents-vote-in-northern-gateway-oil-pipeline-plebiscite/article17949815/ (viewed 28 February 2016).

70 Denis Coderre, "Why Montreal Says No to the Energy East Pipeline," *Montreal Gazette*, 25 January 2016, http://montrealgazette.com/opinion/columnists/opinion-why-montreal-says-no-to-the-energy-east-pipeline (viewed 28 February 2016).

71 In November 2016, the Justin Trudeau-led federal government announced its approval of two of the outstanding pipeline applications, including the expansion of Kinder Morgan's Trans Mountain line. At the same time, however, it rejected the Northern Gateway pipeline: "It has become clear that this project is not in the best

interest of the local affected communities, including Indigenous Peoples." See John Paul Tasker, "Trudeau Cabinet Approves Trans Mountain, Line 3 Pipelines, Rejects Northern Gateway," CBC News, 29 November 2016, http://www.cbc.ca/news/politics/federal-cabinet-trudeau-pipeline-decisions-1.3872828 (viewed 5 January 2017). In October 2017, TransCanada cancelled its planned expansion of the Energy East pipeline in the face of ongoing societal opposition and due to the "changed circumstances," consisting of heightened scrutiny of its environmental impact on the part of a new panel of judges from the National Energy Board. See Alex Ballingall, "TransCanada Ends Bid to Build Energy East Pipeline after 'Careful Review of Changed Circumstances,'" *Toronto Star*, 5 October 2017, https://www.thestar.com/business/2017/10/05/transcanada-ends-bid-to-build-energy-east-pipeline-after-careful-review-of-changed-circumstances.html (viewed 6 April 2018).

4

National Oil Companies and Political Coalitions

Venezuela and Colombia, 1910–76

MARCELO BUCHELI

Few industries are as politicized as oil and gas. As the chapters in this volume show, after the First World War most countries of the world became aware of the political and strategic importance of oil and gas, and this led them to develop policies regulating the operations of private firms in that industry. The type of regulations varied depending on economic issues such as whether the countries were net producers or consumers of crude oil; the domestic technical capability to produce, refine, or transport oil and oil products; and the access to the capital necessary to invest in an expensive industry.[1] Linked to these technical and economic issues, internal politics also determined the type of regulation adopted by different countries.

In this chapter I focus on the latter to argue the following three points: (1) political regimes whose survival depends on the loyalty of a small coalition develop policies towards the oil and gas industry in which the rents are distributed as a private good among the members of that coalition; (2) conversely, regimes whose survival depends on the loyalty of a large coalition develop policies by which the rents generated by the oil industry are distributed as a public good among the members of that coalition; and (3) the decision to create a national oil company is related to the strategies followed by a regime to ensure the loyalty of its supporting coalition. I illustrate my argument through a comparative analysis of the oil policies in Colombia and Venezuela during the twentieth century and the conditions that led to the creation of their national oil companies, ECOPETROL and PDVSA, respectively.

At the time of this writing, Venezuela is the world's eighth largest crude oil exporter while Colombia ranks eighteenth (and fourth in the Americas after Venezuela, Canada, and Mexico).[2] These two neighbouring countries also entered the twenty-first century as opposite images of each other in terms of oil policy. While the left-wing administrations of Venezuelan presidents Hugo Chávez (1999–2013) and Nicolás Maduro (2013–) were seen by the international business media as hostile towards foreign oil companies, the centre-right Colombian administrations of Alvaro Uribe (2002–10) and Juan Manuel Santos (2010–18) were the darlings of international oil investors because of their open-door policy towards the industry. Their differences were reflected in the way they managed their respective national oil companies: Chávez increased government control of PDVSA, while the Colombian government made ECOPETROL public in the international stock markets.

The chapter is divided into four sections, the first of which briefly discusses the dominant theoretical approaches used to analyze the relationship between extractive multinationals and government, and it proposes the selectorate theory as an alternative lens. The second and third sections analyze how changing political coalitions affected oil policies in Venezuela and Colombia, respectively. The fourth and concluding section discusses the implications of this comparison and the potential of the selectorate theory for historical analyses of the relationship between firms and governments.

Oil, Politics, and Multinational Corporations

During the 1960s and 1970s the world witnessed a wave of less developed countries' governments creating national oil companies with the expropriated assets of foreign multinationals.[3] Scholars developed different interpretations of why this process was taking place. One interpretation is known as "obsolescing bargaining power," which argues that the larger the amount of fixed assets a multinational has invested in a country, the lower the bargaining power it will have vis-à-vis the host government if the latter decides to change the contractual terms or even to expropriate the firm's assets. These scholars point to how these characteristics make firms operating in the extractive industries particularly vulnerable to hostile government action.[4] For Stephen Kobrin, a government's decision to expropriate a foreign firm and create a national one is completely rational.[5] He maintains that, with technology becoming more easily available over time and with a larger segment of the domestic population having the skills to run a firm, it does not make sense for a poor country to keep a crucial industry like oil or mining in the hands of foreign firms. Neo-Marxist scholars, on the other hand, interpret the use of expropriation policies to create national state-owned firms in less developed countries as attempts to overcome losses that were the result of foreign capital's historical exploitation (in the form of multinational firms) of their resources.[6] More recent studies, inspired by neo-institutional theories, posit that expropriations of private property in general are the result of an incomplete institutional framework in which the executive does not have enough veto points to control its actions and therefore can act arbitrarily against private investors when considered politically or economically beneficial to do so.[7] Finally, another stream of scholarship highlights the fact that most expropriations in the oil industry have taken place in times of high international crude oil prices.[8] They argue that the chances that a democratically elected government will use expropriation as a way to create a national firm are lower than the chances that a dictatorial regime will do so.

The above interpretations have some potential shortcomings when used to understand oil policies from a historical perspective. First, companies have avoided losing bargaining power vis-à-vis the host government by approaching members of the domestic elite and making sure they see economic benefits from the multinationals' operations.[9] Second, historical evidence has shown that multinationals do not always share the global agendas of their countries of origin, as is implicitly assumed by the neo-Marxist scholars.[10] Rather, as has often happened, a poor country that is in conflict with a multinational might find an ally in the multinational's government, which might not be interested in supporting that particular firm. In fact, some national firms that resulted from expropriation found funding sources in multilateral institutions that were dominated by the expropriated multinationals' home countries.[11] And, third, as several historical and contemporary cases have repeatedly shown, multinational corporations can have very friendly relationships with dictatorial regimes and have often been expropriated after transitions to more pluralistic regimes.[12]

This chapter uses the *selectorate theory of political survival* developed by Bruce Bueno de Mesquita, Alastair Smith, Randolph Siverson, and James Morrow as its main theoretical lens.[13] I believe this approach can help scholars to overcome the problems stated above. Selectorate scholars work under the assumption that all types of rulers (whether they are dictators or elected officials) have a constituency to whom they need to respond.[14] Similarly, they maintain that even the most powerful dictator needs to engage in politics (including negotiations and compromises) in order to ensure the loyalty of the coalition that keeps him or her in power (which they define as the *winning coalition*). Thus, they argue that the main goal in economic policy (in both authoritarian and pluralistic regimes) is to ensure the political survival of those in power (either an individual, a junta, or a political party). This means that, when necessary, those ruling a country will follow economic policies that go against their ideology or that do not translate into more growth or efficiency but that ensure the loyalty of their winning coalition. If the ruler's survival depends on a small coalition (say a few generals and some families), these authors maintain, he/she will develop economic policies that particularly benefit the members of that coalition. Conversely, if the ruler's survival depends on a large coalition (e.g., voters of a particular party, large labour unions, or a large revolutionary army), he/she will develop economic policies that seek to distribute economic rents among the members of that winning coalition.

There are three main benefits of using this theoretical approach to analyzing oil policy in a historical and comparative perspective. First, doing so removes the constraints created by an analysis based on the dichotomy between democracy and dictatorship. Such a simple dichotomy does not allow us to analyze the rulers' strategies for political survival. Second, it removes the constraints of analyzing government policy as something that results from particular ideologies. And third, it allows us to understand why governments might change their policies even without any dramatic changes in the technical characteristics of the industry (e.g., why some governments might choose not to expropriate even when capable of running the industry in question).

Using the selectorate theory of political survival, this chapter conducts a comparative study between the oil policies of Venezuela and Colombia. This allows us to have a better understanding of how different regimes operated, regardless of how their rulers were elected. Even though both countries differ significantly in terms of their political history, the fact that they both share the same institutional origin (Venezuela and Colombia are both inheritors of the Spanish legal system regarding subsoil wealth and, between 1819 and 1831, were actually a single country) permits a more accurate comparison than would be the case if we compared one of them with, say, one of the Persian Gulf oil kingdoms. Both countries also share a long border and are well aware of each other's political developments (something particularly important given the fact that, for decades, they had not agreed on where their borders started and ended).

Oil and Domestic Economy in Venezuela and Colombia

During the period under study the role of oil in the domestic economy differed between Venezuela and Colombia. While between the 1920s and 1940s Venezuela became a petro-state par excellence, the Colombian economy depended mostly on the exports of coffee, with oil being the second largest export at a distant second place. As Table 4.1 shows, during the period under study, the Venezuelan production of crude oil was far higher than was the Colombian production. The weight of oil exports in total exports was also higher for Venezuela than for Colombia, as Table 4.2 illustrates (with, for Colombia, most of the remaining exports being coffee). Table 4.3 shows the importance of exports for both economies and indicates that Venezuela was more dependent on the international markets than was Colombia.

There are important geological differences between both countries, and these need to be taken into consideration when conducting a comparative study. While most of the Venezuelan crude oil comes from the easily accessible Gulf of Maracaibo (which permits direct access to the Caribbean Sea) the Colombian oilfields are located inland about 480 kilometres from the nearest port. This was something that worked to the advantage of the Colombian government when it confronted foreign firms. As this chapter discusses, the differences in the relative importance of oil in both countries shaped different types of political coalitions, each of which had its own distinctive political strategies.

Venezuela: Enlarging Political Coalitions and Changing Oil Policy

Venezuela entered the twentieth century as one of Latin America's poorest countries, but by the post-Second World War period it had the continent's highest per capita GDP.[15] The main driver of this change was the country's increasingly important role as one of the world's largest oil exporters. During this period Venezuela was ruled by different political regimes, including military dictatorships and pluralist democracies. This section shows how the different regimes used their oil wealth as a way of ensuring the loyalty of their winning coalition and, therefore, their rulers' political survival.

TABLE 4.1
Oil production (thousands of barrels), 1910–67, Venezuela and Colombia

	Venezuela	Colombia		Venezuela	Colombia
1910	0	0	1939	205,956	22,037
1911	0	0	1940	184,761	26,067
1912	0	0	1942	147,675	10,487
1913	0	0	1943	177,631	13,261
1914	0	0	1944	257,046	22,291
1915	0	0	1945	323,415	22,825
1916	0	0	1946	388,200	22,250
1917	120	0	1947	434,905	21,846
1918	333	0	1948	490,015	23,734
1919	425	0	1949	482,316	22,589
1920	457	0	1950	546,783	23,353
1921	1,433	67	1951	622,216	24,465
1922	2,201	323	1952	660,254	24,807
1923	4,201	425	1953	644,244	28,469
1924	9,042	445	1954	691,812	29,650
1925	19,687	1,007	1955	787,438	30,495
1926	36,911	6,444	1956	899,212	31,013
1927	63,134	15,014	1957	1,014,457	33,953
1928	105,749	19,897	1958	950,796	35,829
1929	137,472	20,285	1959	1,011,452	44,710
1930	136,669	20,346	1960	1,041,708	64,232
1931	116,613	18,237	1961	1,065,790	84,418
1932	116,541	16,414	1962	1,167,916	98,154
1933	117,720	13,158	1963	1,185,511	97,221
1934	136,103	17,341	1964	1,241,782	100,370
1935	149,113	17,600	1965	1,267,602	98,262
1936	165,452	20,513	1966	1,230,503	104,757
1937	186,230	20,599	1967	1,292,917	114,739
1938	181,440	21,582			

Note: No data available for 1941.

Source: American Petroleum Institute, *Petroleum Facts and Figures* (New York: American Petroleum Institute, various years).

TABLE 4.2

Oil exports as percentage of total exports, 1911–70, Venezuela and Colombia

	Venezuela	Colombia		Venezuela	Colombia
1911	0	0	1941	94.3	23.0
1912	0	0	1942	89.4	7.4
1913	0	0	1943	91.2	9.15
1914	0	0	1944	94.4	16.4
1915	0	0	1945	92.5	15.8
1916	0	0	1946	91.8	11.9
1917	0	0	1947	94.7	13.4
1918	0	0	1948	95.9	14.1
1919	0	0	1949	97.0	17.4
1920	1.9	0	1950	96.2	16.4
1921	8.8	0	1951	95.8	15.2
1922	11.4	0	1952	94.4	14.8
1923	18.3	0	1953	93.8	12.6
1924	30.6	0	1954	93.7	11.3
1925	41.6	0	1955	93.5	10.3
1926	62.4	8.5	1956	93.3	12.6
1927	63.2	20.5	1957	92.4	14.6
1928	76.6	19.3	1958	91.9	14.0
1929	76.2	21.3	1959	91.0	15.0
1930	83.2	23.2	1960	86.0	16.7
1931	84.0	16.1	1961	91.7	15.2
1932	84.6	23.3	1962	92.3	12.7
1933	89.6	13.5	1963	92.0	16.9
1934	90.6	18.5	1964	93.4	13.3
1935	91.2	20.4	1965	92.9	16.0
1936	89.0	17.9	1966	92.3	13.8
1937	88.3	19.8	1967	92.1	11.8
1938	93.3	20.8	1968	93.5	6.4
1939	93.9	18.2	1969	91.9	9.2
1940	94.0	23.8	1970	90.7	7.9

Sources: Leonardo Villar and Pilar Esguerra, *Comercio Exterior y la Actividad Económica en Colombia en el siglo XX: Exportaciones Totales y Tradicionales* (Bogotá: Banco de la República, 1999); Montevideo-Oxford Latin American Economic History Database, http://www.lac.ox. ac.uk/moxlad-database.

TABLE 4.3
Total exports as percentage of the GDP, 1918–80, Venezuela and Colombia

	Venezuela	Colombia		Venezuela	Colombia
1918	0	0	1950	29.4	15.6
1919	0	0	1951	30.5	17.1
1920	18.2	0	1952	31.8	16.4
1921	20.6	0	1953	31.6	17.6
1922	18.7	0	1954	31.3	15.2
1923	18.1	0	1955	32.8	14.8
1924	18.8	0	1956	33.3	15.0
1925	21.4	18.5	1957	35.7	15.3
1926	20.7	20.7	1958	31.7	16.2
1927	22.2	20.3	1959	29.0	17.6
1928	26.6	21.6	1960	30.0	16.6
1929	30.9	22.4	1961	27.6	14.8
1930	32.0	26.5	1962	26.5	15.2
1931	37.2	24.3	1963	24.4	14.4
1932	33.6	23.5	1964	30.5	14.0
1933	38.3	22.1	1965	28.8	15.0
1934	40.5	20.7	1966	26.7	13.5
1935	39.7	22.8	1967	32.9	14.7
1936	37.7	23.2	1968	27.6	14.6
1937	25.1	23.1	1969	29.5	14.4
1938	22.2	22.9	1970	22.4	12.7
1939	18.7	19.9	1971	24.4	12.3
1940	30.9	23.4	1972	22.9	13.2
1941	35.2	17.5	1973	28.2	13.4
1942	24.2	20.0	1974	43.1	12.2
1943	26.2	24.2	1975	32.6	13.9
1944	26.6	23.6	1976	29.6	12.7
1945	20.5	22.0	1977	26.6	11.6
1946	24.0	21.2	1978	23.3	13.1
1947	22.4	18.9	1979	29.6	13.6
1948	23.9	19.3	1980	32.5	13.5
1949	20.4	18.5			

Source: Montevideo-Oxford Latin American Economic History Database, http://www.lac.ox.ac.uk/moxlad-database.

Authoritarianism and the Rise of Venezuela's Oil Industry

Political and economic instability characterized Venezuela between its creation as a sovereign state in 1830 and the 1908 coup that brought General Juan Vicente Gómez to power. Gómez's regime lasted until 1935, and during his rule Venezuela transformed itself from an impoverished and politically weak country into a major actor in the global oil industry that would later become an important player in global geopolitics.[16] As early as 1909, Gómez encouraged the arrival of foreign multinationals by using legislation whereby the president himself had the power to individually decide concession terms.[17] Gómez made sure that all concessionaires signed an agreement with the government rather than becoming owners of the oil resources.[18] This meant that Gómez maintained the previous legislation, which held that subsoil resources were the property of the state. However, in many respects Gómez was the best kind of ruler a multinational could wish for: in 1918, his minister of development drafted new legislation increasing taxes and royalties on foreign multinationals. Both the multinationals and the US and British governments strongly protested against this change. Gómez responded by firing the minister and proposing that the foreign firms write the legislation themselves. "You know about oil. You write the laws. We're amateurs in this area," Gómez is said to have told the multinationals.[19] The companies complied and wrote new legislation – legislation that ruled the oil industry between 1922 (the year in which Royal Dutch Shell discovered the rich Los Barrosos-2 well) and 1943.[20]

Starting in 1922, Gómez awarded a large number of oil concessions to the private sector, which was comprised mostly of large landowners who sold these concessions to foreign oil firms.[21] Many of the concessionaires included Gómez's closest allies, who profited handsomely from the industry and who became Gómez's winning coalition.[22] In 1928, Gómez established some new "fees" for the foreign firms, and in 1930 he approved some new laws that granted better working conditions to the oil workers.[23] After 1930, as a way to maximize the rents received by the state, Gómez made corporations compete with each other for concessions.[24] The point of these measures was to maintain political stability and to make the government more capable of extracting wealth from the oil industry, thereby keeping the loyalty of its winning coalition. The Venezuelan oil industry witnessed some changes after Gómez's death in 1935. When the new ruler, General Eleázar López Contreras, took power, he announced nationalist reforms in the oil sector that would benefit the middle class. In this way, he was trying to legitimize his rule by enlarging the size of the government's winning coalition, but

National Oil Companies and Political Coalitions 105

without going so far as to approach the working class, which he continued to repress. In fact, the higher taxes on foreign firms translated into higher benefits for those in the military and those in the elite who were close to López Contreras.[25]

In 1941, López Contreras named General Isaías Medina as his successor. Although not interested in radically changing the political system, Medina permitted more political freedoms than his predecessor and, in 1942, sought ways to increase oil rents for the government by establishing an income tax on the oil multinationals. Medina also increased the value added generated by the oil industry in Venezuela by forcing foreign firms to refine larger amounts of crude in the national territory rather than in the adjacent Dutch island of Aruba (as they had done until then). The multinationals' protests against their home governments were futile. In the midst of the Second World War, the American and British governments were more interested in keeping oil flowing than in alienating the Venezuelan government.[26] The strongest opposition, however, came from home. Pro-democracy organizations and frustrated young army officials believed that the new flows of oil money were still distributed among those close to Medina's inner circle, leading them to overthrow Medina in 1945 and install a new civilian government.[27]

Oil and the Postwar Enlargement of Venezuela's Government Winning Coalition

The end of the dictatorial period brought important changes to the Venezuelan oil industry. The main political organization behind these changes was the *Acción Democrática* (AD) political party, which won the 1947 presidential elections. AD's winning coalition was comprised mostly of oil workers, labour unions, and the middle class, which explains this government's oil policies. By the late 1940s, oil had radically changed the Venezuelan social landscape, with a larger number of domestic white-collar workers and technicians working for the oil firms and an increasingly important urban middle class.[28] In 1948, the AD government revolutionized the global oil industry by, for the first time, establishing equal participation of the state and foreign firms in the industry's profits: the so-called 50-50 system, by which the government decreed that the profits made by the oil industry should be distributed between the firms and the government in equal proportion. Moreover, the government demanded that the oil multinationals invest in housing, health, and education.[29] As a way of averting domestic hostility, the oil multinationals went further and developed their own policies regarding social spending and the training of the domestic workforce.[30]

The new democratic regime was interrupted for a whole decade when, in 1952, General Marcos Pérez Jiménez overthrew the AD government. General Pérez Jiménez tried to turn the clock back by dissolving the pro-AD oil labour federation, decreasing social investment, and distributing among his closest allies the enormous oil wealth Venezuela received in those years.[31] This means that, during this regime, the government relied on a smaller winning coalition than did the previous AD government.

AD returned to power in 1958 after a coup perpetrated by sympathetic officials. During this new period, the party realized that, in order to avoid new coups in the future, it needed to enlarge its winning coalition and not to rely only on labour unions or the middle class. As a result, the AD government increased the budget for the military, promised to respect the property rights of the landowning oligarchy, decreased taxation, and slowed down social reforms. The social programs that remained were not funded by taxes on the domestic private sector but only by those paid by foreign firms.[32] In this way, oil provided the AD government with the resources to enlarge its winning coalition. Once AD had achieved domestic stability it embarked on a global campaign to create collective action mechanisms among oil-producing countries to maximize the rents they obtained from the industry. In fact, Venezuela was a crucial actor in creating OPEC in 1960.[33]

During the 1960s, political competition in Venezuela was between the centre-left AD and the centre-right Comité de Organización Política Electoral Independiente (COPEI). Although COPEI criticized AD's policies towards multinationals for discouraging private investment, after winning the 1969 elections it joined AD's nationalist agenda and, in 1971, nationalized natural gas. By this time, Venezuela had a sizable middle class with the necessary technical skills to run the industry, a sophisticated industrial elite, and a stable democratic political regime.[34] Both parties needed the support of a civilian population that expected its welfare to continue growing.[35] These circumstances provided the perfect conditions for both parties to consider the need to nationalize the oil industry and to create a state-owned corporation.[36] With an American government supportive of the Venezuelan regime, the multinationals simply started preparing themselves for the inevitable and gradually decreased their fixed assets and increased their marketing activities.[37] Finally, on 1 January 1976, the Venezuelan government took control of the domestic oil industry and created the state-owned enterprise Petróleos de Venezuela (PDVSA). Foreign firms immediately became

National Oil Companies and Political Coalitions   107

contractors of PDVSA and received an indemnity.[38] Between 1977 and 1999, PDVSA was an important employment generator for AD's base. This changed after 1999, with the administration of Hugo Chávez, which used PDVSA's rents to ensure the loyalty of Chávez's winning coalition, which was comprised of the lower class. Chávez's political strategy ended the political duopoly shared by COPEI and AD for the second half of the twentieth century, making his own movement the most important political force in Venezuela in the early twenty-first century.

Colombia: Coffee, Oil, and Bipartisan Politics

As happened with the Venezuelan case, Colombia entered the twentieth century after a chaotic and violent nineteenth century. This period culminated with the bloody and destructive War of the Thousand Days (1899– 1902) between secular and pro-free market liberals, on the one hand, and religious and protectionist conservatives, on the other. The war ended with a conservative triumph, which started an era of relative peace and economic growth led by coffee exports that lasted from 1903 to 1930. This period is known as the Conservative Hegemony, and it was characterized by the conservative dominance of the electoral process and a consensus between conservatives and liberals regarding the country's economic policy: both parties agreed on the need to promote coffee exports and foreign direct investment. During the nineteenth century, Colombia went through several export booms and busts, which created lots of economic uncertainty and fuelled political instability.[39] The leadership of both parties saw the rise of coffee as a reliable export crop in the early twentieth century as an opportunity to finally achieve both economic and political stability.[40] The members of the conservative winning coalition of the first half of the twentieth century were coffee exporters, members of the incipient industrial elite, the military, and the Roman Catholic Church. Even though elections took place, clientelism was rampant and regional powers had the ability to mobilize voters.[41]

Conservative Rule and Oil Policy

Colombia's potential as a crude oil producer was already known by the end of the First World War, when several foreign firms competed for concessions.[42] The first serious discovery took place in 1918, and it was made by the US-based firm Tropical Oil Company, which was later purchased by a subsidiary of the Standard Oil Company of New Jersey. The latter acquired Tropical through its Canadian subsidiary International Petroleum Company, taking advantage of Colombia's location and production costs in comparison to the US and Canada.[43] Shortly afterwards, the government changed the oil legislation, increasing taxation and royalties and thus leading Standard Oil (with the support of the US government) to successfully challenge the decision in the Colombian Supreme Court.[44]

The policies the Colombian government adopted in the following years can be explained by the evolution of the winning coalition and its ability to keep the government in power. Between the First World War and the Great Depression the coffee exporters organized themselves, creating the Federación Nacional de Cafeteros de Colombia (FNCC). This organization achieved enormous political and economic power and became highly influential in the government. The FNCC resulted from several meetings that took place in the early 1920s, at which the coffee bourgeoisie (those involved in the export of coffee but not the small landholders) created a group to pressure the government to help them after having faced the First World War crisis, which shut down European markets. Formally established in 1927, the FNCC continued its close relationship with the government by obtaining tariff protectionism and state funding for some of its activities. In the following years, the FNCC influenced government decisions in terms of taxation and monetary policy (particularly those related to exchange rates). Additionally, the FNCC used its funds to invest in social programs benefiting the small coffee growers, thus creating a mass of supporters with potential political influence.[45] Throughout the twentieth century, the Colombian government protected Colombian coffee exporters from the competition of foreign investors, gave coffee growers generous subsidies and low taxes, and allowed the FNCC to have a say in most issues pertaining to economic policy.[46] In time, one of the FNCC's political strengths came to be its ability to politically mobilize coffee farmers and rural workers.[47] High technological entry barriers in the oil sector, low ones in the coffee sector, and strong government support for the latter led many members of the Colombian elite to orient their efforts towards participating in the coffee industry and to avoid making any serious attempts to enter the oil industry, leaving this activity in the hands of the foreign multinationals.[48]

Despite the importance of coffee, the Colombian government placed big hopes in the country's potential as an oil exporter. Being short of domestic capital, the Colombian government wooed foreign investors who competed with each other for concessions. In 1913, the British oil firm Pearson and Son applied for a concession, but it was eventually overpowered by American interests, which had the backing of the US government.[49] In 1918, the American firm Tropical Oil discovered oil in the region of Santander and later, in August 1920, sold its properties to Standard Oil of New Jersey. The American multinational soon faced two interrelated problems: first, the oilfields were located 480 kilometres away from the Caribbean coast (where it could be exported), which meant the need to apply for a concession for a pipeline that would connect the oilfields with the port city of Cartagena. Second, Colombia was in the midst of negotiations with the US government regarding the payment of American reparations to Colombia for its support of the separation of the Colombian province of Panama, which gave the US control over what would become the Panama Canal Zone. In exchange for the pipeline concession, the Colombian government asked Standard Oil of New Jersey to lobby Washington on Colombia's behalf and to have the $25 million reparation approved by the Senate. The multinational built a coalition comprised of American senators who represented states with an important oil production and refining industry (including those where Standard Oil of New Jersey had a significant presence), senators who were not very politically competitive (and were therefore easier to bribe), and senators who leaned towards an activist state with regard to social issues. In the end, this coalition ensured that the payment of reparations to Colombia was approved. Once this was settled, Standard Oil was guaranteed its control of the Santander fields until 1951.[50]

During the 1920s, some social changes led to gradual shifts in the composition of the electorate. A growing middle class and a highly belligerent working class (particularly in the oil and banana sectors) became an important constituency of the liberal party's left wing, which criticized what it considered to be extremely favourable policies towards oil multinationals. In 1927, concerned about electoral challenges, the conservative party (under the leadership of Minister of Industry José Antonio Montalvo) proposed in Congress a new law that would increase taxes and create the legal grounds for the expropriation of foreign property on the part of the oil industry by declaring subsoil wealth the property of the state.[51] Surrendering to pressures from the US Department of State, the conservative Colombian government eventually dropped the project, leaving it without a potential resource to capture members of the liberal coalition at a time when the latter was creating a larger base.[52] During the impasse with the foreign firms, the Colombian government did not attempt to increase its bargaining power by enlarging its winning coalition by approaching the labour movement (as happened in Venezuela in 1976). On the contrary, in the year 1927, when the oil multinationals faced a strike, Minister Montalvo himself contacted the foreign firms and implored them not to give in to the unions while, at the same time, demanding that the government repress the strikers.[53] Montalvo sought an alliance with the domestic elite, proposing the creation of a joint venture with British investors. The Colombian elite declined the offer, aware of their technical inability to invest in a national oil company and concerned about alienating foreign investors.[54] In fact, that same year members of the liberal left-wing faction approached Montalvo and offered their support, which he rejected.[55]

The Liberal Republic, the Great Depression, and Export Protectionism

In 1930, liberal Enrique Olaya took power in a country facing the challenges of the Great Depression. Contrary to what happened in other Latin American countries, Colombia chose to face the crisis by reinforcing its economic model, which was based on coffee exports. Olaya unsuccessfully attempted to increase taxation on coffee exports and to increase government control over the industry. The final result of the struggle between the government and the FNCC was an even more powerful coffee organization that, in 1931, succeeded in convincing the government to abandon the gold standard, thus giving monetary authorities more leeway to determine foreign exchange rates (which moved in the direction and amount needed by the FNCC).[56] In 1933, Olaya again attempted to increase government control and taxation on the coffee sector but was again defeated, succeeding only in giving the FNCC more power over government economic policy.[57]

As for foreign oil firms, Olaya's administration did not dramatically depart from his conservative predecessors. In fact, while approaching the US, he promoted even friendlier terms for foreign investors. He decreased taxes and royalties for foreign firms, something that was celebrated not only by the multinationals but also by the national industrial elite.[58]

The biggest challenges to oil companies came after the 1934 election of progressive liberal presidential candidate Alfonso López Pumarejo. This candidate came to power with strong support from the liberal left, labour unions, and even the Communist Party. Once in power, López rewarded his winning coalition with unprecedented social reforms and by offering government support to labour unions. López took the US oil multinational Standard Oil Company of New Jersey to court after a debate over the firm's concession deadline: the government claimed the concession ended in 1946, while the multinational claimed it ended in 1951. During this legal conflict, the government received strong support from the labour movement and the political left. In the end, however, the Colombian Supreme Court ruled in favour of the multinational and the deadline remained 1951. After this brief conflict, and to the frustration of the liberal left, the government decreased its hostility towards foreign multinationals.[59]

Conservative Consolidation of Friendly Policies towards Foreign Oil Companies

López's winning coalition collapsed in the 1946 elections. Some factions of the liberal party were afraid of the left turn the party seemed to be taking, while those on the left were impatient with what they considered to be an intentional slowing down of social reforms. As a result, the liberals went to the 1946 elections divided between a centre and a left-wing candidate, thus permitting an easy conservative triumph. Liberal left-wing candidate Jorge Eliécer Gaitán was particularly critical of what he considered to be the sell-out policies of the oil sector.[60] In 1948, while a presidential candidate, Gaitán was assassinated, sparking violence that spread nationwide. The conservative government of Mariano Ospina attempted to control the chaotic situation by restricting political freedoms, turning his regime into a semidictatorship. This type of regime continued with President Laureano Gómez (1950–51), who attempted to change the Colombian Constitution to give himself more power. His attempt was thwarted by the military coup led by General Gustavo Rojas Pinilla, who stayed in power for four years before Colombia returned to civilian rule, with the liberals and conservatives sharing power for sixteen years.[61]

During the tumultuous times that followed Gaitán's assassination (known in the historiography as *La violencia*, 1948–58), the conservative party's winning coalition was comprised of the industrial elite and those connected to the interests of the FNCC. During this period, the industrial elite remained uninterested in developing the oil industry itself, while the FNCC wanted an economic policy that focused on coffee interests. As a result, friendly policies towards foreign oil firms continued. In 1951, the concession to Standard Oil of New Jersey expired, and the multinational peacefully transferred its properties to the Colombian government. The multinational was not expelled from the country but, rather, remained working as a subcontractor of the newly created state-owned enterprise ECOPETROL.[62] Given that ECOPETROL was created at a time when the government was supported by a winning coalition that did not include either the labour movement or the working class, no attempts were made to use this state firm to redistribute rents among those segments of the population. The Colombian elite benefited from having a source of employment for highly skilled labour and from subcontracting activities with ECOPETROL. Thus, the Colombian government did not use ECOPETROL as a tool to redistribute wealth and to build a larger political coalition that included the working class. This, however, did not mean that ECOPETROL did not have a powerful and belligerent labour union. Quite the contrary: since its creation this firm's labour union has been one of the most powerful unions in Colombia. However, its political alliances have not been with the traditional parties in power but, rather, with more radical left-wing organizations, including (at some points) illegal ones, thus more often than not putting the union at odds with the national government.[63]

Conclusion

This chapter proposes using selectorate theory to analyze government policies towards oil multinationals and the origin of national oil companies. I conduct a comparative study of Colombia and Venezuela in the twentieth century, a period during which these two countries experienced divergent political and economic processes. I show how the policies towards the oil sector evinced in each country responds to their regimes' respective strategies for political survival. Whether a military dictatorship, an elected civilian government, or a civilian authoritarian regime, the government aimed to ensure the loyalty of the political coalition that kept it in power. The cases studied show different types of winning coalitions. The Venezuelan military dictatorships of the first half of the twentieth century maximized the rents their small coalitions obtained from the oil industry by focusing on taxation policies that benefited this small group. This translated into limited challenges to the operations of foreign multinationals. Elected governments were not necessarily supported by much larger coalitions, as the Colombian case shows. The enormous power of the coffee export lobby, the reluctance of the Colombian elite to side with the labour movement, and a clientelist political system that permitted regional politicians to mobilize voters did not generate incentives for the government to expropriate foreign firms, or to create a national oil company run by labour unions, or to redistribute wealth among the members of the working class. A movement supported by a larger winning coalition, as in the case of Venezuela's AD, developed more aggressive policies towards oil multinationals. It is worth highlighting, however, that, by the time of the 1976 nationalization of the oil industry, AD's coalition was not limited to the labour movement but included members of the middle class and even market-friendly conservative politicians. This explains the differences between Venezuela's PDVSA, as a firm that ensured the loyalty of oil workers to AD, and Colombia's ECOPETROL, which the government did not use as a political tool.

This chapter also uses selectorate theory to explain the policies governments adopt towards foreign investors in the oil sector. I am aware that political coalitions are complex and hard to define in simple terms such as "a regime allied to the working class" or "a regime allied to the traditional elite." However, the logic of selectorate theory allows us to overcome the problems of approaches that conduct their analyses by relying upon a clear-cut dichotomy between democracy and dictatorship. The potential of selectorate theory to analyze the relationship between firms and states is enormous and can be applied to countries other than Venezuela and Colombia, and industries other than oil. Calls integrating theoretical developments into business history emphasize the usefulness of management theories.[64] Political scientists, however, developed selectorate theory. The strategies developed by states always affect the operations of firms, particularly in politically sensitive industries such as oil and gas.

Acknowledgments
An earlier version of this chapter was presented at the Political Regulation in Natural Resources, 1850–2000: A Global Perspective Workshop, Norwegian University of Science and Technology, Trondheim, Norway, August 2013. I thank Andreas Dugstad Sanders, Oscar Granados, Ishva Minefee, Helge Ryggvik, Pal Sandvik, Espen Storli, and Gail Triner for their useful feedback. This chapter builds on previous empirical analyses developed in Marcelo Bucheli, "Canadian Multinational Corporations and Economic Nationalism: The Case of Imperial Oil Limited in Alberta (Canada) and Colombia, 1899–1938," *Entreprises et histoire* 54 (2009): 67–85; Marcelo Bucheli and Ruth Aguilera, "Political Survival, Energy Policies, and Multinational Corporations: A Historical Study for Standard Oil of New Jersey in Colombia, Mexico and Venezuela in the Twentieth Century," *Management International Review* 50, 3 (2010): 347–78; a historiographical study in Marcelo Bucheli, "Major Trends in the Historiography of the Latin American Oil Industry," *Business History Review* 84, 2 (2010): 339–62; and theoretical discussions in Marcelo Bucheli and Jin-Uk Kim, "The State as a Historical Construct in Organization Studies," in *Organizations in Time: History, Theory, Methods,* ed. Marcelo Bucheli and R. Daniel Wadhwani (Oxford: Oxford University Press, 2014), 241–62; and Marcelo Bucheli and Minyoung Kim, "Attacked from Both Sides: A Dynamic Model of Multinational Corporations' Strategies for Protection of Their Property Rights," *Global Strategy Journal* 5, 1 (2015): 1–26.

Notes

1 Raymond Vernon, *Sovereignty at Bay: The Multinational Spread of US Enterprises* (New York: Basic Books, 1971).

2 Central Intelligence Agency, *The World Factbook, 2013–2014* (Washington, DC: CIA, 2013).

3 Stephen Kobrin, "Expropriation as an Attempt to Control Foreign Firms in LDCs: Trends from 1960–1979," *International Organization* 28, 3 (1984): 329–48.

4 Nathan Fagre and Louis Wells, "Bargaining Power of Multinationals and Host Governments," *Journal of International Business Studies* 13, 2 (1982): 9–23; David Smith and Louis Wells, *Negotiating Third World Mineral Agreements* (Cambridge: Ballinger Publications, 1975); Louis Wells, "The Multinational Business Enterprise: What Kind of International Organization?," *International Organization* 25, 3 (1971): 447–64; Vernon, *Sovereignty at Bay*; Bo Jonsson, *Staten och malmfälten: En studie i svensk malmfältspolitik omkring sekelskiftet* (Stockholm: Almqvist and Wiksell, 1969).

5 Stephen Kobrin, "Foreign Enterprise and Forced Divestment in LDCs," *International Organization* 34, 1 (1980): 65–88.

6 Paul Baran, *Monopoly Capital* (New York: Monthly Review, 1968); Fernando Henrique Cardoso and Enzo Faletto, *Dependency and Development in Latin America* (Berkeley: University of California Press, 1979); Andre Gunder Frank, *Capitalism and Underdevelopment in Latin America: Historical Studies of Chile and Brazil* (New York: Monthly Review Press, 1969).

7 Shannon Blanton and Robert Blanton, "What Attracts Foreign Investors? An Examination of Human Rights and Foreign Direct Investment," *Journal of Politics* 69, 1 (2007): 143–55; Witold Henisz, "The Institutional Environment for Economic Growth," *Economics and Politics* 12, 1 (2000): 1–31; Nathan Jensen, "Democratic Governance and Multinational Corporations: Political Regimes and Inflows of Foreign Direct Investment," *Industrial Organization* 57, 3 (2003): 587–616; Nathan Jensen, "The Multinational Corporation Empowers the Nation-State," *Perspectives on Politics* 3 (2005): 544–51; Nathan Jensen, *Nation-States and the Multinational Corporation: A Political Economy of Foreign Direct Investment* (Princeton: Princeton University Press, 2008).

8 Praasha Mahdavi, "Why Do Leaders Nationalize the Oil Industry? The Politics of Resource Expropriation," *Energy Policy* 75 (2014): 228–43; David A. Jodice, "Sources of Change in Third World Regimes for Foreign Direct Investment," *International Organization* 34, 2 (1980): 177–206.

9 Jean Boddewyn and Thomas Brewer, "International-Business Political Behavior: New Theoretical Directions," *Academy of Management Review* 19, 1 (1994): 119–43; Stephen Haber, Armando Razo, and Noel Maurer, *The Politics of Property Rights: Political Instability, Credible Commitments, and Economic Growth in Mexico, 1876–1929* (Cambridge: Cambridge University Press, 2003).

10 Noel Maurer, *The Empire Trap: The Rise and Fall of US Intervention to Protect American Property Overseas, 1893–2013* (Princeton: Princeton University Press, 2013).

11 Ibid.

12 Marcelo Bucheli and Jin-Uk Kim, "The State as a Historical Construct in Organization Studies," in *Organizations in Time: History, Theory, Methods*, ed. Marcelo Bucheli and R. Daniel Wadhwani (Oxford: Oxford University Press, 2014), 241–62.

13 Bueno de Mesquita, Alastair Bruce, Randolph Siverson Smith, and James Morrow, *The Logic of Political Survival* (Cambridge, MA: MIT Press, 2003).

14 Ibid.

15 Victor Bulmer-Thomas, *The Economic History of Latin America since Independence* (Cambridge: Cambridge University Press, 1994).

16 The most detailed accounts of Gómez's political strategies and his policies towards oil can be found in Brian McBeth, *Dictatorship and Politics: Intrigue, Betrayal, and Survival in Venezuela, 1908–1935* (Notre Dame: University of Notre Dame Press, 2008); and *Juan Vicente Gómez and the Oil Companies in Venezuela, 1908–1935* (Cambridge: Cambridge University Press, 1983). Both works emphasize how Gómez managed to keep his political rivals divided and used the oil rents as a means to ensure his survival.

17 Brian McBeth, *La política petrolera venezolana: Una perspectiva histórica, 1922–2005* (Caracas: Universidad Metropolitana, 2015), 43.

18 Ibid., 44.

19 Rómulo Betancourt, *Venezuela: Oil and Politics* (Boston: Houghton Mifflin, 1978), 27.

20 McBeth, *La política petrolera venezolana*, 44.

21 Ibid.

22 Edwin Lieuwen, *Petroleum in Venezuela: A History* (Berkeley: University of California Press, 1970), 18–19.

23 McBeth, *La política petrolera venezolana*, 43–44.

24 McBeth, *Juan Vicente Gómez and the Oil Companies in Venezuela*.

25 Franklin Tugwell, *The Politics of Oil in Venezuela* (Stanford: Stanford University Press, 1975), 18.

26 McBeth, *La política petrolera venezolana*, 45–46.

27 Tugwell, *Politics of Oil in Venezuela*, 44–45; Betancourt, *Venezuela*.

28 Miguel Tinker-Salas, *The Enduring Legacy: Oil, Culture, and Society in Venezuela* (Durham, NC: Duke University Press, 2009), 171–205.

29 Tugwell, *Politics of Oil in Venezuela*, 44–47.

30 Tinker-Salas, *Enduring Legacy*.

31 McBeth, *La política petrolera venezolana*, 46–47.

32 Lieuwen, *Petroleum in Venezuela*.

33 Terry Karl, *The Paradox of Plenty: Oil Booms and Petro-States* (Berkeley: University of California Press, 1997), 112.

34 Jonathan Di John, *From Windfall to Curse? Oil and Industrialization in Venezuela, 1920 to the Present* (University Park: Pennsylvania State University Press, 2009), 15–32.

35 Tinker-Salas, *Enduring Legacy*.

36 McBeth, *La política petrolera venezolana*, 51–54.

37 Francisco Monaldi, Rosa Amelia González, Richard Obuchi, and Michael Penfold, "Political Institutions, Policy-Making Process and Policy Outcomes in Venezuela," in *Working Paper* (Washington: Inter-American Development Bank, 2006).

38 McBeth, *La política petrolera venezolana*, 54–57.

39 José Antonio Ocampo, *Colombia y la economía mundial, 1830–1910* (Bogotá: Siglo 21, 1984), 47–50.

40 Marco Palacios, *Coffee in Colombia: An Economic, Social, and Political History* (Cambridge: Cambridge University Press, 2002), 25–76.

41 Marco Palacios and Frank Safford, *Colombia: Fragmented Land, Divided Society* (Oxford: Oxford University Press, 2002), 266–95.

42 Marcelo Bucheli, "Negotiating under the Monroe Doctrine: Weetman Pearson and the Origins of US Control of Colombian Oil," *Business History Review* 82, 3 (2008): 529–53; Xavier Durán, "El petróleo en Colombia, 1900–1950: Especuladores y empresas multinacionales," in *Ecopetrol: Sesenta años de historia, 1951–2011*, ed. Juan Benavides (Bogotá: ECOPETROL, 2011), 1–36.

43 Marcelo Bucheli, "Canadian Multinational Corporations and Economic Nationalism: The Case of Imperial Oil Limited in Alberta (Canada) and Colombia, 1899–1938," *Entreprises et histoire* 54 (2009): 67–85.

44 Jorge Villegas, *Petróleo, oligarquía e imperio* (Bogotá: Ancora, 1975), 60–72.

45 Roberto Junguito and Diego Pizano, *Instituciones e instrumentos de la política cafetera en Colombia, 1927–1997* (Bogotá: Fondo Cultural Cafetero, 1997), 50–67.

46 Palacios, *Coffee in Colombia*, 198–226.

47 Ibid.

48 Marcelo Bucheli and Luis Felipe Sáenz, "Export Protectionism and the Great Depression: Multinational Corporations, Domestic Elite, and Export Policies in Colombia," in *The Great Depression in Latin America*, ed. Paulo Drinot and Alan Knight (Durham, NC: Duke University Press, 2014), 129–59.

49 Bucheli, "Negotiating under the Monroe Doctrine."

50 Xavier Durán and Marcelo Bucheli, "Holding Up the Empire: Colombia, American Oil Interests, and the 1921 Urrutia-Thomson Treaty," *Journal of Economic History* 77, 1 (2017): 251–84.

51 Jorge Orlando Melo, "De Carlos E. Restrepo a Marco Fidel Suárez," in *Nueva Historia de Colombia*, vol. 2, ed. Alvaro Tirado Mejía (Bogotá: Planeta, 1989), 220–45.

52 René De la Pedraja Tomán, *Petróleo, electricidad, carbón y política en Colombia* (Bogotá: Ancora Editores, 1993), 28–33.

53 Ministerio de Industrias Colombia, *Memoria Presentada al Congreso de 1927* (Bogotá: Imprenta Nacional, 1927).

54 De la Pedraja Tomán, *Petróleo, electricidad, carbón y política en Colombia*, 33.

55 Efraín Estrada, *Sucesos Colombianos, 1925–1950* (Medellín: Universidad de Antioquia, 1990).

56 Mariano Arango, *Política económica e intereses cafeteros* (Medellín: Universidad de Antioquia, 1979), 60–63.

57 Marco Palacios, *El café en Colombia: Una historia económica, social y política* (Bogotá: Planeta, 2002), 438.

National Oil Companies and Political Coalitions 117

58 Marco Palacios, *Entre la legitimidad y la violencia: Colombia, 1875–1994* (Bogotá: Norma, 2003).

59 De la Pedraja Tomán, *Petróleo, electricidad, carbón y política en Colombia*, 73.

60 Richard Sharpless, *Gaitán of Colombia: A Political Biography* (Pittsburgh: University of Pittsburgh Press, 1978).

61 Marco Palacios, *Between Legitimacy and Violence: A History of Colombia, 1875–2002* (Durham, NC: Duke University Press, 2006), 135–70.

62 International Petroleum Company, *Annual Report* (New York: International Petroleum Company, 1951–52).

63 Renán Vega, Luz Ángela Núñez, and Alexander Pereira, *Petróleo y protesta obrera: La USO y los trabajadores petroleros en Colombia*, vols. 1 and 2 (Bogotá: Nomos, 2009).

64 Geoffrey Jones and Walter Friedman, "Business History: Time for Debate," *Business History Review* 85, 1 (2011): 1–8; R. Daniel Wadhwani and Marcelo Bucheli, "The Future of the Past in Management and Organization Studies," in *Organizations in Time: History, Theory, Methods*, ed. Marcelo Bucheli and R. Daniel Wadhwani (Oxford: Oxford University Press, 2014), 3–30.

5

Managing Russia's Resource Wealth
Coalitions and Capacity
STEPHEN FORTESCUE

Russia is an unusual place in terms of history, location and size, climate and resources. The application of the questions posed by the editors of this collection to Russia's management of its resource wealth and the rents derived from it provides the opportunity to test the universality of the hypotheses and findings that have emerged from the analyses of other countries studied in this volume.

The purpose of this book, as set out by the editors in its introduction, is to examine how various "large" factors form and influence the political economies of resource-rich countries. The editors suggest that, since the second half of the nineteenth century, three partially related factors have emerged to which, in one way or another, most resource-rich countries have responded. The first is the rising state capacity for control and regulation; the second is a nationalist desire to exercise control over a country's resource wealth and the rents derived from it, excluding foreign influences in order to do so; and the third is democracy.

Neither resource nationalism nor democracy are irrelevant in Russia's case, but neither are they dominant or determining. Resource nationalism has not been a major factor in Russia because, throughout its history, it has largely been able to exploit its natural resources on its own. At times it has recognized the need for financing and technology from abroad, and whether and how such foreign contributions to the Russian resource sector should be permitted have been a matter of serious debate and policy action.[1] But

Managing Russia's Resource Wealth 119

Russia has generally managed to obtain both financing and technology without giving up ownership or even control of its natural resources. Resource ownership issues are not a major part of the Russian psyche,[2] limiting the relevance of resource nationalism to the issue of whether foreigners should have access to its resource wealth. In Russia, it is strategic considerations that have been most important. Tellingly, whereas I suspect that, on most occasions in this volume, when the word "nationalization" is used it refers to a state taking over the assets of a foreign firm, in the Russian case it almost always refers to the state taking over the assets of a private domestic firm.

Regarding the third "large" factor mentioned above, democracy has always struggled to gain a foothold in Russia. While the control of resources and their rent flows was certainly a political issue during the turbulent period of the 1990s, which could possibly be described as democratic, it was not a dominant one. The so-called oligarchs, who had moved from their origins in the financial sector to the resource sector in the mid-1990s, were certainly not popular. But it was not until Putin came to power and created a regime that, while not indifferent to the popular mood, can hardly be described as democratic, that serious efforts were made to curb the oligarchs' economic power and political influence, including through the nationalizations mentioned in the previous paragraph.[3]

While democracy might not have been a major factor in shaping Russia's control of its natural resources, Marcelo Bucheli's approach to Venezuela and Colombia (Chapter 4, this volume) could be considered a variation of the democratic factor. He discusses how the breadth of the coalitions that control states affects the way resource wealth is managed. This is an approach that I apply to the Russian case. Given that Russia has largely been able to exclude itself from the resource nationalism strand of recent history, I instead emphasize the state's administrative and technical capacity to manage its resource wealth.

Administrative and Technical Capacity

I suggest that an important aspect of a country's political economy, one that plays a major role in determining how and how well it manages its resource wealth and the rents deriving from it, is its administrative and technical capacity. If a country possesses such capacity it is well able to manage its resources without recourse to foreign involvement, which takes resource nationalism out of play as a factor. While having such capacity by no means guarantees that it will use resource rents well, it is a necessary first step in doing so – both in order for it to extract rents and for it to apply them to the needs of society in an efficient way. The efficient extraction of rents means the maximization of such rents over the long term, which, as we see in a case study below, is a complex technical task that requires not only engineering skills but also considerable capacity to design and implement efficient taxation systems. To then efficiently apply the extracted rents to the needs of society is also a complex task, requiring sophisticated policy and administrative capacity.

Without being naïve about its efficiency, I would suggest that Russia is a modern society with complex needs and with the technical and administrative capacity to meet those needs. Further, it came to possess that capacity before resource wealth began to dominate its economy. It is widely recognized that countries that discovered resource wealth after they modernized have a far better record of managing that wealth well than do those whose resource wealth was being exploited (generally by foreign if not imperial powers) before an independent modern state was created. It is less widely recognized that Russia can be included in the former category.

The Bolsheviks famously had a radically modernizing ideology, with a strategy – particularly once Stalin gained power – of achieving modernity through transferring wealth from the agricultural sector to manufacturing. They struggled throughout the life of the Soviet Union to achieve a balance between coercive and more "rational," in the Weberian sense, methods of achieving their goal.[4] Particularly after the death of Stalin coercive methods declined and the system came to be dominated by a creaky but elaborate and arguably modern technical and administrative bureaucracy.

Unfortunately for the Soviets, for various reasons and despite the presence of a modern bureaucracy, their development model of transferring wealth from agriculture to industry ran out of steam before they had reached their goal of prosperous and powerful modernity. As growth rates declined and living standards started to fall in the 1970s, they turned to a new model, based on the export of natural resources, above all oil and gas. The proceeds of such exports were used to import the food (mostly feed grains for livestock) and the technology needed to modernize the Soviet Union's industry.

The system showed its considerable capacity to achieve major goals by building a large hydrocarbon-exporting sector in West Siberia, despite at times spoiling efforts from the West. This was a tribute to its technical and administrative capacities. But, arguably, its failure to manage the transition from the industrialization model to the resource export model provided a major contribution to the system's ultimate collapse.[5] The large start-up

Managing Russia's Resource Wealth

investments needed to develop the West Siberian oil and gas fields starved the rest of the already struggling economy of money. Even when the returns started to flow, the imports funded by them were insufficient either to satisfy the expectations of consumers or to resolve serious productivity and profitability issues in industry. Particularly when oil prices fell sharply in the 1980s, the system collapsed.

In the early post-Soviet period the economic concerns of policy makers and consumers were not focused on the resource sector. Their all-consuming priorities were getting goods and food into the shops, macroeconomic issues, and halting or at least managing the decline of industry. But hydrocarbons were not going to go away, and they soon came to occupy a dominant place in political and economic debate. The political concerns were focused on ownership and control, although between state and domestic private claims rather than between state and foreign claims. The fate of the economy rested on how to get the balance right between the reproduction and extraction of resource rents. A significant proportion of the oil industry was privatized and placed in the hands of the so-called oligarchs through the highly controversial "loans for shares" scheme of the mid-1990s. The non-privatization of the monopoly gas producer Gazprom, and management's subsequent application to it of rent-extraction, was hardly less controversial.

When Vladimir Putin rose from nowhere to the presidency at the beginning of the new millennium one of his priorities was to seize back for the state control of both oil and gas, above all in order to gain access to rapidly increasing rents as oil prices began to rise. The arrest of Mikhail Khodorkovsky, the owner of the biggest Russian producer, Yukos, in October 2003, and the subsequent transfer of most of Yukos's assets to the state-owned Rosneft, was the first major development in this regard. Although it was not followed by the total nationalization that many expected, the state's share of the oil sector has steadily increased since then.[6] Despite constant predictions to the contrary, output has continued to increase, and tax revenues from the sector have grown enormously. Just as the state dominates the hydrocarbon sector, so the hydrocarbon sector dominates the economy and its tax budget. Table 5.1 shows its oil rents (defined as the difference between the value of crude oil production at world prices and the total costs of production) as a percentage of GDP compared to some other major oil producers. Hydrocarbons, with oil by far the biggest earner, account for 25 percent of GDP, 50 percent of government revenues, and 70 percent of export earnings.[7]

TABLE 5.1

Oil rents as percentage of GDP, selected countries, 2013

Country	Rent as % GDP	Country	Rent as % GDP
Algeria	21.6	Kuwait	57.5
Angola	34.6	Nigeria	13.6
Azerbaijan	33.9	Norway	8.3
Ecuador	16.2	Russia	13.7
Iran	22.8	Saudi Arabia	43.6
Kazakhstan	23.8	Venezuela	23.6

Source: World Bank data, https://data.worldbank.org/indicator/NY.GDP.PETR.RT.ZS.

Has the domination of the sector that dominates the economy been achieved by a state with a modern administrative and technical capacity? I would expect that to be the case. However, many disagree. It is widely held that Russia is a highly personalist regime, dominated by crony relationships, with a large proportion of those relationships and the rent-seeking that is fundamental to their existence being based in and around the hydrocarbon sector. In this view, Putin and his cronies control the sector and use the rents derived from it to control the rest of society. Such a regime does not need and indeed is highly destructive of administrative capacity. Indeed, in Putin's Russia, the bureaucracy is both incompetent and rapacious.[8]

My contention is that, while such phenomena are undoubtedly present, the personalist view ignores the significant modern elements of the Russian system, including its involvement in the political and policy processes of groups with institutionalized interests and significant professional capacity.[9] In the case study below, the activities of such groups in the oil sector are described.

Small versus Big Coalitions

The issue of small versus big coalitions is presented in detail in Bucheli's chapter in this volume. While a big coalition system is by no means the same as a democratic one, there are some similarities.[10] Bucheli argues that when a small coalition controls resource rents, it divides up those rents between its few members, creating extreme wealth inequalities and oppressive and/ or unstable political regimes. When a large coalition controls resource rents, they are likely to be treated as a public good and distributed accordingly. It could be argued that one of the reasons that the Soviet turn to a resource-export model did not work was that too small a coalition controlled the

Managing Russia's Resource Wealth 123

distribution of the resource rents. Although social needs – in the form of food imports – were not totally ignored,[11] the lion's share went to the military-heavy industry coalition that had long dominated the political economy. It made very poor use of the rents it received.

It could be argued that the personalist regime that is claimed to exist in Russia today is also an example of a small coalition: a small group of Putin clients controls the rents. These clients are from various silovik groups that, while on occasion competing among themselves, ensure that limited rent leaks outside the boundaries of the coalition.[12] Again, I would argue that this is an oversimplified view of the Russian system. While keen to look after his cronies and the institutions from which they – and he – come, Putin ensures that rents are distributed within a much broader coalition, including what could be called the social sector – that is, his electorate among pensioners, state-sector workers, and workers in industrial sectors subsidized by the government. They compete for resource rents among themselves as well as with silovik groups. When resource rents were plentiful, they were all able to get a share without the competition being too disruptive. As rents have become scarcer, Putin has kept the broad coalition together by endeavouring to spread the pain and, to the extent that that is not possible, by inducing patriotic fervour among the population. As a result, people are prepared to accept some belt tightening while the defence sector expands and non-competitive non-resource sectors are subsidized and protected from foreign competition. Those kept out of the coalition are entrepreneurial and innovative industry, along with the non-patriotic section of the population, which is likely to be concentrated among private-sector employees. Whether this coalition is sustainable in circumstances of reduced resource rents brings us to the second major task set in this volume: determining whether the various political economies that develop in different resource-rich states are successes or failures.

Success or Failure

Outside commentators generally see Russia's political economy as a failure, usually including its resource and rent management arrangements as a major part of the problem.[13] It is not surprising that resource curse theory, as outlined in the introduction to the volume, has been applied to contemporary Russia.[14] In this view, resource rents are appropriated and squandered by corrupt elites, an aggressive military and security sector, and/or non-productive social groups and industries. It could well be that, ultimately, the resource sector will be squeezed dry. Certainly the reliance on resource rents makes it difficult for new productive sectors of the economy to develop.

To that political economy explanation of the problem is added the more technical economic Dutch disease analysis. Although there is debate as to whether Russia suffers from Dutch disease, certainly some of its symptoms are present.[15] The ruble goes through long periods of real appreciation, with occasional spectacular busts. The massive devaluations give a kickstart to the non-resource economy (albeit a kickstart that, it seems, weakens over time). Then the ruble begins to appreciate again, and the non-resource sector once again struggles to be competitive with imports and on export markets.

Both the rent-destroying and Dutch disease phenomena are undoubtedly present in Russia and prevent it from reaching its full potential. They could well lead to its eventual failure, with a Russian collapse ensured as much by sustained low oil prices as was the Soviet collapse. But we should not ignore either the benefits that resource rents have brought to broad sectors of Russian society in the form of high levels of prosperity or the resilience of both the economy and the society it serves. This is as one would expect if Russia is indeed a broad coalition system with a reasonably modern administrative and technocratic capacity.

But there are extensive theoretical and empirical literatures that tell us that broad coalitions and modern administrative and technocratic capacities bring their own problems. The public choice literature in the Western world and the *ekonomika soglasovaniia/vedomstvennost* literature on the Soviet Union and post-Soviet Russia describe the way that modern policy making and administrative systems can be overwhelmed by the demands of the members of broad coalitions for their share of limited rents.[16] The elaborate consultation and negotiation processes that are typical both of broad coalitions and modern policy and administrative systems contribute to slow and lowest-common-denominator outcomes that may eventually prove so inefficient as to threaten the sustainability of the system.

Case Study

Ideally two case studies should be undertaken to illustrate the points made above: one looking at the production of resource rent, the other at its distribution. The first would test whether Russia has sufficient administrative capacity to efficiently manage the reproduction of resource rents; the second whether rents are distributed within a broad coalition. Here I undertake the first by examining the recent policy process associated with oil tax regimes.

Managing Russia's Resource Wealth

The second I do not undertake but, rather, refer readers to other work on the Russian budget process, where they will find an elaborate and reasonably formalized process for the distribution of budget revenues – largely hydrocarbon rents – among a range of well-organized bidders.[17] Under current difficult circumstances, the social welfare and defence sectors are being asked to accept some pain, but they are still relatively favoured, while investment in infrastructure and human capital is being squeezed hard. However, even with the social sector still being somewhat favoured in budget allocations, standards of living are falling. Putin has offset the possible negative effects of this development on his electorate's willingness to remain in the coalition by appealing to its patriotic instincts through an aggressive foreign policy and the pursuit of "enemies" at home and abroad. With that political strategy as background, there are signs that the budget formation process – the distribution of resource rents – is under strain. These issues cannot be described in detail here, but they include increasing pressure on those producing economic forecasts to adjust them to desired rather than to likely outcomes; the dragging of tax arrangements into the budget process, which has previously dealt exclusively with expenditure and in which the provider of tax revenues – the hydrocarbon sector – is not well represented; and general pressure on consultation procedures.[18]

The case study I present here looks at the stage before distribution: Does the Russian political economy have the capacity to produce the rents needed to keep a broad coalition happy? Does Russia have the technical and administrative capacity to efficiently extract rents? Are there any signs that, while having that capacity, Russia is susceptible to the "modern" problem of bureaucratic deadlock? My focus is the oil tax system.[19]

During the Soviet period tax was essentially an irrelevant concept. With complete state ownership and central planning, whether an enterprise incurred a surplus or a loss was determined by plan indicators, and enterprise performance and remuneration was based on the ability to operate according to those indicators. If revenue was an artificial concept and profit a meaningless one, there was no room for taxation as we would understand it.

In the early years of post-Soviet Russia a system of taxation was introduced in the oil sector; however, the state had little capacity to enforce it. Statutory rates were set at levels so high that the sector, particularly with regard to crude output, would be unprofitable and unsustainable if taxes were collected at those rates.[20] However, taxes were not paid at the statutory rates, as producers, usually on an individual basis, constantly negotiated special deals.[21]

Putin decided to create a more efficient tax system. The basic approach was of simplification, with minimal differentiation and exemptions, which would allow for lower rates but a higher overall take through improved collection.[22] The basic profits tax was cut to a flat rate of 24 percent. Of taxes specific to the oil sector, export duties were retained (differentiated only between rates for crude and refined products) as part of the continuing commitment to protect domestic fuel prices from rises flowing through from increases in global crude prices. Royalty payments were replaced by the minerals extraction tax (MET; in Russian *nalog na dobychu poleznykh ispokaemykh*, NDPI), an undifferentiated levy on output, with the amount paid per unit of output based on the global oil price.

The main advantage of the system was that it was easy to administer, or, to put it more bluntly, difficult to game. The two big taxes, MET and export duties, were based on measurements of output and the global oil price, which could not be easily manipulated by producers. Output passed through pipelines and ports that were independently monitored. When, in 2004, the Ministry of Natural Resources claimed that oil companies were understating output to avoid MET, there was considerable scepticism among those involved in regulating the sector that such manipulations were possible except on a very minor scale in Chechnya and the north Caucasus.[23] With MET levied on output rather than sales, transfer pricing also lost much of its tax-evading salience.[24]

Thus, the approach was adopted because it was easy to administer, a recognition of the weaknesses of the state's capacity to administer and enforce more sensitive arrangements that would have relied on either a much greater capacity to monitor firm performance or a much greater trust in firms to provide accurate data. However, it was always recognized that the system – because of its very simplicity – was crude in its incentive structure. Once it came to be seen that the costs incurred through the crude incentive structure were becoming greater than the benefits gained through ease of administration, the state's policy process went into action. After strong growth in the first half of the decade, by 2005 oil output was levelling off (see Table 5.2), a consequence, in the eyes of many, of underinvestment resulting from excessively high tax rates.[25] More specifically, it was argued that tax arrangements also produced particularly perverse investment incentives with regard to high-cost oil.

The tax arrangements of the 1990s had had some differentiation for cost, but not enough (it was said) to encourage the extraction of high-cost oil.[26] The problem was made much worse by the new tax arrangements introduced

TABLE 5.2
Russian crude oil output, million tonnes, 2000–13

Year	Output	Year	Output
2000	327	2007	497
2001	352	2008	494
2002	384	2009	501
2003	426	2010	512
2004	463	2011	518
2005	475	2012	526
2006	486	2013	531

Source: https://vseonefti.ru/upstream (Russian website "All about Oil").

in the early 2000s. There was no recognition of the cost side of firms' balance sheets, meaning low-cost and high-cost oil were treated equally.

There are two categories of high-cost oil. First, there is oil from brownfields – that is, established fields from which the easily recoverable oil has been taken. The remaining oil in individual wells or in reservoirs bypassed in the original exploitation of the field is more expensive to recover. Russia has a particular problem in this regard since its mature wells have been damaged by the crude recovery techniques that were applied in the late Soviet period in order to maximize short-term recovery.[27]

Brownfield oil is a major component of Russian oil output. An Ernst and Young report of 2013 stated that 80 percent of Russian reserves were in developed fields and that 62 percent of current output came from "difficult" fields.[28] The brownfields are said to have a natural decline rate of about 10 percent per annum. For a while the decline rate was reduced to about 2 percent through enhanced recovery techniques under ruling tax arrangements.[29] But, as the remaining oil became more difficult to gain access to and the cost of enhanced recovery climbed, it was strongly argued that output could be maintained only by granting tax concessions for marginal oil in the brownfields.[30]

The other category of high-cost oil is what I call "frontier" oil – that is, oil that is found in entirely new geographical locations that bring enormous challenges in terms of technology and infrastructure. For Russia, this means the continental shelf, particularly in the Arctic, and, somewhat ambiguously as far as policy makers are concerned, East Siberia.[31]

As cheap West Siberian oil peaked the tax disincentives relating to high-cost oil became a major issue. In essence, the problem was a looming output gap as mature fields in West Siberia peaked before new fields in East Siberia and on the continental shelf came on line. As already indicated, total output levelled out sharply from 2005. In a 2013 report it was noted that new fields in East Siberia had begun making a contribution by the end of the 2000s but that those and planned newer fields could not contribute more than 100 million tonnes per annum (about 20 percent of current output) before 2025. The gap would have to be made up from the brownfields. It was claimed that getting Russian recovery rates from the brownfields to an internationally competitive 43 percent would allow an extra 4 billion tonnes to be recovered (roughly eight years of current total output).[32]

The problem was first identified and publicized by producers, with Lukoil expressing its concerns most persistently. A report used in the account of the output gap above was written by that privately owned company.[33] In placing the problem on the agenda and in proposing solutions, Lukoil and other producers were not only able to operate in the public arena but also to have direct access both to policy participants, including Putin, and to policy arenas, including membership of government policy-making forums. They also found ready support among relevant state agencies. I now describe the policy debate in which producers and state agencies participated in some detail.

In general terms, the demand from producers was for a decrease in the tax burden on the sector and, more specifically, for changes in tax arrangements that would increase the incentive to extract high-cost oil. First, tax concessions had to be offered to producers investing in frontier fields – essentially the state-owned companies and above all Rosneft – to ensure that they came on line as soon as possible. But that in itself would not be enough: the gap could only be closed if tax concessions were also given to producers in mature fields to make it profitable for them to extract residues in exploited wells and deposits that had been passed over as unprofitable during the initial exploitation.

The message was received, and in 2006 tax concessions were granted. MET was set at zero for the early stages of East Siberian operations (the shelf was excluded from the concessions at the last minute, probably because of intense negotiations that were being contemplated over special tax regimes for the foreign companies that were seen as essential for shelf operations). Cuts were granted for brownfield operations that were over 80 percent depleted. These cuts were not particularly generous and were subject to heavy and expensive monitoring conditions. It has been claimed that this, plus lack of agreement between producers and tax authorities as to how depletion was to be measured, led to limited use of the brownfield concessions.[34]

Managing Russia's Resource Wealth 129

Pressure was maintained for more concessions. A full review of the tax system by the Ministry of Energy at the end of the decade led to proposals for new concessions and for adjustments to the old. New concessions were granted on the shelf, and there was some clearing up of monitoring and definitional issues in the brownfields,[35] although monitoring remained a significant cost for producers.[36] From late 2014 the so-called "tax manoeuvre" brought further assistance. It consisted of a sharp decrease in export duty matched by an increase in MET.[37]

By this stage something like 50 percent of Russian oilfields enjoyed some sort of tax concession.[38] Producers, while admitting that the concessions had had some beneficial impact, insisted that more was needed to guarantee avoidance of the output gap.[39] Regulators and analysts complained that, with so many narrowly specific concessions, the system was becoming too complicated to administer, while signs of fiddling were also detected.[40] While lobbying and policy action around further concessions by no means ceased,[41] at this point attention turned to a fundamental change to the taxation system – one that, in its very structure, took account of costs.

In response to demands for such a change, the Ministry of Energy proposed a "tax on financial result" (TFR, *nalog na finansovyi rezul'tat*) levied at a fixed rate (proposed at 60 percent) on the difference between revenues and costs. The Ministry of Finance, fearing the effect on budget revenues, was fiercely opposed.[42] Among its concerns was the potential for such a tax to be manipulated by producers through the inflation of reported costs, a reflection of the ministry's ongoing concerns about administrative capacity.[43]

Despite strong lobbying by producers and Minister of Energy Novak, the responsible deputy prime minister, Arkady Dvorkovich, quickly made it clear that, given Ministry of Finance opposition, there would be no immediate general move towards a cost-sensitive tax system.[44] Producers responded by accepting the fact that the broad implementation of such an approach might be a long-term project,[45] but they agreed that an experimental application to a number of "pilot" projects should be undertaken as soon as possible.[46]

The Ministry of Finance believed that the pilots, and indeed the whole TFR approach, was just a ploy to get tax concessions for deposits that had so far missed out on gaining them without having to deal with any countervailing increases in revenues elsewhere.[47] Despite support for the pilots from Dmitry Medvedev and the sectoral ministries (i.e., energy and natural resources), the Ministry of Finance was able to stymie the progress of draft legislation through the government. Running out of patience, at the end of

2014 one of the most important oil-producing regions, the Khanty-Mansiisk Autonomous Region (KhMAO), exercised its right as a constituent unit of the Russian Federation to prepare legislation – not without, it is heavily implied in press reports, the encouragement and assistance of the Ministry of Energy.[48]

Despite the Ministry of Energy proposing amendments to the KhMAO bill that might placate the Ministry of Finance,[49] the latter refused to sign off on the "opinion" that the government was required to affix to legislation, with the result that the bill was unable to be formally presented to the Duma.[50] On 25 June 2015, Medvedev chaired a meeting on the pilots, at which it was decided to sign off on the KhMAO bill subject to specific amendments that would specify the characteristics that would make a deposit eligible for pilot status.[51] The "opinion" was duly issued.[52]

Meanwhile, as it gave ground in the fight over TFR and in a radical change of tactics, the Ministry of Finance proposed its own cost-based tax, the tax on marginal revenue (NDD, *nalog na dobavlennyi dokhod*).[53] While there were hints that this was just another ministry ploy to delay things further,[54] it appears that the ministry recognized that it was going to have to give ground in principle, particularly as falling oil prices were showing up the limitations – for the federal budget – of the existing system.[55] Clearly, it thought that proposing its own cost-based system would give it greater control over the process. Its thinking appeared to be justified when, at a meeting of the presidential commission for the hydrocarbon sector in October 2015, Putin – albeit in typically ambiguous words – supported the Ministry of Finance. The official transcript of the meeting is limited to Putin's opening comments. He stressed the importance of major investment in the sector (after in a newspaper article a fortnight earlier Minister of Finance Siluanov had suggested that given global conditions oil companies were investing too much),[56] and referred to the connection between investment and tax rates:

> The hydrocarbon sector traditionally plays a major role in forming the revenue side of the federal budget. Considering that, it is necessary to evaluate the effectiveness of any decisions taken on the tax burden of the sector and its influence on the economy as a whole with the maximum degree of precision. We must ensure that any extra extractions from the sector do not lead to cuts in the investment programs of energy companies and do not have a negative multiplier effect on related sectors. I know about the discussions going on in the sector, and indeed agree in part with the Ministry

Managing Russia's Resource Wealth 131

of Finance, but we must, undoubtedly, constantly monitor the situation as it unfolds in the sector. Let's return to the issue at some future meeting of the commission after monitoring the situation.[57]

What he meant was variously interpreted by commentators,[58] but it certainly led to a greater willingness on the part of the Ministry of Energy to work with the Ministry of Finance on developing the NDD approach.

Given that both ministries were proposing essentially the same thing, one might have expected the process now to be straightforward. This was not the case because the two sides continued to pursue radically different goals, as their bureaucratic responsibilities would lead one to expect. The Ministry of Finance, with responsibility for budget stability at a time of increasing budget pressure, was determined that any taxation changes would be at least revenue-neutral. Producers were deeply suspicious that its true intentions were to increase their tax burden[59] – suspicions that were only strengthened as falling revenues forced the ministry to openly call for increased taxation of the hydrocarbon sector. As far as the Ministry of Finance was concerned any tax concessions granted to one part of the sector had to be offset by increases elsewhere. The ministry was well aware of the dangers to the budget of concessions for high-cost oil when an ever-increasing share of Russian reserves – up to 70 percent – was seen as high-cost.[60]

The interests of the Ministry of Energy were quite different. It was essentially a representative of the oil companies, with a state responsibility for maintaining oil output at high levels. It wanted to ensure that no producer – indeed no element of the production profile of any producer – was worse off as a result of the changes, something that put it inherently at odds with the Ministry of Finance. It tried to reassure its opponent that any losses of revenue would be short-term as the new tax incentives encouraged producers to invest in high-cost operations that would quickly deliver increased output, the taxation of which would offset any short-term revenue losses.[61]

The struggle became an immensely complicated and often highly technical saga to determine: the basic rate at which the new tax should be levied; what could be counted as a cost and what, if any, upper limit should be imposed on claimable costs; to what extent existing taxes should remain; to which deposits (if not all) the new tax should be applied; and whether the pilots should proceed. The most contentious issues were, and remain, whether producers of frontier oil should be subjected to the new tax (the position of the Ministry of Finance) or whether they should be able to choose to remain under current arrangements, including current tax concessions, and the pilots, on which the Ministry of Finance has conceded, as long as any loss of tax revenue be compensated for elsewhere. Where that "elsewhere" might be remains a bone of contention.

Many deadlines have been missed, and despite regular claims that agreement is close and draft legislation near to completion, no draft has appeared. And it remains unclear whether, when, and in what form the new tax will appear. How serious a matter this is for the Russian oil industry also remains unclear. At a time when, within the global oil industry, there is more concern about demand than supply, Russia has continued to produce at record levels. However, there remain concerns that this cannot be maintained. For the moment, continuing declines in West Siberian output are offset by increasing output elsewhere, and there is confidence among some that brownfield output will quickly recover when the right price and tax circumstances encourage investment.[62] But there is still a fear that there are not enough new fields in prospect to match the eventual depletion of West Siberia, or at least not with a cost structure that will allow an adequate return to producers and the state's coffers.

One interesting aspect of the debate is that the Ministry of Finance, in moving to a cost-based approach, has had to downplay its concerns over the state's capacity to administer such a system. In response to analysts' concerns that a cost-based system would lead to artificially inflated costs, a ministry source is reported to have said that, although there was some risk, current administrative capacity was adequate to keep control of the situation.[63]

The final outcome of the oil tax policy debate is as yet far from clear, much less the results should the new approach be implemented. We have witnessed a policy process that is sophisticated and that has been carried on by informed participants. However, we have also witnessed some predicted problems. A multitude of well-informed participants relentlessly pursues its own narrow interests. Existing taxation arrangements have become, as they did in the 1990s, so littered with special deals that they are impossible to administer. But efforts to simplify things and to address the incentive problems of the existing system are endlessly debated, negotiated, and adjusted. The process displays the procedural games and ambit claims that delay policy resolution and that are typical of bureaucratic policy regimes.

Conclusion

In the introduction to this volume we are asked: What forms a resource-rich country's political economy? In Russia's case, the answer begins in late Soviet

Managing Russia's Resource Wealth 133

times, when its existing growth-oriented political economy – based on the transfer of resources from agriculture to industry – ran out of steam and forced change. However, the Soviet Union's attempt to shift to a resource-rent model failed: the demands on it from a small and highly inefficient coalition were too great; society, essentially left out of the coalition, responded with ever-worsening labour morale; and an administrative and technocratic capacity that was impressively sufficient to create a resource-export regime was not sufficient to efficiently manage rent distribution. A sharp reduction in rents when oil prices fell drove the system into collapse.

The new system that followed has, it could be argued (although many would not agree), a broader coalition and a better distributive capacity. This means that it has produced better results than it is generally given credit for. But it faces major problems of resource-specific and more generic natures. These include crony rent-seeking (which, while not necessarily unique to resource-rich countries, is certainly well-favoured in such countries) and Dutch disease issues. But there are also what could be called the problems of modernity. The first is the deadlock tendencies of complex bureaucracies, as seen in the case study. A complicated issue is addressed professionally and expertly, but it is very difficult to get an outcome. The second modernity problem involves managing a broad coalition, especially when the rent pie is stagnant or shrinking. In the current Russian case of a stagnant rent pie, Putin has had to undertake foreign adventures to help maintain the coalition, and these are likely to have severe long-term costs. And this is occurring in circumstances in which there is little room for appeals to resource nationalism (something that is common in other resource-rich countries). At the same time, there are some signs, albeit not yet critical, of strain on the distributive capacity of the state, specifically within the budget formation process.

It could be argued that true democracy would help deal with these problems, and that could well be the lesson of other chapters in this volume. Democracies are of course not entirely free of the phenomena described, but one likes to think they suffer from them to a lesser degree than do non-democracies.

The prospects for democracy in Russia are unfortunately not good. Given this, will the problems just summarized ultimately win out over the country's undoubted wealth and capacity? With ongoing crony rent-seeking, with Dutch disease making diversification very difficult, with a broad coalition that needs an increasingly costly aggressive foreign policy to keep it intact, and with a policy-making capacity that struggles to resolve difficult issues, one is not optimistic. Although, at the same time, none of these phenomena is yet so threatening as to suggest imminent collapse.

The broad lesson of my analysis is that modern technical and administrative capacity and a broad coalition can enable a nation to benefit from resource exploitation and, indeed, are probably necessary conditions for any sustained benefits from resource wealth. But they are far from sufficient to guarantee success.

Notes

1 There were times in the Soviet period when Western technology, including in the resource sector, was welcome. But there was never any chance of foreign ownership being accepted. Putin has worked particularly hard, and has often struggled, to get the foreign investments and technology that he recognizes are essential without offering ownership. Minority equity stakes in strategic firms are welcome, albeit under tight strategic investment legislation. See Stephen Fortescue, "The Russian Law on Subsurface Resources: A Policy Marathon," *Post-Soviet Affairs* 25 (2009): 160–84; Stephen Fortescue, "Private Enterprise in the Russian Oil Sector," in *Russian Energy and Security up to 2030*, ed. Susanne Oxenstierna and Veli-Pekka Tynkkynen (Basingstoke: Palgrave, 2014), 161–91.

2 Peter Rutland, "Petronation? Oil, Gas, and National Identity in Russia," *Post-Soviet Affairs* 31 (2015): 66–89.

3 Stephen Fortescue, *Russia's Oil Barons and Metal Magnates: Oligarchs and the State in Transition* (Basingstoke: Palgrave, 2006).

4 On Weberian rationality in the Soviet system, see T.H. Rigby, "A Conceptual Approach to Authority, Power and Policy in the Soviet Union," in *Authority, Power and Policy in the USSR*, ed. T.H. Rigby, Archie Brown, and Peter Reddaway (London and Basingstoke: Macmillan, 1983), 9–31.

5 Thane Gustafson, "Soviet Oil Policy and Energy Politics, 1970–1985," National Council for Soviet and East European Research, 1985, https://www.ucis.pitt.edu/nceeer/1985-627-13-Gustafson.pdf; Valeriy Kryukov and Arild Moe, "The Russian Oil Sector," in *The Oxford Handbook of the Russian Economy*, ed. Michael Alexeev and Shlomo Weber (New York: Oxford University Press, 2013), 344–45.

6 Fortescue, "Private Enterprise in the Russian Oil Sector."

7 Rutland, "Petronation?," 67.

8 Vladimir Gel'man, "The Vicious Circle of Post-Soviet Neopatrimonialism in Russia," *Post-Soviet Affairs* 32 (2016): 455–73.

9 Stephen Fortescue, "Institutionalization and Personalism in the Policy-Making Process of the Soviet Union and Post-Soviet Russia," in *Russian Politics from Lenin to Putin*, ed. Stephen Fortescue (Basingstoke: Palgrave, 2010), 21–50.

10 North, Wallis, and Weingast discuss at length the differences between and difficulties of moving from what they call "limited access orders" (something like the big coalitions spoken of here) and "open access orders" (essentially democracies). See Douglass C. North, John Joseph Wallis, and Barry R. Weingast, *Violence and*

Social Orders: A Conceptual Framework for Interpreting Recorded Human History (New York: Cambridge University Press, 2009).

11 A common concept in the Brezhnev period of the late Soviet Union was the "social contract," often summed up in the humorous aphorism: "They pretend to pay us and we pretend to work." In other words, the state promised a guaranteed minimum standard of living in return for a minimum commitment to productive activity. It could be argued that that was an important component of a broad coalition. Even if it was, however, the state was unable to keep its side of the bargain in that it failed to provide anything for the people to buy with what they earned. The result was that the population largely stopped even pretending to work and dropped out of the coalition.

12 Siloviki are members of the elite with a background (or currently holding positions) in the security forces.

13 Clifford G. Gaddy and Barry W. Ickes, "Putin's Rent Management System and the Future of Addiction in Russia," in *The Challenges of Russia's Politicized Economic System*, ed. Susanne Oxenstierna (London: Routledge, 2015), 11–32.

14 Rudiger Ahrend, "Can Russia Break the 'Resource Curse?'" *Eurasian Geography and Economics* 46 (2005): 584–609.

15 Shinichiro Tabata, "Observations on Russian Exposure to the Dutch Disease," *Eurasian Geography and Economics* 53 (2012): 231–43; Masaaki Kuboniwa, "Diagnosing the 'Russian Disease': Growth and Structure of the Russian Economy," *Comparative Economic Studies* 54 (2012): 121–48.

16 *Vedomstvennost* is a difficult word to translate. The word *vedomstvo* (a bureaucratic agency) is its root, and it refers to the habit of such agencies to pursue their own interests – and the interests of whatever sector of society or the economy for which they are responsible – with no consideration of the common interest. *Soglasovanie* is the Russian word for bureaucratic consultation and sign-off, with the late Soviet economy being characterized by some as dominated by *vedomstva* using *soglasovanie* procedures to the point of deadlock and stagnation. See Stephen Fortescue, *Policy-Making for Russian Industry* (London and Basingstoke: Macmillan, 1997), 2–11. On such phenomena more broadly, see Francis Fukuyama, *Political Order and Political Decay: From the Industrial Revolution to the Globalisation of Democracy* (London: Profile, 2014).

17 See the special issue on the Russian budget, *Post-Communist Economies* 29, 4 (2017): 449–537.

18 Stephen Fortescue, "The Role of the Executive in Russian Budget Formation," *Post-Communist Economies* 29, 4 (2017): 523–37.

19 Resource taxation is an immensely complex issue. For a useful primer, see Ross Garnaut, "Principles and Practice of Resource Rent Taxation," *Australian Economic Review* 43 (2010): 347–56. For an outline of different international approaches specifically in terms of a comparison with Russian practice, see Michael Alekseev and Robert Conrad, "The Russian Oil Tax Regime: A Comparative Perspective," *Eurasian Geography and Economics* 50 (2009): 93–114.

20 The main taxes within the oil sector in the 1990s, in addition to profits tax and other levies to which all businesses were subjected, were a royalty payment and export

duty levied as a percentage of sales, with some cost-based differentiation of the royalty rate. There was also a cost-differentiated excise duty and a mining levy. See Benoit Bosquet, "The Role of Natural Resources in Fundamental Tax Reform in the Russian Federation," in *Policy Research Working Paper* (Washington, DC: World Bank, 2002), 1–66.

21 Vlad Ivanenko, "The Statutory Tax Burden and Its Avoidance in Transitional Russia," *Europe-Asia Studies* 57 (2005): 1031.

22 Goohoon Kwon, "Post-Crisis Fiscal Revenue Developments in Russia: From an Oil Perspective," *Public Finance and Management* 3, 4 (2003): 506.

23 Dmitrii Butrin, "Chekisty ot prirody," *Kommersant,* 13 August 2004.

24 Vadim Visloguzov, "Vsia vlast' – nalogu!," *Kommersant,* 1 October 2004.

25 Kryukov and Moe, "Russian Oil Sector," 354–58.

26 Bosquet, "Role of Natural Resources in Fundamental Tax Reform," 13.

27 Thane Gustafson, "The Origins of the Soviet Oil Crisis," *Soviet Economy* 1, 2 (1985): 103–35. Their critics claim that the oligarchs compounded the problem with their expanded use of enhanced recovery techniques to maximize short-term profits. See Thane Gustafson, *Wheel of Fortune: The Battle for Oil and Power in Russia* (Cambridge, MA, and London: Belknap Press of Harvard University Press, 2012), 216.

28 Cited in James Henderson, *Key Determinants for the Future of Russian Oil Production and Exports,* OIES Paper, WPM 58 (Oxford: Oxford Institute for Energy Studies, 2015), 9.

29 *Global Trends in Oil and Gas Markets to 2025* (Moscow: Lukoil, 2013), 46; Henderson, *Key Determinants for the Future of Russian Oil Production and Exports,* 56.

30 *Global Trends in Oil and Gas Markets to 2025,* 49.

31 East Siberia is the most accessible of the frontier oil. Gustafson stresses the extreme frontier nature of East Siberian oil – an area of relatively small, scattered, geologically complex and relatively low-quality fields in an extremely forbidding and infrastructure-free region – "an oilman's nightmare." Henderson talks of it rather as a conventional greenfield region. With whom policy makers agree determines whether the region wins tax concessions. Ibid.; Gustafson, *Wheel of Fortune,* 465–69; Henderson, *Key Determinants for the Future of Russian Oil Production and Exports,* 40.

32 *Global Trends in Oil and Gas Markets to 2025,* 47–49.

33 Ibid.

34 Margarita Panchenkova and Irina Kezik, "Oshibka na 1,3 trln rub.," *Vedomosti,* 5 July 2013.

35 Oksana Gavshina, Dmitrii Kaz'min, and Elena Mazneva, "Naplastovanie l'got," *Vedomosti,* 2 August 2012.

36 *Taxation in the Oil and Gas Sector – Big Changes on the Way,* Tax Flash Report. Russia, Issue 22 (340) (Moscow: PricewaterhouseCoopers, July 2013).

37 Henderson, *Key Determinants for the Future of Russian Oil Production and Exports,* 38.

38 Margarita Panchenkova, Alina Fadeeva, and Mikhail Serov, "My ne khoteli by bezhat' v odnu storonu, a potom rezko v druguiu," *Vedomosti,* 12 April 2015.

39 Ekaterina Derbilova, Mikhail Serov, and Natal'ia Biianova, "Sanktsii otrazhaiutsia na vsekh!," *Vedomosti,* 26 June 2014; *Global Trends in Oil and Gas Markets to 2025,* 48.

40 Kirill Mel'nikov, "Ia v etoi zhizni malo chego opasaius,'" *Kommersant*, 4 October 2012; Sergei Titov and Galina Starinskaia, "Neftianuiu otrasl' zhdet nalogovyi eksperiment," *Vedomosti*, 31 October 2013; Sergei Donskoi and Valerii Kriukov, "Strategiia: Novoe regulirovanie dlia trudnoi nefti," *Vedomosti*, 21 October 2014; Anna Fadeeva, "Kak mozhet izmenit'sia nalogooblozhenie neftianoi otrasli, *Vedomosti*, 8 December 2015.

41 Margarita Papchenkova and Petr Tret'iakov, "Eksportozameshchenie," *Vedomosti*, 15 June 2015.

42 Evgeniia Pis'mennaia and Dmitrii Kaz'min, "Konechno, my opasaemsia," *Vedomosti*, 16 March 2011; Dmitrii Kaz'min, "Minfin poprosil neftianikov zabyt' o sverkhpribyliakh," *Vedomosti*, 21 October 2011.

43 Margarita Papchenkova, "Sokrashchat' raskhody, vidimo, pridetsia," *Vedomosti*, 12 January 2015.

44 "Zasedanie Pravitel'stva (2013 god, No38)," 30 October 2013, https://government.ru/meetings/7856/.

45 Kirill Mel'nikov, "Ia v etoi zhizni malo chego opasaius,'" *Kommersant*, 4 October 2012.

46 Ekaterina Derbilova and Timofei Dziadko, "Razve ia pokhozh na cheloveka, kotoryi chto-to prodaet?" *Vedomosti*, 5 September 2013.

47 Iurii Barsukov and Kirill Mel'nikov, "Minfin gotov meniat' nalogi na l'goty," *Kommersant*, 18 November 2014. The proposed pilots were indeed deposits without current tax concessions.

48 Margarita Papchenkova and Ol'ga Churakova, "Novyi nalog neftianikam," *Vedomosti*, 3 December 2014; Margarita Papchenkova, "Prem'er rassudit spor ob eksperimente," *Vedomosti*, 26 June 2015.

49 Margarita Papchenkova, Alina Fadeeva, and Mikhail Serov, "My ne khoteli by bezhat' v odnu storonu, a potom rezko v druguiu," *Vedomosti*, 12 April 2015.

50 Iurii Barsukov, "Manevry bez finansovogo rezul'tata," *Kommersant*, 16 March 2015.

51 Margarita Papchenkova, "Neftianiki dobyli nalogovuiu," *Vedomosti*, 29 June 2015.

52 "Zakliuchenie Pravitel'stva na zakonproekt o novom podkhode k nalogooblozheniiu v neftianoi otrasli," 1 August 2015, https://government.ru/activities/19130/.

53 Margarita Papchenkova, "Minfin podgotovil zakonoproekt o naloge na dobavlennyi dokhod," *Vedomosti*, 26 August 2015.

54 "Riski prevaliruiut nad zadachei uvelicheniia dobychi," *Kommersant*, 21 December 2015.

55 It is a system that gives a very high percentage of oil revenues to the state when prices are high, but this means that, as they fall, the loss of earnings is borne almost entirely by the state.

56 Anton Siluanov, "Brat' ili ne brat," *Vedomosti*, 6 October 2015.

57 "Zasedanie Komissii po voprosam strategii razvitiia TEK i ekologicheskoi bezopasnosti," 27 October 2015, https://kremlin.ru/events/president/news/50571.

58 Iurii Barsukov, "S bol'shim voprositel'nym TEKom," *Kommersant*, 28 October 2015; Margarita Papchenkova, "Minenergo nadeetsia provesti nalogovyi eksperiment dlia neftianikov," *Vedomosti*, 11 November 2015.

59 Margarita Papchenkova and Aleksandra Prokopenko, "Nalogovaia reforma v neftianoi otrasli natolknulas' na biurokraticheskuiu pomekhu," *Vedomosti*, 14 August 2016.

60 "No Can Do in Doha," *The Open Wall*, 18 April 2016. https://www.khodorkovsky. com/no-can-do-in-doha/.

61 Alina Fadeeva, Margarita Papchenkova, Alena Makhneeva, Ivan Peschinskii, "Strany OPEK ne mogli dogovorit'sia mezhdu soboi s 2008 goda," *Vedomosti*, 19 December 2016.

62 Galina Starinskaia, "Padenie dobychi nefti 'Lukoilom' v Zapadnoi Sibiri uskorilos,'" *Vedomosti*, 6 June 2016.

63 Margarita Papchenkova, "Nalog na dobavlennyi dokhod opasen dlia neftianoi otrasli," *Vedomosti*, 28 September 2016.

6

Regulatory Regimes for Petroleum Production in Brazil

GAIL D. TRINER

Two important, but largely separate, themes address the overall topic of economic "regulation" with respect to non-renewable natural resources: regulation of the gains from extraction (the level and distribution of government revenues) and regulation of the activities and actors involved in production. This chapter focuses on the latter topic with respect to petroleum in Brazil.[1] At the end of the twentieth century and the beginning of the twenty-first, discoveries of oil deposits moved Brazil from being the largest developing country petroleum importer to potentially joining the group of major exporters. The dramatic change in energy prospects followed immediately upon what appeared to have been a similarly sweeping change of the political economy regime governing the country. After establishing itself as one of the most assertive protectionist economies of the mid-twentieth century, Brazil, at the end of the century, assumed a leadership role among emerging economies in opening its markets to dynamic competitive global practices. Doing so required revamping economic governance and regulation. This chapter explores fundamental tensions arising from these two significant transitions. The rapidly developing petroleum sector provided one of the most challenging venues for applying new regulatory principles – and one of the most important. The shifts in political economy regime, geological technology, and production capacity have directly shaped the regulatory environment. This chapter analyzes the political economy history of petroleum in Brazil, with an emphasis on specific defining situations:

establishing the industry in the 1950s; facing severe financial constraints while also discovering significant new reserves in the 1980s; and, finally, attempting to realize the transformation from importer to exporter in a technologically challenging scenario. Its themes emphasize aspects of public governance that have shaped the sector: controlling access to the sector, capitalization, and using petroleum as a tool for the wider goal of industrial development.

The chapter concludes that recent governance reforms have changed the actors and permissible actions without mitigating the deeply entrenched ambitions that originally governed the structure of Brazil's petroleum sector: energy security, sophisticated industrialization, national control of the industry, and public-sector financial gains. The switch from a highly protected environment to (relative) market-oriented openness in one of the most important sectors of the Brazilian economy has been fragile and subject to reversal. This chapter makes two contributions. First, it recasts the earlier interpretations of political history of petroleum in Brazil in terms consonant with recent political economy and institutional analyses.[2] Second, bringing that history forward in time, it offers one of the first extensions of the political history of petroleum, and it blurs the distinction between history and policy analysis. The result offers insight into one of the most important economic transformations on the current horizon for Brazilians.

History of Petroleum in Brazil in a Nutshell

To be clear, in past decades, the political importance of petroleum production in Brazil has far outstripped its economic role. Petroleum policy was in place long before the discovery of oil. Small deposits in the province of Bahia in 1864 were of interest for their potential to manufacture kerosene, mostly for lighting.[3] Active exploration began in 1892, and industrial ambitions motivated further interest. Petroleum arose as a defining national political issue in the early 1930s.[4] Concerns about national sovereignty of control and ownership defined the political rhetoric and controversy that surrounded oil. Brazil's history as a commodity-export-producing (i.e., natural-resource-extracting) colony,[5] its subsequent vulnerability to global demand trends, and its reliance on imports for manufactured goods provided the backstory that justified "economic nationalism." Anticipating phrases that came into use in later years, industrial policy and energy independence were tightly integrated goals. The problem with petroleum in Brazil, however, was that early exploration and geological mapping failed to identify commercially viable deposits, even if they found enough evidence that geological conditions supported the likely presence of petroleum and so kept expectations high.[6]

Framing its importance in terms of national defence and economic security, the Brazilian military and industrial sectors sought a means to finance petroleum exploration. They based their arguments for direct state participation on the externalities of petroleum development. The substance was necessary to fuel the large-scale modern industrial sector that was integral to their concept of Brazil's future. The anticipated externalities included ensuring the supply and allocation of petroleum at government-regulated prices and advancing industrialization by creating domestic demand for sophisticated manufactured products for its own operations. This perspective came to be accepted wisdom at the highest levels of government. In 1939, President Getúlio Vargas announced: "It remains for us now to industrialize petroleum and install large steel, which we will do soon ... Iron, coal and petroleum are the mainstays of any country's economic emancipation."[7] These ideas underpinned the role of the state within the petroleum sector. Reciprocally, over time, the petroleum sector was perhaps the single most important sector of the productive economy in determining industrial policy.

The first Brazilian oil company (the Companhia Petróleos do Brasil), founded in 1932, failed after two years, when the National Department of Mineral Production issued a statement that nothing substantiated the expectation of finding petroleum reserves in the areas under exploration.[8] In the absence of commercially viable deposits at the time, state intervention in petroleum meant supporting its continued exploration as well as building the capacity for refining and distribution. After new finds in 1951, production began in 1954, with output reaching twenty-five hundred barrels per day in the Recôncavo of Bahia (onshore, but close to the coast).[9]

In 1953, the Petroleum Law provided for the formation of Petróleo Brasileiro S.A. (Petrobras) with federal capital, and the law mandated national control.[10] This solution to the nagging concerns of providing support for industry consolidated strategies of state-driven economic nationalism.[11] After two decades of political debate, the state stepped in to provide a substitute for private-sector capital, whether of foreign or domestic origin, in petroleum.[12] Petrobras based its legitimacy on the state's claim of property rights to extracted oil and the firm-ownership model of earlier state-owned enterprises (overwhelming ownership and control by the federal government but organized as limited liability companies with shares tradable on the Brazilian stock exchange). Petrobras became a central player in an activist growth strategy that relied on import-substituting industrialization. The enterprise had three functions within this strategy. First, it was responsible for maintaining the supply of petroleum for the Brazilian economy; second, by virtue of the price differential between imported crude and refined petroleum derivatives, Petrobras provided a source of significant foreign exchange savings for an economy in chronic deficit; and, third, externalities of the petroleum sector spurred further industrial development through both the local demand that Petrobras generated for industrial goods and the physical infrastructure that the firm constructed.

Two factors fundamentally reshaped Brazilian ambitions within the petroleum sector. The global oil crises of 1973–74 and 1978–79 highlighted the attractions of energy independence at the same time that Brazilians were discovering rich offshore deposits of petroleum.[13] Global petroleum embargoes, with associated price increases, escalated the cost of continued reliance on imports (see Figure 6.1). Nevertheless, the Brazilian state continued its aggressive industrial policy. The resulting deterioration of balance of payments and sovereign debt concerns generated by the oil price increases motivated new strategies for oil policy. Domestic exploration regained priority status in national energy policy. Petrobras found new reserves in the early 1970s, primarily in offshore locations (see Figure 6.2),[14]

FIGURE 6.1
Brazil petroleum imports and world prices, 1960–2011

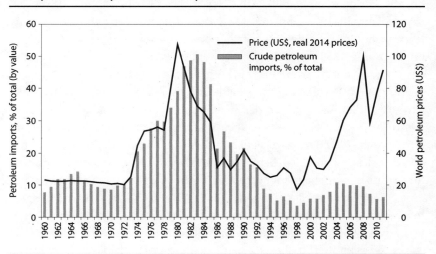

Sources: UN Comtrade database, http://comtrade.un.org; United Nations, Statistical Office, "International Trade Statistics Yearbook" (New York: United Nations, various years); InflationData.com, http://inflationdata.com/inflation/inflation_rate/historical_oil_prices_table.asp.

FIGURE 6.2
Offshore exploration in Brazil

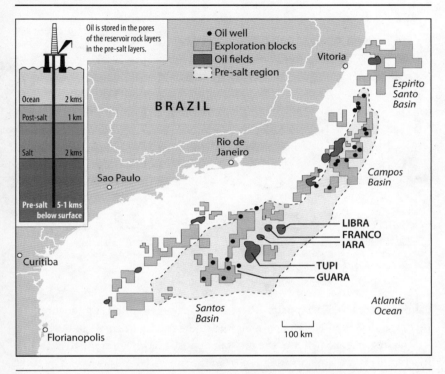

Sources: Adapted from Carrie Cockburn, *Globe and Mail*, and data from Petrobras and Wood Mackenzie.

and new wells began operation through the decade. State investment in exploration activities tripled between 1973 and 1979.[15] Subsequently, production more than tripled from 1979 to 1987.

With time, Brazilian oil deposits proved richest in offshore locations. Offshore production rose from less than 6 percent of total production in 1970 to 91 percent in 2009 (see Figure 6.3.). In 2007, Petrobras confirmed its discovery of massive deposits in the pre-salt layers below the ocean floor, transforming goals of self-sufficiency into expectations for a strong new source of export revenues. The pre-salt deposits are located about three hundred kilometres offshore and at a depth of five to seven kilometres. To access them requires drilling through about two kilometres of shifting salt layers (often with long distances of horizontal hydraulic fracturing [see Figure 6.2]), and this has created enormous technological challenges. Their distance from the mainland has compounded the logistical difficulties of

FIGURE 6.3
Production and reserves, % offshore, 1970–2010

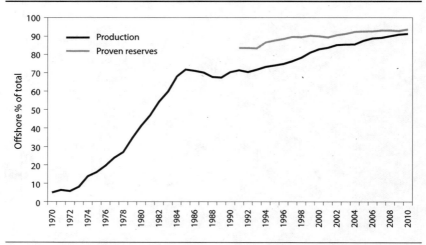

Sources: IBGE (Instituto Brasileiro de Geografia e Estatística), Anuário Estatístico, 1970–90; ANP (Agência Nacional de Petróleo), Anuário Estatístico, 1991–2010.

gaining access to the deposits. These issues have generated significant technological development and have increased the capital intensity of the sector.

The first-order impact of the pre-salt deposits has been small to date, but it is rapidly increasing. Production from the pre-salt deposits began in 2008 and accounted for 0.4 percent of total output; by 2013, these deposits were the source of 15 percent of crude oil production.[16] At the time, the proven reserves of Brazilian deposits were the equivalent of 13 percent of the combined proven reserves within the five largest global producers, and the pre-salt reserves accounted for 85 percent of Brazilian holdings (Table 6.1). By the end of 2011, estimates of the volume of these reserves ranged between 50 billion and 123 billion barrels of petroleum-equivalent.[17]

Regulation of a State-Owned Monopolist: An Oxymoron?

One of the first and strongest signals about the state's preoccupation with oil occurred in 1937, when the Mining Code began to treat hydrocarbons different from how it treated subsoil minerals. In contrast to minerals, the oil itself was to be the property of the state. This distinction removed petroleum from private ownership claims and provided a stronger constraint than the traditional principle of sovereign domain for the subsoil. Opposition to foreign ownership was behind the prohibition of private ownership.[18] As a

TABLE 6.1
Global petroleum reserves for Brazil and top five producers, year end 2009 (billions of barrels of oil-equivalent)

Country	Reserves	Country	Reserves
Brazil		*Top five producers*	
Pre-Salt	90	Saudi Arabia	265
Other	16	Venezuela	172
Total	106	Iran	138
		Iraq	115
Brazil as % of	13.4	Kuwait	102
top five		Total (top five)	792

result, the scope for developing the oil sector in a manner consistent with market conditions capable of attracting sufficient private capital narrowed considerably.[19] By the late 1940s, Juarez Távora, the minister of agriculture, in whose ministry the regulatory authority for oil and minerals resided, understood both that continued exploration would require large-scale state intervention (he phrased it as "monopoly") and that a state monopoly was politically infeasible.[20] Constituting Petrobras as a state-owned enterprise in 1953, with a monopoly for prospecting (and, anticipatorily, producing) and refining petroleum was a major break with earlier principles, which prohibited combining state ownership with monopoly power.[21] The expropriations (with compensation) of Standard Oil of New Jersey and Royal Dutch Shell refineries constituted the major and earliest effects of Petrobras's formation.[22]

By the late 1950s, petroleum policy needed to grapple with the tangible problems of supply and distribution. The rules for operations expanded, and vertical integration of production processes occurred at a rapid pace through the 1960s. In 1963, the monopoly extended to include transport as well as the import and any production of crude petroleum and its refined derivatives. Petrobras also took on responsibility for the broader policy of overall energy self-sufficiency. It became one of the most complicated conglomerate firms of the developing world. Through the decade, the company created subsidiaries for petrochemicals (mostly fertilizers for agro-industrial application, rubber-based products, and plastics), retail distribution, and international expansion for commodity trading and overseas exploration.[23] With the exception of retail distribution, the state-owned enterprise had monopoly rights in each of these areas. Regulating the petroleum sector required that the state regulate only one entity – itself. By statute, the Ministry of Mining and Energy was responsible for overseeing Petrobras, and the National Energy Council formulated energy policy. No pretense of regulatory independence prevailed in this environment.

Although constituted as a publicly traded limited-liability firm (with share ownership confined to Brazilians) Petrobras functioned as an entity that was intended to provide a public good to the Brazilian economy. The public-goods perspective of the firm, [24] its position as the only actor in the sector, and state ownership combined to situate much of the "regulation" of the petroleum industry within the confines of intragovernmental understandings. Codified regulatory practices were few. The company received specific concessions to delineate (and confine) its exploration and production rights. Discussion between Petrobras and the ministry, rather than publicly transparent rules, determined the specific practices of prospecting, producing, refining, distributing, and pricing. Environmental regulation specific to petroleum did not exist until 2000.[25] Product quality, local-content provisions, and occupational safety practices were also not subject to regulation by an administrative body that functioned independently of Petrobras. The company did not ignore these aspects of its operations. Nevertheless, actions resulted from direct negotiation with the Ministry of Mining and Energy or from the company's own initiative; they were neither required nor enforced by regulation.

The regulations that most affected Petrobras were those defining the company's role in the macro-economy and the company's position within the industrial policy of import substitution. These included price and currency controls, output allocation and distribution to critical consumers or deficit regions, pricing, and trade preferences. In all these fields, Petrobras received preferences and exemptions to further the goal of increasing petroleum availability through imports of crude oil, which Petrobras would refine.[26]

The melding of owner/producer with regulator began to face pressure in the 1970s and 1980s. Closed capital markets compounded the problems of international supply uncertainty (in volume and prices – the oil "shocks") as well as financial and fiscal crises.[27] In this economic environment, the state was incapable of investing in its premier enterprise. Financial constraints arose simultaneously with the discovery and development of large offshore deposits. The technology and logistics for offshore production (transportation of equipment and personnel to offshore sites, drilling platforms, etc.) were capital intensive. Channelling increased investment to basic exploration constrained other aspects of the firm's development and maintenance.

How was Petrobras able to invoke the expansion of exploration and technology that was necessary to explore and drill the offshore discoveries in order to transform Brazil from major importer to self-sufficiency? Rethinking the relationship with foreign actors, Petrobras began to structure mechanisms to tap the capital, operational capability, and technology of major oil producers. The firm entered into joint ventures (termed "risk-sharing contracts") with multinational oil-producing and -servicing enterprises. The change reversed the earlier strong prohibitions against foreign presence in Brazil; it was controversial and required careful assessment of relations with outside firms. Petrobras entered into risk-sharing contracts without specific legislative authorization.[28] Prior to the first risk-sharing contracts in 1975, concessions to Petrobras determined its exploration and production rights; the firm negotiated contracts with foreign and domestic entities to provide goods and services for fixed fees. Through joint ventures, Petrobras created partnerships with its providers that divided the risks and potential profits within narrow confines. Risk-sharing provided a means to attract the capital and technology required to develop newly discovered offshore deposits. Simultaneously, it maintained industrial policy, the formality of the Petrobras monopoly, and the public domain of the petroleum. Petrobras retained its monopoly of supply as well as control of all stages of production.[29]

By the end of the 1970s, Petrobras had joint ventures with twenty firms, primarily to develop the offshore deposits of the Campos Basin (see Figure 6.2). Partners included many major global companies, such as Chevron, Elf Aquitaine, Citgo, British Petroleum, Marathon, and Union Oil.[30] The ability for Petrobras to partner with foreign and domestic companies opened the way for private actors to explore, produce, and profit from Brazilian petroleum. Industry participants interpreted the introduction of joint ventures as the first step away from the tightly controlled Petrobras monopoly towards global market competition in supply and production.[31] Nevertheless, the risk-sharing relationship remained between Petrobras and the service provider; it did not invoke oversight by a disinterested regulatory body.[32]

Regulation in an Environment of Open Markets
Disruptions in financial markets resulting from the oil shocks focused at least as much attention on the link between macro-economic policy and the

state's entrepreneurial role as they did on petroleum policy.[33] By the 1980s, macro-economic trends seriously hampered both the state's ability to finance public investment and the creditworthiness of state-owned enterprises.[34] Lack of public-sector capital for investment in the light of fiscal crisis, excessive debt burden, inflation, and political uncertainty left Petrobras and other state-owned enterprises under-financed. Aligning policy to minimize these detrimental circumstances and to benefit from globalizing practices that had transformed other economies during the decade required loosening the grip of import-substituting industrial policy. The Brazilian economy began to introduce many of the neoliberal reforms that addressed the prevailing crises and aligned the regulatory regime with global trends. The pillars of the new strategy were to privatize many state-owned enterprises and to liberalize commerce, reversing the broad economic policies of the mid-twentieth century. The Constitution of 1988 revamped governance procedures.[35] It remodelled the economic role of the state to include regulating, planning, and incentivizing but not producing. Opening the macro-economy to wider international participation and market forces in the late twentieth century required the establishment of a new regulatory framework to accommodate new actors. The reformed regulatory regime was in continual tension with entrenched interests and practices.

Even as the Constitution mandated the privatization of state-owned enterprises, it also continued to treat humanly produced goods differently from how it treated strategic natural resources. Petroleum, natural gas, other hydrocarbons, and nuclear minerals remained the property of the state, and Petrobras remained a state enterprise.[36] Petrobras and energy policy makers faced strong incentives to open the firm to large outside investment as they tried to balance rapidly escalating capital needs to extend and deepen offshore capability within the limits of strong fiscal constraint and prohibition against competition. The government's goals in reforming the petroleum sector were similar to those throughout other sectors of the economy, but the strategy was different. Given Petrobras's iconic role as a proud national symbol, privatization was never seriously considered as a strategy in the oil sector.[37] The state's response was to "flexibilize" the monopoly, beginning in 1995 with an amendment to the Constitution. In 1997, a new petroleum law operationalized the Constitutional Amendment.[38] In this framework, the state retained resource ownership while private actors, including foreign companies, could obtain exploration and production rights.[39] In addition, the Petroleum Law opened other activities, such as refining and transportation, to private (including foreign) investors. The law required open access to pipelines, maritime tankers, and other transport; producers could not operate proprietary facilities.[40]

Developing an effective regulatory framework to replace the previously close interconnection between state and state-owned firm was an immediate challenge in order to attract private investors. The Petroleum Law of 1997 provided for the National Council for Energy Policy (Conselho Nacional de Política Energética [CNPE]) to set energy policy and the National Petroleum Agency (Agência Nacional de Petróleo [ANP]) to administer policy and laws as a regulatory agency within the Ministry of Mining and Energy.[41] Building the regulatory structure and establishing the ANP became an exercise in demonstrating transparency in public governance.[42]

The most important responsibilities of the ANP were to enforce practices that promoted competition and investment, ensured consumer rights, and guaranteed supplies.[43] Its specific activities also included demarcating and managing the annual competitive auction of concessionary blocks for exploration and production, collecting and distributing royalties, expediting licences, overseeing the sector's transportation infrastructure, and securing the supply of oil through the National System of Stockpiles. From 1999 to 2007, the ANP held annual open auctions for oil companies to bid for concessions.[44] As a further indication of the ANP's broad scope of regulatory influence, local content provisions came into effect as a result of the agency's criteria for evaluating auction bids rather than by legislative action.[45] The ANP's specific responsibilities vested it with significant statutory control over the sector.[46] In all, the framework left room for substantial discretion, but it seemingly created an environment that separated regulatory procedures from commercial activity.

Opening the sector to private participants was politically contentious and necessitated wide implementation of regulatory changes, but it did not challenge Petrobras. Dominance by one firm and the lack of a technologically qualified pool of possible regulators free from personal histories with Petrobras limited the ANP's independent effectiveness. By 2006, Petrobras still retained 95 percent of the domestic market in petroleum-derivative products. Many of the ongoing problems of petroleum supply remained unsolved.[47] ANP actions were concentrated in retail outlet (gas station) inspection and controlling market entry in the exploration segment of the industry.[48] Even in exploration, the ANP's actual powers could be challenged. For example, in 2008, federal court action halted the eighth round of bidding for offshore sites in a conflict over the concentration of contracts awarded to a single bidder – Petrobras.[49]

Beyond broadening the sector's actors, enabling Petrobras's ability to raise capital in private equity markets offered a second avenue to the overarching goal of building the capital and technology of the petroleum sector. Doing so supported the firm's growth without requiring public-sector resources. However, the crucial caveat that the federal government would retain a majority share of Petrobras (minimally, 50 percent plus one ordinary share) remained in place. Issuing equity on the São Paulo stock exchange raised the equivalent of US$807 million in 2001. Even more radically, Petrobras raised US$5.1 billion by selling equity shares on the New York Stock Exchange in 2002. Opening the enterprise to private capital allowed it to grow extremely rapidly while maintaining the state's control.

Capital expansion had important implications for both petroleum and capital markets. For Petrobras, the new capital financed the company's ever-increasing offshore production and technology development through larger partnerships as well as its own development investments. Increased capital was a major factor that contributed to positioning Petrobras as a major global petroleum company in all aspects of production and technology development. Although not the topic of this chapter, the governance practices and procedures for financial capital within Brazil were, arguably, more affected by the Petrobras stock issuance than the first-order effects on the firm.[50]

Regulating the Pre-Salt

The confirmation of pre-salt deposits in 2007 motivated another regulatory overhaul. The revamped approach, legislated in 2010, applied both to production and to the rents captured by the state. The cornerstone of the reform was to treat deposits in the pre-salt layers differently from how traditional (onshore or post-salt offshore) oil was treated. New regulatory structures apply only within the "pre-salt polygon." Most important, the state reinserted itself into the exploration and production of pre-salt deposits.[51] The long and intimate connections between Petrobras and the formation of the institutions governing petroleum provided the basis on which the regulations of 2010 rest.

Separating the pre-salt deposits from other petroleum production allowed the state to delineate rent-seeking and protectionism without directly affecting the reforms that apply to traditional petroleum operations. With the exception of exclusive concessions to Petrobras (discussed below) production- (or profit-) sharing, rather than fixed-price, concessions structure the relations between petroleum companies and the government.[52] The defining feature of the concession is that the government, separately from Petrobras, is a full partner in each project and receives a share of profits as partial compensation for access to the pre-salt concession. Profit-sharing is a major break with the history of non-renewable resource management in Brazil. Since the earliest Portuguese settlement, access to resources had been allocated through fixed-price concessions.[53] The Constitution maintained this practice, until legislation in 2010 changed this provision.[54] The motivation for changing allocation practices derived from the extent and certainty of reserves, and the state's expectation of being able to command a higher share of the profits from producers. Profit-sharing contracts determine the state's compensation, based on the level of "profit oil." "Profit oil" is the portion of production that Petrobras and its partners share with the state after excluding "cost oil," allowing sector participants to recover costs of discovery, development, and production. Cost oil is not subject to an upper limit.[55] Further, the state will receive payment (its share of profit) in petroleum. These terms indicate the extent to which the Brazilian government believed itself to be in a seller's market with respect to its new reserves.[56]

The state formed Pré-Sal Petróleo S.A. (PPSA) to represent the state's pecuniary interests in the pre-salt operations and to mitigate information asymmetries between the state and oil companies.[57] PPSA is a separate limited-liability corporation, wholly state-owned and managed by the ANP.[58] The entity functions as a commodity trading company, assuming the commercial and price risks of the petroleum received as the state's share of profit. The new company appoints one-half of the operating oversight committee for each pre-salt consortium, including the president of each committee, who has veto power over the committee's decisions.[59] No mechanisms are in place to avoid potential conflicts of interest between PPSA, the ANP, and Petrobras. Concerns have circulated about using control of the petroleum sector and Petrobras to manage the macro-economy (interest rates, prices, and consumer demand).[60] Further, a corporate body to manage the contracts within the purview of the ANP once again creates a situation in which the regulator regulates itself and gives the state a direct mechanism for controlling the operations of petroleum producers. At least as seriously, no provisions suggest that resolving conflicts can be achieved in a manner that assures a third party of regulatory independence.

In addition to redefining its interests, the state re-established a very privileged position for Petrobras. The company purchased the exclusive rights (*cessão oneroso*) to 5 billion barrels of petroleum-equivalent in the pre-salt deposits as part of the 2010 framework.[61] Although it accounted for less than 6 percent of the then identified pre-salt reserves, the size of the concession was notable. The exclusive concession has also experienced "privilege creep" (for want of a better term). Subsequent regulatory action (July 2014) granted a second exclusive concession for as much as 9.6 to 15.2 billion barrels in a newly discovered pre-salt field.[62] The exclusive concessions fall outside the profit-sharing framework. Nevertheless, they establish important terms for other pre-salt projects. The first concession estimated the value of the unextracted oil to be US$42.5 billion. The valuation determined the controversial terms of the "signing bonus" that Petrobras paid to the state.[63] In addition to the signing bonus, Petrobras agreed to pay royalties at the level of 10 percent of production, twice the base rate of traditional petroleum royalties, on the assumption that the higher rate attached to especially rich wells would apply.[64] The exclusive concession also provided for local content of goods and services for 37 percent of the development phase of the project and 55 to 65 percent during production.[65]

Beyond Petrobras's exclusive concession, the profit-sharing law guarantees – or requires – that the firm participate in the profit-shared projects to the minimum extent of 30 percent and that it serve as lead manager in each project. To date, major international partners in the development of oil and gas include Statoil, Maersk Energy, BP Energy, Repsol, Shell, and the Chinese companies of Sinochem, CNPC, and CNOOC.[66] If competitive bidding were to occur during ANP auctions, the firm would bid against itself in alternative projects. The guaranteed participation in all pre-salt development and the exclusive concession of 2010 motivated another major expansion of the firm's capital. In order to meet the terms of the signing bonus and to finance the development of capital-intensive technology to gain access to the pre-salt deposits,[67] the firm issued equity for a value of US$69.6 billion on the New York Stock Exchange in September 2010. The novelty of the capital expansion, in addition to its size, was to motivate further enhancement of Petrobras's governance practices and profit motives to satisfy investors,[68] even while maintaining the state's status as the majority shareholder.

The pre-salt regulatory regime has been criticized from the perspectives of constitutionality and pragmatism. The Constitution of 1988 prohibits extending discriminatory favours to state-owned or mixed enterprises that are not extended to all actors. Both the Constitution and its amendment for petroleum explicitly anticipate an open market. Attempting to circumvent these provisions, the state made the case that exemptions for national strategic interests cover the special conditions accorded to Petrobras.[69] Similarly,

Petrobras's share in development and production consortia calls into question requirements for competitive public bidding for all government contracts and gives the firm the ability to veto any project. Further, the structure of PPSA is not only constitutionally questionable but also opens the way to conflicts of interests with the regulatory agency. Weaknesses in the profit-sharing regulations also remain. The bases for calculating the profit to be shared are complicated and obscure. The absence of a limit on the share of gross output that may constitute cost oil minimizes the incentive for productivity, just as it creates incentive to overstate costs. Finally, the state's share of profits is incremental to the signing bonus and royalty payments, and royalties on pre-salt deposits will be at the rate of 15 percent rather than the base rate of 5 percent required of traditional oil (with payments doubled for especially rich wells). Other petroleum-producing states using these arrangements accept shares of profit as full compensation for depleting the supply of a non-renewable natural resource, replacing royalties.[70] In sum, the practices invoked for regulating extraction from the pre-salt deposits have resurrected many protectionist practices of earlier regulatory regimes, with an added layer of rent-seeking on the part of the state.

Conclusion

Risk is a characteristic of oil production. Analysts typically identify three types of risk in the sector: discovery, production, and regulatory.[71] Discovery risk was extremely high in the middle of the twentieth century for the Brazilian industry. After the confirmation of extensive offshore deposits, more recently extended to the pre-salt layers, discovery risk plummeted. As the technology to drill ever-deeper wells and to penetrate the salt layer has advanced, the production risks have increased. Serious accidents have hindered operations off the Brazilian coast,[72] and the infamy of the 2010 Deepwater Horizon accident in the Gulf of Mexico suggests the scale of potential damage and costs associated with these risks. In the middle of the twentieth century, advocates of open markets may have characterized the nature of petroleum regulation in Brazil as sub-optimal for maximizing growth and innovation, but risks and applicability of regulation were narrow and stable. In the early twenty-first century, regulation has arisen as an important risk.

The nature of the recent regulatory risks has revealed the profound nature of Brazilian sensitivities with regard to regulating petroleum. Carving out the pre-salt deposits for separate regulation reintroduced previously targeted practices of protection and gave reason for scepticism about the robustness of the institutions shaping the newly opened Brazilian economy.

These practices included discriminatory royalties for pre-salt production while also collecting "signing bonuses," rules favouring Petrobras, shifting contractual regimes to allocate greater rents to the state. The formal demise of Petrobras's monopoly in the traditional segments of the industry has been of diminished importance since the extent of the pre-salt deposits has become evident. The new procedures have enshrined Petrobras's position in Brazilian petroleum production, while preserving the ability to capture the benefits of foreign capital and technology partnerships. Further, instituting a separate entity (PPSA) to ensure the state's interests in pre-salt contracts has highlighted the re-emergence of strong political interests that continue to emphasize the state's role in non-renewable natural resources as an issue of national sovereignty,[73] as well as responding to those who simply lay claim to the resource wealth for the state. In sum, the sovereign claim to resource wealth and control has remained in place. One logically consistent manner of interpreting the changes to petroleum governance since 2007 is that, with the disappearance of discovery risk and enormous profit potential, the state has relied on historical precedent to structure its claims to future returns. These positions have wagered that the returns to private-sector participants, after all costs, will suffice to keep them in Brazil.

Since the discovery of the pre-salt deposits, the global petroleum industry has continued to change dramatically. Price trends, even more recent discovery of additional deposits (especially in the shale and tar sands of North America), and the fallout of a massive corruption scandal dating from 2014 have dampened Brazilian prospects within global ranking tables. However, whether Brazil becomes a major actor in global markets or not, oil will become an important export product for the national economy. The first auction of production rights to the pre-salt deposits in 2014 demonstrated the results of regulatory actions. The one bid, led by Petrobras and PPSA, included Shell, Total, and two state-owned Chinese oil companies (CNOOC and CNPC) as partners. Other global companies withheld participation, citing objections to the structuring of PPSA and the shifting parameters of regulatory requirements.[74]

Has the state learned to manage the political economy issues associated with past experiences with commodity boom (among others, with sugar, coffee, rubber, iron ore, or soy)? The governance reforms since discovery of pre-salt deposits have been motivated by rent-seeking (i.e., the distribution of petroleum in excess of what is mediated by "markets") rather than by technological or administrative needs within the industry.

Regulatory Regimes for Petroleum Production in Brazil   155

Two important and related changes have gained traction in petroleum governance: foreign ownership is present in the sector and the state has diluted its share of ownership. Both changes reflect the height of the barriers created by capital within the sector. Other regulatory reforms highlight the persistence of tools developed to serve a state-directed economy. Protecting the role of Petrobras and reinserting the state as an actor within the sector have provided further evidence of the staying power of the state's efforts to capture rents and to allocate privilege selectively. This chapter does not make a case for any specific policy regime in preference to others; rather, assessing the trajectory of petroleum governance reveals the deeply entrenched effects of earlier policy and offers historical experience as a tool for assessing current policy choices.

Acknowledgments

This chapter benefits from comments on an earlier version at the workshop on the history of natural resource regulation, held at NTNU (Norwegian University of Science and Technology), Trondheim, Norway (August 2013); the workshop on energy in the Americas, held at the University of Calgary (October 2014); and the session on the history of natural resource regulation held at the World Economic History Congress, Kyoto (August 2015). Fellowship support from a Fulbright Fellowship (2012) and the Woodrow Wilson Center for International Scholars (2012–13) permitted the resources and time for research and writing. Research assistance from Ícaro Gama was indispensable.

Notes

1 This chapter is about the political economy history and institutions of petroleum. It is not about the (perhaps related) political economy of corruption. As such, the chapter does not analyze the very significant corruption scandal (the *Petrolão*) that has enmeshed the entire Brazilian economy since late 2014, with Petrobras at its centre. While irregularities have been revealed in the past with respect to Petrobras accounting and contracting, the scope and depth of political "payola" networks in this instance take Brazilian corruption experience (more broadly than that limited to Petrobras) to new levels.

2 The subject has not received much scholarly attention since the earlier regulatory regime. See José Luciano de Mattos Dias and Maria Ana Quaglino, *A questão do petróleo no Brasil: Uma história da Petrobras* (Rio de Janeiro: CPDOC/SERINST Petróleo Brasileiro, 1993); Laura Randall, *The Political Economy of Brazilian Oil* (Westport, CT: Praeger, 1993); John D. Wirth, ed. *Latin American Oil Companies and the Politics of Energy*, Latin American Studies Series (Lincoln: University of Nebraska Press, 1985); Peter Seaborn Smith, *Oil and Politics in Modern Brazil* (Toronto: Macmillan of Canada, 1976); Peter S. Smith, "Petrobrás: The Politicizing of a State Company, 1953–1964," *Business History Review* 46, 2 (1972).

3 Dias and Quaglino, *A questão do petróleo no Brasil.*

4 Maria Augusta Tibiriçá Miranda, *O petróleo é nosso: A luta contra o 'Entreguismo,' pelo monopólio estatal – 1947–1953, 1953–1981* (Petrópolis: Vozes, 1983).

5 Very long histories of dependence on commodity exports and foreign markets for sugar, coffee, rubber, soy, iron ore, and many other primary products shaped a widespread aversion to foreign participation in the Brazilian economy. Some of the major works on this topic include Celso Furtado, *The Economic Growth of Brazil: A Survey from Colonial to Modern Times,* trans. W. de Aguiar Ricardo and Eric Charles Drysdale (Berkeley: University of California Press, 1963); Caio Prado Jr., *História econômica do Brasil* (São Paulo: Editora Brasilense, 1993). Globally, oil is one of the resources to which the curse has most applied. See, for example: Thad Dunning, *Crude Democracy: Natural Resource Wealth and Political Regimes* (Cambridge and New York: Cambridge University Press, 2008); Michael L. Ross, *The Oil Curse: How Petroleum Wealth Shapes the Development of Nations* (Princeton and Oxford: Princeton Univesity Press, 2012); Terry Karl, *The Paradox of Plenty: Oil Booms and Petro-States* (Berkeley: University of California Press, 1997).

6 Maurício Vaitsman, *O petróleo no Império e na República* (Rio de Janeiro: Editora Interciência, 2001); John W.F. Dulles, *Vargas of Brazil: A Political Biography* (Austin: University of Texas Press, 1967), 237.

7 Getúlio Vargas, *A política nacionalista do petróleo no Brasil* (Rio de Janeiro: Tempo Brasileiro, 1964), 54–55. Discurso [speech] em Leopoldina, Minas, 24 October 1939.

8 Paulo Roberto de Almeida, "Monteiro Lobato e a Emergência da Política do Petróleo no Brasil," in *Potência Brasil: Gás natural, energia limpa para um futuro sustentável,* ed. Omar L. de Barros Filho and Sylvia Bojunga (Porto Alegre: Laser Press, 2008).

9 Vaitsman, *O petróleo no Império e na República,* 183.

10 Brasil, Colleção das Leis do Brasil, Lei 2004, 3 October 1953.

11 Edelmira del Carmen Alveal Contreras, *Os desbravadores: A Petrobrás e a construção do Brasil Industrial* (Rio de Janeiro: Relume Dumará and ANPOCS, 1993), 71.

12 Gail D. Triner, *Minerals and the State in Brazilian Development* (London: Pickering and Chatto, 2011), chaps. 5 and 7; Maria Antonieta P. Leopoldi, "O Difícil Caminho do Meio: Estado, Burguesia e Industrialização no Segundo Governo Vargas, 1951–1954," in *Vargas e a crise dos anos 50,* ed. Angela de Castro Gomes (Rio de Janeiro: Relume Dumaná, 1994), 178.

13 Hsu Yuet Heung O'Keefe, *A crise do petróleo e a economia brasileira* (São Paulo: Instituto de Pesquisas Econômicas, 1984).

14 Humberto Quintas and Luiz Cezar P. Quintans, *A história no petróleo no Brasil e no mundo,* Coleção Direito do Petróleo (Rio de Janeiro: IBP, Freitas Bastos Editora, 2010), 70.

15 Ilmar Penna Marinho Jr., *Petróleo: Política e poder: Um novo choque do petróleo?* (Rio de Janeiro: José Olympo Editora, 1989), 389.

16 Agência Nacional de Petróleo, *Anuário estatístico* (Rio de Janeiro: ANP, various).

17 Bryan W. Blades, "Production, Politics, and Pre-Salt: Transitioning to a PSC Regime in Brazil," *Texas Journal of Oil, Gas and Energy Law* 7, 1 (2011): 32. Updated estimates offer a similarly wide range.

18 Juarez Távora, "O código de minas e desenvolvimento," *Geologia e metallurgia* 14 (1956): 164–65. CPDOC: AN c 1928.0202; letter to Goés Monteiro from Monteiro Lobato, 3 May 1940.

19 Miranda, *O petróleo é nosso*, 28.

20 de Almeida, "Monteiro Lobato e a Emergência da Política do Petróleo no Brasil," 14.

21 Thomas J. Trebat, *Brazil's State-Owned Enterprises: A Case Study of the State as Entrepreneur* (Cambridge and New York: Cambridge University Press, 1983), 42.

22 Mário Victor, *A batalha do petróleo brasileiro*, vol. 72, Relatos do Brasil (Rio de Janeiro: Ed. Civilização Brasileira, 1970), 295–98.

23 Petrobras, "Relatório Anual/Annual Report," Petrobras, from 1999, at http://www.investidorpetrobras.com.br/ (Petrobas investor relations website); Contreras, *Os Desbravadores*, 72–100.

24 I am not arguing that providing petroleum was a public good as understood by economists and political scientists: I am arguing that the Brazilian state and the firm regulated petroleum as a club good.

25 Marilda Rosado de Sá Ribeiro, "Aspectos Ambientais da Indústria do Petróleo no Brasil," in *Direito internacional ambiental e do petróleo*, ed. Sidney Guerra, Lier Pires Ferreira Júnior, and Adherbal Meira Mattos (Rio de Janeiro: Editora Lumen Juris, 2009), 139–56; David Zylbersztajn and Sonia Agel, "A Reforma do Setor de Petróleo de 1997: Racionalidade, Concepção e Implementação," in *Petróleo: Reforma e contrarreforma do setor petrolífero brasileiro*, ed. Fabio Giambiagi and Luiz Paulo Vellozo Lucas (Rio de Janeiro: Elseveir, 2013), 73–75.

26 Randall, *Political Economy of Brazilian Oil*; Dias and Quaglino, *A questão do petróleo no Brasil*.

27 Albert Fishlow, "Lessons from the Past: Capital Markets during the Nineteenth Century and the Interwar Period," *International Organizations* 39, 3 (1985): 383–439; Werner Baer, *The Brazilian Economy: Growth and Development*, 4th ed. (Westport, CT: Praeger, 1995).

28 Quintas and Quintans, *A história no petróleo no Brasil e no mundo*, 73–76. Earlier prohibitions in Petrobras contracting practices arose from political and ideological sensitivities rather than from legal necessity.

29 Fausto Cupertino, *Os contratos de risco e a Petrobrás: O petróleo é nosso e o risco deles?*, Coleção Realidade Brasileira (Rio de Janeiro: Civilização Brasileira, 1976), 15–18.

30 Petrobras, "Relatório Anual/Annual Report," 1979, 15.

31 Getúlio Carvalho, *Petrobras: Do monopólio aos contratos de risco* (Rio de Janeiro: Forense-Univeristária, 1977).

32 As always, the judicial system remained available to adjudicate disputes.

33 Armando Castelar Pinheiro and Fabio Giambiagi, "The Macroeconomic Background and Institutional Framework of Brazilian Privatization," in *Privatization in Brazil: The Case of Public Utilities*, ed. Armando Castelar Pinheiro and K. Fukasaku (Rio de Janeiro: BNDES-OECD, 1999), 1–23.

34 Eliana Cardoso, "From Inertia to Megainflation: Brazil in the 1980s," *NBER Working Paper*, No. 3585 (Cambridge, MA: National Bureau of Economic Research, 1991).

158   Gail D. Triner

35 The new Constitution was developed to support the re-emergence of civilian rule
    after the military regimes of 1964–85. The neoliberal changes in Brazil were similar
    to macro-economic policy changes occurring globally through national policies and
    restructuring on the part of international organizations (e.g., the World Bank, the
    International Monetary Fund, GATT/WTO, etc.). This chapter does not address the
    question of whether Brazil was a "follower" in these policy changes or whether
    broadly similar conditions across many countries with similar ISI/protectionist
    policy regimes and suffering from the oil crises consolidated a global change of
    policy regime.
36 Brasil, Constituição dos Estados Unidos do Brasil, 5 October 1988, Rio de Janeiro,
    Impresa Nacional, Article 176. On petroleum, see Cláudio A. Pinho, Pré-sal: História,
    doutrina e comentários às leis (Belo Horizonte: Editora Legal, 2010), 29; William
    Freire, Comentáriosao código de mineração (Rio de Janeiro: Aide Editora e Comércio
    de Livros, 1995), 168; Gilberto Bercovici, Direito econômico do petróleo e dos recur-
    sos minerais (São Paulo: Editora Quartier Latin do Brasil, 2011), 244.
37 Although Petrobras remained a state-owned enterprise, the firm did privatize some
    subsidiaries that were not central to its supply and production functions, such as
    fertilizers and retail distribution.
38 Constitutional Amendment 09, 9 November 1995, and the Petroleum Law enabled
    the constitutional amendment (Lei 9478, 6 August 1997); Amaury de Souza and
    Carlos Pereira, "A Flexibilização do Monopólio do Petróleo no Contexto das Re-
    formas dos Anos 1990," in Petróleo: Reforma e contrarreforma do setor petrolífero
    brasileiro, ed. Fabio Giambiagi and Luiz Paulo Vellozo Lucas (Rio de Janeiro: Elseveir,
    2013), 50.
39 To date, only one Brazilian company has engaged in oil exploration (it declared
    bankruptcy in 2013), although a number of Brazilian firms participate in many
    aspects of petroleum-servicing.
40 Paulo Valois Pires, A evolução do monopólio estatal do petróleo (Rio de Janeiro:
    Editora Lumen Juris, 2000), 129; Edna Maria B. Gama Coutinho, "O Que Mudou
    na Indústria do Petróleo?," in Informe Infra-estrutura: Área de projetos de infra-
    estrutura, ed. BNDES (Rio de Janeiro: BNDES, 1998), 3–4; Ricardo Pinto Pinheiro,
    Abastecimento Nacional de Combustíveis no Ambiente de Flexibilização do Mono-
    pólio de Petróleo, ed. Secretaria de Energia Ministério de Minas e Energia Brasil,
    Departamento Nacional de Combustíveis (Rio de Janeiro: Departamento Nacional
    de Combustíveis, 1996).
41 Pires, A evolução do monopólio estatal do petróleo, 129; Coutinho, "O Que Mudou
    na Indústria do Petróleo?," 1–2.
42 Gesner Oliveira and Thomas Fujiwara, "Brazil's Regulatory Framework: Predict-
    ability of Uncertainty?," in Texto para Discussão no. 147 (São Paulo: Fundação
    Getúlio Vargas, 2006).
43 Ricardo Pinto Pinheiro, Seminário: A Agência Nacional do Petróleo: Estruturação
    e Funcionamento, ed. Secretaria de Energia Ministério de Minas e Energia Brasil,
    Departamento Nacional de Combustíveis (Rio de Janeiro: Instituto Brasileiro de
    Petróleo, 1997).

Regulatory Regimes for Petroleum Production in Brazil 159

44 ANP, http://www.anp.gov.br/?id=516 (ANP website). The first auction in 1998 (Rodada Zero) allowed Petrobras to establish which of its pre-existing concessions it would keep.
45 Local content provisions have also proven slippery; precise definitions do not exist and the conditions for waiving the provisions are rather nebulous. See Luiz Cezar P. Quintans, *Direito do petróleo: Conteúdo local* (Rio de Janeiro: IBP, Freitas Bastos Editora, 2011), 10–26.
46 ANP, "Competências da ANP, http://www.anp.gov.br (viewed 27 November 2012); Haroldo Lima, *Petróleo no Brasil: A situação, o modelo, a a política atual* (Rio de Janeiro: Synergia, 2008), 60–63.
47 Refining capacity constraints continued to plague the industry. See Marcello de Mello Corrêa, "O Setor de Petróleo e Gás Nautral no Brasil Após 1990 – Regulação e Desenvolvimento" (master's thesis, Universidade Federal Fluminense, 2004), 28–29.
48 Oliveira and Fujiwara, "Brazil's Regulatory Framework," 28.
49 Luiz Paulo Velozo Lucas, "A Derrota de um Modelo de Sucesso," in *Petróleo: Reforma e contrareforma do setor petrolífero brasileiro*, ed. Fabio Giambiagi and Luiz Paulo Vellozo Lucas (Rio de Janeiro: Elseveir, 2013), 135.
50 Raising capital from Brazilian investors on the São Paulo exchange aided the promotion of pension fund, mutual fund, and individual investment. International markets (the New York Stock Exchange, in the form of the ADRs [American Depositary Receipts]) bound Petrobras to international corporate governance standards with respect to financial transparency and such operational areas as safety, human resources, and environmental protections.
51 The change, not in accord with the 1995 Constitutional Amendment, was instituted legislatively rather than through a constitutional framework. See Pinho, *Pré-sal*, 37 and 52. "Especialistas Criticam Possível Mudança na Lei do Petróleo," *O Valor Econômico*, 18 November 2007.
52 Lei 12351, 22 December 2010; Brasil, "Coleção das Leis e Decretos," Imprensa Nacional, 22 December 2010.
53 Triner, *Minerals and the State in Brazilian Development*, chap. 2.
54 The new principles for allocating rights also ignores the fact that many analysts believed that the fixed-price concessionary system was successful. See Lucas, "A Derrota de um Modelo de Sucesso," 139. See also Adriano Pires and Rafael Schechtman, "Os Resultados da Reforma: Uma Estratégia Vencedora," In *Petróleo: Reforma e contrarreforma do setor petrolífero brasileiro*, ed. Fabio Giambiagi and Luiz Paulo Vellozo Lucas (Rio de Janeiro: Elseveir, 2013), 81–103.
55 Recovery and development costs vary considerably across sites; it is not feasible to set a standard. See Paulo César Ribeiro Lima, *Pré-sal: O novo marco legal e a capitalização de Petrobras* (Rio de Janeiro: Synergia, 2011), 30.
56 Although legislative principles motivated the changes in governance, high oil prices from about 2000 to 2014 added incentive to state rent-seeking in anticipation that high prices would continue to prevail.
57 Ministério das Minas e Energia, "Novo Marco Regulatório: Pré-Sal e Áreas Estratégicas" (Rio de Janeiro: Ministério das Minas, 2009), 24.

160   *Gail D. Triner*

58 Lei 12304, 2 August 2010; Brasil, "Leis." PPSA was officially constituted on 2 August 2013.

59 Luiz Cezar P. Quintans, *Contratos de petróleo: Concessão e partilha – Propostas e leis para o pré-sal* (Rio de Janeiro: Benício Biz and Instituto Brasileiro de Petróleo, 2011), 99.

60 Blades, "Production, Politics, and Pre-Salt," 49; Luiz Cezar P. Quintans and Renata Gualberto Rosa, "As Inconsistências da Lei da Partilha," *O Estado de São Paulo*, 10 July 2010; Kelly Lima, "Sistema de partilha pode ser inviabilizado," *O Estado de São Paulo*, 6 May 2010.

61 Lei 12276, 30 June 2010.

62 The stated purpose of expanding the exclusive concession is to accelerate the development of unexpectedly rich reserves in the Libra Field (International Law Office Newsletter, 26 August 2014), http://www.internationallawoffice.com/newsletters/detail.aspx?g=246b85e4-40a1-4736-b40a-bd15ab5c0483 (viewed 27 August 2014); and *O Estado de São Paulo*, 14 July 2014, http://economia.estadao.com.br/noticias/geral,e-preciso-tirar-a-petrobras-do-palanque-imp-,1528294.

63 While advocates for state intervention in petroleum believed the state's compensation was too low, financial analysts opined that Petrobras had over-compensated the state for the transaction.

64 The 1997 Petroleum Law maintained royalties at 5 percent of production, but it contained a provision subjecting especially rich sites to additional "special participation" payments on a sliding scale, to a maximum of 10 percent. See Lindbergh Farias, *Royalties do petróleo – as regras do jogo* (Rio de Janeiro: Agir, 2011), 26. Since then royalty rates have been revised upward to 15 percent.

65 Although not the subject of this chapter, one can argue that the local content requirements of the pre-salt concessions have been instrumental in the massive corruption scandal that has roiled the state and Petrobras since 2014.

66 ANP Anuário Estatístico 2014, 19–24. These firms and others often form project-specific partnerships, which tends to hide their total participation.

67 As an indication of the capital-intensity, the estimated global oil prices necessary for pre-salt production to break even in August 2014 was US$120/barrel. The prevailing spot price at the time was approximately US$100/barrel. See *Oil Price Newsletter* "Five Regions Where Big Oil Is Foolishly Chasing Profits," http://oilprice.com/Energy/Crude-Oil/Five-Regions-Where-Big-Oil-Is-Foolishly-Chasing-Profits.html (website showing crude oil prices, viewed 19 September 2014). In addition, Petrobras issued US$10 billion in bonds to the Chinese Development Bank, payable in oil over ten years. See Edmar de Almeida, "The Role of China in Brazilian Oil and Gas Industry" (São Paulo: Energy Economics Group, Institute of Economics, Federal University of Rio de Janeiro, 2014).

68 This was the largest equity issue in global stock exchange history. Petrobras adopted accounting procedures in both the Brazilian and US equity exchanges that adhere to higher levels of transparency. See Petrobras, "Relatório Anual/Annual Report," 2010. The scandal from 2014 (the *Petrolão*) seems to demonstrate that enhanced accounting practices and transparency have not insulated the firm from fraudulent reporting.

69 Blades, "Production, Politics, and Pre-Salt," 42.
70 Quintans, *Contratos de petróleo*, 98. Blades, "Production, Politics, and Pre-Salt," 38–41, refers to production-sharing regimes with royalties provisions as "hybrid production-sharing agreements" and states that royalties constitute a portion of the cost oil in profit-sharing agreements.
71 Fernando Antonio Slaibe Postali, *Renda mineral, divisão de riscos e benefícios governamentais na exploração de petróleo no Brasil* (Rio de Janeiro: BNDES, Area de Comunicação e Cultura, Gerência de Comunicação e Marketing, 2002).
72 The first serious accident in Brazilian offshore production occurred in March 2001. The tangible costs of this accident were eleven lives, one sunken drilling platform, and a massive oil spill. See Petrobras, "Relatório Anual/Annual Report," 2001, 11. Other, lesser, accidents have occurred since then.
73 Zylbersztajn and Agel, "A Reforma do Setor de Petróleo de 1997," 65.
74 Some of the largest companies pulling out of the bidding included ExxonMobil, BP, and Chevron. This auction occurred before the corruption scandal became public.

PART 2

IMPACT OF IMPERIALISM ON RESOURCE POLICY

7

Regulating Oil Concessions in British West Africa

The Case of Nigeria and the Gold Coast during the Colonial Period

JON OLAV HOVE and JOHN KWADWO OSEI-TUTU

There is no gainsaying that the quest for natural resources was one of the main driving forces behind European colonial expansion in Africa and Asia beginning in the second half of the nineteenth century. Within the British Empire, colonial governments introduced legislation and regulatory systems to guide the exploitation of all kinds of resources. Though British colonies operated within the overall policy directives and goals of the British Empire, each colonial government exercised a large degree of autonomy to tailor natural resource regulatory regimes to local social-political realities. One natural resource that was considered to be of strategic and economic importance to the British Empire was oil, traces of which were discovered in British West African colonies in the 1890s. In the 1930s, global oil companies took an interest in further exploring these traces in Nigeria and the Gold Coast. This forced the colonial governments concerned to consider developing sets of regulatory measures to manage exploration, prospecting, and mining activities.

Though the two colonies held relatively equal status (apart from size) within the British imperial hierarchy in West Africa and were governed through similar administrative structures, each had socio-cultural and resource ownership peculiarities that influenced colonial policy in the emergent oilfield. These peculiarities led to policy convergences and divergences that affected colonial regulation of the resources in both colonies. It is therefore misleading to generalize about a monolithic "colonial experience" – something that is inherent in many accounts of imperial development policy.[1] Rather, for a fuller understanding of the workings of postcolonial oil regulatory regimes, it is crucial to analyze their colonial origins.

The general theme of this chapter concerns the establishment of regulatory mechanisms for oil exploration, prospecting, and production in Nigeria and the Gold Coast in the late colonial period between the 1930s and 1950s. This work is relevant because, overwhelmingly, studies of the growth of the oil industry in the two countries focus on the post-independence period. In the case of Nigeria, the focus has been on the oil industry after 1960, when oil had been found in commercial quantities. The themes explored in these studies include the relationship between oil companies and successive civilian and military governments, the impact of the oil industry on the general economic as well as political development of the country, and the environmental consequences of oil production. Other themes include insurgency in the Niger belt and how the optimistic start of the Nigerian oil boom, with promises of economic growth and social progress, has turned into what several researchers have described as a "resource curse."[2] In the case of Ghana, whose oil industry is currently in the beginning phase, the last decade has seen an emphasis on petroleum exploration legislation, petroleum revenue management, and the development of local content.

However, there is limited coverage of pre-1950s oil exploration in British West Africa. Even scantier in the historiography of the oil industry are writings about the processes informing the development of legislation and policy for regulating exploratory and prospecting concessions during this period. An exception is Phia Strewn's article, which offers an insight into oil exploration in Nigeria in the colonial period.[3] Notably, while this chapter also focuses on the early stages of oil exploration in West Africa, its point of departure is the negotiations that underpinned the regulations governing the exploration and prospecting concessions granted to two multinational oil companies – a Royal Dutch Shell and British Petroleum – that jointly sought to explore the viability of developing an oil industry in the two British West African colonies. Our approach is comparative, and we organize the chapter chronologically into four sections. The first section looks at negotiations and the regulation of oil exploration prior to the Second World War; the second at exploration during the war; and the third and fourth at the postwar negotiations pertaining to onshore and offshore exploratory licences up to the 1950s.

Explorations for Oil in West Africa prior to the Second World War

As was typical of colonial state formation in African territories, the British established the Gold Coast and Nigeria as colonial states around 1900. The formation of the two states involved the unification of territories containing multiple independent and socio-culturally heterogeneous Indigenous states through a combination of protectorate agreements, conquest, annexations, and mandates. Thus, the Gold Coast Colony was an amalgamation of several autonomous territories, namely, the Gold Coast Protectorate (established in 1874), the Asante Kingdom (by conquest in 1901), and the Northern Territories (annexed in 1902). Nigeria was the product of a merger in 1914 of the Southern Nigeria Protectorate and the Northern Nigeria Protectorate (both established in the 1900s).[4] The addition of half of former German Togoland to the Gold Coast and half of the German colony of Cameroon to Nigeria under the League of Nations mandate arrangements in 1919 (and later as United Nations mandates until 1960) completed the process of colonial state formation in the two British territories.[5]

Even prior to the establishment of the Gold Coast and Nigeria as colonial states, Europeans and Africans were exploring for and mining a wide range of minerals, particularly gold and diamonds, under Indigenous regulatory systems.[6] Therefore, one of the key issues with which the Nigerian and Gold Coast governments had to contend was the various degrees of organized opposition to their attempts to appropriate resources as well as to subvert Indigenous control over those resources. The earliest opposition to colonial resource appropriation occurred in the Gold Coast between 1889 and 1890, when the British initiated legislation to "vest Waste Lands, Forest Lands and Minerals in the Queen." In gist the new legislation, "The Crown Lands Bill of 1894," sought to vest control of the land, forest, and mineral resources in the British Crown, which would then exercise the power to grant concessions with or against the wishes of the colonized societies. Opposition was mobilized and led by traditional authorities (chiefs) as well as by the Western-educated and commercial elites who argued that the 1894 bill was a means to take from the people all their land and sources of revenue. They held that, contrary to the claims of the colonial authorities, there were no "waste lands" in the Gold Coast Colony and that all existing land belonged to either the "stool," or ruler (in trust for their entire society), or to family heads (in trust for members), or to individuals (through allotments or purchase).[7] Due to the sustained and coordinated opposition, which was organized through protest, petitions, and a deputation to London to present the case to higher authority, the Crown Lands Bill was not enforced. Nonetheless, a compromise measure was instituted under the Concessions Ordinance of 1900, which recognized the rights of local rulers to issue concessions to prospecting companies but insisted that such grants should be regularized through validity certificates issued by the Gold Coast government.[8] The move by the government to appropriate the natural resources and control concessions in the Northern Territories through the Land and Native Rights Ordinance of 1931 was less acrimonious.[9] Consequently, there existed within the territory different systems for regulating concessions.

With regard to oil, exploration and prospecting activities in the Gold Coast commenced in the 1890s when the West African Oil and Fuel Company sunk four wells in the Apollonia area, west of Cape Three Points in the western part of the colony. Results from a series of exploration activities on the part of this and other companies in 1903, 1909–13, and 1923–25 were not encouraging.[10] In Nigeria in 1903, with similarly discouraging results, the Nigeria Bitumen Corporation, which was instituted in 1905 by the Nigeria Properties and the West African Development Syndicate, began exploring for oil, bitumen, and coal in the Lekki Lagoon region of the Lagos Colony.[11]

In the interwar years, several imperial entrepreneurs were operating in the British Empire. These entrepreneurs were individuals who were adept at identifying business opportunities in the colonies, taking initial risks in acquiring concessions in resource-rich territories and in mobilizing investments to exploit resources.[12] In Nigeria, Major Seaborn Marks was an archetype of the imperial entrepreneur in the oil industry. He had established a considerable network in the British Empire through his previous positions as director of the British Burmah Petroleum Company (for over two decades) and as a managing director of the Nigerian Electricity Supply Corporation and the Associated Tin Mines of Nigeria Limited. In his opinion, a new oil drilling technique developed in Germany during the First World War offered new hopes for profitability in the oil industry in West Africa, particularly in Nigeria.[13] This possibility for profit stimulated his interest in the oil business, and, in 1931, Marks applied to the Nigerian government for a three-year monopoly over oil concessions between Lagos and Benin City in south-central Nigeria.

The Nigerian government was receptive to Marks's proposals but had reservations concerning the size of the territory for which he asked. Thus, while it was willing to grant an "exploration licence" over a "very considerable area" within Marks's proposed operational territory, these rights would not cover prospecting and mining.[14] However, the negotiations were suspended due to the global economic depression in the early 1930s. When negotiations resumed in May 1936, Marks tabled a new proposal to extend the "exploration" area to cover the entire Niger Delta. The Nigerian government was comfortable with Marks's request for only "exploration" rights and had communicated to the Colonial Office its inclination to accede to Marks's application.[15] However, the expressions of interest in Nigeria on the part of oil multinationals complicated the negotiations.

In August 1936, shortly after Marks resumed negotiations with the Nigerian government, the Anglo-Iranian Oil Company (later known as the British Petroleum Company, or BP) and the Anglo-Saxon Petroleum Company (a Royal Dutch Shell subsidiary) applied through the Colonial Office to the British imperial government (hereafter London) for permission to send a joint geological scouting party to the British colonies of Nigeria and Kenya as well as to the mandated territory of Tanganyika.[16] Initially, purely on a first-come-first-served basis, the Nigerian government was inclined to accept Marks's application.[17] Yet, as the wording of a telegram from the officer administering the government of Nigeria to the Colonial Office suggests, local officials did not discount the presence of imperial economic or strategic interests in favour of the established oil companies. The telegram read:

All terms and conditions in connection with Marks [sic] application have been discussed locally and Marks notified that his application has been referred to you. No information is available here which would justify my varying the Governor's recommendation. If however for Imperial or other reasons of which I am unaware you consider preference should be given to the Anglo Iranian/Anglo Saxon application I suggest that you should refuse to approve that of Marks.[18]

In their discussions of the matter officials in London expressed a clear preference for the two oil conglomerates. Two main reasons for London's decision were expressed by officials in the Colonial Office and the petroleum department in the British Ministry of Fuel and Power. The first concerned the strategic value of oil "for defence purposes, in view of the uncertain prospects of sources of supply via the Mediterranean in certain circumstances."[19] The second was that officials believed that the combined efforts of the two companies would lead to quicker results. For London, Marks was only an oil "speculator" without the experience, financial outlays, and technical know-how to "embark on oil exploration & marketing on his own." It feared, therefore, that Marks would resell his rights at a large profit without yielding to the government the maximum "amount [of money] which [...] idle mounts took out of it."[20] Subsequently, the colonial government in Nigeria was informed that explorations would be put in the hands of the Anglo-Iranian/Anglo-Saxon group, primarily for reasons of defence.[21]

Following negotiations in London between officials of the Colonial Office and representatives of the two companies it was agreed that, under four conditions, the Anglo-Iranian Oil Company and the Anglo-Saxon Petroleum Company would have an exclusive oil exploration licence over the entirety of Nigeria. The first condition was that the companies would pay an unspecified nominal, or "small," fee to be decided in conjunction with the Nigerian government. Given that Marks's concession fee was set at £100, it was expected that the conglomerates would pay "something above £100."[22] The second condition was that the staff of the Nigerian Geological Surveys department would be attached to the companies' field survey party. The third was that copies of all geological data obtained in the course of the survey would be lodged with the colonial government.[23] The fourth condition was that the interests of Indigenous communities in potentially oil-rich areas should be secured through consultation by Nigerian government agents. To wit: "The licensee will not enter upon any land until Government officers have been able to consult and explain to the natives of the area, if any, the reasons for such entry in order to allay any anxiety that the natives might have as to disturbances of their rights."[24] However, at a later date, officials in Nigeria noted that it was "perhaps undesirable to grant a licence to explore anywhere in Nigeria and that some occupiers of land might resent the entry of geologists, even though they offered compensation."[25] This suggests either that the spectre of the 1890s' protests in the Gold Coast Protectorate still occupied the official mind or that similar protests had begun to surface in Nigeria as well. In any case, Colonial Office officials made clear to the companies "the fact that the surface in Nigeria was in the hands of the native authorities" and that the colonial government therefore was "not in a position to pledge any grant of land rights." The companies were therefore advised to negotiate with local communities with regard to land surface rights regarding any future drilling. In the meantime, the companies were "assured that it would be reasonable to proceed with exploration on the assumption that if they were successful in locating oil the [colonial] Government would give them all the help they could."[26]

The oil conglomerates accepted the conditions and sent out a survey party in 1937 in lieu of the issuance of an official operating licence. However, the issuance of the licence was delayed due to its diplomatic implications for existing trusteeship (mandate) arrangements. While the agreement stated that the two companies would have exclusive exploration rights in all parts of the colony, Article 6 of the Cameroons Mandate prohibited concessions that had the character of a general monopoly. The legal dilemma in relation to the Cameroons concerned whether the grant of "sole rights" for exploration could be interpreted as, de facto, conferring an exclusive "concession license" for prospecting and mining, in which case it would be a violation of the mandate agreement.[27] In diplomatic circles the issue, however it was interpreted, was considered to be problematic, particularly in view of German complaints that companies operating in British mandate areas did not offer "greater opportunities for sharing mineral resources."[28] Throughout the entire discussion, officials in the Colonial Office agreed unanimously that the grant of sole exploration rights to the two companies was in the interest of the people of the trust territory. However, to avoid provoking German criticism, the Colonial Office decided that the word "sole" should not only be removed from all existing licences but also excluded from licences yet to be signed.[29] In other words, a change was made in the wording but not in the content of the licence.

Up until the Second World War, the Anglo-Iranian Oil Company and Royal Dutch Shell continued explorations work in both Nigeria and the Cameroons. In 1940, they merged their operations under a joint venture company called Shell-D'Arcy, which after then reported to the Colonial Office that its geological surveys had given "good hopes" that Nigeria held commercially viable oil reserves. However, due to the difficulties posed by the Second World War, Shell-D'Arcy suspended its activities. The Colonial Office accepted the company's proposal for a moratorium on its operations for the duration of the war and twelve months thereafter without variance to the other agreed terms of their exploration licence.[30]

Exploration for Oil during the Second World War

During the war, apparently encouraged by the successes achieved in Nigeria, Shell-D'Arcy turned its attention to the Gold Coast.[31] In the same period, unnamed American oil companies also approached the Colonial Office and indicated an interest in exploring for oil in the Gold Coast. In view of this growing interest, the Colonial Office instructed the Gold Coast government to bring local mining legislation up to date by, among other measures, vesting the power of granting oil concessions in the British Crown.[32] Given the complexities of Indigenous land rights and regulatory systems, this measure would, colonial officials believed, make it possible for the local colonial government to protect the rights of all property holders in oil-bearing areas where, depending on the drilling techniques applied, drilling activities on one property could affect adjacent properties.[33] Obviously, London was intent on forestalling or limiting the possibility of litigations that could delay the development of the oil industry in West Africa. However, the Gold Coast government, because of the "serious political upheaval" it had experienced in the 1890s, was apprehensive about the latest measure to vest the power to grant concessions in the Crown. Gold Coast officials stressed particular worry about the timing of the measure, stating unequivocally that it would be "impolitic during the continuation of war to vest mineral rights in the Crown owing to [the] bitter political opposition this would certainly arouse,"[34] given "the extreme touchiness of the Gold Coast natives concerning his land and anything appertaining to it."[35] They recommended, instead, that all oil-prospecting activities should be "prohibit[ed]" until after the war.[36]

Unconvinced that the "atmosphere [would] be more propitious for handling this thorny subject after the war," officials in London pressed home the need for the Gold Coast to immediately initiate measures to vest control of petroleum concessions in the Crown.[37] This urgency underscored the fact that international oil conglomerates were giving greater attention to the Gold Coast. In December 1943, Shell-D'Arcy informed the British Ministry of Fuel and Power that it was anxious to complete negotiations in anticipation of, after the war, starting exploration activity on four concessions covering approximately four hundred square kilometres that it had acquired from the Gold Coast Petroleum Company, a subsidiary of the large trading company known as the United Africa Company. In addition, the company asked for rights over a further 520 square kilometres along the coast of the colony.[38]

However, the Gold Coast government disagreed and tried to parry the pressures from London, thus bringing the matter of land rights in the Gold Coast to a head. In addition to concerns about the implications of upheavals during the war, the colonial government's reluctance to dabble in the land question was predicated on concerns about the disruptive effect that any upheaval would have on ongoing negotiations between Governor Sir Alan Burns and elements within the emerging political elite regarding a new constitution for the Gold Coast.[39] During discussions in London, apparently not wanting the people of the Gold Coast to blame him for "taking away the African's land," Governor Burns flippantly suggested that "the only way in which anything could probably be done was by the Labour Party here [in the United Kingdom] starting an agitation for the nationalisation of land or at any rate mineral rights in the Gold Coast!"[40] In any case, the Gold Coast government doubted whether oil existed in commercially viable quantities in the colony. Apparently exasperated by the constant pressure from London, the governor lamented: "There may be no oil there, and we should have had our political trouble for nothing. If oil is found there may be more trouble, but it would be worth it."[41]

As a compromise, the Gold Coast government agreed to allow Shell-D'Arcy to start explorations on the four concessions they had already acquired from the Gold Coast Petroleum Company but refused to issue an exploration licence for the additional 520 square kilometres that the company requested. Moreover, Gold Coast officials were aware that, should Shell-D'Arcy find commercially viable oil reserves, they would have no option but to succumb to London's demand for legislation to vest the oil resources in the Crown. As it turned out, the Gold Coast government's suspicions about the non-existence of oil in commercial quantities proved to be correct.[42] Shell-D'Arcy's explorations on the Gold Coast concessions in 1947 yielded disappointing results, and the company announced that it was no longer interested in searching for oil in other parts of the colony.[43] The company redirected its energies to explorations for oil in Nigeria.

Postwar Oil Prospecting in Nigeria
Shortly after the Second World War, Shell-D'Arcy resumed exploration in Nigeria and the mandated territory of the Cameroons, this time with success. In 1949 it therefore applied to the Nigerian government for a prospecting licence in order to commence test drillings. However, before beginning the costly prospecting stage, the companies wanted to clarify the terms of the subsequent mining lease in order to assess the profitability of a future oil industry in Nigeria.[44] Whereas earlier negotiations of the exploration licence were relatively frictionless, negotiations of the mining lease reached a stalemate as the postwar interests of the Nigerian government and the oil companies came into conflict.

The postwar political situation in Nigeria had changed radically. Locally, communities in the oil-bearing regions of a densely populated area of southeastern Nigeria, particularly around Owerri, began to mount opposition to the intrusion of oil companies on their land. The people in this area refused to let the oil companies enter and occupy their land on any terms. On 13 July 1949, one government official noted: "it was not a case of how much rent and compensation they would receive, but simply that the land was theirs and they would not voluntarily be moved."[45] On 18 July 1949, another reported apprehensively to the Colonial Office: "the Exploration Parties have already met with considerable opposition, including sabotage of equipment and, on one or two occasions, physical violence, but it is certain that the future holds in store even fiercer opposition probably incited by politicians and backed by sections of the Press."[46]

The fears of Nigerian government officials that happenings in Owerri could have political consequences in other localities as well as in the entire colony were justified. An organized protest was welling up in all parts of the colony of Nigeria against the Minerals Ordinance, the Public Lands Acquisition Ordinance, and the Crown Lands (Amendment) Ordinance, which sought to transfer control of and regulatory power over minerals and lands from Indigenous to colonial authorities. The people believed, perhaps rightly, that these "obnoxious" laws constituted a move by the Nigerian government to appropriate Nigeria's resources for the British Crown. As James S. Coleman has noted, for these anti-colonial politicians the title "Crown" was synonymous with "the idea of rapacious and exploitive imperialism progressively asserting its control over African minerals and lands." The Nigerian government therefore believed that African politicians like Nnamdi Azikiwe (a co-founder of the National Council of Nigeria and the Cameroons and the Zik Group of newspapers) were turning the cause of the local inhabitants into an anti-colonial nationalist issue.[47]

Notwithstanding the political difficulties, the Nigerian government was determined to develop the colony's oil resources. Consequently, it set about to devise a new mining lease that would ensure Nigerian participation through private partnerships with oil companies and/or government participation.[48] The idea of public participation was inspired by resource regulation measures that had been recently introduced in Pakistan, which stipulated that a percentage of shares in new oil companies be reserved for nationals.[49] This reform, the government hoped, would limit local opposition and convince "moderate and responsible Nigerian opinion" that the interests of Nigeria were being protected.[50]

However, the oil companies vigorously opposed the Nigerian government's demand for participation and profit sharing. As representatives of the companies argued, the Nigerian government would receive an adequate share of profits through royalties and local taxes. Moreover, the companies feared the precedent that Nigerian participation would create for their operations in other parts of the world, "particularly the South American ones."[51] The situation in late 1949 was summed up neatly by the governor of Nigeria, Sir John Macpherson, who remarked that the companies opposed the idea of public participation because it would place them "in a difficult position when it came to negotiating with countries like Ecuador or Pakistan, but ... we could not possibly use such an argument with our people [in Nigeria]."[52]

The British government had strong interests in the development of the oil resources of Nigeria. The Ministry for Fuel and Power took the side of the oil companies and urged the Colonial Office to convince the Nigerian government to abandon its demand for participation. According to the ministry, oil production in Nigeria would be valuable from a strategic point of view in the event that supplies from the Middle East were interrupted. Furthermore, Nigeria could become an oil source in the Sterling area, something that was of particular importance in view of the postwar dollar shortage. Since colonial governments elsewhere in the Empire had been satisfied with similar terms, it was thought Nigeria should accept them as well.[53]

The deadlock between the oil companies and the Nigerian government placed the Colonial Office in a difficult position. On the one hand, the British government was committed, through policy declarations, to the economic and social development of the colonies. The development of an oil industry would, officials thought, greatly contribute to the development of Nigeria. As one official argued, the main function of colonial governments was to "persuade Colonial peoples and their representatives to adopt enlightened and sensible points of view in dealing with such matters as economic development, and that if they cannot do it, our whole Colonial policy will have failed."[54] On the other hand, the Colonial Office sought to direct and control the political reform process in the colonies so that it moved towards self-government in a distant future. In order to achieve this, politicians considered to be "moderate and responsible" had to be encouraged and included in the development of the territories, while issues that could be exploited by anti-colonial nationalist politicians like Nnamdi Azikiwe had to be avoided. Therefore, when discussing policies for economic development, officials had to take account of political conditions in order to ensure that the British government did not lose control of the political process and, consequently, economic development projects. As one official put it: "our great task of developing Africa [...] will inevitably remain unfulfilled unless we are prepared, as I believe we are, to take the genuine political difficulties seriously."[55]

In any case, Colonial Office officials agreed they could not undermine the decision of the local government in Nigeria. Thus, the parliamentary undersecretary of state, David Rees-Williams, told representatives of the oil companies that the secretary of state for the colonies was "not prepared to bring pressure to bear on the Nigerian Government to act in a way which they thought to be contrary to their own interest."[56] Clearly, officials in London preferred to facilitate continued negotiations between the companies and the Nigerian government, hoping that the former would yield since, given the massive investments they had incurred in Nigeria, they had too much to lose if they withdrew.[57]

Although officials in the Colonial Office and the colonial government in Nigeria insisted on terms they thought would be more acceptable to Nigerian politicians, this should not be equated with sympathy towards the conviction and opinions of the local inhabitants in Owerri or anti-colonial politicians in Nigeria. In fact, colonial officials generally considered opponents of oil exploration, like the people of Owerri, as "irrational," "fanatically attached to their land," and "intensely hostile to anything which savours to their naturally suspicious minds of an attempt to tamper with it [i.e. their land]."[58] Criticism of the oil companies that provided "the civilised world with mineral oils" was equally irrational and irresponsible.[59] The insistence of British officials on terms considered more acceptable to Nigerians was largely for self-interest. As in the Gold Coast case, the Nigerian government sought to avoid political difficulties that could challenge its position and the orderly development of the colony.

In November 1949, the Executive Council, whose membership now included four Africans, agreed unanimously that, in view of the benefits that the colony (and the British Empire) would gain from a future oil industry, it was necessary to encourage the oil companies rather than frustrating them with demands that might drive them away from Nigeria. The council decided that the government would be content with the payment of a royalty of 12.5 percent ad valorem on oil proceeds and the establishment of a new locally based oil company with a local Nigerian representative on the board of directors. Yet the governor was urged to persuade the companies to "agree to form a company in Nigeria and to offer for local subscription a proportion of the shares of that [new local] Company."[60] The companies rejected outright the demand to offer Nigerians shares subscription in an eventual Nigeria-based company, though they would consider appointing a Nigerian to the

Regulating Oil Concessions in British West Africa 177

board.[61] The Nigerian government yielded, and by the end of 1950 the companies were issued a prospecting licence to start drilling for oil.[62]

Meanwhile, other companies were also taking an interest in Nigeria's oil potential. In 1952, the Socony-Vacuum Oil Company of the United States applied for an exploration licence in areas of Nigeria that were not covered by Shell-D'Arcy's exploration licence.[63] The news of Socony-Vacuum's interest was welcomed both in Lagos and London. There was, as one official put it, "everything to be said for having the oil potentialities of the territory as thoroughly examined as possible."[64] Subsequently, Socony was given an exploration licence in 1953.[65] Also, the stakes were raised in the course of the 1950s, when some oil companies proposed to conduct offshore exploration in Nigeria's territorial waters and continental shelf.

Oil Exploration on the Continental Shelf

By 1956, Shell-D'Arcy found oil in commercial quantities in Nigeria and a new company called Shell-BP was formed to mine this oil. Production of crude oil began in 1958, and, in 1960, 840,000 tons of crude oil was exported.[66] While operations in Nigeria were still formally a joint venture, Shell had taken a leading position: the personnel engaged in Nigeria were largely from Shell and the venture was considered locally to be a Shell undertaking.[67]

In 1956, Shell-BP applied to the government of the newly (1954) federated colonial state of Nigeria for exploration rights on the continental shelf.[68] The area sought by the company was considerable: already its onshore concessions covered two-thirds of the coastal areas of Nigeria, and it now sought the adjoining continental shelf.[69] This presented a challenging legal dilemma for both the Nigerian government and the Imperial government in Britain. The Nigerian government did not have sovereignty over the continental shelf, and in order to grant Shell-BP's request the continental shelf would have to be appropriated. Also, the question of the boundaries between the trust territory of Cameroons to the east, the French colony Dahomey to the west, and the island Fernando Po to the south needed to be settled. Also troublesome was how to ensure the interests of Nigeria's coastal Indigenous polities when it came to their (potential) rights to a share of the revenue accruing from the oil industry.[70]

While Shell-BP wanted to obtain an exploration licence over the shelf as soon as possible, the Colonial Office saw reasons not to hasten the annexation. As one official noted, the continental shelf could very well be treated as a reserve area and saved for later oil exploration. Furthermore, the proposed area was considered "far too large an area to give to one company alone especially when that company already has nearly 40,000 square miles of land concessions." In view of the expense of offshore drilling, it would be more to the advantage of the Nigerian government to have "several companies examining medium sized portions of the Continental Shelf than giving a very large slice to one admittedly large company."[71] This issue was also broached during a meeting with A.C.F. Armstrong, permanent secretary in the Ministry of Lagos Affairs, Mines and Power at the Colonial Office in May 1957.[72] Armstrong was then told the content of a draft letter to the Nigerian government, which stated:

> We [the Colonial Office] are revising our views on the size of the areas which should be granted to an individual oil company for exploration and prospecting. We do not feel that it would be in your best interest to grant the whole of the Continental Shelf which is adjacent to Shell/B.P.'s licensed mainland areas to the company. They should, of course, get some part of it, but as we see it, your best interest would be served by sharing the Shelf between several companies so as to secure the quickest possible evaluation of oil prospects.[73]

Armstrong was furthermore told that the Nigerian government should not hurry the annexation of the continental shelf but, rather, take the necessary time to decide on the size of the areas to be given to individual companies: "Once it is annexed, of course, you will have at your disposal a very large reserve area for future exploration, which it would be a pity to tie up in advance with one company."[74]

However, the relationship between officials of Shell-BP and those of the Colonial Office and Nigeria remained close and, sometimes, got personal. For instance, in September 1957 the deputy governor general of Nigeria, Sir Ralph Grey, wrote the Colonial Office on behalf of the company. He had, he said, taken an interest in matters related to oil exploration and "had some Shell people staying with [him] for a night or two." He had also spoken to Mr. Bridges, the general manager of Shell-BP in Nigeria, about the company's desire to get exploration rights over the continental shelf. According to Grey, the company "fully realised that they cannot go on indefinitely getting 'favoured Company' treatment" and that "it might not be politically possible for the Government to give one sole Company exclusive rights." Instead, the general manager noted that he "would prefer to have 100 percent rights in areas of the Shelf chosen by his Company to having, say, 50 percent rights over the whole of the Shelf." In other words, Shell-BP wanted exclusive rights for preferred areas and proposed that it "do some more survey work in order that they can be selective in applying for their areas." Deputy Governor General Grey thought the general manager's approach "very reasonable": "after all the capital that his company have [sic] put into oil exploration in Nigeria and the initiative they have shown [...] they have some claim on the goodwill of the Government if it is a matter of deciding between competing claims."[75]

In London, relations between Shell-BP and the Colonial Office were also close. In May 1958, Under-Secretary of State Sir Hilton Poynton wrote, in an internal minute, that he had been "at a lunch party the other day given by the Shell Company to Sir R. Stapledon [the governor of Eastern Nigeria]" and the "question of the Continental Shelf in Nigeria had come up."[76] At no point did anyone question the appropriateness of Shell hosting a lunch for the governor of Eastern Nigeria that included officials from the Colonial Office. But the good relationship between the oil companies and British officials appeared to be of decreasing significance due to the political changes taking place in Nigeria. In the late 1950s, the colony was fast approaching independence, and the extent of self-government was already considerable. Thus, it was largely the federal Nigerian government and not the Colonial Office that would have the final say regarding the division of exploration rights on the continental shelf of Nigeria.

Furthermore, in the late 1950s, American oil companies were looking to Nigeria as an alternative source of oil, particularly after the Suez Crisis that followed upon Egypt's nationalization of the Suez Canal. These companies – including the Standard Oil Company of California, the Standard Oil Company of New Jersey, the Pan American International Oil Company, and Socony Mobil Oil Company (which had already obtained an exploration licence under the name Socony-Vacuum Oil Company in 1953) – focused on the prospects of the Nigerian continental shelf.[77] In this manner, the federal government of Nigeria had several alternatives to Shell-BP

In 1960, Nigeria became independent from British Colonial rule, and Shell-BP lost the exclusive position that it had enjoyed in the colonial period. The company nonetheless continued to play a significant role in the emerging Nigerian oil industry. In 1956, the exploration licences were expiring and the company started relinquishing acreages as it converted existing licences (allowing geological and geophysical explorations only) into prospecting licences that gave rights to drill and to produce oil in smaller areas. And, as Shell-BP relinquished acreages, other companies, primarily

American, came in. Consequently, "the concessionary map of Nigeria came to resemble a mosaic of competing interest."[78] In this process, offshore exploration licences were also granted to four different companies, one being Shell-BP. Its dominant role, at the time of independence, is reflected in the federal government's preparation of a new taxation regime for the oil industry. As one taxation expert put it, the "dominant position which the expenditure of Shell-BP has had, and is continuing to have, in the economy of Nigeria makes it evident that in the best interests of the country no proposal in this report should be pressed to a point at which it would endanger the continuance of such activities."[79]

Conclusion

This chapter set out to explore the processes that informed the establishment of regulatory regimes for oil exploration, prospecting, and production in two British West African colonies – Nigeria and the Gold Coast – during the first half of the twentieth century. The results show that, though the oil industry in West Africa took off first in Nigeria in the 1950s, and much later in Ghana, the foundations for the industry were laid during the colonial period through the pioneering activities of and risks taken by multinational oil conglomerates, particularly (Dutch) Shell and British Petroleum (Shell-BP) between the 1930s and the 1950s.

Significantly, the development of regulatory regimes for the exploitation of oil was carried out through separate negotiations between the oil multinationals and the respective governments of the two colonies. While the former operated on a global scale and sought to impose a uniform business structure to facilitate efficient control of their ventures, the latter sought to adapt regulatory regimes to local socio-political and economic conditions. In the case of the Gold Coast, the government was unwilling to revise existing regulations because of fears of local unrest, at least as long as prospects for a future oil industry were uncertain. In this manner, the exploration for oil was arrested even before it got properly under way.

In Nigeria, the government initially welcomed the oil companies and sought to facilitate their exploratory activities by amending necessary regulations. However, the emergence of anticolonial movements made the colonial government more mindful of the interests of Indigenous states whose territories contained petroleum resources and the interests of politicians considered to be "moderate" as opposed to anticolonial. Yet, in the course of negotiations with the oil companies, the colonial government was unwilling to jeopardize a future oil industry that could accelerate the economic

Regulating Oil Concessions in British West Africa

development of the territory in question. The end product of the negotiations therefore reflected the interests of the oil companies rather than those of local politicians and Indigenous societies.

Thus, the focus on separate negotiations of regulatory systems underscores the idea that, whereas the British colonial empire may be seen as an imposing imperial unit, the reality was that, in the oil sector, its component parts exercised large degrees of autonomy. If we broaden this notion of fragmentation to how we perceive other aspects of British colonial rule, it becomes clear that it would be proper for researchers to look for specificities in particular cases rather than to talk generally about "the colonial experience." Indeed, considering how things developed differently in the Gold Coast and Nigeria despite the proximity and connections between the two colonies, it is evident that even greater variances must be expected when investigating developments in colonies in other parts of the world.

Notes

1 Several accounts have given invaluable insights into centrally generated colonial development policies but without relating them to actual practices in individual colonies. See, for instance, J.M. Lee, *Colonial Development and Good Government* (Oxford: Clarendon Press, 1967); D.J. Morgan, *The Official History of Colonial Development*, vols. 1–5 (London: Macmillan, 1980); P.J. Cain and A.G. Hopkins, *British Imperialism: Crisis and Deconstruction, 1914–1990* (London: Longman, 1993); D.K. Fieldhouse, *Merchant Capital and Economic Decolonization* (Oxford: Clarendon Press, 1994). Examples of accounts that focus on a singular experience of underdevelopment include Walter Rodney, *How Europe Underdeveloped Africa* (Abuja: Panaf Publishing, 2009); Samir Amin, *Neo-Colonialism in West Africa* (Harmondsworth: Penguin Books, 1973).

2 For an overview of relevant research on the Nigerian oil industry, see Ann Genova and Toyin Falola, "Oil in Nigeria: A Bibliographical Reconnaissance," *History in Africa* 30 (2003): 133–56; Heather J. Hoag, *Developing the Rivers of East and West Africa: An Environmental History* (London: Bloomsbury, 2013), 149.

3 Phia Steyn, "Oil Exploration in Colonial Nigeria, c. 1903–58," *Journal of Imperial and Commonwealth History* 37, 2 (2009): 249–74.

4 Southern Nigeria Protectorate was itself an amalgamation of the Crown Colony of Lagos, established in 1861, and Niger Coast Protectorate, established in 1894 (formerly Oil Rivers Protectorate, established in 1884). The Niger Delta is the location of the bulk of Nigeria's oil.

5 On mandates, see Anthony Anghie, "Colonialism and the Birth of International Institutions: The Mandate System of the League of Nations," in *Imperialism, Sovereignty and the Making of International Law* (Cambridge and New York: Cambridge University Press, 2004), 115–95. For a general history of colonialism in Ghana and Nigeria, see Roger Gocking, *History of Ghana* (Westport, CT: Greenwood Press,

2005); Toyin Falola and Matthew M. Heaton, *A History of Nigeria* (Cambridge: Cambridge University Press, 2008).

6   See, for instance, Raymond E. Dumett, *El Dorado in West Africa* (Oxford: James Currey, 1998).

7   For land ownership and tenure systems as well as the impact of land commercialization on urban areas in the Gold Coast, see Naaborko Sackefio-Lennoch, *The Politics of Chieftaincy: Authority and Property in Colonial Ghana, 1920–1950* (Rochester, NY: University of Rochester Press, 2014).

8   The Gold Coast land dispute during the late nineteenth century is described in detail in David Kimble, *A Political History of Ghana* (Oxford: Clarendon Press, 1963), 330–57.

9   The land tenure system prevailing in the Gold Coast in the interwar period is explained by the colonial government in *The Gold Coast Handbook 1937* (London: West Africa Publicity Ltd., 1937).

10 See account of early oil drilling activities in *Report on the Geological Survey Department for the Financial Year 1938–39* (Accra: Gold Coast Government, 1939), 20–22. A copy of this report can be found in RG 7/1/778, Accra, Public Records and Archives Administration Department (hereafter PRAAD).

11 Steyn, "Oil Exploration in Colonial Nigeria," 252.

12 A relevant example of a similar imperial entrepreneur is Duncan Rose, who was able to secure all the necessary concessions for what became the Volta River Project in the Gold Coast (Ghana) before he was bought out by the large Canadian aluminum producer Alcan. See Jon Olav Hove, "The Volta River Project and Decolonization, 1945–57: The Rise and Fall of an Integrated Aluminum Project," in *Aluminum Ore*, ed. Robin S. Gendron, Mats Ingulstad, and Espen Storli (Vancouver: UBC Press, 2013), 185–210.

13 See letters from Major Seaborn Marks to the Chief Secretary, Lagos, Nigeria, 16 June 1931, and to Secretary of State for the Colonies, 11 December 1931, CO 583/181/1, London, The National Archives (hereafter TNA).

14 Sir Donald Cameron, Governor of Nigeria, to James Henry Thomas, Secretary of State for the Colonies, 31 August 1931, CO 583/181/1, TNA.

15 Bernard Henry Bourdillon, Governor of Nigeria, to William Ormsby-Gore, Secretary of State for the Colonies, 2 October 1936, CO 852/34/7, TNA.

16 A.C. Hearn, Anglo-Iranian Oil Company, to Sir John Shuckburgh, Assistant Under-Secretary of State for the Colonies, Middle East Division, 10 August 1936, CO 852/34/7, TNA.

17 Bernard Henry Bourdillon to William Ormsby-Gore, 26 October 1936, CO 852/34/7, TNA.

18 Officer Administering the Government of Nigeria to the Secretary of State for the Colonies, 16 November 1936, CO 852/34/7, TNA.

19 Note of a meeting to discuss oil development in Kenya and Nigeria, 27 November 1936, CO 852/34/7, TNA; Sir Cecil Bottomley, Assistant Under-Secretary of State for the Colonies, to Bernard Bourdillon, 27 November 1936, CO 852/34/7, TNA.

20 Gerard Clauson, 19 November 1936, CO 852/34/7, TNA.

21 Sir Cecil Bottomley, Assistant Under-Secretary of State for the Colonies, to Bernard Bourdillon, 27 November 1936, CO 852/34/7, TNA.

Regulating Oil Concessions in British West Africa   183

22 £100 in 1936 would be worth approximately £6000 in 2014, not a considerable fee for the two companies in question. Calculated with www.measuringworth.com, a website that calculates relative worth over time.

23 Note of a meeting with representatives of the Anglo-Iranian and Anglo-Saxon Oil Companies held in the Colonial Office, 3 December 1936, CO 852/34/7, TNA.

24 Letter from G.E.J. Gent, Colonial Office, to the Anglo-Iranian Oil Company Limited, 21 December 1936, CO 852/34/7, TNA.

25 Bernard Henry Bourdillon to William Ormsby-Gore, 21 May 1937, CO 852/74/9, TNA.

26 Note of a meeting with representatives of the Anglo-Iranian and Anglo-Saxon Oil Companies held in the Colonial Office, 3 December 1936, CO 852/34/7, TNA.

27 W. Dave, 21 September 1937, CO 852/74/9, TNA.

28 Gerard Clausen, 24 September 1937, CO 852/74/7, TNA; Sir G. Bushe, 28 September 1937, CO 852/74/9, TNA; J.B. Sidebotham, 24 September 1937, CO 852/74/9, TNA; O.G.R. Williams, 24 September 1937, CO 852/74/9, TNA.

29 Originally suggested by Sir G. Bushe, 28 September 1937, and decided by Sir Bottomley, 4 October 1937, CO 852/74/9, TNA.

30 T.G. Cockrane, Anglo-Saxon Petroleum Company Limited to the Under-Secretary of State, Colonial Office, 24 December 1940, CO 852/276/4, TNA. According to Jedrezj George Frynas, this joint venture was established in 1937. See Jedrzej George Frynas, *Oil in Nigeria: Conflict and Litigation between Oil Companies and Village Communities* (Hamburg: Lit Verlag, 2000), 9.

31 See letter from G.W. Lepper, Ministry of Fuel and Power, to R.H. Burt, Colonial Office, 10 December 1943, CO 852/529/1, TNA.

32 Secretary of State for the Colonies to Officer Administering the Government, 17 April 1942, RG 7/1/777, PRAAD.

33 See, for instance, minute by Sidney S. Abrahams, Legal Adviser to the Colonial Office, 24 June 1942, CO 852/464/15, TNA.

34 Governor of the Gold Coast to Secretary of State for the Colonies, 11 July 1942, RG 7/1/777, PRAAD.

35 T.R.O. Mangin, 24 June 1942, RG 7/1/777, PRAAD.

36 Governor of the Gold Coast to Secretary of State for the Colonies, 11 July 1942, RG 7/1/777, PRAAD; Governor of the Gold Coast to Secretary of State for the Colonies, 1 August 1942, RG 7/1/777, PRAAD.

37 See, for instance, minute by R.H. Burt, 14 April 1944 and O.G.R. Williams, 2 May 1944, CO 852/643/6, TNA.

38 G.W. Lepper, Ministry of Fuel and Power, to R.H. Burt, Colonial Office, 10 December 1943, CO 852/529/1, TNA.

39 Sir Alan Burns to Oliver Stanley, 26 July and 17 August 1944, CO 852/643/6, TNA.

40 Gerald Creasy, 13 May 1944, CO 852/643/6, TNA.

41 Sir Alan Burns, 1 July 1944, RG 7/1/777, PRAAD.

42 Commercially significant offshore discoveries of oil in Ghana were announced in 2007, and production in the Jubilee Fields at the Cape Three Points area began in 2010.

43 "Shell" Overseas Exploration Company Limited to the Colonial Office, 17 August 1948, RG 7/1/778, PRAAD.

44 Letter from Shell Overseas Exploration Company quoted in Dr. W.L.F. Nuttall, British Ministry of Fuel and Power, to R.H. Burt, Colonial Office, 19 February 1949, CO 852/982/5, TNA.

45 Dr. W.L.F. Nuttall to R.H. Burt, 13 July 1949, CO 852/982/5, TNA.

46 C.J. Pleass, Development Secretary, Nigeria, to L.H. Gorsuch, Colonial Office, 18 July 1949, CO 852/982/5, TNA.

47 James S. Coleman, *Nigeria: Background to Nationalism* (Berkeley: University of California Press, 1963), 283.

48 H.M. Foot, Chief Secretary to the Governor of Nigeria, to R.H. Bugler, General Manager, Shell Company of West Africa Ltd., 23 September 1949, CO 852/982/5, TNA.

49 The Nigerian government was informed of the Pakistani regulations in a telegram from Secretary of State for the Colonies to Sir J. Macpherson, Governor of Nigeria, 11 September 1949, CO 852/982/5, TNA.

50 H.M. Foot, Chief Secretary to the Governor of Nigeria, to R.H. Bugler, General Manager, Shell Company of West Africa Ltd., 23 September 1949, CO 852/982/5, TNA.

51 Note of a meeting with representatives from Shell, 12 August 1949, CO 852/982/5, TNA.

52 Sir John Macpherson to Sir Hilton Poynton, Colonial Office, 25 October 1949, CO 852/982/5, TNA.

53 Victor Butler, Ministry of Fuel and Power, to C.G. Eastwood, Colonial Office, 26 August 1949, and Dr. W.L.F. Nuttall to N.L. Mayle, Colonial Office, 11 October 1949, CO 852/982/5, TNA.

54 Assistant Under-Secretary of State, Gerard Clauson, 4 October 1949, CO 852/982/5, TNA.

55 A.B. Cohen, 5 October 1949, CO 852/982/5, TNA.

56 Note of a meeting with representatives of Shell, 6 September 1949, CO 852/982/5, TNA.

57 See, for instance, minutes by R.H. Hobden, Colonial Office, 19 August 1949, and R.H. Burt, 20 August 1949, CO 852/982/5, TNA.

58 C.J. Pleass to L.H. Gorsuch, 18 July 1949, CO 852/982/5, TNA.

59 Gerard Clauson, 4 September 1949, CO 852/982/5, TNA.

60 Sir John Macpherson to the Secretary of State, 14 December 1949, CO 852/982/5, TNA.

61 I.D. Davidson, Shell, to A.H. Poynton, Colonial Office, 28 December 1949, and Davidson to Poynton, 26 January 1950, CO 852/982/5, TNA.

62 Sir John Macpherson to the Secretary of State, 11 March 1950, CO 852/982/5, TNA.

63 Governor of Nigeria to Secretary of State for the Colonies, 11 June 1952, CO 852/1203/6, TNA.

64 H.A. Harding to Dr. W.L.F. Nuttall, 25 June 1952, CO 852/1203/6, TNA.

65 Jêdrzej George Frynas, Matthias P. Beck, and Kamel Mellahi, "Maintaining Corporate Dominance after Decolonization: The 'First Mover Advantage' of Shell-BP in Nigeria," *Review of African Political Economy* 27 (2000): 407–25.

66 Frynas, *Oil in Nigeria*, 9.

Regulating Oil Concessions in British West Africa

67 James Bamberg, *British Petroleum and Global Oil, 1950–1974* (Cambridge: Cambridge University Press, 2000), 110.
68 Telegram from the Governor General's Deputy, Nigeria, to Secretary of State for the Colonies, 27 November 1956, CO 1029/256, TNA. For the political development of Nigeria in the late colonial period, see Falola and Heaton, *History of Nigeria*.
69 E.A.C. Bent, Colonial Office, 21 May 1957, CO 1029/256, TNA.
70 See memoranda by D.G. Gordon Smith, 18 February 1957, CO 1029/256, TNA.
71 E.A.C. Bent, Colonial Office, 21 May 1957, CO 1029/256, TNA.
72 E.A.C. Bent, Colonial Office, 28 May 1957, CO 1029/256, TNA.
73 Draft letter from J.M. Kisch to A.C.F. Armstrong, not issued, CO 1029/256, TNA.
74 Ibid.
75 Sir Ralph Grey to Sir Hilton Poynton, 2 August 1957, CO 1029/256, TNA.
76 Minute by Sir Hilton Poynton, 5 May 1958, CO 1029/256, TNA.
77 A.C.F. Armstrong to J.M. Kisch, 25 June 1957, CO 1029/255, TNA.
78 Bamberg, *British Petroleum and Global Oil*, 110.
79 Report of investigation by the Oil Taxation Study Group, Nigerian Mineral Oil Taxation, CO 1029/257, TNA.

8

Regulating Oil in Iran and India

The Anglo-Iranian Oil Company and Burmah Oil, 1886–1953

NEVEEN ABDELREHIM and SHRADDHA VERMA

During the first half of the twentieth century, access to oil became crucial for both economic and strategic reasons. No modern state could do without oil, but since the known deposits were irregularly spread around the globe, most states had to rely on outside supplies for their needs.[1] This combination of relative scarcity and high criticality meant that oil became a very politically contested issue. For oil-rich states, the consequence was that their regulatory frameworks for this natural resource could come under pressure from foreign powers or from foreign companies, while for oil-importing states the consequence was that the policies of exporting states had direct implications for their supply of this resource. Thus, regulation of oil was never a purely domestic issue.

This general point is clearly illustrated by the history of oil regulations in Iran and India in the first half of the twentieth century. Although these two states were very differently situated when it came to oil (Iran was one of the largest producers in the world while India had limited oil resources), they were both firmly within the British sphere of influence politically. In addition, in both countries British companies dominated the oil industries.

Persia (renamed Iran in 1935) was one of the countries in which Britain gained enormous power and influence due to its control over Iran's main export product – oil – through the Anglo-Iranian Oil Company (AIOC). Iranian oil became crucial to Great Britain during the Second World War, and Britain's control over that oil in the postwar years was an essential source

*Regulating Oil in Iran and India*187

of revenue for the British state. AIOC made money not only from the sale of oil but also from the taxes it levied on Iran. In 1950, AIOC made £170 million from oil sales and an amount equal to 30 percent of the profits in taxes.[2]

Oil was also important for India, but for very different reasons. India depended on imported oil and oil products to meet its needs. Foreign oil companies, which established successful businesses in India while India was a formal colony of Britain, dominated the oil industry. The major company in India was the Burmah Oil Company (BOC), a British company that imported kerosene and other oil-related products into India from Burmah. BOC also owned the Assam Oil Company, the only major oil producer in India at this time. After its independence from Britain in 1947, India moved away from importing oil products, with both the refining of imported oil and oil prospecting becoming increasingly important for its government.[3]

This chapter takes a historical political economy perspective in exploring the activities of AIOC and BOC from the time of their establishment until 1953. BOC and AIOC were both British companies based in, and run from, Britain, with BOC owning AIOC jointly with the British government. We compare the operations of AIOC and BOC in Iran and India, respectively, and their relationship with the host governments as well as with the British government from the start of the twentieth century until the 1950s. This period is of particular importance for both countries. In Iran, after many years of AIOC producing oil with Iranian government support, a wave of economic nationalism led to the government nationalizing it in 1951. India gained independence in 1947, and the new Indian government rapidly established many of the institutions that were important to its economy until 1992, some of which limited the importance of BOC. In both countries oil was an important natural resource, although for different reasons, and we explore the interactions of the state in relation to oil, AIOC, and BOC. It is worth noting that, before Indian independence and before Iran's wave of economic nationalism, the two companies benefited from their relationship with the British government, and the British could directly or indirectly influence how their regulatory regimes were designed and implemented.[4] However, after the Second World War, this gradually changed, and the two companies lost their special standing in their host countries.

Some scholars have argued that regulations pertaining to different countries developed in different ways in order to address wider concerns such as fighting communism and advancing special relationships.[5] For other scholars, the existence of oil companies was a spillover of "British imperialism," with British officials believing that British firms should dominate the oil market to protect the home country's uncertain balance of payments.[6] White suggests that "nationalisation appeared a distinct possibility in a number of Britain's decolonizing territories because many anti-colonial movements taking shape by the 1950s espoused some form of socialism."[7]

In relation to Iran, Bostock and Jones argue that virulent Iranian economic nationalism "can't be treated solely as an endogenous factor to British business. Iranian policies were a reaction to the close relations between British business in Iran and the British government."[8] Das Gupta (1971) and Vedavelli (1976) have studied the oil industry in India, and they discuss issues relating to all the oil companies in that country, covering both the pre- and post-independence period. Our chapter extends their work by providing an in-depth study of the interactions of BOC, the largest of the oil companies operating in India at this time. We also extend the previous studies by providing a comparison of AIOC in Iran to BOC in India, and we focus explicitly on the regulatory context faced by both these companies.

Our research builds on existing research by integrating the above perspectives with a view of two different colonial experiences (BOC and AIOC), both of which were important to British imperial interests. One of these experiences occurred within a setting of formal colonization (i.e., AIOC in India) and the other (i.e., BOC in Iran) did not. Our contribution also lies in exploring the operations of two major British oil companies in pre- and postcolonial periods by using political economy theory to analyze the imperial influence on both companies and how this changed over time. We attempt to show the continuing importance of British companies within the oil industry during this period, and we highlight the ongoing negotiations between the oil companies and their respective governments.

The chapter is structured as follows: first, we provide a brief outline of the political economy of both Iran and India; second, we use a political economy perspective to analyze the events affecting AIOC and BOC both before and after the Second World War (until 1953), focusing particularly on the regulations and other state interactions faced by both companies.

Political and Economic Context of Iran

The early years of the twentieth century witnessed an atmosphere of discontent with and protest against the despotic rule of the Qajars and foreign intervention.[9] Patriotic and nationalistic sentiments among the urban middle and religious classes led to the creation of a parliament (Majlis), whose first session was held in 1906. In 1907, the Russians and the British signed an agreement that divided Persia into northern and southern spheres of

Regulating Oil in Iran and India

influence. The civil war, which lasted from 1908 until 1911, erupted after the Parliament refused to grant concessions demanded by Russia and England. Russian troops entered Iran and killed many prominent Constitutionalists. Other cities rose in rebellion against Muhammad Ali Shah (1872–1925), and he was forced to flee to Russia.[10]

The twentieth century was a period of profound transformation for the Iranian economy. After centuries of underdevelopment and economic stagnation, with only a marginal role in world markets, the economy of Iran began to change in terms of structure, productivity, and international impact. The role of the state in the economy underwent significant changes both in the scope and the nature of government intervention. Under the influence of internal and external forces, and with increasing revenues from oil exports, the state moved beyond its traditional roles and took on major responsibilities for economic development. Understanding the political economy of Iran is important if one is to gain insight into the ways in which it regulated its oil resources.

For Iran, oil played an important role in facilitating its ability to engage in global markets and gave it the opportunity to become more involved in oil production for export.[11] Iran's participation in the world economy was greatly enhanced by its strategic location and by its prized oil resources.[12] Indeed, Iran's oil reserves accounted for the greater part of the total assets of the petroleum industry of the Middle East, and the country became a major supplier of oil to Britain following AIOC's initial oil exploration.

AIOC established the world's largest oil refinery in Abadan, and the company continued to expand its oil production from this major installation. Iran, via AIOC's activities, consequently became the second largest exporter of crude petroleum in the world, having the third largest oil reserves during the period under discussion. Iranian oil supplies were a major source of soft currency generation and tax revenue for the British government,[13] and it was essential to Britain's balance of payments.[14] In fact, Iran was not militarily strong, but its geo-strategic location made it invaluable.[15] Iran was the oldest oil-producing country in the Middle East region, accounting for 74.2 percent of the net income of the oil industry in the period between 1913 and 1947.[16]

Government Interactions, Regulation, and AIOC Pre-Nationalization

The first oil concession ever granted in the Middle East was to William D'Arcy in Iran in 1901. The D'Arcy Concession was typical of a traditional concession, with a sixty-year term, starting in 1901 and lasting to 1961, including almost all territories of Iran except for the five northern provinces, which were the traditional preserve of Russia. According to the concession, the concessionaire enjoyed the exclusive right to explore, develop, exploit, and transport petroleum, in return for which the Iranian government was entitled to 16 percent of the net profit on all operations.[17]

In 1908, D'Arcy finally discovered a huge oilfield, and his company, Anglo-Persian Oil Company (which was now partly owned by BOC), became a leading contender on the international oil markets.[18] After the discovery, a pipeline was built from the oilfields to the coast, and a refinery was constructed at Abadan.[19] This discovery was to radically alter the face of the world oil industry.[20] In 1914, the first Lord of the Admiralty, Winston Churchill, was keen to see the British Navy start using oil rather than coal power for its ships. As a result, after prolonged negotiations, Churchill, on behalf of the British government, bought 51 percent of the Anglo-Persian Oil Company with the aim of establishing a new kind of organization.[21] Anglo-Persian changed its name to AIOC in 1935.

Between 1921 and 1940, Reza Shah's regime brought about major institutional changes in Iran. The rise to power of Reza Khan opened a new period in Anglo-Iranian relations. The decade beginning from 1923 was the most active in laying the foundations for the resurgence of Iran in accordance with Reza Khan's ideas. Once Reza Khan had consolidated his power, first as prime minister, then as shah, there were three important aspects of British policy towards Iran that called for his attention. First, Reza Khan was determined to centralize all authority in Iran. Second, and involved with Reza Khan's ambitious modernization program, was the position of the Anglo-Iranian Oil Company. Third, AIOC's installations and its refinery at Abadan had become the greatest industrial complex in the Middle East. It was a splendid modern technological achievement and it pointed to the emerging importance of oil in the world supply of energy. Nevertheless, its presence was an object of suspicion and resentment, a symbol of national frustration. At the same time, AIOC was a crucial source of revenue and an industrial training facility. After the First World War, the Iranian media and Reza Shah objected to this concession because little money was being paid to the Iranian government. This caused acrimony regarding how the agreement between Iran and Britain was being carried out, and Reza Shah tried to minimize involvement with the latter. For its part, the British government, due to its ownership of AIOC, controlled all Iran's oil resources.

The Great Depression of the 1930s and the rise of protectionism around the world also prompted and intensified interventionist policies in Iran, much as it did in most Latin American countries. The government managed the expansion of international trade through such techniques as the foreign exchange controls imposed in 1936. Despite many advances in domestic and foreign economic policy, however, in the years before the Second World War, Iran remained an exporter of raw materials and traditional goods and an importer of both consumer and capital goods.[22] In 1933, a new concession was ratified by the Majlis (Iranian Parliament), which extended the life of the original D'Arcy concession by thirty-two years. The key features of the 1933 agreement between Iran and AIOC were an increase in the royalty paid to Iran and the implementation of Iranianization.[23]

Following the outbreak of the Second World War, and especially after Germany's invasion of the Soviet Union in June 1941, the Persian Gulf and Iran's vast oil resources became critical for the success of the British Navy. Iran declared itself neutral, but Reza Shah, who had established strong cultural and technological ties with Germany, was perceived as problematic by the Allies. By 1941, Britain and the Soviet Union turned their attention to Iran and saw the newly opened Trans-Iranian Railway as an attractive transport route from the Iranian Gulf to the Soviet Union. In August 1941, Britain and the USSR invaded Iran, arrested Reza Shah, sent him into exile, allowed his political system to collapse, and limited the functions of Iran's constitutional government. They permitted Reza Shah's son, Mohammad Reza Shah Pahlavi, to succeed to the throne.[24] In January 1942, Britain and the USSR signed an agreement with Iran to respect Iran's independence and to withdraw their troops within six months of the war's end. In 1945, the USSR refused to announce a timetable for leaving Iran's northwestern provinces of East Azerbaijan and West Azerbaijan, where Soviet-supported autonomy movements had developed.[25]

The departure of Reza Shah and the presence of foreign troops from 1941 to 1946 created a new environment within which a variety of groups found opportunities to participate in the political process.[26] This led to a relatively chaotic political situation because, at the time, Iran lacked well-established political and policy-making institutions to coordinate the multitude of conflicting demands that had emerged. The only issue that seemed to unify large segments of the population was the desire to gain control of the oil industry and to appropriate larger shares of its revenues. Iran's political system became increasingly open. Political parties were developed, and in 1944 the

Iranian parliamentary elections were the first genuinely competitive elections in more than twenty years.

The AIOC, which was owned by the British government, continued to produce and market Iranian oil, and the British government made far more money from petroleum taxation than Iran made from royalties.[27] In the beginning of the 1930s, some Iranians had begun to support the nationalization of the country's oilfields. After 1946 this became a major popular movement. The years preceding nationalization witnessed a series of failed proposals, on the one hand, and a succession of Iranian governments and institutional changes, on the other, reflecting the increasing influence of political organizations opposed to AIOC.[28] Until 1951, when the Iranian Parliament nationalized its oil industry, there were no existing legal frameworks in place during the negotiating process between the two parties, and the concessions signed were typically those between Iranian rulers and oil companies. These concessions were validated in the Iranian Parliament and became legally binding once agreement was reached. Due to the absence of relevant legislation, the rulers did not encounter any legal restrictions on the type of contracts, or the terms and conditions, they could agree upon.

The Iranian prime minister Musaddiq's nationalization of AIOC on 1 May 1951 angered the British government and seemed part of a growing pattern of putting pressure on British control of the oil industry.[29] From this arose the whole question of British influence in the Middle East.

Government Interactions, Regulation, and the AIOC Post-Nationalization

Financial difficulties caused by an international British-led embargo on Iranian oil as well as deliberate boycott attempts by the intelligence services of the United States undermined the Musaddiq government. Musaddiq's actions brought him into conflict with the pro-Western elites of Iran and with the shah, Mohammed Reza. The shah dismissed Musaddiq in mid-1952, but massive public riots condemning this action forced him to reinstate Musaddiq a short time later. British intelligence sources, working with the American Central Intelligence Agency (CIA), and the shah began to engineer a plot to overthrow Musaddiq. At this point, the shah left the country for "medical reasons." While British intelligence backed away from the debacle, the CIA continued its covert operations in Iran. On 19 August 1953, the military, backed by street protests organized and financed by the CIA, overthrew Musaddiq. The shah quickly returned to take power and, as recognition of American help, signed over 40 percent of Iran's oilfields to US companies.[30]

The strong nationalist sentiment in Iran against the British monopoly over Iran's oil resources coincided with the United States' desire to reorganize the geographic distribution of world oil markets. The British plan was to allocate designated Middle East exports among various oil-exporting countries and not to restructure the oil industry towards increased concessionary access for US oil companies.[31] Even during the British oil embargo of 1952–53, when all foreign revenues to Iran originated from non-oil exports, trade remained in surplus. Interestingly, while the British government encouraged non-oil exports during the embargo, it was only concerned about weathering the temporary foreign exchange shortages and did not pursue it as a long-term strategy.[32]

In 1954, negotiations restarted between the coup government and international oil companies, resulting in an agreement with a consortium whose shareholders consisted of seven major American oil companies and AIOC. The agreement attempted to reconcile the concessionary regime with the Iranian Nationalization Act. It covered almost all the areas previously under the concession of the AIOC while applying the principle of nationalization and turning AIOC's assets in Iran over to the state-owned National Iranian Oil Company (NIOC). The stage was set to bring Iranian oil back into production and onto the world market. The American government waived the application of its anti-trust laws in the Iranian case, and, subsequently, the Anglo-American intercompany talks ended with the signing of a memorandum of understanding on 9 April 1954. The memorandum provided for the formation of a consortium in which the shares would be 40 percent for AIOC (which became the British Petroleum Company in December 1954); 14 percent for Royal Dutch Shell; 8 percent each for the five US companies of Standard Oil (NJ), Socony, Socal, Texas, and Gulf; and 6 percent for Compagnie française des pétroles (CFP). Thus, Iran agreed to pay a sum of £76 million, of which £51 million was paid in cash and the balance of £25 million was to be paid in ten yearly instalments of £2.5 million each. This was meant not only to compensate for AIOC's nationalized assets in Iran but also to settle the claims and counter-claims of both parties. The Iranian government refused, however, to consider the company's suggestion to set up a company with mixed Iranian and British directors that would operate in Iran on behalf of NIOC. NIOC offered employment to British staff but this was not accepted. The prime minister of Iran also insisted on his anti-sabotage bill as a measure designed to convict the British in case of any future misadventure at Abadan.[33]

Subsequently, NIOC, faced with an increasing demand for oil in Iran, embarked on the construction of a network of pipelines from the southern refineries to the northern centres of oil consumption in order to market its oil products. In theory, NIOC was in charge, but the consortium of foreign companies managing oil production rapidly took control of the production and distribution of Iranian oil, passing 50 percent of the profits on to the Iranian state.

Oil revenues recovered and imports sharply increased to the extent that Iran developed a large trade deficit and started borrowing from abroad.[34] Oil production increased, with the result that AIOC's crude production recovered more rapidly from the Iranian crisis than did its refinery runs. Meanwhile, greater reliance needed to be placed on processing contracts with other companies.[35] AIOC's policy of exporting crude oil was more flexible once it no longer depended on refining a large proportion of the output within the area.[36] In April 1955, the agreement was modified and each of the major US companies gave up 1 percent of its holdings so that a 5 percent share could be made available for nine smaller independent US oil companies to hold through the joint organization.

Political and Economic Context of India

India, in direct contrast to Iran, had only limited reserves of oil and, as such, relied on imports of oil and related products such as kerosene. Due to geographical proximity, India, pre-independence, was a natural market for oil and oil-related products from Burma. And BOC, the major oil company in Burma, was able to develop this market, beginning in 1902, and very quickly became the largest oil company in India.

India, being an important colony of the British Empire, was of strategic, political, and economic importance to Britain.[37] This colonial relationship governed the trading relations between India and Britain. During the period of colonization, the economy of India was, arguably, run in the interests of Britain. For example, under policies made in Britain, India produced raw materials and foodstuffs that were exported to Britain, and, using these raw materials, Britain manufactured goods that were exported back to India. This import/export policy, which left India as a supplier of raw materials to the British and as a market for British goods, was very much in the interests of the British economy and, hence, of particular importance to Britain.[38]

India gained independence from Britain in 1947, and, under an Indian government, post-independence conditions were very different from pre-independence conditions. At independence, India inherited a predominantly agrarian economy. Foreign capital dominated industry in India, with British firms being in control, either directly or through managing agencies. With some notable exceptions, such as Tata and Birla, Indian industry was characterized by low technology, low productivity, low wages, and labour-intensive goods, and it was concentrated in only a few selected areas, such as textiles. In addition, there was little production of capital goods and a dearth of industrial infrastructure, modern banking, and insurance. Thus, India's economy was very underdeveloped, with low per capita income, poor economic growth, many living below the poverty line, and little industrialization.[39]

Inheriting an economy that needed modernizing, economic growth and Indianization was a priority for the government of India (GOI). The GOI introduced a mixed economy into India, in which there was a role for both private and public enterprise and in which socialist ideals operated within a secular democracy. The key elements of the economic system that were implemented soon after independence included central planning of the economy, the development of a large public sector, state control of the corporate sector (including licensing of private enterprise), price controls over key resources, the control of foreign exchange, and the use of import-substituting policies. A resolution on industrial policy, issued on 6 April 1948, stated that the aim of the government of independent India was to establish a social order whereby justice and equality of opportunity would be secured for all people. This would be achieved by careful planning of the whole of the economy, a highly regulated economy, and strong government involvement in industry and the business sector.[40] Thus, post-independence, BOC faced a very different business environment. However, it still remained the most important oil company in India throughout the period of analysis.

In the next sections, we offer an analysis of pre-independence government interactions and the regulatory environment in relation to BOC, followed by an analysis of how these changed post-independence.[41]

Government Interactions, Regulation, and the Burmah Oil Company Pre-independence

BOC was set up in Glasgow in 1886, when the British annexed Upper Burma and granted oil concessions to BOC. It grew steadily in its early years, dealing successfully in fuel oil, wax, and kerosene, both in Burma and in Britain. As the only major British oil company at the time, BOC was important to the British Empire. That the British government granted concessions to BOC and not to its non-British rivals was important in helping the company grow in its early years, and this favourable treatment enabled it to set up a successful oil business.[42]

In 1902, BOC started to trade kerosene in India through a managing agent in Calcutta, and it successfully grew this trade in kerosene both by entering into price wars and by negotiating with other oil companies, including Asiatic Petroleum (a joint marketing subsidiary of Royal Dutch and Shell) and Standard Oil, two key rivals. In 1905, it concluded a kerosene agreement with Asiatic Petroleum, agreeing to sell its excess production to other oil companies. In addition to the price wars and negotiations, BOC benefited from continued British support when entering the Indian market. It was able to gain protection from some competition from both the British government in Burma and the British government in India, which refused to grant licences for oil exploration or production to non-British rivals.[43] This helped BOC's economic interests by ensuring that key resources were held by British companies and British interests within the Empire.

In 1903, the British government required oil for its new oil-burning warships not only to support the defence of the Empire but also to protect its economic imperial interest. The British Admiralty turned to BOC for this oil, BOC being the only significant oil company within the British Empire. The British government chose not to regulate the oil market but, instead, negotiated a long-term agreement between the Admiralty and BOC, signed in 1905, for the long-term supply of fuel oil. The close links between the British government and the company also led to the Admiralty requesting that BOC assume the managerial and financial burden of prospecting for oil in Persia, further increasing the links between it and the British government.

The oil agreement was expected to be beneficial to both parties, and it led to BOC becoming an important company to the British government (indicated by the presence of a government representative on its board of directors). In practice, BOC did not benefit as much as expected from the deal as the British government did not recompense it for all it had to do to provide oil under the agreement. However, it did benefit in other ways. The links between the British government and BOC led to the former setting up AIOC in conjunction with BOC, which became one of the latter's important assets.[44]

The links between BOC and the British government were again strengthened during the First World War. BOC was able to provide both fuel oil and kerosene to India when other oil companies curtailed shipments there in 1917, providing vital oil supplies for the British government in India.[45] Again the oil needs were met through cooperation between the British government and BOC rather than through regulatory measures.

In the 1920s, BOC continued to trade successfully in India and did so through government support, diversification, and the negotiation of agreements with other oil companies operating in India. Government support came through the British government refusing to grant oil concessions to BOC's foreign rivals, and diversification included the acquisition of Assam Oil Company, one of only two oil producers in India. BOC also entered into agreements with Shell to operate a joint marketing company, Burmah Shell (BS), in India. BS purchased all its oil supplies from its two parent companies, with most of the oil coming from BOC and Shell importing much lower amounts. Shell's initial import quota was later shared with AIOC.[46] In 1928, BOC extended its connection with Shell by acquiring 800,000 ordinary shares of the (British) Shell Transport and Trading Company, increasing this to one million shares in 1929.

This left Standard Oil, which, as BOC's main rival, met 25 percent of the Indian subcontinent's kerosene requirements.[47] Standard Oil responded to the BOC/Shell deal by entering into ongoing price wars with BS, and, in 1927, it contracted with Soviet authorities to buy kerosene cheaply, with the intention of importing this into India. This was a major threat to BOC and Shell. In response, BOC and Shell cut kerosene and oil prices in India before the arrival of cheap Russian oil.

In addition to cutting prices, BOC asked the British government in India to increase the tariffs on imported oil and kerosene, arguing that the import of Russian oil would adversely affect Britain's interests and economic position. This request was referred to the Indian Tariff Board, a board that comprised both Indian and British civil servants and that was chaired by an Indian civil servant.

The Indian Tariff Board set up an inquiry to establish whether the interests of the Indian people would be served by introducing a tariff on oil imports.[48] BOC fully expected the Indian Tariff Board to report in its favour as a British company within the Empire dealing with key resources. However, contrary to BOC's expectations, the Indian Tariff Board did not support BOC's proposals and even criticized the company for charging high prices that were not in the interest of the Indian people.[49]

In this case, the British government in India did not support BS and BOC, indicating a rather complex relationship between company and state. Indeed, different government departments had different ways of dealing with BOC. For example, BOC had good relationships with the petroleum department and the Admiralty but not with the India Office.[50]

The price war with Standard Oil continued intermittently throughout the 1930s. BOC continued to negotiate with Standard Oil and eventually entered into informal price agreements with the US company, thus reducing price wars in the industry. These contracts were often informal, the point being to circumvent anti-trust regulations, particularly in the United States.[51]

The 1930s, with Hitler's rise to power in Germany and the increasingly militaristic stance of imperial Japan, were dominated by the threat of war. BOC's fuel oil contract with the Admiralty was still operative, and British state interaction with BOC continued. Although BOC was unable to fulfill its contractual obligations with the oil from its Burma oilfields, with the Admiralty's consent it used AIOC's refinery at Abadan to provide such fuel oil as the British Navy needed, thus continuing to be an important imperial company.[52]

During the Second World War, BOC continued to produce oil in Burma but undertook, if required by the British government, to destroy its oilfields in order to prevent oil falling into the hands of enemy forces. This became necessary when Japanese forces invaded Burma in 1941–42. After the war, recompense for this became an area of disagreement between BOC and the British government and led to BOC filing a lawsuit against the British government, which the company eventually lost.[53]

Throughout this period the British government exercised little direct regulation of BOC and other oil companies, and a laissez-faire approach generally prevailed. Although avoiding direct regulation, the British government interacted with BOC through the granting of concessions, through establishing links created by negotiated agreements to supply oil to the British Admiralty, and through its policy to support the competitive position of imperial companies such as BOC against non-British companies.

Despite difficulties with various British government departments, BS and BOC were important imperial companies and, as such, were in a favoured position in India. British interests were paramount within the British Empire, allowing for easy remittances of monies to the UK and protection against foreign competition. The companies were allowed to trade without undue government involvement, British staff dominated their key positions, and

Regulating Oil in Iran and India 199

they were closely linked within the management system associated with the British Empire.[54] These conditions changed significantly after India gained independence in 1947.

Government Interactions, Regulation, and BOC/BS in Post-Independence India until 1953

At independence, oil was very much in the control of BOC through Burmah Shell, its joint marketing subsidiary with Shell and other smaller foreign oil companies. BS was by far the largest and most important oil company in India at this time, its being the largest importer of kerosene, owning Assam Oil (the only major oil producer in India), and being a large distributor of oil-related products.[55] Thus oil interests were very much in private-sector hands. And, after independence, they were in the hands of foreign companies, with BS dominating the industry. Post-independence, the new Indian government recognized oil as an important resource for achieving its socioeconomic aims.[56] Thus, building refineries and exploring for domestic sources of oil became increasingly important.

BS continued to remain important in India after independence in 1947. The company was able to retain the oil concessions that it had held before independence, successfully and unproblematically renegotiating these with the newly appointed GOI.[57]

BS faced an increasingly planned and controlled business environment, with the GOI introducing a highly planned economy, nationalizing key industries, and heavily regulating business and economic life.[58] In particular, the economic industrial policy of 1948 held that key resources would be developed in the public sector and be under government control,[59] leading BS to fear that oil might be nationalized or directly regulated by the GOI.

However, very soon after independence, the GOI indicated that it would not nationalize BS or the other smaller foreign oil companies and that it would not enter into activities relating to oil.[60] This included the development of oil refineries. The GOI indicated that the development of oil refineries and oil exploration activities would be left to BS, its being the most significant oil company in India at this time. Thus, BS's fears that the GOI would take over oil activities proved to be groundless.

Although the GOI ruled out nationalizing it, oil remained a very important resource, vital for the rapid economic modernization that the nation desired. Contrary to what happened with regard to other industries, the oil industry was not directly regulated, although regulations relating to price controls and licences were applied to BS and the other oil companies.[61] The

GOI required that many companies in India acquire licences to trade. BS, too, was required to obtain a licence from the GOI to operate in the oil industry, and this enabled the government to formally interact with the company.

In addition to licence and price control legislation, the GOI also engaged in direct oversight of the oil companies through various government officials and departments. The GOI tried to influence the operations of BS through individual meetings with company representatives whenever it felt there was a need to discuss specific issues. It also used the approval process for dividend remittances to the UK to influence the activities of BS.[62]

Although it did not promulgate any direct oil regulations, the GOI aimed to regulate oil through contracts it negotiated with BS to build oil refineries. These contracts included not only provisions relating to the building of the refineries but also provisions relating to the pricing and marketing of the oil products that were the output of the refining process.[63]

In 1948, the GOI discussed establishing refineries in India, requesting BOC and Shell to send delegations to India to discuss oil refinery development and oil exploration.[64] The development of Indian oil refineries was blocked because BS and the other foreign oil companies acted together to stall negotiations. BS led the negotiations and argued that the pricing of the deal was not favourable enough, and so it did not agree to build the refineries that the GOI desired.

In response to this deadlock and BS's delaying tactics, the GOI indicated that it might use foreign experts to help it develop its own oil refineries, perhaps on the Soviet model, but it did not follow through on this. In addition, the GOI also indicated that Indian capital might be raised to fund Indian refineries, but again, it did not follow through on this.[65] Negotiations continued with BS, and it was finally agreed, in 1950, that BS would build an oil refinery at Trombay, near Mumbai (previously Bombay). The GOI also entered into agreements with two other foreign oil companies, Caltex and Standard Vac, to build smaller refineries. This was contrary to the GOI's initial promise to deal only with BS.[66]

The GOI tried to introduce more competition into the oil market rather than relying upon regulation. This meant that BS faced not only more direct competition from new foreign companies looking to enter the Indian market but also competition introduced by the GOI.[67] The GOI created competition by entering into deals with different foreign companies, importing cheaper oil from Romania, and, in the 1950s, using Soviet expertise to try to set up Indian oil companies.[68] This was, perhaps, an attempt to reduce BS's dominance as well as an attempt to deal with the tendency of oil companies to act collectively against the GOI's proposed refinery agreements (particularly early in the period).

Despite these initiatives, BS was able to continue to trade profitably and to stall government-initiated negotiations for the development of oil refineries and oil exploration until price provisions were favourable for it.[69] This indicates that the balance of power was with BS and BOC rather than with the GOI.

Political and economic factors contributed to the relatively weak position of the GOI. Since India was not a major producer of oil, most of its oil needs had to be met by imports. This created foreign exchange issues as, during most of this period, India faced a shortage in this area.[70] Conservation of foreign exchange was important to the GOI and led to various initiatives, for example, obtaining cheaper oil from other foreign states, setting up Indian oil companies, and increasing oil exploration in India in an attempt to increase its own production.[71] Economic considerations were also important in determining BS's relative bargaining strength. The economic legacy of British colonialism left the GOI with a shortage of capital to modernize its economy, a shortage of technical expertise, and a continuing shortage of foreign exchange.[72] This led to oil being left in the hands of foreign private-sector companies, with BS dominating the industry despite the GOI's goal of Indianization. Over time, the GOI tried to increase its control over BS activities through price control and licensing regulations as well as through refinery negotiations, but, throughout the period of analysis, BS managed to retain its position as the largest oil company in India.

Comparison of BOC and AIOC

The situations facing Iran and India were quite different in terms of oil, Iran being oil rich and a large exporter of oil while India imported oil for most of its oil needs. In addition, oil was the most important economic and trading asset in Iran, which had relatively few other resources and trading activities. India, by contrast, was much more diversified than Iran, having both private-sector and public-sector companies in different industries.[73] Furthermore, Iran retained its position as a sovereign state, whereas India was a formal colony of Britain and was ruled by that nation for many years. These very different contexts contributed to both countries dealing differently with the oil companies operating within their purviews both before and after the Second World War.

Before the Second World War, the Iranian government entered into agreements with AIOC to produce oil, and the government and the company shared in the benefits of oil production and export. Thus, for a large part of the period, the Iranian government's and AIOC's interests converged, and both parties benefited from this arrangement. However, as AIOC continued to operate in Iran, nationalistic feelings against the company developed and it was criticized for operating in its own economic interest and that of Britain rather than in the interest of Iran or its Iranian employees, who were treated much less favourably than were its British employees. Iranians believed that oil was the most important issue to their nation because Iran had great natural resources.[74] Iranian people wanted the profits from Iranian oil to go to them, and they wanted their government to make every effort to provide for the welfare of the disadvantaged elements of its own population.[75]

The British government had a complicated relationship with BOC before the Second World War, but, in general terms, BOC was important both in its own right as a major British oil company and also as part owner of AIOC. Thus BOC benefited from British government protection within the Empire and was exempt from regulation.[76] The British government adopted a laissez-faire approach, leaving BOC to enter into price wars and negotiations with its competitors but supporting it by not granting oil concessions to its rivals.

However, in India, nationalistic feeling and anti-imperial concerns against the British rulers of India were channelled into creating an independent nation-state. Once this was achieved, the GOI chose not to nationalize or directly regulate BOC in order to develop an Indian oil industry; instead, it chose to work with BOC, leaving oil-related activities, including building refineries and oil exploration, in the hands of a now foreign company.[77] The reasons for this relate back to the socioeconomic and political context facing India at independence. The GOI's aim was to stimulate economic growth as rapidly as possible, and it planned the development of a large public sector. This – combined with lack of expertise in oil production and exploration, the need for large amounts of capital, and a lack of foreign exchange – may have contributed to a policy of cooperation rather than a policy of nationalization. Due to these factors and BOC's dominant position, BOC and BS certainly appear to have had stronger bargaining power than did the GOI at the beginning of this period. They were able to stall negotiations that were considered unfavourable and only entered into refinery agreements when they deemed the contracts favourable. The power of the GOI increased over this period, and it was able to introduce more competition into the market, enter into agreements for refinery development and oil exploration with BOC and BS, and increase control over prices via licences and price control regulations. These regulations were applicable to all industries in India but, in 1953, were still dependent on BOC and other foreign oil companies due to India's continuing economic difficulties. This contributed to the GOI not directly regulating BOC and the other foreign oil companies in India, despite this being contrary to its own industrial polices and its strong regulation of other industries and businesses.

Another difference between Iran and India relates to post-independence events. India showed much more stability than did Iran. At independence, it inherited an established political system and civil service, enabling its leaders – after initial problems relating to the partition of India and Pakistan and a large and violent migration of people across the new borders – to create stability in the country. This was also possible due to strong support for the Congress Party, which had, as the Indian National Congress, led the fight for independence. The strong public support for the Congress Party continued after independence. Of particular importance was the policy of Nehru, who wished to remain independent of foreign powers, especially Britain, the United States, and Russia. Nehru's foreign policy allowed foreign powers less direct intervention in the affairs of India.[78] This did not occur in Iran, which, by contrast, was very unstable after the nationalization of AIOC – and foreign powers were instrumental in determining events in Iran.

Finally, we can see that India's continuing relationship with BOC led to its being able to develop its oil industry. Several new oil refineries were built and oil exploration led to the discovery of new oilfields in 1953, strengthening the GOI's position in relation to oil. The nationalized AIOC in Iran fared less well, and this led to the Abadan Crisis, whereby, under British pressure, foreign countries agreed not to purchase Iranian oil and the Abadan refinery was closed. AIOC withdrew from Iran and increased the output of its other reserves in the Persian Gulf. Musaddiq broke off negotiations with AIOC when Britain warned tanker owners that receipts from the Iranian government would not be accepted on the world market. The United States, through the International Court of Justice, tried to settle the dispute, but both the British government and Musaddiq rejected a 50/50 profit-sharing arrangement, with recognition of nationalization. The nationalization crisis became acute as Britain's boycott of Iranian oil eliminated a major source of government revenue and ensured that Iranians were rendered poorer and unhappier by the day.

Conclusion

The history of AIOC in Iran reveals a number of distinct features. The first is the dominant role played by the company in creating a modern economic sector in Iran. The second is the close relationship between the company and the British government, which could be seen as a centre of diplomatic rivalry. Finally, and perhaps most importantly, Iran's historical legacy and AIOC's dominant position in the economy led to severe and acrimonious conflicts between British commerce and the Iranian government.[79]

As for BOC, one can see political involvement in its operations throughout the period of analysis. Although there was little direct regulation of BOC before the Second World War, the British government, adopting a laissez-faire approach, supported BOC and not its non-British rivals and also approved oil agreements between BOC and the British Admiralty. Before the Second World War, BOC was an important imperial company both in its own right as a major British oil company and as part owner of AIOC.

After Indian independence, BOC's socioeconomic and political context changed significantly. Despite these changes, BOC continued to be the most important oil company in India, and its interactions with the GOI helped shape the oil industry in that country until 1953. Contrary to the strongly regulated and highly controlled economy implemented by the GOI in other areas, it effected little direct regulation of BS and the oil industry in post-independence India. This was due to BS's relatively strong bargaining position and the GOI's political and economic weakness in relation to foreign exchange, technical expertise, and capital. The GOI tried to influence BS in other ways – for example, through price control and licencing regulations, refinery negotiations, and government oversight. Despite this, however, BS and BOC managed to retain their position within the oil industry in India throughout our period of analysis.

As the evidence suggests, there are interesting contrasts in the ways that both oil companies were able to stall negotiations and become independent. The comparative study developed in this chapter might also help scholars to assess the social, economic, and political contexts of oil companies during times of nationalization and independence. Specifically, the results of this study have wider implications for an understanding of the political economy of oil companies and how they may enhance their bargaining positions.

Regulating Oil in Iran and India 205

There is scope for further investigation on the part of companies looking to strengthen their social, economic, and political positions.

We also underline one of the key findings in Jon Olav Hove and John Kwadwo Osei-Tutu's chapter on the political regulation of oil in British West Africa. Although these chapters cover partially different time periods, different areas, and different relations with Britain, they both support the view that colonial experiences are not monolithic. Both studies also conclude that, despite local resistance, in Iran and India, as in Nigeria and the Gold Coast, the interests of British and foreign oil companies remained important in both pre- and postcolonial periods.

Notes

1 Marcelo Bucheli, "Multinational Corporations, Totalitarian Regimes and Economic Nationalism," *Business History* 50, 4 (2008): 533–54.
2 See http://www.coldwar.org/ (Cold War Museum website, viewed 25 October 2015).
3 Thomas Anthony Buchanan Corley, *A History of the Burmah Oil Company*, vol. 2, *1924–1966* (London: Heinemann, 1988), 309–29.
4 Stephanie Decker, "Building up Goodwill: British Business, Development and Economic Nationalism in Ghana and Nigeria, 1945–1977," *Enterprise and Society* 9, 4 (2008): 602–13; Stephanie Decker, "Corporate Political Activity in Less Developed Countries: The Volta River Project in Ghana, 1958–66," *Business History* 53, 7 (2011): 993; John Wilson, "Strategies of State Control and Economy, Nationalisation and Indiginization in Africa," *Comparative Politics* 22, 4 (1990): 402.
5 Steve Marsh, "Anglo-American Crude Diplomacy: Multinational Oil and the Iranian Oil Crisis, 1951–1953," *Contemporary British History Journal* 21, 1 (2007): 28.
6 Frances Bostock and Geoffrey Jones, "British Business in Iran, 1860s–1970s," in *British Business in Asia since 1860*, ed. Richard Davenport-Hines and Geoffrey Jones (Cambridge: Cambridge University Press, 1988), 46.
7 Nicholas White, "The Business and the Politics of Decolonization: The British Experience in the Twentieth Century," *Economic History Review* 53, 3 (2000): 551.
8 Bostock and Jones, "British Business in Iran," 46.
9 The Qajars were a Turkic tribe that lived in territories in present-day Azerbaijan, then part of Iran.
10 See http://www.metmuseum.org/toah/ht/11/wai.html (Metropolitan Museum of Art website, viewed 13 January 2016).
11 Hadi Esfahani and Mohammad Pesaran, "Iranian Economy in the Twentieth Century: A Global Perspective," in *Cambridge Working Papers in Economics* (Cambridge: Faculty of Economics, University of Cambridge, 2008), 19.
12 Ibid., 11.
13 Marsh, "Anglo-American Crude Diplomacy," 28.
14 Steve Marsh, "The United States, Iran and Operation 'Ajax': Inverting Interpretative Orthodoxy," *Middle Eastern Studies* 39, 3 (2003): 9

15 Ibid., 1–38.
16 Charles Issawi and Mohammed Yeganeh, *The Economics of Middle Eastern Oil* (New York: Preager, 1962), 121.
17 Shahri Nima, "The Petroleum Legal Framework of Iran: History, Trends, and the Way Forward," *China and Eurasia Forum Quarterly* 8, 1 (2010): 114.
18 Ibid., 57.
19 Ibid., 112.
20 Geoffrey Jones, "Multinational Strategies and Developing Countries in Historical Perspective," working paper, Harvard Business School, 2010, 2.
21 Ibid., 52.
22 See http://www.loc.gov/collections/country-studies/about-this-collection (Library of Congress website, viewed 12 August 2015).
23 Esfahani and Pesaran, "Iranian Economy in the Twentieth Century," 11.
24 Ervand Abrahamian, *Iran between Two Revolutions* (Princeton: Princeton University Press, 1982), 251.
25 See http://www.iranchamber.com/society/articles/globalization_women_struggle_iran1.php (Iran Chamber Society website, viewed 15 January 2016).
26 Abrahamian, *Iran between Two Revolutions*, 251.
27 Ibid., 115.
28 Stephen Kobrin, "Diffusion as an Explanation of Oil Nationalisation," *Journal of Conflict Resolution* 29, 1 (1985): 3–32.
29 Neveen Abdelrehim, Josephine Maltby, and Toms Steven, "Corporate Social Responsibility and Corporate Control: The Anglo-Iranian Oil Company, 1933–1951," *Enterprise and Society* 12, 4 (2011): 824–62; Neveen Abdelrehim, Josephine Maltby, and Toms Steven, "Accounting for Power and Control: The Anglo-Iranian Oil Nationalization of 1951," *Critical Perspectives on Accounting* 23, 7–8 (2012): 595–607; Leslie Rood, "Nationalisation and Indigenisation in Africa," *Journal of Modern African Studies* 14, 3 (1976): 427–47.
30 Ibid.
31 Ibid.
32 Abdelrehim, Maltby, and Steven, "Corporate Social Responsibility and Corporate Control"; Abdelrehim, Maltby, and Steven, "Accounting for Power and Control."
33 Ibid.
34 Esfahani and Pesaran, "Iranian Economy in the Twentieth Century," 12.
35 Edith Penrose, *The Large International Firm in Developing Countries* (London: George Allen and Unwin, 1968), 114.
36 Issawi and Yeganeh, *Economics of Middle Eastern Oil*, 79.
37 The British Empire has been studied from many different perspectives, including Barbara Bush, *Imperialism and Postcolonialism* (Harlow, UK: Pearson Education, 2006); Peter Cain and Mark Harrison, eds., *Imperialism: Critical Concepts in Historical Studies* (London: Routledge, 2001); Peter Cain and Anthony Hopkins, *British Imperialism, 1688–2000* (London: Longman, 2002); Leela Gandhi, *Postcolonial Theory: A Critical Introduction* (Edinburgh: Edinburgh University Press, 1998); Anita Loomba, *Colonialism/Postcolonialism* (Abingdon: Routledge,

2005); Ronald Robinson and Jack Gallagher, *Africa and the Victorians: The Official Mind of Imperialism* (London: Macmillan, 1961); Edward Said, *Culture and Imperialism* (London: Vintage, 1994); Edward Said, *Orientalism* (London and Henley: Routledge and Keegan Paul, 1978).

38 Vijay Joshi and Ian Little, *India, Macroeconomics and Political Economy, 1964–1991* (Oxford: India Paperbacks, 1998), chaps. 1 and 3; A. Vaidyanathan, "The Indian Economy since Independence (1947–70)," in *The Cambridge Economic History of India*, vol. 2 (New Delhi: Cambridge University Press, 1982); Dietmar Rothermund, *An Economic History of India from Pre-Colonial Times to 1991* (London: Routledge, 1993), chaps. 9 and 10.

39 Ibid.

40 GOI, Industrial Policy Resolution, 1948, National Archives of India.

41 Government interactions post-independence have been explored in relation to the accounting profession and company law by Shraddha Verma, "The Influence of Empire on the Establishment of the Institute of Chartered Accountants of India after independence," in *Accountancy and Empire: The British Legacy of Professional Organization*, ed. Chris Poullaos and SukI Sian (London: Routledge, 2010), 192–214; Shraddha Verma and Sid Gray, "The Setting up of the Institute of Chartered Accountants of India: A First Step in Creating an Indigenous Accounting Profession," *Accounting Historians Journal* 33 (2006): 131–56; Shraddha Verma and Sid Gray, "The Development of Company Law in India: The Case of the Companies Act 1956," *Critical Perspectives on Accounting* 20, 1 (2009): 110–35.

42 Thomas Anthony Buchanan Corley, *A History of the Burmah Oil Company*, vol. 1, *1886–1924* (London: Heinemann, 1988).

43 Ibid.

44 Ibid.

45 Ibid.

46 Thomas Anthony Buchanan Corley, *A History of the Burmah Oil Company*, vol. 2, *1924–1966* (London: Heinemann, 1988).

47 Ibid.

48 GOI, report regarding the grant of protection to the oil industry, Calcutta, 1928–1929, National Archives of India.

49 Ibid.

50 Correspondence between petroleum department and India office, National Archives of India, PRO POWE 33/456.

51 Corley, *History of the Burmah Oil Company*, vol. 2, chap. 1.

52 Ibid., chap. 2.

53 Ibid., 309–29, and chaps. 3 and 8. Claims by Burmah Oil Company, The National Archives, UK, Foreign Office file FO 371/159783; Burmah Oil Company and subsidiary companies, The National Archives, UK, Board of Trade file BT 228/6.

54 Ibid., 309–29.

55 GOI, report of the Oil Price Inquiry Committee (Damle Report) 1961, BP Archives and National Archives of India.

56 *Times of India*, "Evolution of National Oil Policy," 25 June 1956.

57 Assam Oil Company note – position of alluvial area as at 31.12.1950, BP Archives, ARC ref 47644w; Concession agreements with various states in India, BP Archives, ARC ref 47644w.

58 Joshi and Little, *India, Macroeconomics and Political Economy*, chaps. 1 and 3; Vaidyanathan, "Indian Economy since Independence"; Rothermund, *Economic History of India*, chaps. 9 and 10.

59 GOI, industrial policies of 1949, 1956, National Archives of India.

60 Notes of discussion between GPI and BS in 1949, BP Archives, ARC ref 47644w.

61 GOI, Report of the Oil Price Inquiry Committee (Daimler Report) 1961, BP Archives and National Archives of India.

62 Notes of discussion between GPI and BS in 1949, BP Archives, ARC ref 47644w; Corley, *History of the Burmah Oil Company*, 2:309–29.

63 GOI, text of agreements with the oil companies, BP Archives and National Archives of India; GOI, Report of the Oil Price Inquiry Committee (Daimler Report) 1960, BP Archives and National Archives of India.

64 Biplap Das Gupta, *The Oil Industry in India: Some Economic Aspects* (London: Frank Cass and Co., 1971); Rangaswamy Vedavalli, *Private Foreign Investment and Economic Development* (Cambridge: Cambridge University Press, 1976).

65 GOI, Report of the Oil Price Inquiry Committee, 1960, BP Archives and National Archives of India; *Amrita Bazar Patrika* (newspaper), 23 June 1949; Oil possibilities in India, confidential BS/BOC memo, 20 June 1950, BP Archives; Corley, *History of the Burmah Oil Company*, 2:313.

66 GOI, establishment of oil refineries in India, text of agreements with the oil companies, Ministry of Production, 1951–53, BP Archives and National Archives of India.

67 BOC letter, W.J. Condon to Mr. Abraham, 10 October 1949, on competitors, BP Archives, ARC ref 47644w; BS letter, 11 October 1950, on Gulf Oil (India) Ltd, BP Archives; BOC note, 28 February 1951, on Gulf Oil (India) Ltd, BP Archives; Letter, geological department to BOC, 27 November1950, on SVOC being granted certificate of approval, BP Archives.

68 GOI, Report of the Oil Price Inquiry Committee (Daimler Report), 1960, BP Archives and National Archives of India; *Amrita Bazar Patrika* (newspaper), 23 June 1949, "Oil Possibilities in India," confidential BS/BOC memo, 20 June 1950, BP Archives, ARC ref 47644w; Corley, *History of the Burmah Oil Company*, vol 2, 313.

69 *Amrita Bazar Patrika* (newspaper), 23 June 1949, "Oil Possibilities in India," Confidential BS/BOC memo, 20 June 1950, BP Archives, ARC ref 47644w; Gupta, *Oil Industry in India*; Corley, *History of the Burmah Oil Company*, 2:309–29.

70 Joshi and Little, *India, Macroeconomics and Political Economy*, chaps. 1 and 3; Vaidyanathan, "Indian Economy since Independence"; Rothermund, *Economic History of India*, chaps. 9 and 10.

71 Gupta, *Oil Industry in India*; Vedavalli, *Private Foreign Investment and Economic Development*.

72 Joshi and Little, *India, Macroeconomics and Political Economy*, chaps. 1 and 3; Vaidyanathan, "Indian Economy since Independence"; Rothermund, *Economic History of India*, chaps. 9 and 10.

73 GOI, industrial policies of 1949, 1956, National Archives of India.

Regulating Oil in Iran and India

74 BP 080924, Gist of Tudeh pamphlet distributed among depot labour on 1 August 1949, 1. BP Archives, Coventry.
75 *Times Newspapers*, 26 September 1952, 4, Issue 52427.
76 Corley, *History of the Burmah Oil Company*, 2: 309–29.
77 GOI, Report of the Oil Price Inquiry Committee (Daimler Report), 1960, BP Archives and National Archives of India; *Times of India*, "Investment in Three Refineries over RS 50 Crore," 17 March 1955.
78 Hermann Kulke and Dietmar Rothermund, *A History of India* (London and New York: Routledge, 1990); Paul Brass, *The Politics of India since Independence* (Cambridge: Cambridge University Press, 1994).
79 Bostock and Jones, "British Business in Iran," 46.

9

"In the National Interest"

Regulating New Caledonia's Mining
Industry in the Late Twentieth Century

ROBIN S. GENDRON

New Caledonia is a French-ruled archipelago in the southwest Pacific Ocean, east of Australia and north of New Zealand. It is also home to the world's most extensive bodies of nickel ore, an estimated 25 percent of global reserves. Despite the crucial role that foreign investment played in the early development of these reserves, however, by the mid- to late twentieth century access to them was severely restricted by the French state. By the 1960s in particular, the French state considered New Caledonia's nickel industry a vital strategic asset that needed to be marshalled primarily for the benefit of France. In practice, this meant preserving preferential access to these reserves for the French company Société Le Nickel and denying access to other major nickel producers, especially North American ones such as the International Nickel Company (INCO). Yet doing so required the French government in Paris to (re)assert political responsibility over New Caledonia's mining industry, thereby depriving the local territorial government of the political autonomy it had previously enjoyed. The subsequent dispute between French and territorial authorities over the development of New Caledonia's nickel industry helped inaugurate a broader debate about the nature of the relationship between France and New Caledonia and, by the 1970s, propelled the emergence of an independence movement in the territory.

Regulating access to natural resources is inherently a political decision. In this case, the question of foreign access to New Caledonia's nickel reserves

"In the National Interest" 211

became a, if not the, central issue in discussions of New Caledonia's political and economic development in the late twentieth century. This chapter explores the regulatory regime governing New Caledonia's nickel industry and the effects it had on the territory and its relationship with France in the late twentieth century, though with a focus on the 1960s and 1970s. During this period of significant growth and technological change in the nickel industry, stakeholders in both France and New Caledonia adopted different attitudes towards the forces of internationalization that gripped the industry, including, notably, a rapid expansion in the number of companies involved therein and in the diversity of their sources of nickel ore. For the French authorities, internationalization in the nickel industry was a process to be resisted in so far as possible and required the preservation of a strong French stake in the industry, one able to resist the expansion of (North) American political, economic, and cultural interests that, from the French perspective, seemed to be the principal beneficiaries of globalization. Many Caledonians, in contrast, including most of the territory's political and economic elite, viewed the opening of New Caledonia's nickel industry to foreign investment, technology, and markets as vital to the territory's prosperity and development. Ironically, despite the significant political tensions engendered by these inherently contradictory attitudes, the force of events gradually mitigated the differences between most French and Caledonian stakeholders. After rejecting foreign investment completely throughout most of the 1960s, the French government moved towards a cautious openness to it, albeit reluctantly, while the initial enthusiasm for foreign investment among Caledonian stakeholders cooled as scepticism about the costs and benefits to be derived from it mounted.

The Nickel Industry in New Caledonia, 1863–1945

Following the discovery of nickel in New Caledonia in 1863 by engineer Jules Garnier, the territory became the world's largest producer of the metal in subsequent decades, a position it lost only after exploitation of the vast nickel deposits of the Sudbury basin in Ontario, Canada, came fully online in the 1890s and early 1900s. Nonetheless, New Caledonia enjoyed a "nickel boom" from 1873 to the turn of the twentieth century due, in large part, to the entrepreneurialism of individuals such as Australians James Paddon and John Higginson, who recognized the industrial and commercial potential of New Caledonia's nickel and who, with the backing of mostly British and Australian capital, founded many of the territory's first mines and mining companies, including Société Le Nickel (SLN), established in 1876. Indeed, during this early period, the development of New Caledonia's mining industry depended heavily on foreign entrepreneurs and foreign capital, with French interests only gradually replacing British and Australian interests, which had dominated the industry initially.[1] The growing involvement of the Paris branch of the Rothschild family with SLN exemplifies this process: the Rothschilds first invested in this company in 1880 and by 1890 had taken a controlling interest in it. In subsequent decades, SLN came to dominate New Caledonia's nickel industry, controlling the bulk of the territory's richest mining concessions and operating its only smelters, particularly after its merger with Société Caledonia in 1931.[2] The French government introduced legislation in 1913 (amended in 1916 and again in 1924) to reduce the influence of non-French companies in New Caledonia by curtailing the mining concessions granted to them, yet legal constraints offer only a partial explanation for the gradual disappearance of foreign-owned companies from the territory.[3] Japanese nickel companies continued to purchase nickel ore from the territory's *petits mineurs* through the 1930s and well into the post-1945 years, but high production and transport costs, among other factors, discouraged direct foreign investment in the territory by the 1920s and 1930s.[4] Canada's International Nickel Company, for example, held concessions in the territory after 1902 thanks to the participation in its establishment by Caledonian-based companies; it sold these interests in 1926, however, focusing instead on its operations in North America and elsewhere.

By the 1930s, therefore, New Caledonia's nickel industry was focused around a single French company, SLN, with foreign companies' involvement in the industry restricted to the purchase of relatively small amounts of nickel ore from the territory's *petits mineurs*.[5] Though New Caledonia was by then no longer the most important source of nickel in the world, SLN enjoyed a largely comfortable and profitable existence within what had become its own little *chasse gardée*. Indeed, in addition to the slight legislative protection mentioned above, SLN's dominance of New Caledonia's industry received even greater protection from a gentleman's agreement reached with the International Nickel Company of Canada (INCO) in 1932. This agreement, negotiated in part with the help of the French government, essentially divided the global nickel market between the two companies, with INCO agreeing not to compete with SLN for much of the European market, a situation that also allowed SLN to charge a higher price for nickel in Europe than was charged by INCO, the industry's price-setter, in North America.[6] But in guaranteeing SLN's position in Europe, INCO also indirectly guaranteed its position in New Caledonia, confirming that the world's largest nickel company had no interest in mining or refining nickel in the territory. During the Second World War, a further agreement with INCO and the Australian and American governments helped keep SLN's smelter at Doniambo running at full capacity, with a guaranteed market for its nickel matte despite the loss of much of SLN's traditional market to German occupation during the war.

The Evolving Political Economy of the Nickel Industry in the 1940s and 1950s

SLN entered into the post-1945 period firmly and comfortably ensconced at the centre of New Caledonia's nickel industry, politically and legally abetted and financially subsidized by governments in both France and the territory, and bolstered through the informal protection of INCO, the industry's dominant company. Despite the difficulties it experienced during the war, SLN remained the world's third largest nickel producer and a key component of France's plans for postwar industrial recovery. And yet the storms were gathering. During the 1940s and 1950s, changes were beginning to take effect in both New Caledonia itself and within the global nickel industry that ultimately eroded SLN's unchallenged position as the dominant, indeed the only, major nickel company to exploit the riches of New Caledonia's vast nickel reserves. In New Caledonia, public opinion was turning against SLN, despite the jobs it provided in its mines and smelter and the financial contribution it made to the territory's coffers. By the 1950s, many Caledonians were demanding that its "soulless monopoly" of the territory's nickel industry be broken.[7] Externally, the global nickel industry was evolving rapidly from the small "gentleman's club" that had characterized it in the prewar period. More companies, new technologies, and the seemingly sudden availability of reserves in new parts of the world dramatically altered the dynamics of the industry. In New Caledonia, the convergence of these two factors, beginning in the 1950s, touched off a momentous and acrimonious debate about the role of foreign investment in New Caledonia's nickel industry.

Within New Caledonia, SLN's "public relations" problems stemmed from the company's dominance of almost all facets of life in the territory – political, economic, and otherwise. Although Caledonians appreciated the high standard of living that they enjoyed thanks to SLN and its operations, they nonetheless harboured a great deal of resentment towards the company. The source of this resentment generally lay in the widespread belief that the company exploited New Caledonia's rich natural resources for its own advantage, returning insufficient economic and other benefits to its people after repatriating the company's large profits to France for the benefit of its shareholders, mainly the Rothschilds. Moreover, many Caledonians greatly resented the company's tremendous political influence in Paris and Nouméa, the territorial capital, which enabled it to maintain its dominant position in New Caledonia.[8] This influence, and its status as a virtual monopoly, also gave the company the ability to solicit, perhaps even extort, financial or other concessions from metropolitan and/or territorial authorities – from reductions in export duties in the late 1940s to assistance with the construction of a dam at Yaté in the mid-1950s, for example – all in the name of maintaining the viability/prosperity of the company and, through it, the territory's nickel industry.

Opposition to SLN and its position/influence in New Caledonia was not a recent phenomenon, but it gained momentum with the establishment of a new political party in the territory in the early 1950s. Under the leadership of Frenchman Maurice Lenormand, the Union Calédonienne, founded in 1953, emerged as the most forceful and effective critic of SLN and its virtual monopoly over New Caledonia's nickel industry, particularly once it gained control of the territory's executive branch of government in 1957.[9] Lenormand's and his party's criticism of SLN did not scuttle all new territorial subsidies for the company's operations – the Territorial Assembly did grant some fiscal concessions in 1956 and 1960 – but the company faced much more serious political opposition in the late 1950s and early 1960s than it ever had before in New Caledonia. By the early 1960s, even many of the company's traditional allies and supporters, including Gaullist and ultraconservative senator Henri Lafleur, had joined the Union Calédonienne in opposing SLN's continual demands for concessions and subsidies. When SLN returned to the Territorial Assembly in 1964 with a renewed request for tax exemptions to help finance its ongoing program of expansion, the assembly baulked. With SLN having reported record, and rapidly growing, net profits in the 1960s, many of the territory's elected officials openly wondered why the company could not finance its expansion itself (when it obviously had the resources to do so) without further imposing on the public purse. Increasingly exasperated with SLN's demands, many Caledonians came to the conclusion that, until its monopolistic position in New Caledonia's nickel industry was broken, the territory and its people would be at SLN's mercy.[10] What was needed, they decided, was new investment in the industry.

Not coincidentally, Caledonians reached this conclusion at the same time that foreign/non-French mining companies began displaying renewed interest in New Caledonia's nickel reserves. The postwar nickel industry had changed dramatically from the early twentieth century when INCO and SLN had "constituted a world oligopoly" that controlled most of the world's reserves of nickel, produced most of the world's nickel, and shared the market between them, especially after INCO's merger with Mond Nickel in 1928 made it by far the world's biggest and most important nickel company.[11] INCO in particular became so large and so dominant in the industry, a position only reinforced by the Second World War and the misfortunes suffered by its competitors (including SLN and Falconbridge Nickel), that, in the late 1940s, the American government unsuccessfully pursued anti-trust proceedings against the company. Frustrated in that effort, the US government nonetheless had a significant effect on the structure of the nickel industry in the early 1950s with a two-pronged decision to begin stockpiling nickel and (concerned about INCO's near monopoly on production of this newly classified strategic mineral) to encourage competition in the industry by entering into supply contracts with companies such as Falconbridge, paying a premium of forty cents over the market price for 100 million pounds of nickel, a subsidy of $40 million to the smaller Canadian company. Thus encouraged, and in response to the increased demand for military armaments stimulated by the outbreak of the Korean War in 1950 and the broader rearmament that accompanied it in NATO countries in particular, as well as growing demand for nickel in civilian industries (stainless steel, automotive, aeronautical, etc.), a host of new companies entered the nickel industry in the 1950s, including Sherritt Gordon in Canada; Amax, Kaiser, Freeport Minerals, and Hanna Mining in the United States; and eventually Japanese and Australian companies as well.[12] Though INCO remained the industry leader, its position began to erode under this increased competition: it produced 85 percent of the world's nickel outside the Soviet/Communist-bloc in 1950 but only two-thirds by 1960 and 50 percent by 1970.

At the same time, new technologies facilitated a geographical expansion within the industry, which had previously focused mostly on exploiting the sulphide ores in colder countries like Canada. Thanks in large part to a refining process developed and fairly widely licensed by Sherritt Gordon, however, the new entrants into the nickel industry began to turn their attention to the world's reserves of lateritic nickel in more tropical regions, including Guatemala and Indonesia. Falconbridge was the first of the nickel companies to expand into these more tropical regions with a major purchase of nickel mines in the Dominican Republic in 1955 financed, in part, with the subsidies provided to it by the US government. Yet very quickly other companies followed suit, and by the 1960s the geographical focus of the nickel industry was shifting away from Canada.[13] Faced with the long-term erosion of its market position, with rising costs and diminishing reserves in its traditional Canadian base, even mighty INCO was compelled by the 1960s to explore international projects as a way to shore up its dominance of the global nickel industry.[14]

In short, by the end of the 1950s, the nickel industry was undergoing a process of fairly rapid evolution characterized by a growing number of participants in the form of increasingly multinational mining companies, a more level technological playing field, and fierce competition for access to and control of the world's nickel reserves, especially the tropical laterite ores that constituted some 80 percent of all nickel reserves. In an industry that was already globalized – Falconbridge, for example, mined its ores in Canada yet refined them in Norway while INCO had refineries in Canada, Wales, and the United States – the 1960s and 1970s witnessed a vigorous and aggressive internationalization. Gone were the days when a gentleman's agreement could divide the global nickel market between companies for their mutual benefit. Instead, the nickel industry became highly competitive, geographically dispersed, and interdependent, though it was still largely dominated by multinational companies from developed countries. With such extensive nickel reserves – up to 25 percent of the world's total – it was inevitable that New Caledonia would attract significant attention from international mining companies in this new, more globalized environment. However, the various industry stakeholders in New Caledonia, including the French government, SLN itself, the *petits mineurs*, and territorial leaders in and embodied by the Territorial Assembly, responded very differently to the challenges and opportunities of this new environment.

Clashing Views on Investment in New Caledonia's Nickel Industry in the 1960s

For SLN, the postwar years represented an unprecedented opportunity to expand and modernize its production to meet the growing demand for nickel in the years after 1950. Accordingly, beginning in 1953, it embarked on an ambitious program of expansion that, by the early 1960s, saw the number of its employees double to more than 3,000, its production of nickel matte more than quadruple to 26,000 from 6,000 tons, and its share of world nickel production rise from 10 to 18 percent.[15] Between 1964 and 1966, the company developed plans to expand even further, doubled and then doubled again to up to 100,000 tons annually, by building a new generating plant and enlarging the capacity at its Doniambo smelter. It ran into difficulties, however, as previously discussed, when it sought public assistance to help finance this expansion. The French government was not the source of SLN's problems; despite some misgivings about SLN's dominance of New Caledonia's economy and, especially, the antagonism that many Caledonians felt towards it, the French authorities generally supported SLN's expansion on the grounds that it would ultimately benefit the territory as a whole.[16] Instead, it was Caledonian leaders who increasingly objected to SLN's plans, and their opposition, most famously articulated in a detailed memorandum adopted almost unanimously by the Territorial Assembly in July 1966 that roundly criticized SLN, proved to be a formidable obstacle to the implementation of the company's planned expansion.[17] In particular, from 1963 through 1966, the assembly refused to vote for the tax breaks and other concessions that the company felt it needed to make its 1960s round of expansion economically feasible. Instead, the assembly, backed by most of the *petits mineurs* – some of the territory's wealthiest and most influential individuals[18] – and the territory's press, insisted that the prosperity of New Caledonia's nickel industry depended on breaking SLN's monopoly and opening it to new investment, particularly from foreign companies.[19]

This insistence on permitting foreign investment in New Caledonia's all-important nickel industry contributed to a political crisis that played out in the territory over the course of the 1960s, with important political and economic consequences for New Caledonia as a whole. Increasingly concerned about the political leanings and intentions of the leadership of the Territorial Assembly – the Union Calédonienne routinely triumphed in territorial elections from the mid-1950s to the early 1970s – the French government moved to strengthen its control over the territory by stripping the local authorities of most of the power they had been granted just a few years before. In 1956, the French National Assembly had responded to growing nationalist agitation throughout the French Empire by enacting a series of reforms, known as the *loi-cadre Defferre*, which devolved significant responsibility for economic and social policy, including the regulation of natural resources, to the elected assemblies and representative bodies in the French colonies. Through the *loi-cadre*, New Caledonia, like other French colonies, had gained important measures of autonomy from French rule, including, notably, the right to have the members of the executive branch of the territorial government selected from and by the elected members of the Territorial Assembly.[20] In 1959, however, just three years after the passage of the *loi-cadre*, the French government began reversing the liberal thrust of its reforms in New Caledonia by depriving the territory's head of government, the Union Calédonienne's Maurice Lenormand, of his power over the police, the civil service, and communications in the territory. Then, in December 1963, the National Assembly in Paris passed the Jacquinot Law, which transformed the governing council of New Caledonia's Territorial Assembly, of which Maurice Lenormand had been the head, from an executive into a consultative body and restored executive authority to the territory's appointed governor. Five years after that, the National Assembly passed another series of laws – the Billotte Laws – that removed even more powers from the Territorial Assembly, including responsibility for issuing mining permits.[21] In essence, over the course of the 1960s, the French government reasserted its control over New Caledonia's political and economic development despite the bitter protests of most Caledonians. Whereas France's other colonies and territories obtained greater autonomy or even their independence from France in the 1950s and 1960s, New Caledonia had been recolonized.

Differences between Nouméa and Paris over the role of foreign investment in New Caledonia's nickel industry offer only a partial explanation for the controversial recolonization of the territory that occurred in the 1960s. Equally important, the French government deprived the Territorial Assembly of many of its powers for fear that the Union Calédonienne's stated commitment to autonomy for New Caledonia masked its true intention of pursuing the territory's ultimate independence from France, though in fact the two issues were inextricably linked. The French were concerned about the ultimate loyalty to France of Maurice Lenormand and his colleagues in the Union Calédonienne, while these individuals, though denying any ulterior motive, did anticipate that economic diversification through foreign investment would help loosen the stranglehold that, between them, SLN and Paris held over New Caledonia and its political and economic development.[22] Yet, clearly, the recentralization of political powers was also designed in large part to give the French government maximum control over the development of New Caledonia's nickel and broader mining industries. Since the local authorities – principally but not exclusively the Union Calédonienne – could not be trusted to keep foreign interests from penetrating the nickel industry, control over it had to be restored to Paris to ensure that the industry developed in line with French policy and French interests.

Consistent with its approach to most industrial endeavours in the post-war period, the French government's response to the internationalization of the nickel industry beginning in the 1950s was to promote and support a French company as a "national champion" capable of competing and prospering in the international market. In this case, it already had such a champion in SLN, the second or third largest global producer of nickel and a key partner in French industrial development. SLN still supplied France with 72 percent of its nickel in the 1960s.[23] Moreover, this was a company that enjoyed deep and close ties with the French political and business establishment – Georges Pompidou, prime minister of France from 1962 to 1968, was a former executive with the Rothschild-owned bank that controlled SLN, for example – and that could be relied upon to promote French interests in New Caledonia and elsewhere. It was for this reason that the French authorities supported SLN's controversial program of expansion and modernization in the early to mid-1960s.[24] After all, a prosperous nickel industry benefited both New Caledonia and France, but, as Charles de Gaulle warned Caledonians when he visited in September 1966, the territory's rich mineral resources could not be developed outside the "national interest" of France itself.[25] And if, as happened by 1966, the French government recognized that SLN's monopoly of New Caledonia's nickel industry could not be maintained because so many Caledonians were hostile towards it, then it insisted that any new company established in the territory also had to be French.

Through SLN, preferably, or even through the establishment of a second major French company in New Caledonia's nickel industry, France expected to retain an important stake, albeit a minority one, in a vital global industry dominated by (North) American companies. For French officials such as Jacques Foccart, de Gaulle's influential foreign policy advisor, any penetration of New Caledonia's nickel industry by non-French companies would only weaken French interests, particularly if INCO, by far the world's largest nickel producer, began to operate in New Caledonia, as so many Caledonians hoped it would, in the 1960s. According to Foccart, INCO already enjoyed a quasi-monopoly on global nickel production; giving it access to New Caledonia's rich reserves of nickel would only strengthen its position in the global industry at the expense of French interests.[26] SLN itself made a similar argument in response to complaints from Caledonians about its own apparent monopoly of the industry there.[27] In effect, the French government and SLN argued that reserving access to New Caledonia's nickel reserves, and through them its broader nickel industry, for French companies was a crucial form of protection for SLN, French industry, and the broader French nation, including New Caledonia itself, against the overwhelming power and market influence of a dominant company like INCO. For Foccart and others, a company like INCO, with its price-setting power, its market access, its access to massive amounts of foreign capital, and its political influence in the United States, Canada, Britain, and elsewhere, would be next to impossible for the French government to influence or control once installed in New Caledonia.[28]

Moreover, Foccart, Georges Pompidou, and Charles de Gaulle himself worried that once in New Caledonia, (North) American nickel companies, INCO or others, would inevitably facilitate not only the penetration of American economic interests into the French Pacific but also American political and cultural influences as well. For individuals who remembered vividly the American presence in New Caledonia during the Second World War – the territory was home to the largest American naval base in the Western Pacific, the staging ground for much of the reconquest of the Pacific – and the difficulties that caused for France, including President Roosevelt's reluctance to endorse continued French sovereignty over the territory after the war, this was a bitter prospect.[29] Thus, the only way to preserve the French character of New Caledonia over the long term, they felt, was to insulate it from the pervasive and pernicious influence of American companies.

From the French perspective, therefore, the postwar expansion and internationalization of the nickel industry created opportunities for France and for French companies like SLN but it also created the risk that, unprotected, French industry would not be able to compete with its mostly American competitors. Not surprisingly, many Caledonians did not see the situation in quite the same terms. For them, the internationalization of the nickel industry presented a variety of opportunities, notably: (1) to break SLN's monopoly on the territorial industry as well as the political and economic influence that went with it; and (2) to maximize the benefits New Caledonia derived from the exploitation of its vast mineral resources. To many Caledonians, it seemed, the best way to do this was to allow foreign investment to develop and modernize the industry and expand its global reach. Foreign investment, therefore, was something to be welcomed, not feared. Protectionism, in contrast, had enabled SLN to develop into a coddled, inefficient, and technologically outdated company unwilling or incapable of developing the industry without relying heavily on public assistance.[30] With no real competition in New Caledonia, with almost exclusive access to the best of the territory's nickel reserves, SLN had very little incentive either

"*In the National Interest*" 221

to develop the industry fully – by developing the technology to exploit lower-content nickel ores, for example – or to maximize the economic and social benefits the territory and its inhabitants derived from its operations. And without competition in the industry, the territorial government had no real leverage over SLN and would remain hostage to its continual demands.

Caledonians felt that opening New Caledonia's nickel industry to foreign investment and competition would contribute enormously to its modernization and its expansion. Between 1966 and 1967, when the debate about the nature and structure of New Caledonia's nickel industry reached its peak, New Caledonia's press engaged in an extensive discussion of the benefits and costs of foreign investment. With only a few exceptions – the Rothschild-owned and thus SLN-affiliated newspaper *La France Australe* being the most notable – the territory's press enthusiastically supported allowing foreign companies to enter New Caledonia's nickel industry. Doing so, it argued broadly, would revitalize the industry, providing new outlets in particular for the territory's *petits mineurs;* it would provide jobs for the territory's workers and especially its youth; it would bring prosperity and (some small) diversification to the territory's economy and increase the revenues received by the territorial government; it would introduce new technologies to the industry, especially ones enabling the development of New Caledonia's extensive reserves of low-grade laterite ores; and it would give Caledonian nickel access to new markets around the world, including in the United States, that would position the New Caledonian industry to take advantage of the boom in demand.[31] Keeping New Caledonia closed to foreign investment, on the other hand, would see the nickel boom pass the territory by as companies like INCO pursued opportunities elsewhere – the press made a big point of the discovery of a major nickel body in nearby Australia, for example – leaving the territory saddled with an inefficient, backwards industry. The choice facing New Caledonia, stated one letter writer in *Le Journal Calédonien,* was simple: either the industry welcomed foreign investment and thereby integrated fully into the modern global nickel industry or it stagnated.[32]

These conflicting attitudes towards foreign investment on the part of stakeholders in Paris and Nouméa were not unique. In broad terms, though the situation is hardly as binary as it seems, they replicated a decades-long debate about the merits of globalization and free trade that has been going on around the world between advocates who see them as vehicles for prosperity and those who worry about the loss of sovereignty, national (or local) interest, and/or local control that they entail. In New Caledonia, the debate was complicated by the colonial relationship that existed between the territory and the French government, or was re-imposed on the former by the latter between 1963 and 1968, yet even there the positions staked out by the opposing sides did not remain static. Indeed, the years following the late 1960s witnessed more of a convergence in their attitudes towards foreign investment, with the French government gradually warming to the idea of allowing non-French companies to operate in New Caledonia's nickel industry, while over the years many Caledonians became more sceptical about the benefits and more concerned about the social, economic, and/or environmental costs of foreign investment.

Converging Views on Investment in New Caledonia's Nickel Industry Post-1968

Ironically, it was SLN itself that initially undermined the argument for keeping New Caledonia closed to foreign companies. As part of its expansion program announced in 1965, SLN entered into a partnership with the American company Kaiser Aluminum. Though neither a merger nor a full joint venture – the principal benefit to SLN came through Kaiser's agreeing to market SLN's products in the United States – it nonetheless represented an implicit acknowledgment on the part of the French company that, in light of the ongoing internationalization of the nickel industry, it too needed foreign assistance to reach its full potential, an irony not lost upon its Caledonian critics. At that point, the French government still insisted that SLN was the best option for the further development of New Caledonia's nickel industry, even if it began to waver on whether it was the only option. Within several years, however, it had begun to change its mind, albeit reluctantly. By late 1966, public pressure from within the territory compelled the government to announce that a second company would be allowed to operate in New Caledonia, though it insisted that this company too had to be French. When no such company or combination of companies could be enticed to enter the industry – highlighting a flaw of an industrial strategy that relied on national champions – the government again yielded and permitted foreign involvement in the new company, though only on a minority basis. This development led to the establishment in 1969 of a company called COFIMPAC, with the Canadian multinational INCO holding a 40 percent stake and the rest owned by a consortium of the French government geological agency BRGM and French companies, including Ugine-Kuhlman, the Banque de l'Indochine, the Banque nationale de Paris, and the Compagnie financière de Paris et des Pays-Bas.[33] Through COFIMPAC's ownership structure and a variety of other requirements, such as the company being based in Paris and the French government holding a veto over the nomination of the company's president, it was clear that the French government had no intention of allowing foreign interests to exert influence on New Caledonia via this new company, a commitment the government reaffirmed by its concomitant final passage of the Billotte Laws stripping control over the mining industry from the Territorial Assembly of New Caledonia.

COFIMPAC ultimately collapsed in 1972, a casualty, at least in part, of its complicated ownership structure, which proved too fragile to withstand the end of the global nickel boom in the early 1970s. One by one, unable to provide their share of the company's funding under the gloomier conditions of the end of the boom, the French investors withdrew. Even the French government's BRGM had earlier sought to reduce its stake in the company. Caledonian critics blamed the French government and its officials in the territory for the collapse of COFIMPAC, pointing to their palpable hostility towards INCO and foreign investment in general as key factors, and renewed their opposition to the Billotte Laws and the lack of local control over the mining industry.[34] Indeed, frustration with the constraints of French rule – of which the Billotte Laws were a major component – contributed directly to the emergence of a full-fledged independence movement in New Caledonia in the 1970s.[35] It took until the 1980s and the outbreak of nationalist violence in New Caledonia, however, to convince the French government to restore a greater degree of autonomy to the territory, leading to the conclusion of the Matignon Accord in 1988 and the subsequent Nouméa Accord of 1998, by which New Caledonia secured fairly comprehensive self-government.[36] Throughout this period, foreign investment remained minimal in the territory's mining industry, though the French government did relax its restrictions somewhat, and INCO, for one, remained forever hopeful that it would be allowed to operate on its own.[37] Overall, though the French government demonstrated a greater openness to free trade and foreign investment beginning in the 1970s,[38] it was not until after the advent of self-government in the late 1980s that New Caledonia's new provincial governments began reaching agreements with companies such as INCO and Falconbridge regarding the development of the Goro and Koniambo reserves, respectively.

For their part, Caledonian stakeholders maintained their overall enthusiasm for foreign investment as a means to develop the territory's nickel industry from the 1970s into the 1990s. For many of them, including in particular the emergent Kanak nationalist movement, foreign investment was a useful and necessary tool for economic development, but it was also, as it had been in the 1960s, tied closely to their political aspirations for autonomy and even independence from France.[39] Even so, that enthusiasm began to be tempered fairly early on by growing scepticism about the actual benefits and/or the potential costs associated with further development of the nickel industry by foreign companies. One of the earliest examples of this growing scepticism can be found in a report prepared by Roland Caron, member of the Territorial Assembly and secretary of the SOENC, the largest of New Caledonia's unions, following his visit to INCO's mines and smelters in Sudbury, Ontario, in July 1971. Having heard and believed for so long that INCO would bring a new era of prosperity and technological progress to New Caledonia, Caron had been shocked and dismayed by the environmental degradation, safety and health problems, and other issues he witnessed in Sudbury.[40] INCO, or foreign investment in general, Caron had learned, would be no magic elixir for the problems that beset New Caledonia and its nickel industry, an assessment reinforced by INCO's decade-long operation (from the late 1970s to the late 1980s) of the mine at Tiebaghi, which experienced the same types of labour unrest, industrial accidents, and health and environmental concerns as did most mining or other industrial projects. The more that INCO operated in New Caledonia, in fact, the less it seemed like a saviour to many Caledonians.[41] By the time that it finally obtained approval in the 1990s to proceed with its Goro nickel project, INCO faced a torrent of criticism from environmental groups, non-governmental organizations, Kanak groups, community activists, and others that significantly and adversely affected the project's implementation.

Conclusion

The internationalization of the nickel industry beginning in the late 1950s had a significant effect on New Caledonia, touching off a profound debate about the merits and desirability of foreign investment in the territory, particularly during the key period from the 1960s to the early 1970s. Fearful of the potential loss of sovereignty and of the state's ability to promote the "national interest," the French government actively resisted the installation of foreign companies in New Caledonia's nickel industry. Doing so, however, aroused the hostility of many Caledonians, who viewed foreign investment as key to diversifying and modernizing the territory's economy, breaking the power of the Société Le Nickel, and increasing local self-government. In this response, Caledonians differed significantly from the general pattern established in the post-Second World War period, when

"In the National Interest"	225

peoples and governments in colonial territories and newly independent or developing countries viewed global capitalism with suspicion and resisted the incursions of multinational corporations into their national economies.[42] New Caledonia also differed from most if not all other colonial territories or developing countries during this period in that it alone neither gained nor asserted greater regulatory control over its natural resources, instead actually seeing its regulatory powers over mining and natural resources reduced significantly by the French state from the late 1950s to 1969, despite vociferous protests from within Caledonian society.

In the end, the French authorities were largely able to prevent foreign investment from penetrating New Caledonia until the late 1980s but only by reasserting political control over it, in effect recolonizing the territory after it had been granted a significant degree of autonomy in the 1950s, a development that further antagonized much of the territory's political leadership and population and helped inaugurate a full-fledged independence movement by the early 1980s. The regulation of New Caledonia's mining industry and strict French controls over access thereto played a key role in the territory's political evolution in the late twentieth century, but it was only after Caledonians secured self-government again between 1988 and 1998 that foreign companies were truly welcomed into the territory. By that time, however, much of the early enthusiasm for them had waned in the face of growing environmental and societal concerns about the impact of mining.

Notes

1 Virginia Thompson and Richard Adloff, *The French Pacific Islands: French Polynesia and New Caledonia* (Berkeley: University of California Press, 1971), 244.

2 By the early 1950s, SLN produced 70 to 80 percent of New Caledonia's nickel; it controlled the biggest and richest mining concessions in the territory; and its exports of nickel generated the vast majority of the territory's export and tax revenues. See Pierre Legoux, *Première note d'orientation sur un Plan de Développement minier du Territoire de la Nouvelle Calédonie*, 13 April 1964, Centre des archives contemporaines (CAC), Ministère de l'Industrie, vers 19771394, art 33, dossier 3.

3 It was fairly easy, for example, to circumvent the law through the establishment of a subsidiary based in New Caledonia or even in France itself.

4 Thompson and Adloff, *French Pacific Islands*, 408.

5 *Petits mineurs* literally means "small miners," though this is a very misleading term. By the mid-twentieth century, the term had come to designate those mining companies that did not themselves process or refine the ore they produced, depending instead upon SLN's smelter at Doniambo for processing or, for example, simply exporting raw ore for refining in Japan. The *petits mineurs*, however, included or were

owned by some of the wealthiest and most influential individuals and families in New Caledonia, including Senator Henri Lafleur, Édouard Pentecost, and Maurice Lenormand, and at times mined up to 30 or 40 percent of New Caledonia's nickel ore. See Yann Bencivengo, "Petits mineurs," in *101 mots pour comprendre: La mine en Nouvelle-Calédonie*, ed. Yann Bencivengo (Nouméa: Éditions Île de Lumière, 1999), 167–68.

6 Thompson and Adloff, *French Pacific Islands*, 403–4. It has been argued that INCO agreed to concede the European market to SLN in order to preserve its market position in North America until such time as the world economy, and demand for nickel, rebounded. It is equally possible, however, that the agreement was inspired at least in part by INCO's anti-trust concerns. The agreement allowed SLN's global market share to increase to 17 percent from 10 percent, thereby reducing the perception of INCO's dominance of the industry.

7 John Connell, *New Caledonia or Kanaky? The Political History of a French Colony* (Canberra: National Centre for Development Studies, Australian National University, 1987), 124 or 30–31.

8 Édouard Pentecost, one of the greatest of the *petits mineurs*, accused many French officials, including the high commissioners in Nouméa (the territorial governors), of having sold themselves to SLN at the expense of the territory's interests. See A. Lafond, *Note au sujet du rapport sur "les positions de M. Edouard Pentecost,"* 28 November 1966, CAC, DOMTOM, vers 19840122, art 2, dossier 3.

9 In 1956, the French National Assembly passed a *loi-cadre* enacting a series of reforms to the administration of France's colonial empire. Intended to allow the inhabitants of the colonies more influence over their internal affairs, thereby, it was hoped, nullifying calls for full independence, the *loi-cadre* replaced New Caledonia's appointed governing council with elected members of the Territorial Assembly, or self-government, as it is known in the tradition of the British Commonwealth and its self-governing dominions.

10 Thompson and Adloff, *French Pacific Islands*, 408.

11 Jorge Niosi, *Canadian Multinationals*, trans. Robert Chodos (Toronto: Garamond Press, 1985), 86.

12 Ibid., 87–88.

13 Following its displacement of New Caledonia as the centre of the nickel industry in the early twentieth century, Canada had produced up to 80 percent of the world's nickel through the mid-twentieth century. By 1979, however, Canada's share of global nickel production had fallen to 28 percent. See Niosi, *Canadian Multinationals*, 88.

14 For a discussion of INCO's "internationalization" in the 1960s and 1970s, see J.H. Bradbury, "International Movements and Crises in Resource Oriented Companies: The Case of INCO in the Nickel Sector," *Economic Geography* 61, 2 (1985): 129–43.

15 Thompson and Adloff, *French Pacific Islands*, 405.

16 In the mid-1950s, an analysis by the French Senate concluded that, after all, "a healthy metallurgical industry in New Caledonia is better than no industry at all." See France, minutes of the National Assembly, 27 August 1954, as cited in Thompson and Adloff, *French Pacific Islands*, 407.

17 Jean Le Borgne, for one, detailed his criticism of SLN in his memoir. Le Borgne was a Union Calédonienne minister who served on New Caledonia's governing council in the late 1950s and early 1960s. See Jean Le Borgne, *Nouvelle-Calédonie, 1945–1968: La confiance trahie* (Paris: L'Harmattan, 2005).

18 See note 5 above.

19 In March 1965, for example, just as the Territorial Assembly was due to consider another of SLN's requests for assistance, *L'Avenir Calédonien* (the official organ of the Union Calédonienne) carried an editorial whose title stated that the installation of new mining and metallurgical companies was the key to New Caledonia's development and its future. See "Le Développement de la Nouvelle Calédonie par l'installation de nouvelles entreprises minières et metallurgiques reste la clé de notre avenir," *L'Avenir Calédonien*, 22 March 1966, 1.

20 For a further discussion of the *loi-cadre* and its effects on French colonies, see Robert Aldrich and John Connell, *France's Overseas Frontier: Départements et territoires d'outre-mer* (Cambridge: Cambridge University Press, 1992), 65–69; Robert Aldrich, *France and the South Pacific since 1940* (Honolulu: University of Hawaii Press, 1993), 33–75.

21 Connell, *New Caledonia or Kanaky?*, 253.

22 For an exploration of this point, see Robin S. Gendron, "At Odds over INCO: The International Nickel Company of Canada and New Caledonian Politics in the 1960s," *Journal of the Canadian Historical Association* 20, 2 (2009): 112–36.

23 Thompson and Adloff, *French Pacific Islands*, 405.

24 For a discussion of the evolution of postwar French industrial policy, in particular the French state's policy of focusing on successful enterprises or "national champions," see Matthias Kipping, "Les relations gouvernement-monde des affaires dans la France de l'après-guerre: Adaptations et adaptabilité d'un système original," *Histoire, Économie et Société* 20, 4 (2001): 577–96.

25 *Allocution prononcée par le Général de Gaulle, Président de la République, à l'Assemblée Territoriale de la Nouvelle Calédonie le 5 septembre 1966*, Archives territoriales de la Nouvelle Calédonie (ATNC), vers 32J (Lenormand Papers), Numéro d'Ordre 24.

26 Jacques Foccart, *Tous les soirs avec de Gaulle: Journal de l'Elysée, 1965–1967* (Paris: Librairie Arthème Fayard/Jeune Afrique, 1997), 656–57.

27 Jean Guillard, Société Le Nickel, Remarques sur le memorandum approuvé par l'Assemblée Territoriale de Nouvelle Calédonie le 7 juillet 1966 et concernant le développement de l'industrie du nickel et les projets d'implantation de nouvelles usines de traitement par des firmes franco-étrangères, 26 July 1966, CAC, Industrie, vers 19771394, art 33, dossier 3.

28 Foccart, *Tous les soirs avec de Gaulle: Journal de l'Elysée, 1965–1967*, 353.

29 See Kim Munholland, *Rock of Contention: Free French and Americans at War in New Caledonia, 1940–1945* (New York: Berghahn Books, 2005), 165–67.

30 This argument formed a substantial part of the memorandum criticizing SLN that was passed almost unanimously by the Territorial Assembly in July 1966. See "Le fait de la semaine: Ce mémorandum adopté par l'assemblée," *Le Journal Caledonien*, 12 July 1966, 2.

31 For an example of the discussion in the Caledonian press on this subject, see "L'I.N.C.O., ce monster qui fait palir la Kaier Aluminium et la Sté Le Nickel," *Le Journal Caledonien*, 13 September 1966, 5.

32 "De M.H.M. (Nouméa)," *Le Journal Caledonien*, 5 April 1966, 6.

33 Gendron, "At Odds over INCO," 132–33.

34 The 1973 election campaign for New Caledonia's deputy in the National Assembly focused in part on the culpability of the French government in COFIMPAC's demise. The winning candidate, the UC's Roch Pidjot, was returned to Paris with instructions to seek the repeal of the Billotte Laws. Se HAUSSAIRE to MEDETOM, 6 April 1973, CAC, DOMTOM, vers 19940218, art 15, dossier 6.

35 On the emergence of this independence movement, see David Chappell, "The Black and the Red: Radicalising Anti-Colonialism in 1970s New Caledonia," *Journal of Pacific Studies* 27, 1 (2004): 49–62.

36 David Chappell, "The Nouméa Accord: Decolonization without Independence in New Caledonia," *Pacific Affairs* 72, 3 (1999): 373–91.

37 In the 1970s, INCO was allowed to mine nickel at a previously closed chromite mine at Tiebaghi in the north of New Caledonia's main island. According to Roland Gilbert, the former Director of INCO's subsidiary in New Caledonia, INCO very much considered this operation a form of placeholder, keeping INCO in New Caledonia while it attempted to renegotiate its access to the Goro nickel reserves in the south that had been part of the COFIMPAC concessions. Roland Gilbert, telephone interview with the author, 23 April 2012. Still, as noted by many observers, the French state remained intent on preserving control of New Caledonia's nickel industry. Chappell, "Nouméa Accord," 383.

38 See Kipping, "Les relations gouvernement-monde des affaires dans la France de l'après-guerre."

39 On this point, see Leah S. Horowitz, "Towards a Viable Independence? The Koniambo Project and the Political Economy of Mining in New Caledonia," *Contemporary Pacific* 16, 2 (2004): 287–319.

40 "Report on my trip to Toronto and Sudbury," n.d., personal papers of Roland Caron, with the permission of his family.

41 This view was expressed by Laurent Chatenay, a former executive with INCO Océanie, among others. Laurent Chatenay, interview with the author, 19 December 2011.

42 This dynamic both inspired and was inspired by the "dependency theory" of economic development in developing countries that has been elaborated since the late 1940s by scholars such as Andre Gunder Frank and Immanuel Wallerstein. See, for example, Andre Gunder Frank, "The Development of Underdevelopment," *Monthly Review* 18, 4 (1966): 17–31; Immanuel Wallerstein, *World-Systems Analysis: An Introduction* (Durham, NC: Duke University Press, 2004).

PART 3

GROWING INTERNATIONALIZATION OF RESOURCE POLICY

10

Regulating the Regulators

The League of Nations and the Problem of Raw Materials

MATS INGULSTAD

The Great Crash sent economic and political shockwaves around the world. As governments trembled and international trade dropped, with tariffs and agitators on the rise, there was also hope that a new economic order could emerge from the wreckage of the old. Arthur Salter, for many years the director of the economic and financial section of the League of Nations, even suggested that the crash provided an especially favourable moment to eliminate a competition for raw materials as a primary cause of war.[1] The seemingly counter-intuitive argument was premised on the need for a set of international rules that reduced the latitude for restrictive regulations on the national level. If raw materials became available on equal terms to the whole world, their political importance would dwindle, thereby avoiding armed conflicts over natural resources. Purchasing power would replace firepower.

The history of the League of Nations and its activities related to international regulation of the production and distribution of raw materials remains little explored.[2] In part, this is due to the relative obscurity of the League of Nations and its economic work, which recently has developed into a vibrant field of scholarly inquiry.[3] The new international history looks past the League's failure to preserve the peace and investigates its role in matters like the handling of failed states, treatment of minorities, prostitution, drugs, and intellectual cooperation. As Susan Pedersen has noted, particularly in "its efforts to regulate cross-border traffics or problems of all kinds, it emerges rather as a harbinger of global governance."[4] As the well-springs of the international economic system that emerged after 1945 are traced back to the interwar period or even to the First World War itself, the League emerges from the mists as a vessel for experiments in international economic regulation. These experiments prefigured important phenomena like the commodity agreements sponsored by the UN Conference on Trade and Development or the advent of global multilateralized trade negotiations under the watchful eye of the World Trade Organization.[5]

This chapter investigates the attempts to develop an international regime for raw materials to be upheld by a universal organization. This was to a great extent an attempt to regulate how states regulated, setting the acceptable parameters for commercial and trade policies, such as the permissible extent of restrictions on exports and production. This global governance regime was also to determine the leeway for regulation between states and companies on the international level, particularly through the establishment of guidelines for producer cartels in the guise of international commodity agreements. The League's involvement in international economic regulation drew upon different strands of technocratic internationalism rooted in the experiments with raw materials controls during the First World War. These experiences placed the distribution and control of resources on the international agenda and further demonstrated that commodity markets and state policies could and should be regulated.[6]

The League of Nations marked a new departure in international regulation, replete with an internationalized civil service to monitor and nurture developments. It also embodied a new set of norms and rules for the behaviour of states in international political and economic relations more generally.[7] In the clash of ideas over how the world's resources were to be distributed, the League served as an arena, an actor in its own right, and was frequently portrayed as a serviceable apparatus for securing equal access. As the focal point for an international regulatory regime, it could help bridge the gap between enforcement of an open-door regime and the unconstrained sovereign right to determine the scale and scope of natural resource exploration.

Organizing for War, Preparing for Peace

The First World War introduced many changes in the manner in which raw materials were mobilized for war. This related not only to their uses on the battlefield but also to their production, pricing, and distribution behind the front lines. These processes occurred within individual states, which, on both sides, introduced new modes of organizing the flow of raw materials within their economies, often combining state direction and free markets in new ways.[8] The war also encouraged experiments that cut across state borders. Internationalized procurement and distribution were introduced through experimental forms of intergovernmental commodity organizations. The establishment of the inter-Allied international Wheat Executive in November 1916 served as a model for Allied cooperation on other raw materials, such as tin and nitrates. The formation of the Allied Maritime Transport Council in December 1917 heralded a further expansion of what became an intricate inter-Allied structure of committees, councils, and executives. These international bodies assessed requirements and supplies pertaining to many raw materials before allocating the necessary transportation capacity. Staffed by experts, they collected information on requirements and usage, bargained with neutral countries, and sought to regulate consumption, prices, and distribution. Their goals were to secure more resources for the Entente and to withhold them from Germany.[9]

Beyond emphasizing the advantages of coordinated trade in raw materials, the war also highlighted the enormous societal costs of losing access to natural resources. The lesson on the risks of import dependency still resonated after the end of hostilities. In Germany in 1915, Walther Rathenau, the head of the Raw Materials Division (*Kriegsrohstoffabteilung*, KRA), insisted that the war had fundamentally altered the political valuation of raw materials. The economic doctrine of protective tariffs was replaced by an evolving "doctrine of 'protection of raw materials."[10] On the other side of the no man's land, the Entente powers resolved at the Economic Conference in Paris in June 1916 "without delay to render themselves independent of the enemy countries in so far as regards the raw materials and manufactured articles essential to the normal development of their economic activities." This was to be achieved through recourse to subsidies, customs duties, and temporary or permanent prohibitions.[11] The French minister of commerce, Étienne Clémentel, was particularly eager to carve Germany out of the transnational value chains: "Germany was the mistress of foreign minerals which she converted on her territory ... The Allies are to-day in agreement not to leave any longer to others these raw materials essential to the life of a nation."[12] This ambition reveals not only just how crucial raw materials had become to the war capabilities of the modern state but also how trade barriers, substitution, export restrictions, and other ostensibly autarkic measures were imagined as political and economic weapons to enforce the victors' peace. Beyond the maintenance of anti-dumping measures against Germany after the war, Clémentel envisaged joint-Allied cooperation on the basis of joint control of raw materials, suggesting "the beginning of a new economic era, one which permits the application of new methods, founded on control, on collaboration, on everything that can introduce some order into the process of production."[13]

Ideas of the postwar regulation of raw materials were in broad circulation, even if they were by no means universally popular. France and Italy in particular pushed for continuing collaboration and maintenance of economic controls after the end of the war.[14] British eagerness to restore free markets was also tempered by the recognition that the maintenance of controls could prevent potential enemies from organizing a corner in various commodities. Even in Berlin, the hopes of carving out an autarkic territorial sphere in Europe had been balanced against fears of losing access to the world economy.[15] The prospective League became a natural point of convergence for such ideas. According to the statesman-general and strategist of imperial internationalism Jan Smuts, the success of the Allies in controlling and managing supplies naturally gave credence to the idea that a future League of Nations might have uses beyond preventing wars or punishing belligerency. It could also busy itself with the common economic needs of member nations, particularly in controlling food or raw materials that might be subject to shortages.[16] The Italians drew up a draft covenant for the nascent League of Nations that stated that international distribution of raw materials "must be controlled in such a way as to secure to every country whatever is indispensable to it in this respect."[17] These arguments were bolstered by the establishment of the Supreme Economic Council as a continuance of the wartime economic cooperation mechanism. The council maintained coordinated control over access to and distribution of raw materials necessary for the reconstruction of the war-torn continent.[18] Although its powers were limited, and the council proved politically unviable in the face of American opposition, its raw materials section was a forerunner for the League of Nations' involvement in economic and financial questions.

The ambitious European plans for postwar control of raw materials did not go down well in Washington. The US president, Woodrow Wilson, was initially intrigued when the prominent banker Thomas Lamont suggested a scheme for the maintenance of Allied raw materials and shipping control after the war, "a sort of international socialism on a grand scale." But there was substantial opposition from many US business and political elites. The director of the American Food Administration, Herbert Hoover, bluntly predicted that that the US "will not agree to any programme that even looks like inter-Allied control of our resources after peace."[19] In fact, Wilson had already embarked on another course with his programmatic Fourteen Points. The third point called for the removal of economic barriers and the imposition of "an equality of trade conditions among all the nations consenting to the peace."[20] Rather than maintaining and extending control over the markets, Washington wanted to depoliticize the world economy. Raw materials, goods, and capital, rather than armies, should cross borders. The refusal to let the League involve itself in the management of resources cast a long shadow. One of the leading lights of the interwar internationalist movement, Alfred Zimmern, fumed for many years about the opportunities that were lost when the Allied organizations were dismantled. He also lauded the Italian proposal for guaranteed access to raw materials as a safeguard for the of growth and prosperity even for states poor in natural resources. Zimmern saw in it a program of international social justice in which Karl Marx joined hands with Adam Smith: "The League of Nations is to guide 'the invisible hand' in order to minister to the needs of 'proletarian states.'"[21]

Strings on the Guiding Hand: Commercial and Colonial Issues in the Covenant

The competing ideas about the nature of a postwar trade regime became readily apparent during the drafting of the Covenant for the League of Nations. The French delegates proposed a series of measures related to equality of trade, including a ban on import and export duties on raw materials. The stated objective was "to put an end, as far as possible, to international rivalries in the search for raw materials, to suppress many of the causes of the economic conflicts that endanger the world's peace, and to offset the natural inequalities arising from the geographical distribution of resources."[22] To transform this objective into a legally binding obligation proved impossible. When the Americans proposed their own declaration on equality of trade conditions, the British countered with a very different pitch.[23] The heart of the matter was the sharply diverging ideas about equality, as evident in the separation between "sovereign units" and "economic units." The US proposal would enforce equal treatment in the non-discriminatory sense. This would leave every country free to establish the principles of its own economic policy as long as it did not discriminate between domestic and foreign nationals in any way, including in all colonies, mandates, and dependent territories. The British proposal, to American chagrin, limited the applicability to sovereign states, thereby preserving the ability to discriminate against foreign investors within the Empire.[24]

The conflict over principles of commercial policy was complicated by its intimate relationship to the colonial question. Among the spoils of war were the German and Ottoman colonies, placed under international jurisdiction through a system of mandates described in the Covenant's Article 22. Former Ottoman territories in the Middle East were designated as the A-class. They were slated for independence after a period of tutelage under one of the victorious Great Powers. The C-class mandates were territories with small or sparse populations, like German Samoa or Southwest-Africa, for which there were no prospects for independence in the foreseeable future. They could be administered directly under the laws of the mandatory power. The B-class mandates were comprised primarily of former German colonies in Central Africa, and for them the Covenant specified that the mandatory power had "secure equal opportunities for the trade and commerce of other Members of the League."[25] The entanglement with the question of rules for commercial policy raised the issue not only of how important colonial raw materials were to the metropolitan states but also of which legal principles were to guide the development of these resources.[26] For instance, Australia and New Zealand made it known that they wanted to annex Nauru due to its rich phosphate deposits. More interested in access than formal control, the US pushed particularly hard for an open-door policy to the A- and B-class mandates. While equal treatment was written into the Mandate Agreements for the B-class mandates like Tanganyika, it generally did not apply to A- and C-class mandates.[27]

The final outcome of negotiations over trade equality and the open-door principle in the colonies was that the only provisions targeting the postwar trade environment in raw materials were to be found in Article 23 (e) in the Covenant. This charged the members to conform to existing or future conventions to "make provision to secure and maintain freedom of communications and of transit and equitable treatment for the commerce of all members of the league."[28] The British even managed to insert an introduction to the article that robbed it of whatever power it might have possessed. As one contemporary observer remarked, "equitable treatment was left to individual interpretation, far from securing 'equality of treatment.'"[29] A similar fate befell the idea of creating a supranational authority to run all African and Ottoman colonies and supervise the exploitation of their resources.[30] The failure to settle the colonial and trade policy questions would haunt the League until its very end.

Quis custodiet ipsos custodes? The Initial League Involvement with Raw Materials[31]

The new-fangled League began its life without a clear mandate or the regulatory capabilities to intervene decisively in the raw materials field. But the immense problems of the reconstruction of Europe quickly forced it to take an interest in production and the distribution of resources. The undersecretary-general of the League, Raymond Fosdick, despaired of the situation: "Rotterdam is choked with cotton, and the Port of London is full of wool for which there are no buyers, because, although Europe is desperate for these materials, the unbalanced exchange makes it impossible for her to pay for them."[32] This was more than a local European problem. The economic interdependence of the world was increasingly salient as a systemic property, which also served as a constraint on the individual state.[33] In his influential study of the Paris settlement, John Maynard Keynes emphasized that the war had gravely disrupted the supply networks that fed a small number of industrial centres, a "delicate and immensely complicated organization, of which the foundations were supported by coal, iron, transport, and an unbroken supply of imported food and raw materials from other continents." Since these networks sustained the densest aggregation of population in the history of the world, the supplies had to keep flowing to maintain European living standards and stave off starvation. If not, he warned, civilization itself would be under threat: "Men will not always die quietly."[34]

The supply networks for many raw materials were transnational by their very nature. Consequently, many of the bountiful postwar crop of international organizations saw the League as the proper instrument for intervention. At the first Annual Session of the International Labour Organization (ILO) in 1919, the Italian Worker delegate Gino Baldesi urged the League to get a handle on the distribution of raw materials since shortages were driving unemployment. The motion was narrowly defeated. The majority expressed the view that such an intervention would interfere with the states' "absolute right to dispose freely of what belongs to them."[35] Nevertheless, the Baldesi motion became a reference point for subsequent debates and spawned many new initiatives to put the raw materials problem on the agenda for international action.[36] The first meeting of the International Chamber of Commerce in Paris subsequently passed a resolution to "put a stop to rivalries between nations in their search for raw materials" by recommending the abolition of export taxes.[37] In August 1920, the International Miners Congress also unanimously adopted a resolution to establish "an international office for the distribution of fuel, ores and other raw materials indispensable for the revival of normal economic life" with the assistance of the League.[38] In other words, League involvement to secure the circulation of raw materials was widely touted as necessary to restoring ordinary commercial activity, reducing unemployment, and avoiding the eruption of a new conflict. The raw materials problem affected social, economic, as well as political security in ways that made the League a natural node for international action.

League intervention in raw materials was no straightforward matter. Its economic mandate was nebulous at best. The British were especially emphatic in their opposition to League involvement, citing the vagueness of Article 23 as evidence that it lacked standing.[39] However, the League could not remain aloof if the peace itself was under threat. The international Congress convened by the League at Milano in mid-October 1920 adopted a resolution that the League should sanction the principle of abolition of restrictions and barriers of all natures to commercial exchanges, especially for essential raw materials.[40] The Council of the League also appointed a special committee led by the Italian statistician Corrado Gini to investigate the raw materials problem, including assessments of requirements, shortages, and eventual problems caused by monopolies withholding commodities from the markets. But before the Gini committee could report, the problem of urgent shortages disappeared: "the whole economic situation of the world has been revolutionised ... the outstanding fact as regards raw materials is no longer the difficulty experienced by consuming countries in securing supplies, but the difficulty experienced by producing countries in finding outlets for their products."[41] The Gini Report failed to address the intractable dilemma of whether there existed an equal right to access to resources in the territories of all states. The committee merely pitted the incontestable right of states to dispose freely of their raw materials output against the "no less incontestable" undesirability of restrictions on trade in raw materials, which could be used to "impose systematic inferiority" on those states dependent on imports.[42] The League concluded, on the basis of the Gini Report, that raw materials should not be hindered by restrictions or discriminatory regulations and that its supply mechanisms should not be allowed to "degenerate into methods of economic aggression."[43]

Rationalization of Trade in the Service of Peace and Reconstruction

While the most critical raw material shortages disappeared before the Gini Report appeared, the specific problems of pricing and supply were entangled with more general economic problems, such as those related to unemployment, transportation, and distribution. The League experts – particularly the officials with experiences from wartime supply work, like Bernardo Attolico or like Jean Monnet, the life-long schemer for international economic collaboration – continued to see raw materials issues and unemployment as vital problems that required further engagement.[44] One of the most vocal proponents was Arthur Salter, the long-time head of the League Economic and Financial Section, who made explicit the connection between his experiences with wartime commodity administration and the League. He hoped "that the league and the power which it is able to wield [would] be used tactfully, but with strength and resolution, to influence the economic policy of the different countries of the world in such a way as to reduce to a minimum the potential causes of economic disputes."[45] The Preparatory Commission for the League-sponsored Disarmament Conference in 1926 also noted that the political and military importance of raw materials was still considerable as, in order to wage war, any country had to "count upon the total organization of production which [would] include all the factors in the cycle, from raw materials to finished products."[46] Since, for most countries, these factors could not be controlled within national boundaries, the League seemed well suited to take on the tasks of ensuring the availability of resources and reducing their political salience.

The League and its officials drew heavily on the contemporary trends of internationalist beliefs and experiences, such as the concurrent development of international law. The ideas for natural resource regulation addressed an apparent demand for a more regularized form of cooperation on political, economic, and security issues.[47] The icon of interwar functionalist thought, David Mitrany, used the wartime requirements for raw materials as conclusive evidence for the need to develop "new methods of functional economic government." Since the mobilization of resources for war impelled development towards socialism, he professed bafflement at the fact that not all millionaires were conscientious objectors.[48] Several such strands of thought directly inspired League action on raw materials. The persistent idea that dependency on mutual trade could act as a guarantee against aggression pointed towards eliminating tariff barriers and forbidding discrimination against external trade. This was the attempt to foster what Joel Hurstfield called "the holocaust of controls," to return to the free trade practices of an earlier era.[49] Freeing up trade in raw materials had the added advantage that states that had not received mandates, such as Italy, could hope to be consoled by access to colonial resources on equal terms in the mandate territories.[50] For the League Economic and Financial Committee, interdependence and freedom of trade became "indispensable conditions for resumption of normal life." Therefore, further international cooperation was necessary to reduce trade barriers, and, particularly, Article 23 of the Covenant had to be implemented.[51]

The thinking on trade matters in Geneva cut deeper than mere rote recitals of arguments for free trade. It was also informed by an ideology of rationalization that sought to acknowledge the interdependency of the entire world and utilize it in service of the peace.[52] Statistics showing exports and imports of raw materials trade offered a powerful heuristic tool to describe the necessity of cooperation and integration. To the leading proponents of international regulation this suggested that a superstate would naturally follow from the "scientific fact of interdependence."[53] The rationalization ideology appealed to both the technocratic ethos and logos of the League officials, but it was by no means uniform. It comprised an ideal of productivity increases on the micro level through the application of scientific management and new technologies that would lead to cost reductions for the benefit of both consumers and producers.[54] At the macro level, it entailed support for cartels as measures for reducing cyclical price fluctuations and stabilizing the commodity markets by bringing better balance to supply and demand.[55] To realize these gains, the epistemic communities surrounding and encompassing the League's civil servants also dreamed of more internationalized, "possibly autonomous boards" running arrangements for everything from traffic, health, and distribution of raw materials in a manner similar to the Universal Postal Union. Such febrile hopes were stoked by visions that "humanity could be organized in a world society where men's minds are released from the stupid obsession with mutual carnage, and busy with achievements and dreams beyond our ken."[56]

While the most ardent supporters of the League saw rationalization as a third way between free trade and protectionism, there were many barriers to this imagined internationalist functionalism in the organization of raw materials trade.[57] The foremost was political. As the prominent geologist Charles Kenneth Leith put it: "Certainly the world has not reached the utopian condition where any nation can be expected to voluntarily yield up to any super-national body the ownership of a part of its resources."[58] Furthermore, rationalization by way of League-sanctioned commodity cartels was bound to run into resistance from powerful consumers and competitors in addition to the compliance problems facing practically every cartel. The British Stevenson rubber scheme, for instance, suffered intense hostility

Regulating the Regulators 241

from other governments and consumer interests as well as competition from unaffiliated producers and smuggling.[59] While "cartel" was already an odious term in some countries, commodity cartels restricting the output of necessary resources seemed even more sinister. US secretary of commerce Herbert Hoover decried commodity cartels as a revival of "medievalism" that not only violated basic economic principles but also posed a grave national threat to the US.[60] The sheer obstinacy of the US critique earned a rebuke in a later League-sponsored study, which pointedly suggested to the vociferous non-member that the League's economic apparatus could facilitate exactly the type of international cooperation needed to combat such abuse of market power.[61]

The First Multilateral Advances against Trade Restrictions: League Summitry in the Late 1920s

As the idea for a League conference on raw materials supply, prices, and distribution gathered steam, there were different categories of solutions that suggested themselves to contemporary observers. As summarized by Chandler P. Anderson, the "nationalist solution" entailed an adjustment of political borders to allow every nation to be self-contained and self-supporting. The "socialist solution" required the establishment of an international organization on the lines of the wartime international executives to acquire raw materials throughout the world and to distribute them evenly among the members and according to their requirements. The "free trade solution" required the establishment of complete freedom in international trade, removal of all barriers, without contemplating common ownership by all nations. In its stead, this solution required imposition of limitations upon a state sovereignty, effectively limiting its freedom to regulate commercial policy regarding raw materials.[62] Since boundary adjustments and inter- and supranational regulation were out of the question, the League attempted to approach the raw materials problem in the context of general trade issues.[63]

The World Economic Conference of 1927 was held under League auspices in Geneva and clearly represented the "free trade" approach. The conference report warned that private international agreements in the commodity sector could encourage monopolistic tendencies and unsound business practices. This could check technical progress and hinder improvement of production processes that could improve quality and cut costs. It could also endanger the legitimate interests of important sections of society and of particular countries. Furthermore, the conference very definitely condemned export taxes, other export and import prohibitions, as well as privileges granted to state enterprises. The remedy was "free circulation of raw material as one of the essential conditions for the healthy industrial and commercial development of this world."[64] It was within this framework that the benefits of rationalization could accrue through international industrial agreements, although this latter point was rather vague and short on specifics.[65]

The subsequent Diplomatic Conference on Import and Export Restrictions later that year resulted in the first important international action affecting control in raw materials trade. Almost thirty states signed the Convention for the Abolition of Import and Export Prohibitions and Restrictions that charged the contracting parties to reduce current restrictions to a minimum and to refrain from imposing new ones.[66] On the coat-tails of the convention there were also separate agreements covering bones as well as hides and skins. They required the setting of uniform duty levels and the abolition of all import and export duties beyond nominal fees imposed for statistical purposes.[67] While the commodities regulated were themselves rather insignificant, there were hopes that the convention and the protocols would set precedents and generate momentum for international agreement on the basic principles on trade in raw materials.[68] The momentum never materialized. Due to expressed reservations and conditional ratifications the Convention on the Abolition of Import and Export Restrictions only came into effect in 1930 with seven adherents, and it was defunct by mid-1934.[69] While the League also made some headway against the use of quantitative restrictions, the overall impression of its first decade was bleak.[70] The League's three-year Economic Consultative Committee, which met in 1928 and 1929, also made proposals for collective action with regard to capping duties and concerted reductions on groups of commodities, but these were defeated by competing state interests. In retrospect, these efforts take on the appearance of rearranging the deck chairs on the Hindenburg, as the Great Crash was about to send the world economy down in flames.

Regulating Market and State Behaviour in Times of Crisis
The eruption of the Great Depression rekindled the hopes and desires for League intervention in the raw materials sphere.[71] Not only did the degree of state intervention in the economy increase but it also paved the way for more acceptance of market regulation. International trade seemed to be under threat as states imposed higher tariffs or imperial preferences to protect their home producers. Alongside falling demand, the effects on the commodity markets were immediate. Prices dropped so fast and so low that

the floor fell out from under many of the existing private commodity cartel and unilateral valorization schemes. The use of artificial price control and restriction on production and sale suddenly appeared as a necessity. Many industries abandoned their previous opposition to tighter regulation, hoping controls on trade and production could act as a panacea against the ills of the Great Depression.[72] This provided the League with a new field of activities to regulate as well as with more tolerance for intervention.

Commodity agreements as measures for global market rationalization particularly appealed to League officials and committed internationalists.[73] After all, they were essentially arrangements to regulate production, stocks, exports, markets, and prices of raw materials on an international basis, with a view to maximizing the utility of these resources. The participating states could then use regulatory tools like export controls, licensing, tariffs, or state-owned buffer stocks to influence price levels. Further, they could bring balance to supply and demand, thereby eliminating the economic and social costs associated with either over- or under-production. Commodity control agreements were not a new phenomenon: there had been several schemes in operation during the 1920s, like the Franco-German potash cartel. But after the onset of the Great Depression they became far more salient, with the conclusion of new agreements or the extension of existing agreements covering items like platinum, lead, and zinc. They also developed from either privately managed or unilateral affairs like the Indian jute or the Hawaiian pineapple schemes, from industry agreements with varying degrees of governmental support, or were created outright as fully-fledged intergovernmental agreements.[74]

In order to halt the rising tide of economic nationalism the League sponsored the London Monetary and Economic Conference in 1933, hoping to achieve nothing less than a revival of international trade, stabilization of commodity prices, and a restoration of the gold standard.[75] While the gold standard fiasco became the dominant feature of the conference, the price levels for non-monetized raw materials also garnered substantial interest. The Preparatory Committee of Experts called for increased international regulation of trade and distribution to deal with over-production prior to the conference. This prescription of more regulation was plainly incompatible with the usual bromides of trade barrier reductions. It also widened the conflict between the producing countries, who wanted higher prices to re-establish their purchasing power, and the consuming countries, who were reluctant to accept higher prices on the input factors for their hard-pressed industries.[76] The London Conference eventually produced agreement on a set of guidelines for the establishment of commodity agreements. They required that the commodity in question had to be important for world trade, that market conditions called for "special concerted action," that the greatest possible number of producers had to be included, and that the "product must lend itself as much as possible to international regulation." Furthermore, the agreement should be "comprehensive as regards the commodities to be regulated," meaning that related and substitute products should be included in order to avoid serious market dislocations. The price levels should be fair but remunerative.[77]

Viable candidates for international regulation were not lacking. There was already an international tin control scheme dating back to 1931, and the conference considered the regulation of several other commodities (such as copper). Partly due to the efforts of the London conference, the subsequent conclusions and revisions of international agreements covering tin, tea, rubber, and sugar came to differ from those of their predecessors. These new types of schemes were agreements between governments, operated by international agencies, and implemented by domestic legislation coming from the participating governments.[78] However, one feature remained constant: the commodity agreements were subject to the persistent criticism that they privileged producer interests.[79] This condemnation was not merely of a commercial nature but, rather, pointed to the deeper political and strategic rivalry that would eventually undo the League.

The "Have Nots" Have Their Day: The Failure of the Raw Materials Embargo

The governments of exporting nations busied themselves with interventions in the international commodity markets, and this provoked reactions from the major industrial nations that were reliant upon imports. Particularly, Italian, Japanese, and German diplomats fired repeated salvos of bombastic rhetoric about the lack of economic fairness. They cast themselves in the role of "have-not" states deprived of access to raw materials through increasingly tightly regulated markets. Their calls for access to raw materials were entangled with revisionist and expansionist demands for a territorial redistribution, either by the return of lost colonies or by the provision of mandates through the League. The British openly criticized the have-not thesis as a paradox. They suggested that raw materials were not in short supply or subject to restrictive regulations; rather, the problems stemmed from "eccentric" monetary and currency policies. Norman Angell, the Nobel Peace Prize-winning theorist of economic interdependency as an

Regulating the Regulators 245

antidote to war, caricatured the have-nots through poetic tautology: "Why do you need to go to war? To have raw materials within our borders. Why do you need to have them within your borders? In order that we may go to war."[80]

The demands for colonial materials, and particularly Mussolini's threats against Ethiopia, created an increasingly strained atmosphere in Geneva.[81] Foreign Secretary Samuel Hoare therefore went before the General Assembly to reaffirm British support for the League and warned that Great Britain would resort to sanctions if Italy did not halt its policy of aggression. Hoare also suggested that an international effort to provide for equitable access to raw materials could assist in removing the underlying causes of war. This proposal met with approval in Washington, which considered Great Britain to be the motivating force in the imposition of restrictions and control of essential raw materials and now hoped that London would change its course.[82] Mussolini was not swayed by the offer of an international settlement on raw materials as a substitute for colonial expansion. Rather than dispatching his diplomats to Geneva, he marched the Italian army into Ethiopia. This blatant aggression by one member against another compelled a response from the League. Due to Italy's trumpeted dependence on raw materials, an embargo could provide a crucial test case for the utility of sanctions. But the prospective League-enforced embargo on oil, coal, steel, and pig iron to Italy fell apart. France and Britain needed Italy's support against a resurgent Germany, while the Roosevelt administration was constrained by strong neutralist sentiments at home.[83] A relieved Mussolini later remarked to Hitler that minerals sanctions would have forced Italy to retreat within a week.[84] The first attempt at implementing multilateral economic sanctions, using threats to sever the raw materials supply overseen by a universal organization, failed ignominiously. It proved beyond a doubt that the Covenant of the League was a paper shield against determined military aggression.

Rather than ending the debate on the importance of raw materials for the maintenance of national war potential, the Italian triumph stimulated it. For instance, Corrado Gini, the author of the League's 1921 report on raw materials, had spent the intervening years closely aligning himself with the fascist regime.[85] He now explicitly ruled out a supranational bureaucratic allocation of resources through the League as a solution to the international problem of raw materials. Hoare's offer was a mere Platonic manifestation of good will as "there does not seem to be any possibility of an equitable re-distribution of population and raw materials without the use or at least the threat of force."[86] The German minister of the interior, Wilhelm Frick, availed himself of the Ethiopian crisis to demand the return of the German colonies as a precondition for Germany's return to the League.[87] Reich finance minister Hjalmar Schacht seconded him and accused the Great Powers of disregarding the fact that the many controls, cartels, and trade barriers had made access to raw materials a political rather than an economic question. Schacht also warned that, "despite all her love of peace," Germany might be forced to follow the example of Italy and Japan. These powers had solved their problems despite the League rather than through it, and they had managed to lift themselves into the ranks of the haves.[88] Without the prospect of resource embargoes, the question was whether economic appeasement could restrain the jingoistic adventurism of the have-nots.

"An Atmosphere of Extreme Pessimism": The League's Raw Materials Inquiry

The Hoare proposal fell flat due to lack of interest on the part of the Axis powers. Nevertheless, in 1936, Foreign Secretary Anthony Eden again put the proposal before the General Assembly, which, in turn, instructed the council to appoint a commission to inquire into the question of "equal commercial access for all nations to certain raw materials."[89] Undeterred by press reports that suggested Germany and Italy would not participate, the League Council appointed a special committee consisting of members from the League Economic and Financial Committees, along with a group of experts invited in a personal capacity. The Secretariat compiled a memo containing the most frequently debated issues pertaining to raw materials. These included the familiar suggestions for abolition of trade obstacles, a general open-door policy in all colonial territories, admittance of consumer representatives to controlling bodies of certain cartels, and conclusion of international agreements for distribution of raw materials.[90] The more radical suggestions included the transformation of existing colonies into mandates and the introduction of international supervision over raw materials distribution. The most ambitious ideas envisioned international organization of the distribution of raw materials coupled with international control, placing the administration of the existing colonies under international authority, the creation of specially chartered companies to extract resources, an international bank to facilitate payments for resources, and/or an international mines and forests trust administered by the League.[91] While

Secretary-General Joseph Avenol claimed to have no views of his own on these matters, the prominent place awarded to colonial questions in conjunction with the raw materials question ensured that the inquiry caused considerable alarm.[92]

The Secretariat's memorandum condensed the many competing ideas for the extensive and wide-reaching internationalization of raw materials offered by academics, government officials, and internationally oriented activists of many stripes. The committee experts, however, quickly assumed their roles as champions for their respective national interests. For instance, the British privately could see the utility of having Japan add to the world's resource base by tapping ores in underdeveloped areas, but, naturally, political and strategic considerations militated against it.[93] The British representative, Fredrick Leith-Ross, defended the imperial preferences with development rhetoric that prefigured the postwar justification for continued colonial rule. Enforcement of open-door policies might "be harmful to the development of the colonies and even to the welfare of the natives." Brazil faithfully spoke for the producers and stressed the problem of falling prices, while Portugal discounted the value of the colonies. The Polish representative was a forceful exponent for the have-nots, while the Soviet representative mocked the countries that "had no money to pay their trade debts but who had enough to prepare guns for the launching of a future war." The ILO assistant director dismissed the demand for territorial adjustment as the solution to the raw materials problem, "for one would not find one even by exchanging whole continents." Finally, the Czech representative disregarded "any super-nationalization [sic!] of essential raw materials that at the present time would be still less realizable than it was at the time of the 1921 enquiry when these proposals were termed utopian and unrealizable."[94] In short, the committee deliberations brought more than a decade of competing ideas into sharp relief, but any possibility for a workable compromise was hard to see.

Given the political volatility of the colonial question, the raw materials committee singled out supply and payments as the issues that warranted investigation by special subcommittees. The supply committee found hardly any instances of export restrictions detrimental to the interest of the consumers. While some import-dependent states imposed export restrictions, the committee did not wish to contest the view that a country had "first call on its own resources for the benefit of domestic industry." On the other hand, imposing export restrictions to exert political pressure was clearly unacceptable. The committee noted that it had not found, nor had it received word of, any specific instances of such restrictions, even though "the impression undoubtedly prevails that the possibility of such abuses exists."[95] What is more, the committee did not raise any serious objections to the proliferation of cartels and intergovernmental regulatory schemes geared towards market stabilization.[96] The subcommittee on payments had the politically delicate task of pronouncing on exchange policies, widely seen as tools of political encroachment, economic domination, and military rearmament for the Axis powers.[97] However, other self-identified have-nots also criticized the tendency to dismiss raw materials problems as a function of exchange policies. The Polish representative likened it to assuring a starving beggar that the baker's shop was full.[98] The subcommittee nevertheless struck a direct blow at both Japan and the notably absent Germany by concluding that the restoration of normal monetary conditions would "automatically diminish" the difficulties experienced by "certain countries." It also argued the case for abolishing clearings. One of the few points of agreement in the subcommittee was the need for a revival of the 1927 Convention for the Abolition of Import and Export Prohibitions and Restrictions.[99]

The League released the raw materials report in September 1937 with approval from the General Assembly. The committee generally advocated freer flows of trade and credit, but it also noted that "governmental regulation schemes relating to raw materials now in operation, have, generally speaking, been an important factor in the improvement of economic conditions."[100] It downplayed the problem of supply restrictions and highlighted the problem of payments policies. As Patricia Clavin has noted, the conclusions were toned down to avoid having the "three naughty powers react against the League."[101] It is questionable whether this concession to political realities made any difference. The Japanese representative had already warned that "to be quite frank, the raw material question can never be settled satisfactorily without an equitable redistribution of territories."[102] The report challenged this view by stating that only 3 percent of all commercially important raw materials originated in the colonies, which became a staple statistic in subsequent rebuttals to Axis demands for colonial readjustment.[103] The German response was immediate and strident. Adolf Hitler used one of the most ideologically supercharged festivals in the Nazi calendar, the *Erntedankfest*, to engage with the key arguments advanced in the report. He ridiculed the colonial powers for their refusal to return the allegedly worthless colonies to their rightful owners, thereby making a mockery of the modesty and morality supposedly embodied in the League.

He further trumpeted that Germany could not buy what it needed since it was robbed of its purchasing power under the Versailles Treaty. Consequently, it needed to supplement the German *Lebensraum* with colonial territories, no matter what foreign statesmen might have to say about the matter.[104]

Final Invitations from the Great Purchasing Powers

The dim prospects for international cooperation did not stop the League experts in the Economic Committee from formulating a set of principles for raw materials trade in its December 1937 report to the council. The officials suggested that raw materials should not be subject to export prohibitions or restrictions, except under international regulation. Duties should only be levied purely for revenue purposes or to finance industrial development schemes. The principle of non-discrimination should apply: foreign investors should have the same rights and facilities as the inhabitants of both sovereign and colonial territories, although with special provisions to safeguard the interest of native inhabitants in the latter. Any international regulation schemes had to admit effective representation of consuming interests and make information about their operations available. Such schemes had to be designed to keep prices stable, but not excessive, while ensuring adequate supplies.[105] The General Assembly noted these guidelines with approval and urged further study and consultation with a view to implementation. Meanwhile, Secretary-General Avenol invited the interested governments to submit their observations on whether the time was ripe for international action on raw materials and, if so, what form it should take. He thus played the ball directly back into the hands of the national governments.

The British government was the original driving force behind the raw materials inquiry, but its initial response to Avenol's invitation was cautious. Whitehall adopted a wait-and-see stance while asserting that it already conformed to the recommendations. This earned Chamberlain a sharp rebuke in the House of Lords, where there were eager advocates for setting up an economic equivalent to the ILO to address the raw materials problem. They chastised Chamberlain for "fiddling while Rome burns down the rest of the world."[106] As the replies from other governments slowly trickled in it became apparent that the prospects for a multilateral solution were poor. Japan and Poland called for action, but most other governments expressed their reservations or doubted whether the time was ripe.[107] Even the League's Economic Committee concluded that the multilateral path was impassable and instead urged bilateral commercial agreements as the most likely means to effect progressive reduction of export and exchange restrictions, quotas, and customs tariffs. As the US consul wryly commented, although the atmosphere of "extreme pessimism" gradually lifted from Geneva, there was little talk and no action on raw materials.[108] The reason so many governments preferred to postpone or outright ignore the call for a conference or a convention on raw materials was clear enough. There were no discernible indications that either Germany or Italy would offer anything in exchange for the concessions they demanded.[109] This was not a problem with the League per se. A similar fate befell the attempt by former Belgian prime minister Paul van Zeeland to bypass the League and broker a reduction in economic aggression by way of great power diplomacy. Zeeland eventually suggested international control over the colonies, an open-door system modelled on Belgian practices, with privileged and impartial companies to supply raw materials in exchange for industrial goods. These arrangements would fall primarily under the League mandate commission. The response was overwhelmingly negative, perhaps in part because it was hard to accept the notion of Belgium providing an example of colonial best practices.[110]

An international settlement of raw materials problems remained a diplomatic conversation piece until the eve of the Second World War. After the German invasion of rump-Czechoslovakia, Roosevelt asked Mussolini and Hitler to offer guarantees that there would be no more violations of territorial integrity. In return, Roosevelt would take part in talks to open up international trade, based on the familiar argument that if all nations could buy and sell on equal terms then they would have no difficulty in securing resources for the maintenance of their economic life.[111] As a rehash of the Hoare proposal and the League recommendations, it had scant chances of going down well in Rome and Berlin. Hitler scathingly retorted that if the US believed so much in international conferences, why had it not itself become a member of the League? He then provided the answer: "in almost twenty years of the activity of the greatest conference in the world, the League of Nations, it has proved impossible to solve one single decisive international problem."[112] Mussolini was perhaps even more uncharitable as he labelled the initiative "a result of progressive paralysis."[113] While the raw materials problem and international regulation remained a topic for discussion thereafter, there would be no more attempts to grapple with the problem at an international level.[114] The League's own experts could merely warn that a new war would create severe pressure on the available resources and express hope for the free exchange of products and commodities in the postwar world.[115]

Conclusion: Regulators, Mount Up!

In late 1918, the German industrialist and statesman Walther Rathenau proposed "an economic administration of the world" charged with placing raw materials at the disposition of all nations on the same terms. At the time this sounded remarkably similar to ongoing discussions in Paris, Rome, and Washington, but by the end of the 1930s these suggestions were summarily dismissed as a "contribution to Utopian literature."[116] Nevertheless, the idea of reorganizing the global political economy on natural resources thrived surprisingly well throughout the interbellum period. From the later stages of the First World War, the distribution of raw materials was a key concern for the idealists that took upon themselves the task of articulating the organizational principles for regulation at the national and the international levels. The experience of mobilization for war provided a key reference point for the debates on how to manage the peace, and the doctrine of rationalization provided a powerful lens through which the League experts observed patterns in market and state behaviour.

The League served as an arena for debate as well as a canvas upon which different solutions were projected. Beyond its contributions to identifying and diagnosing the problems of raw materials distribution, the multivalent League stood out as the means for solving the many intractable problems related to natural resources. Whether this entailed colonial redistribution, new rules for prohibition of trade restrictions, or the reorganization of entire industries on a global level, the League could be pressed into service as a vehicle for turning aspiration into reality and ambition into regulation. The League served as a natural lightning rod for suggestions to guarantee raw materials supplies as a remedy against starvation and unemployment or for securing investment to exploit untapped ore beds in underdeveloped territories. Many of the various ideas for reducing the threat of war over natural resources also cast the League in the role of a mediator or even of a supranational arbiter. But as the work of the raw materials committee revealed, in the increasingly charged political atmosphere of the late 1930s the League also provided a low-resistance path to the ground for these high-flying ideas. As appealing as the doctrines of international socialism, technocratic supranationalism, or free trade liberalism might have sounded, there was simply no political space for international regulatory solutions, whether in the context of reintegrating or disintegrating markets.

Even as the League failed as a platform for the implementation of a transnational raw materials diplomacy, the ideas that developed during its troubled lifespan quickly resurfaced in the postwar world. The United

Nations oversaw a series of international commodity agreements, such as the international wheat agreement in 1949, followed by tin in 1953, sugar in 1954, coffee in 1962, cocoa in 1972, and finally rubber in 1980.[117] While the League's espousal of commodity agreements was a direct predecessor of the initiatives of the UN Conference on Trade and Development, there were also substantial differences in how the League and the UN would relate to the Third World. A widely shared assumption in the interwar period was that if lesser-developed territories possessed resources of potential importance to the industrialized nations, then they had to be exploited for the benefit of the rest of the world, no matter what Indigenous peoples thought. This approach was inherent in the League's mandate system and underpinned the global order in the interwar period. Despite all the continuities, the postwar UN system would become the forum for a new and radical approach, premised on the idea that the people inhabiting a territory retained the supreme right to decide how resources were to be exploited. The UN's adoption of the Principle of Permanent Sovereignty over Natural Resources in 1962 created new sets of regulatory challenges in addition to inter- and intrastate conflicts. The functionalist utopia of well-regulated commodity markets and well-behaved states engaged in peaceful exchange of natural resources remained as distant as ever.

Acknowledgment
The author would like to acknowledge the generous assistance of the Gerda Henkel Stiftung.

Notes
1 Arthur Salter, *The Causes of War: Economic, Industrial, Racial, Religious, Scientific, and Political* (London: Macmillan, 1932), 20.
2 A few recent exceptions are Michael Fakhri, *Sugar and the Making of International Trade Law* (Cambridge: Cambridge University Press, 2014); Marta Petricioli, "Raw Materials and Peace," in *For Peace in Europe: Institutions and Civil Society between the World Wars*, ed. Marta Petricioli and Donatella Cherubini (Brussels: Peter Lang, 2007), 94–103.
3 Patricia Clavin, *Securing the World Economy: The Reinvention of the League of Nations, 1920–1946* (Oxford: Oxford University Press, 2013). See also Antoine Fleury, "The League of Nations: Towards a New Appreciation," in *The Treaty of Versailles: A Reassessment after 75 Years*, ed. Manfred Boemeke, Gerald Feldman, and Elisabeth Glaser (Cambridge: Cambridge University Press, 1998), 507–23; Patricia Clavin and Jens-Wilhelm Wessels, "Transnationalism and the League of Nations: Understanding the Work of Its Economic and Financial Organisation," *Contemporary European History* 14, 4 (2005): 465–92.

4 Susan Pedersen, "Back to the League of Nations," *American Historical Review* 112, 4 (2007): 1091–117, at 1092. See also Mark Mazower, *Governing the World: The History of an Idea, 1815 to the Present* (London: Penguin, 2012), 153.

5 Yann Decorzant, *La Société des Nations et la naissance d'une conception de la régulation économique internationale* (Brussels: Peter Lang, 2011).

6 Wolfram Kaiser and Johan Schot, *Writing the Rules for Europe: Experts, Cartels and International Organizations* (London: Palgrave, 2014).

7 Klaas Dykmann, "How International Was the Secretariat of the League of Nations?," *International History Review* 37, 4 (2015): 721–44.

8 Wolfgang Michalaka, "From War Economy to 'New Economy': World War I and the Conservative Debate about the 'Other' Modernity," in *Germany, in War, Violence, and the Modern Condition*, ed. Bernd-Rüdiger Hüppau (Berlin: De Gruyter, 1997), 77–98.

9 British Embassy to Balfour, 6 December 1918, The National Archives (hereafter TNA), Kew; War Trade Board to British Embassy, 30 November 1918, FO382-1910, TNA, Kew; Arthur Salter, *Allied Shipping Control: The Allied Maritime Transport Executive* (Oxford: Clarendon Press, 1921); Chandler P. Anderson, "International Executives," *American Journal of International Law* 13, 1 (1919): 85–88; Bernard Baruch and Richard Hippelheuser, *American Industry in the War: A Report of the War Industries Board (March 1921) besides a Reprint of the Report of the War Industries Board of World War I* (New York: Prentice-Hall, 1941), 153ff, 66ff.

10 Walther Rathenau, "Address of Walther Rathenau before the German Society, 1914, on 'Germany's Provisions for Raw Materials,'" in *Fall of the German Empire, 1914–1918*, vol. 2, *Documents of the German Revolution*, ed. Ralph Lutz (Stanford: Stanford University Press, 1932), 77–91.

11 UK Board of Trade, *Recommendations of the Economic Conference of the Allies, Held at Paris on June 14, 15, 16 and 17, 1916* (London: H.M. Stationary Office, Harrison and Sons, 1916).

12 US Department of State, *Foreign Relations of the United States, 1916: Supplement, The World War* (1916), 977–81.

13 Adam Tooze, *The Deluge: The Great War and the Remaking of Global Order* (New York: Viking, 2014), 290.

14 Royal Commission on Wheat Supplies to the Treasury, 29 July 1919, TNA, T 1, 12435; Memorandum of the Italian Delegation, 3 November 1919, TNA, T 1, 12435.

15 Peter Yearwood, "'Real Securities against New Wars': Official British Thinking and the Origins of the League of Nations, 1914–19," *Diplomacy and Statecraft* 9, 3 (1998): 83–109.

16 Jan Smuts, *The League of Nations: A Practical Suggestion* (London: Hodder and Stoughton, 1918), 7–8.

17 David Hunter Miller, *My Diary at the Conference of Paris, with Documents*, vol. 1 (New York: Printed for the author, 1924), 355.

18 Yann Decorzant, "Internationalism in the Economic and Financial Organization of the League of Nations," in *Internationalism Reconfigured: Transnational Ideas and Movements between the World Wars*, ed. Daniel Laqua (London: I.B. Tauris, 2011), esp. 117.

19 William Keylor, "Versailles and International Diplomacy," in *The Treaty of Versailles: A Reassessment after 75 Years*, ed. Manfred Boemeke, Gerald Feldman, and Elisabeth Glaser (Cambridge: Cambridge University Press, 1998), esp. 498n110; Wilton B. Fowler, *British-American Relations 1917–1918: The Role of Sir William Wiseman* (Princeton: Princeton University Press, 1969), 209–13.

20 Dennis Merrill and Thomas Paterson, *Major Problems in American Foreign Relations*, vol. 2, *Since 1914* (Boston: Wadsworth Cengage, 2009), 34–36.

21 Alfred Zimmern, *League of Nations and the Rule of Law, 1918–1935* (London: Macmillan, 1936), 156–59.

22 Harold Temperley, *A History of the Conference of Paris*, vol. 5 (Oxford: Oxford University Press, 1924), 68.

23 David Hunter Miller, *My Diary at the Conference of Paris, with Documents*, vol. 2 (New York: Printed for the author, 1924), 162–67.

24 US Department of State, *Foreign Relations of the United States*, 1919, the Paris Peace Conference, 511–14; David Hunter Miller, *The Drafting of the Covenant*, vol. 2 (New York: G.P. Putnam's Sons, 1928), 16–22.

25 Covenant of the League, art. 22. See "The Covenant of the League of Nations with a Commentary Thereon, Presented to Parliament by Command of His Majesty, June 1919," League of Nations Archive (hereafter LoNA), Geneva, S 585.

26 Susan Pedersen, *The Guardians: The League of Nations and the Crisis of Empire* (Oxford: Oxford University Press, 2015).

27 Anthony Anghie, "Colonialism and the Birth of International Institutions: The Mandate System of the League of Nations," in *Imperialism, Sovereignty and the Making of International Law* (Cambridge and New York: Cambridge University Press, 2004), 141–44.

28 "The Covenant of the League of Nations with a Commentary Thereon, presented to Parliament by Command of His Majesty, June 1919," LoNA, S 585.

29 Temperley, *History of the Conference of Paris*, 5:68.

30 Mazower, *Governing the World*, 168.

31 "Who will guard the guards themselves?": Juvenal, *Satire 6*, 345–50.

32 Raymond Fosdick, "The League of Nations Is Alive," *Atlantic Monthly* 125, 6 (1920): 845–53.

33 Manfred Berg, "The Concept of World Economic Interdependence," in *Genoa, Rapallo, and European Reconstruction in 1922*, ed. Carole Fink, Axel Frohn, and Jürgen Herideking (Cambridge: Cambridge University Press, 1991), 77–93.

34 John Maynard Keynes, *The Economic Consequences of the Peace* (Harcourt: Brace and Howe, 1920), 227.

35 International Labour Office, *Papers Relating to Schemes of International Organization for the Distribution of Raw Materials and Foodstuffs. Studies and Reports B*, 2 (Geneva: International Labour Office, 1920).

36 M. Stencek, memorandum on meeting, 19 December 1921, LoNA, R1199.

37 Benjamin Wallace and Lynn Edminster, *International Control of Raw Materials* (Washington: Brookings Institution, 1930), 322–27.

38 International Labour Office, *The Miners International, Geneva 2–6 August 1920. Studies and Reports A, 7* (Geneva: International Labour Office, 1920).

39 Harold Greaves, *The League Committees and World Order: A Study of the Permanent Expert Committees of the League of Nations as an Instrument of International Government* (London: Oxford University Press, 1931), 54–55.

40 Corrado Gini, *Report on the Problem of Raw Materials and Foodstuffs* (Geneva: League of Nations, 1921).

41 Report to the Council on Certain Aspects of the Raw Materials Problem by the Economic Section of the Provisional Economic and Financial Committee, 21.09.1921, LoNA, R369.

42 Quoted in Wallace and Edminster, *International Control of Raw Materials*, 325.

43 Societé Des Nations, Les Rapports de La Commision Èconomique et Financière Provisioire, Rapport Présenté par la deuxième Commision, 24,09.1921, LoNA, R369.

44 Bernardo Attolico to Eric Drummond, Jean Monnet, and Frank Nixon, 26 November 1921, LoNA, R1199.

45 Salter, *Allied Shipping Control*, 268.

46 Preparatory Commission for the Disarmament Conference, Subcommission B, Report 1, 30 November 1926, LoNA, R 282.

47 Mazower, *Governing the World*, 151.

48 David Mitrany, "Interrelation of Politics and Economics in Modern War," *Annals of the American Academy of Political and Social Science* 192 (1937): 82–88.

49 Joel Hurstfield, "The Control of British Raw Material Supplies, 1919–1939," *Economic History Review* 14, 1 (1944): 1–31.

50 Petricioli, "Raw Materials and Peace," 103.

51 League of Nations, the reports of the Provisional Economic and Financial Committee Report submitted by the Second Committee, 26 September 1921, LoNA, R369.

52 Jo-Anne Pemberton, "New Worlds for Old: The League of Nations in the Age of Electricity," *Review of International Studies* 28 (2002): 311–36.

53 Harold Greaves, *Raw Materials and International Control* (London: Methuen, 1936).

54 Eugene Staley, *Raw Materials in Peace and War* (New York: Council of Foreign Relations, 1937), 9.

55 Michael Fakhri, "The 1937 International Sugar Agreement: Neo-Colonial Cuba and Economic Aspects of the League of Nations," *Leiden Journal of International Law* 24, 4 (2011): 899–922.

56 Charles Howard Ellis, *The Origin, Structure and Working of the League of Nations* (Boston: Houghton Mifflin, 1928), 86, 476. Authorship is often attributed to Konni Zilliacus of the League's Information section. See James Cotton, "'The Standard Work in English on the League' and Its Authorship: Charles Howard Ellis, an Unlikely Australian Internationalist," *History of European Ideas* 42, 8 (2016): 1089–104.

57 Greaves, *Raw Materials and International Control*; Greaves, *League Committees and World Order*.

58 Charles Kenneth Leith, "The Political Control of Mineral Resources," *Foreign Affairs* 3, 4 (1925): 541–55.

59 Shakila Yacob, *The United States and the Malaysian Economy* (New York: Routledge, 2008), 95–97.

60 Joseph Brandes, *Herbert Hoover and Economic Diplomacy: Department of Commerce Policy, 1921–1928* (Pittsburgh: University of Pittsburg Press, 1962), 76–80.

61 League of Nations, *Raw-Material Problems and Policies* (Geneva: League of Nations, 1946), 45.
62 Chandler P. Anderson, "International Control and Distribution of Raw Materials," *American Journal of International Law* 19, 4 (1925): 739–42.
63 Karl Kapp, *Memorandum on the Efforts Made by the League of Nations towards a Solution of the Problem of Raw Materials* (Geneva: International Institute of Intellectual Co-operation League of Nations, 1937), 65.
64 "Report of the World Economic Conference Adopted on May 23, 1927," *Annals of the American Academy of Political and Social Science* 134 (1927): 174–206.
65 Louis Pauly, *The League of Nations and the Foreshadowing of the International Monetary Fund* (Princeton: International Finance Section, 1996), 18.
66 "International Convention for the Abolition of Import and Export Prohibitions and Restrictions," *League of Nations Official Journal* (May 1928): 728.
67 League of Nations, *Raw-Material Problems and Policies*, 47.
68 Lynn Edminster, "Control of Exports of Raw Materials: An International Problem," *Annals of the American Academy of Political and Social Science* 150, 1 (1930): 89–97.
69 Bob Reinalda, *Routledge History of International Organizations: From 1815 to the Present Day* (New York: Routledge, 2009), 256; Pawan Arora, *Material Management* (New Delhi: Global India Publications, 2009), 177.
70 Martin Hill, *The Economic and Financial Organization of the League of Nations: A Survey of Twenty-Five Years' Experience* (Washington: Carnegie Endowment for International Peace, 1946), 46–51.
71 Wallace and Edminster, *International Control of Raw Materials*, 233.
72 J.W.F. Rowe, *Markets and Men: A Study of Artificial Control Schemes in Some Primary Industries* (Cambridge: Cambridge University Press, 1936), 18–19.
73 Fakhri, "1937 International Sugar Agreement."
74 League of Nations, *Raw-Material Problems and Policies*, 50; International Labour Organization, *Intergovernmental Commodity Control Agreements* (Montreal: ILO, 1943).
75 Rodney Morrison, "The London Monetary and Economic Conference of 1933: A Public Goods Analysis," *American Journal of Economics and Sociology* 52, 3 (1993): 307–21.
76 Kapp, *Memorandum on the Efforts Made by the League of Nations*, 84–88.
77 Extract from the Report of the Economic Commission of the London Monetary and Economic Conference on the work relating to the coordination of production and marketing, approved by the conference 27 July 1933, Appendix A in ILO, *Intergovernmental Commodity Control Agreements*.
78 Kurt Wilk, "International Affairs: International Administrative Regulation: The Case of Rubber," *American Political Science Review* 36, 2 (1942): 323–37.
79 Kenzō Hemmi, "International Commodity Agreements: Reality and the Future," *Developing Economies* 2, 4 (1964): 358–72.
80 Norman Angell, *This Have and Have-Not Business: Political Fantasy and Economic Fact* (London: H. Hamilton, 1936), 133.
81 "Il Duce Again Blocks League Peace Effort," *Chicago Daily Tribune*, 11 September 1935.

82 Herbert Feis, "Sir Samuel Hoare and International Commodity Controls," 13 September 1935; Feis to Moore, 16 September 1935; Feis to Hull, 12 December 1935. All located in Library of Congress, Washington, Herbert Feis Papers, box 125, Strategic Materials 1935.

83 Warren Kuehl and Lynne Dunn, *Keeping the Covenant. American Internationalists and the League of Nations, 1920–1939* (Kent: Kent State University Press, 1997), 98.

84 Cristiano Andrea Ristuccia, "The 1935 Sanctions against Italy: Would Coal and Oil Have Made a Difference?," *European Review of Economic History* 1 (2000): 85–110.

85 Elisabetta Tollardo, *Fascist Italy and the League of Nations, 1922–1935* (London: Palgrave, 2016).

86 Corrado Gini and Robert K. Merton, "Problems of the International Distribution of Population and Raw Materials," *Annals of the American Academy of Political and Social Science* 189 (1937): 201–14.

87 Kurt Johannesen and H.H. Kraft, *Germany's Colonial Problem: The Necessity for Redistributing the World's Raw Material Resources – Facts and Arguments Supporting Germany's Claim to the Return of Her Colonies* (London: Thornton Butterworth, 1937), 37.

88 Hjalmar Schacht, "Germany's Colonial Demands," *Foreign Affairs* 15, 2 (1937): 223–34.

89 League of Nations, "Raw Materials, Question of Equal Commercial Access" November 1936, LoNA, R 4433.

90 *Spectator,* 5 March 1937.

91 Committee for the Study of the Problem of Raw Materials, general aspects of the problem as brought out by the principal statements made and publications issued since September 1935, 24 February 1937, LoNA, R4433.

92 Kapp, *Memorandum on the Efforts Made by the League of Nations,* 95.

93 Memorandum, the raw materials inquiry and the "open door," 15 April 1937, NA, FCO 98/606.

94 All quotes in this paragraph are from Kapp, *Memorandum on the Efforts Made by the League of Nations,* 89–105.

95 World Control of Raw Materials, draft memorandum for the raw materials inquiry, 28 April 1937, and notes on the memorandum that it proposed should be circulated to Dominion Representatives at the Imperial Conference, n.d., NA, FCO 98/606.

96 League of Nations Committee for the Study of the Problem of Raw Materials, first subcommittee, provisional draft report, 25 June 1937, LoNA, R4434.

97 This view also permeated postwar historiography but has been forcefully challenged. See Albrecht Ritschl, "Nazi Economic Imperialism and the Exploitation of the Small: Evidence from Germany's Secret Foreign Exchange Balances, 1938–1940," *Economic History Review* 54 (2001): 324–45.

98 Memorandum, the raw materials inquiry and the "open door," 15 April 1937, NA, FCO 98, 606.

99 Addendum to the report of the second subcommittee, 23 June 1937, LoNA, R4434.

100 League of Nations Committee for the Study of the Problem of Raw Materials, final report, quoted in ILO, *Intergovernmental Commodity Control Agreements.*

101 Quoted in Clavin, *Securing the World Economy,* 184.

102 Declaration by Mr. Shudo at the preliminary meeting, 24 June 1937, LoNA, R4434.
103 Hubert Henderson, *Colonies and Raw Materials* (New York: Farrar and Rinehart, 1939), 4, 10.
104 Max Domarus, *Hitler. Reden 1932 bis 1942, Teil I Triumph, Zweiter Band* (Leonberg: Pamminger and Partner, 1988), 739–41.
105 League of Nations Economic Committee, report to the council on the work of its forty-seventh session, 9 December 1937, NA, FO 371, 22566.
106 Extract from House of Lords debate, 13 April 1938, 682. A copy is located in NA, FO 371, 22566.
107 League of Nations, Commercial Access to Raw Materials, 23 March 1939, NA, FO 371, 24043; League of Nations, Commercial Access to Raw Materials, 24 September 1938, NA, FO 371, 22566.
108 Consul in Geneva to the Secretary of State, 12 July 1938, US Department of State, *Foreign Relations of the United States 1938*, 1:924.
109 Frederick Leith-Ross to Ashton Gwatkin, 27 June 1938, NA, FO 371/22566; Gwatkin to Leith Ross, 1 July 1938, NA, FO 371/22566.
110 Clavin, *Securing the World Economy*, 188.
111 President Roosevelt to Chancellor Adolf Hitler, 14 April 1939, US Department of State, *Foreign Relations of the United States 1939*, 1:130–33.
112 Adolf Hitler, *Der Führer antwortet Roosevelt. Reichstagsrede vom 28. april 1939* (Munich: NSDAP Zentralverlag, 1939), 32–33.
113 Lloyd Gardner, *Economic Aspects of New Deal Diplomacy* (Madison: University of Wisconsin Press, 1964), 169.
114 League of Nations, *Raw-Material Problems and Policies*, 66–67.
115 League of Nations Economic Committee, *Observations on the Present Prospects of Commercial Policy* (Geneva: League of Nations, 1939).
116 Staley, *Raw Materials in Peace and War*, 197, n30.
117 R.J. Barry Jones, ed., *Routledge Encyclopedia of International Political Economy* (New York: Routledge, 2001), 189.

11

Regulating the Natural Resources in the Antarctic Region

A Historical Review

BJØRN L. BASBERG

Antarctica is, for most people, associated with a pristine ice- and snow-covered continent with a heroic history of exploration. Commercial ventures have been few and are not associated with the continent but with the surrounding sea – the Southern Ocean (also known as the Antarctic Ocean). Sealing dominated during the 1800s. Whaling was the main commercial activity of the 1900s to about 1970. More recently, fisheries and ship-borne tourism have become dominant. So an analysis of the Antarctic as an area of economic and commercial activity throughout history – and any regulations of its resources – must involve more than just the continent. Indeed, commercial activities and exploitative industries have been concentrated in the seas and sub-Antarctic islands around the continent rather than on the continent itself. We must therefore position the borders of the Antarctic as an economic area north of the 60th parallel – the "political" boundary of the Antarctic – at least as far north as the Antarctic Convergence (the Polar Front). It would be natural to include even some islands that lie slightly north of the Antarctic Convergence.

As an economic region, the Antarctic is unique. The continent itself is, of course, extremely homogeneous: ice-covered and with relatively few accessible resources. The climate, especially temperatures, is extreme. Neither the continent nor the islands have any Indigenous inhabitants, any national or non-dependent states, or, for that matter, any currency in the traditional sense, all of which make the Antarctic extremely unusual in an economic

FIGURE 11.1
The Antarctic region

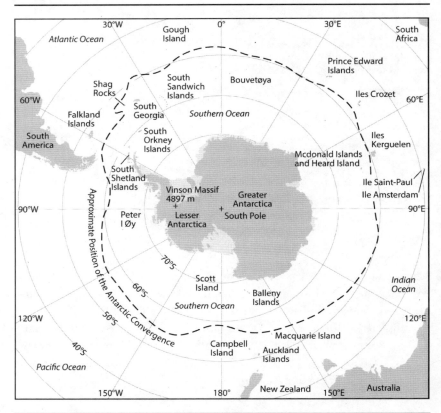

Source: Redrawn from R.K. Headland, *A Chronology of Antarctic Exploration* (London: Bernard Quaritch, 2009), 14.

context. These characteristics, among others, account for the difficulty in obtaining economic statistics for the region. They have also posed difficulties when it comes to developing sustainable management procedures, resulting in some unique legal systems.

Antarctic Industries
In his Antarctic chronology, polar historian Robert K. Headland distinguishes between three apparent exploitative periods in Antarctic history: sealing, whaling, and fishing. Writing in the 1980s, he viewed mineral extraction as a "potential fourth" and iceberg/fresh water exportation as a "conceivable fifth."[1] If we limit the concept of industry to exploitation of

resources, then sealing, whaling, and fishing are obviously the only ones that, so far, have been extensively developed. Mineral exploitation has not occurred. The export of ice and water has so far been too limited to justify using the term "period."

When adopting a wider definition of industries to include the non-exploitative industries, the main phases, or periods, will have to be redefined. Exploration and science will then have to be considered as the first Antarctic activity that included economic or commercial aspects. Such activities have had a more or less continuous presence throughout the human history of the region. There have, of course, been phases of development within this long period, the "Heroic Age" of exploration from the late nineteenth century being one. The post-Second World War period, with permanent stations and thus a much more extensive logistical activity, is another.

Together with research, tourism has, for the last few decades, been the dominant activity in the Antarctic. As is the case with science, tourism is a non-exploitative industry but, obviously, a commercial one occupying a main development period, as listed in Table 11.1.

Sealing in the Antarctic and at islands throughout the Southern Ocean started towards the end of the eighteenth century.[2] The industry was from the start dominated by British and American sealers who took fur seals (for the pelt) and elephant seals (for the oil). The market was found in the US, Europe, and also in China (Canton). Typically, the sealers arrived at an island or area and worked there until there were no more seals and then

TABLE 11.1
Antarctic industries: Main divisions and chronology

Sector		Period
Exploration and science		18th century–present
Sealing		19th century
Whaling		1904–80s
Fishing		1960s–present
Tourism		1960s–present
Other industries:	Animal breeding	20th century
	Philately	20th century
	Water supply and export	20th century
	Ship register	1980s–present
	Bio-prospecting	21st century

Source: Revised from B.L. Basberg, "Perspectives on the Economic History of the Antarctic Region," *International Journal of Maritime History* 18, 2 (2006): 301.

moved on to new grounds. This pattern lasted throughout the nineteenth century – a period that lacked any regulations or management procedures.[3]

To some extent, whalers also visited Antarctic waters in the nineteenth century during the American heyday of pelagic whaling. However, this industry mainly operated further north in the Atlantic, Pacific, and Indian Oceans – and in the Arctic. I have therefore not included it as an Antarctic industry. When it came to regulations, whaling during this period was similar to sealing in that it lacked any control regimes. The first control regimes in the Antarctic region came with the development of twentieth-century whaling – the industrialized, so-called modern whaling with its new technology of steamships and grenade harpoons.

"The Allardyce Era": The First Antarctic Whaling Management Regime

The whalers began working at South Georgia in the 1904–05 Antarctic summer and at the South Shetlands in 1905–06. At that time sovereignty issues had not been resolved, and obviously no regulations concerning a potential whaling industry existed. William Lamond Allardyce (1861–1930) was governor of the Falkland Islands from 1905 to 1915. His service in the Falklands thus coincided with the start of Antarctic whaling, when he was responsible for the introduction of the whaling regulations there.[4] Mr. Allardyce and his government were quick to recommend formal declaration of the islands as British territory and to introduce legislation regulating the industry. An Ordinance to Regulate the Whale Fishery of the Colony of the Falkland Islands was introduced in 1906. Based on the Newfoundland Whaling Act, 1902, the main components were:

- regulation based on leases of land and whaling licences (terms, conditions, numbers)
- regulation of the maximum number of whale catcher boats for each floating factory or shore station.

Thus, the regulations put restrictions on the equipment allowed. There were no restrictions on number of whales caught, on hunting grounds, or on the duration of the whaling season.

The Falkland Islands Dependencies were formally defined in 1908 (including South Georgia, the South Sandwich Islands, the South Orkney Islands, and the South Shetland Islands), making it possible to provide the regulations with more authority. Legislation, introduced gradually after 1906, involved:

- appointment of government supervisors (magistrates and whaling inspectors at South Georgia [1908] and the South Shetlands [1912])
- requirement of "full utilization" of the whale carcass to reduce waste and control of catches; the whaling companies should not catch more than they could process with the available equipment
- protection of mothers and calves
- no further increase in the number of leases or licences
- regulation of sealing and preservation of penguins.

Allardyce also proposed legislation on conservation of plants and other wildlife.

Whether he deserves to be called a "conservationist" is not obvious. He did not oppose the whaling industry as such. To the contrary, he was in favour of it and saw its potential for contributing to the revenue of the colony. This was, in fact, also his mandate.[5] Allardyce served in the Falkland Islands in a period when the economy was not in the best shape, and he saw the potential of the whaling industry to increase the income of the colony. He also to some extent favoured British whaling interests. At least this was the way the Norwegian whaling community viewed his policy. However, Allardyce was also concerned about maintaining a "sustainable" industry – one that would last. In his budget speech in 1911 he indicated clearly that he was interested in more than short-term financial issues: "The policy of this Government will continue to be that of endeavouring to establish a permanent industry rather than the rapid collection of a large revenue."[6]

Whaling in the Falkland Island and the Dependencies increased, reaching a maximum of one licence in the Falklands and altogether twenty-two in the Dependencies (South Georgia, the South Shetland Islands, the South Orkney Islands, and the South Sandwich Islands) in 1911 (Table 11.2).

TABLE 11.2
Whaling licences, Falkland Islands and Dependencies, 1904–11

Whaling ground	Beginning	Licences
Falkland Islands	1906	1
South Georgia	1904	7
South Shetland Islands	1906	10
South Orkney Islands	1911	4
South Sandwich Islands	1911	1

Source: I.B. Hart, *Whaling in the Falkland Islands Dependencies, 1904–1931: A History of Shore and Bay-Based Whaling in the Antarctic* (Newton St. Margarets, UK: Pequena, 2006).

The gradual increase in the number of shore stations, factory ships, and whale catchers at the main whaling grounds of South Georgia and the South Shetlands indicates the increase in the number of licences and restrictions on equipment and, thus, shows how the industry was affected by the management regime. It is possible to distinguish three phases:

1. 1904–1910: Development of the industry and annual increase in the number of licences
2. 1910–1914/15: Restrictions of licences
3. 1914–1918/20 (First World War years). At South Georgia whaling increased: more catchers were permitted (increased from twenty-two to more than thirty) at the British stations to maximize oil production. At the South Shetlands whaling diminished: factory ships were redirected to merchant shipping (mostly Norwegian).

Thus, especially at South Georgia, the effect of the Allardyce regime in terms of limiting the expansion of the industry was moderate during the years between 1910 and 1914.

The ordinance focused on the regulation of input (licences, catchers). This obviously also affected the output (oil production). However, the output was clearly also affected by other factors. The relationship between input and output factors may be illustrated by the number of whales caught per catcher. There were large annual variations, indicating that limiting the number of catchers alone was not sufficient to regulate output. The annual number of whales per catcher increased for several years. One possible factor that may explain this is the continuous reinvestments in larger, more efficient catchers. Another factor is the duration of the whaling season. Such factors were not part of the Allardyce management regime. The decrease in the input/output ratio during the last years of observation must also be explained by factors beyond the control regime: the availability of whales in the coastal waters.

An indication that the whole whale carcass was being utilized is the quantity of oil obtained per whale. After some years with no increase, there was a consistent increase, and this was clearly an effect of the Allardyce policy of "full utilization." There was also, for the same reasons, a rapid increase in bone and meat meal production.[7]

Were the regulations initiated by William Allardyce successful? They obviously put a "brake" on potential expansion: approximately 120 applications for licences were refused.[8] And the catches were more fully utilized.

However, the regime introduced no quotas, no protection of individual species (humpback whales were caught too extensively in the early years), and no limits to the duration of the whaling season.

Allardyce's policy had its problems and challenges. The First World War expansion (due to war needs) overruled the restriction on the number of catchers at South Georgia. However, during the 1920s the regime was, to a large extent, again practised at South Georgia and the South Shetlands. No more licences were issued and the number of catchers was stable until 1929. As to the development of the industry, however, the management system became insufficient and irrelevant as unlicenced and pelagic whaling developed in the 1920s. After the 1931 crises, whaling in the Falkland Island Dependencies never regained its position, becoming of minor importance compared to other areas as whaling extended to the high seas of the Southern Ocean – beyond national jurisdiction.

What would have happened if the management regime had continued to influence the entire industry? Whaling historian Ian Hart suggests one answer: "It is ironic that had Governor Allardyce's early far-sighted whale conservation policies continued, rational harvesting could have been maintained, the whale stocks would have been preserved for biological posterity and the ensuing slaughter would have been prevented."[9] This may be a too optimistic assessment. As we have seen, the policy did not prevent increase, but its main deficiency was obviously that it lacked geographical cohesiveness. Allardyce himself was aware of this problem, as may be seen in a statement from 1911: "Until such time as there is an international agreement on the subject, little practical protection can be afforded to the whale."[10]

From Voluntary Agreements to the International Whaling Commission

In the early years, as we have seen, most whaling took place in British-controlled waters and limits were placed on the number of concessions, the hunting equipment, and the processing of the catch. In the first years of pelagic whaling from the 1920s, these rules became gradually more irrelevant, leading to severe over-exploitation. But after the economic crisis of the industry at the beginning of the 1930s, the two major whaling nations, Great Britain and Norway, jointly introduced quotas in an attempt to regulate catches. The motivation had little to do with conservation: the intention was to provide better market conditions and to save the industry. Cooperation within these rules (the "voluntary agreements") was certainly reluctant, and some companies did not participate at all. Quota agreements to some extent worked from 1932 to 1934, and the total number of whaling operations was reduced. In the second half of the 1930s, conflicts between the whaling nations escalated. The effect of the regulations was also undermined as new nations, Japan and Germany in particular, began whaling.[11]

During the late 1920s there were international initiatives and meetings involving many nations, the aim being to create an international agreement on the regulation of whaling. A result was the Convention for the Regulation of Whaling, adopted by twenty-six delegate nations at a meeting at the League of Nations in Geneva in 1931. It was a first, albeit small, step towards a regulation regime. It banned, among other things, the catching of right whales and calves. It required the full utilization of the carcass. The companies were to submit whaling statistics. Any whaling operation would require a licence or a concession. Although the convention did not impose quotas on the major whale species that were hunted on the Antarctic grounds (blue whale, fin whale, sperm whale), neither Norway nor Britain signed the agreement at the beginning. This was done only in 1932 and 1934, respectively.

As was the case with the bilateral Norwegian-British relationship, the late 1930s saw little progress with regard to international cooperation on the management of whaling. An international conference in London in 1937, which was aimed at restricting catches, ended in fiasco. An important new phase in international cooperation was only reached at the end of the Second World War with a conference in Washington, DC, that resulted in the International Convention for the Regulation of Whaling and the establishment of the International Whaling Commission (IWC) in 1946.[12] The meeting in the US capital was initiated by the Americans, who now saw an opportunity for a new start in whaling diplomacy after the disruption of the war. The conference was chaired by Dr. Remington Kellogg. He had taken part in the international negotiations during the 1930s and became the US commissioner to the IWC until 1967. He was thus instrumental to the development of the organization.[13]

The new international management regime established by the IWC introduced restrictions on the volume of the catch, the length of the whaling season, and catching areas. However, the way the catching quota system was organized – by way of a maximum of so-called Blue-Whale-Units (BWU) – provided inadequate protection; only gradually was the beginning number of 16,000 reduced. There were strong disagreements between the dominant whaling nations regarding how regulations should be monitored. Nations threatened to leave the IWC and, in fact, two nations (Norway and the

Netherlands) left the commission for some years. Disagreements also led to the temporary abandonment of the international BWU quota system. It was replaced by national quotas that led to *increased* total catches in the Antarctic waters around 1960 – a period referred to as "the Whaling Olympics." These years, and indeed the entire period from the foundation of the IWC, have been referred to as "twenty years of failure."[14] This involved the failure to resolve the major challenges faced by the IWC and the failure to agree on a proper management regime.

Some progress was eventually made. In 1963, the hunting of blue and humpback whales was prohibited. This was long overdue. The catch of blue whales had peaked back in 1931, which gives an indication of the extent to which the stocks had been exploited. Then the 1970s – albeit only after Antarctic whaling had come to an end for Britain, Norway, and the Netherlands – saw some changes that improved the management regime. The BWU-system was replaced by quotas for the different species. A "new management procedure" was adopted, and eventually (in 1982) the IWC agreed to a moratorium on all commercial whaling in Antarctic waters.

Restrictions and quotas notwithstanding, the postwar catches exceeded what the whale populations could withstand. When restrictive quotas were imposed on some species, the whalers moved to others. When the blue whales could not be taken, the whalers concentrated instead on smaller species – fin and sei whales, which, in any event, were more abundant. In the last phases of Antarctic whaling even the little minke whales, which no one had bothered with before, were hunted. The Antarctic whaling industry came to an end not chiefly because of the restrictions but because of failing catches and, therefore, failing profits as whales became scarcer.

With the exception of Japan's "scientific whaling" of minke whales, there is no whaling in the Antarctic today. Other marine resources are exploited instead. Few want whaling back. Even many decades after most whaling companies withdrew, whale populations are still far from regaining their former numbers. Besides, there are few signs that the 1982 whaling moratorium is being challenged. The IWC is still "in business," but for many years the organization has not been a forum for whaling nations (that was the case from the beginning) but, rather, for nations and non-governmental organizations interested in the protection of whales. At least to some extent, this shows how the attitudes towards whales have shifted from their being an exploitable resource to their being a symbol of the struggle to protect nature and the environment.[15]

The Antarctic Treaty and Resource Management

By the 1930s, almost all of the Antarctic continent and coastal waters had been claimed by seven nations: France, Australia, New Zealand, Britain, Chile, Argentina, and Norway. Following the Second World War, there was an increased focus on scientific activity in the region as well as on international cooperation. This development escalated in the 1950s, and the International Geophysical Year (IGY) (1957–58), in particular, was a major event for further international cooperation in the Antarctic. More than fifty research stations were opened and research programs were coordinated. In 1958, as a result of IGY, the Special (later Scientific) Committee on Antarctic Research (SCAR) was set up.

Twelve countries participated in scientific activities in the Antarctic during IGY and also initiated the foundation of SCAR. In addition to the original seven claimants, there was the United States, the USSR, Japan, Belgium, and South Africa. Not being among the claimant nations led the United States, in particular, to take an active role in negotiations for a more permanent international agreement on the Antarctic, and in October of 1959 representatives of the twelve nations met in Washington, DC. The result was the Antarctic Treaty, signed on 1 December 1959.[16]

The treaty came into force in 1961. The most important elements (specified in fourteen articles) were those that saw that the seven original sovereignty claims were kept in abeyance. The treaty area, south of sixty degrees latitude, was to be devoted to peaceful purposes and international scientific cooperation. The treaty guaranteed access to the region for scientific research, and an inspection system was established to prevent military activities. Exchange of information was to take place freely.

Being negotiated and agreed in the middle of the Cold War era, the Antarctic Treaty was a remarkable achievement. One reason for its success may be that, geopolitically, Antarctica was comparatively unimportant. But another reason was that the treaty gave both the United States and the USSR more influence in the area. The Antarctic Treaty gradually grew in importance and significance, with more countries participating. As of today (2018), there are fifty-three parties: twenty-nine so-called consultative parties (including the original twelve signatory states) and twenty-four non-consultative parties.

The protection of the environment was an important goal of the Antarctic Treaty, and the development of measures for the preservation and conservation of resources began right away.[17] A system for the protection of animal and plant life was agreed upon in 1961. Measures for their conservation were agreed upon in 1964. However, issues relating to the large exploitative resources were not settled by these measures. The management of the whaling industry was left to the IWC – an institution outside and independent of the Antarctic Treaty. Mineral exploitation and fisheries were handled within the treaty, but it took years before any management regimes were in place.

Fisheries

The start of fisheries in the Antarctic was closely tied to whaling. The whaling companies that operated in South Georgia made several attempts at fishing as early as 1904, but fisheries failed to gain any significance at that time. This was not on account of a lack of fish; rather, the companies chose to concentrate on something that was obviously more profitable at the time – whales.

The first notable expansion in commercial fisheries coincided with the conclusion of the whaling epoch. Soviet trawlers started fishing in the Southern Ocean in the area around South Georgia at the end of the 1960s. New fishing areas were opened during the 1970s, especially around other sub-Antarctic islands but also further south. Several nations joined. East Germany, Poland, and Bulgaria were especially active – as later on were Japan and Chile.[18]

During this period, fisheries in the Antarctic region were based on several species of fish. The first species to be focused upon was Antarctic cod, but for most of the time two other species of fish dominated: toothfish (Antarctic and Patagonian) and mackerel icefish. And there have been substantial fisheries for squid and, especially, for krill, which, in terms of total catch size, has far exceeded that of the other fisheries.

For many years Antarctic fisheries were not restricted in any way, with severe overfishing and depleted stocks being the consequence. For a long time it looked like fisheries were following the same course as had earlier Antarctic industries. In particular, there was a growing concern that krill, being a key ecosystem species, was being heavily over-exploited. By the mid-1970s, participants in the Antarctic Treaty began work to develop a management regime. A research program on krill – Biological Investigation of Marine Antarctic Systems and Stocks (BIOMASS) – was also undertaken by the treaty's scientific committee (SCAR). Then a conference was held in Canberra in 1980 that resulted in the Convention for the Conservation of Antarctic Marine Living Resources (CCAMLR). It came into effect in 1982 as a convention within the Antarctic Treaty system.

As the name indicates, CCAMLR is about "conservation." Indeed, it became the first international fisheries management regime that had the conservation of ecosystems as a prime objective.[19] Strictly regulated fishing zones were introduced throughout the entire Southern Ocean. While the Antarctic Treaty is limited to the area south of the 60th parallel, the CCAMLR area extended as far north as the Convergence (the Polar Front). Thus, it also included the important fishing grounds around the sub-Antarctic islands.

It is difficult to estimate the size of the fisheries during the years before regulations were introduced, but it rapidly developed into an industry that annually engaged several hundred fishing vessels and thousands of fishers. The annual reported catch of toothfish has ranged between 15,000 and 20,000 tonnes in recent years, while 2,000 to 4,000 tonnes of icefish have been caught per year.[20] These figures are modest compared to those of fisheries elsewhere in the world.

During several years in the 1980s, the annual catch of krill was as high as 400,000 to 500,000 tonnes. The catches diminished during the 1990s – about 100,000 tonnes annually. This was primarily due to developments in the USSR – at the time the main participant in this fishery. After the USSR's political collapse, Russia did not continue the krill fishery on a very large scale. CCAMLR set a krill quota of 5 million tonnes in 1993. This figure has never been reached. However, there has lately been substantial international interest in this resource. Traditionally, krill have been used as feed for farmed fish, but the market for its oil for other products is growing. With a high concentration of omega-3 fatty acids and other special qualities, krill is becoming increasingly attractive for potential use in nutritional supplements, cosmetics, and pharmaceuticals.

The fisheries today are largely well regulated, and CCAMLR is seen as successful. However, the challenges of regulating such activities in the vast Southern Ocean remains enormous, and unregulated and unreported (as well as illegal) fishing remains extensive. There are also other challenges. In recent years CCAMLR has been discussing how to keep protected marine areas from exploitation (so-called marine protected areas – MPAs). The Ross Sea and an area in East Antarctica was considered, but it was difficult to reach consensus among the members. CCAMLR's executive secretary explained the outcome of the 2014 annual meeting this way: "A range of views and national interests on complex issues such as MPAs in international waters creates a challenging environment for reaching consensus."[21] This statement reflects well the problems faced in Antarctic resource management

Regulating the Natural Resources in the Antarctic Region 271

– not only relating to fisheries today.[22] However, progress is also being made. At the thirty-fifth annual meeting of CCAMLR in October 2016, the members agreed to establish the Ross Sea MPA.[23] Having entered into force in December 2017, the 1.55-million-square-kilometre area is the largest in the world of its kind.

Minerals

The search for minerals has been important in Antarctic exploration from the beginning. Geology and mineralogy were key components in every scientific expedition. With accumulating knowledge of the mineral deposits on the continent and the sea floor, hopes grew for commercial exploitation, especially of coal, iron, rare metals, and, later, hydrocarbons. Mining plans were formulated early – in South Georgia as early as 1890. However, mineral resources have never been extracted in the Antarctic, and there are several reasons for this.[24] First is the region's inaccessibility, which makes the costs of extraction too high compared with alternatives found elsewhere. However, as the technological frontiers shift (as offshore oil drilling closer to the Arctic indicates), and mineral deposits in more accessible areas are gradually depleted, pressure to exploit Antarctic mineral resources has increased. It became a difficult and controversial issue within the Antarctic Treaty beginning in the 1970s. The so-called voluntary moratorium on mineral resource activities was agreed in 1977, but negotiations to arrive at a permanent agreement regarding mineral exploration and extraction continued in the 1980s.[25] The 1988 Convention on the Regulation of Antarctic Mineral Resource Activities (CRAMRA) was never fully ratified. Eventually, the Protocol on Environmental Protection to the Antarctic Treaty was agreed in 1991. It bans mineral exploitation for fifty years.

From Maritime Industries to Bio-Prospecting

Individual tourists have been observed in the Antarctic since the late nineteenth century, but tourism did not develop into an industry until the 1960s and 1970s. In recent years about twenty thousand visitors are recorded annually, most of whom come aboard cruise ships. The activity poses needs for management and regulations, and since 1991 most of the industry has been guided by the International Association of Antarctic Tour Operators (IAATO), a voluntary member organization (not within the Antarctic Treaty system) that provides guidelines, procedures, and regulations for how activities should be conducted.[26] IAATO is especially concerned with guidelines relating to environmental issues (pollution, behaviour relating to wildlife, etc.). The guidelines also relate to historic heritage and aim to minimize adverse effects on historic sites.

Another maritime activity in the Antarctic has been maritime transport, especially with regard to logistical support for the many research stations. To a certain degree, this can be seen as an integral part of the scientific sector. Many nations employ their own research vessels for such services. Commercial shipping companies have also been involved since the establishment of the earliest research stations in Antarctica.

Shipping is still essential for supplying the research bases, though air transport has become increasingly significant. Other forms of economic activity in the Antarctic area in recent years are small in scale and rather unusual. The export of ice and water has not yet progressed beyond the experimental stage but may have great commercial potential on account of the raw material's exotic origin and the obvious growth in the international market. Philately is a commercial activity that has grown along with the rising number of visitors. Today stamp sales are a source of income at bases on the continent and the islands visited by cruise ships. Governments also regard it as an exercise in sovereignty.

Attempts have also been made to exploit the special status of the sub-Antarctic islands in another way. The shipping register of the French island of Kerguelen includes seventy-some French and other ships.[27] Such commercial activities obviously have limited effects on the environment and consequently pose few challenges to the management regimes. There are, however, new activities that may change this situation.

One activity that is still only modest in extent but will probably increase in importance is bio-prospecting – the search for organisms, molecules, and genes with the intention of exploiting them commercially. This has been a worldwide activity, but in recent decades scientists and businesses have turned their attention towards Antarctica. On land and in the sea there have been discoveries of substances in fish, invertebrates, and bacteria that have diverse potential commercial applications. Some organisms have qualities that prevent damage from the formation of ice crystals, thus having potential for improving the quality of frozen food products. In addition to uses in nutritional products, there are also possible medical applications, for example, in the treatment of cancer. There has been talk of great economic possibilities, and biotechnology and pharmaceutical companies have already been granted numerous patents.

As an activity with minor adverse environmental consequences, bio-prospecting is apparently a business well suited to vulnerable Antarctica.

Regulating the Natural Resources in the Antarctic Region 273

However, patents fundamentally concern exclusivity and property rights, which, in turn, may concern issues of sovereignty. How this should be handled within the Antarctic Treaty system has already been discussed for some time.[28] Such development may also indicate that scientific cooperation is being increasingly displaced by commercial competition in the Antarctic region.[29]

Conclusion

The exploitative industries – sealing, whaling, and fisheries – have several similarities. For example, in periods with no or limited regulation, the catching led to over-exploitation and depletion of stocks. The industries moved from one area (island, catching ground) to another around the Southern Ocean, and they explored further and further south to hitherto unexploited grounds.

The historical development may have taught us something about the need for regulations. Early sealing was never regulated. Whaling was regulated, but probably too late. Fisheries were regulated, although not right from the start, and time will tell if it was early enough and sufficient. The newer activities (tourism, science) also face strict regulations that clearly limit their operations and expansion.

When it comes to differences between the industries, a major shift has obviously been from traditional exploitative industries to non-exploitative industries, corresponding to general trends in many economies that are moving from primary to secondary and eventually to service industries. The increased accessibility of the Antarctic region is yet another major trend affecting how activities and associated businesses can be undertaken. This is relevant, for example, when it comes to mineral exploitation. Such exploitation has so far been banned, but to reach a consensus on this issue within the Antarctic Treaty took the organization through a crisis – which clearly shows the fragility of this regime. History has shown that commercial rivalry for Antarctic resources has been a challenge to the establishment of regulations and management. When it comes to minerals, at least some sort of regulation has preceded exploitation.

Acknowledgments

An earlier version of this chapter was presented at a workshop entitled "The History of Regulation of Natural Resources in a Global Perspective," NTNU (Norwegian University of Science and Technology), Trondheim, 20–21 August 2013. It relies on several of my earlier publications, especially B.L. Basberg, "Perspectives on the

Economic History of the Antarctic Region," *International Journal of Maritime History* 18, 2 (2006): 285–304; and J-G. Winther, ed., *Norway in the Antarctic: From Conquest to Modern Science* (Oslo: Schibsted, 2008). I have received valuable comments and suggestions from the workshop participants and organizers as well as from Robert K. Headland and Paul Berkman. The section titled "The Allardyce Era" is based on my paper of the same title, which was delivered at a workshop titled "The Decimation of Whales: An Example of Non-Sustainable Management," Commander Chr. Christensen's Whaling Museum, Sandefjord, June 2007.

Notes

1 In the revised edition, only the "potential fourth" period is still included. See R.K. Headland, *A Chronology of Antarctic Exploration* (London: Bernard Quaritch, 2009), 35. There are quite a few publications that review the Antarctic industries throughout history. See, among others, M.W. Holdgate, "The Use and Abuse of Polar Environmental Resources," *Polar Record* 22, 136 (1984): 25–49; G. Decon, *The Antarctic Circumpolar Ocean*, Studies in Polar Research (Cambridge: Cambridge University Press, 1984); R. Laws, *Antarctica: The Last Frontier* (London: Boxtree, 1989).

2 For a recent review of this industry, see B.L. Basberg and R.K. Headland, "The Economic Significance of the Nineteenth Century Antarctic Sealing Industry," *Polar Record* 49, 251 (2013): 381–91.

3 There were occasional critiques from conservationists. In fact, concerns were raised as early as the 1780s, when the industry was at its very beginning. See H.G.R. King, "An Early Proposal for Conserving the Southern Seal Fishery," *Polar Record* 12, 78 (1965): 313–16.

4 For biographies of Allardyce, see Henry R. Heyburn, "William Lamond Allardyce, 1861–1930: Pioneer Antarctic Conservationist," *Polar Record* 20, 124 (1980): 39–42; Stephen Palmer, "William Lamond Allardyce," in *Dictionary of Falklands Biography*, ed. D. Tatham (Ledbury: ABC Print, 2008), 37–42.

5 For a critical view of Allardyce as a conservationist, see D.G. Burnett, *The Sounding of the Whale: Science and Cetaceans in the Twentieth Century* (Chicago: University of Chicago Press, 2012), 30ff.

6 Palmer, "William Lamond Allardyce," 39.

7 B.L. Basberg, "Survival against All Odds? Shore Station Whaling at South Georgia in the Pelagic Era, 1925–1960," in *Whaling and History: Perspectives on the Evolution of the Industry*, ed. B.L. Basberg, J.E. Ringstad, and E. Wexelsen (Sandefjord: Commander Chr. Christensen's Whaling Museum, 1993), 157–68.

8 I.B. Hart, *Whaling in the Falkland Islands Dependencies, 1904–1931: A History of Shore and Bay-Based Whaling in the Antarctic* (Newton St. Margarets, UK: Pequena, 2006), 310ff.

9 Ibid., 274.

10 South Georgia Archives, Scott Polar Research Institute, Cambridge, 8 July 1911, quoted from Palmer, "William Lamond Allardyce," 40.

11 J.N. Tønnesen and A.O. Johnsen, *Den moderne hvalfangsts historie: Opprinnelse og utvikling*, vols. 1–4 (Oslo: Norges Hvalfangstforbund, 1959–70), 3:414ff. See also a

Regulating the Natural Resources in the Antarctic Region   275

one-volume version in English by the same authors, *The History of Modern Whaling* (London: C. Hurst and Co, 1982), 433ff. The challenges faced by international whaling diplomacy in this period were recently investigated by K. Dorsey, *Whales and Nations: Environmental Diplomacy on the High Seas* (Seattle: University of Seattle Press, 2013).

12 Tønnesen and Johnsen, *Den moderne hvalfangsts historie*, 4:173; Tønnesen and Johnsen, *History of Modern Whaling*, 499. There is a large literature on the history of the IWC from historians as well as social scientists. For recent contributions focusing on the relationship between politics and science, see Burnett, *Sounding of the Whale*, esp. chaps. 4 and 5; and Dorsey, *Whales and Nations*. On the development of the International Whaling Commission and the many difficult discussions about resource management, see R.T. Friedheim, ed., *Towards a Sustainable Whaling Regime* (Edmunton: CCI Press, 2001). On the management of whaling in the context of international law, see A. Gillespie, *Whaling Diplomacy: Defining Issues in International Environmental Law* (Cheltenham: Edward Elgar, 2005).

13 Dorsey, *Whales and Nations*, 41.

14 Gillespie, *Whaling Diplomacy*, 4. On these years of crises in the IWC, see also Burnett, *Sounding of the Whale*, 405ff; and Dorsey, *Whales and Nations*.

15 M. Haugdahl, "Fornuft og følelser? Forståelse og forvaltning av hval og hvalfangst" (unpublished PhD thesis, NTNU, Tronheim, 2012).

16 There is an extensive literature on the history and development of the Antarctic Treaty and the associated Antarctic Treaty system. This section relies especially on R. Trolle Andersen, "The Political Drama during the Cold War and the Development of Antarctic Co-operation" and "Resource Management and Protection of the Environment," both in J-G. Winther, ed., *Norway in the Antarctic: From Conquest to Modern Science* (Oslo: Schibsted, 2008), chaps. 5 and 6. See also A. Jørgensen-Dahl and W. Østereng, eds., *The Antarctic Treaty System in World Politics* (London: Macmillan Academic, 1991); O.S. Stokke and D. Vidas, eds., *Governing the Antarctic: The Effectiveness and Legitimacy of the Antarctic Treaty System* (Cambridge: Cambridge University Press, 1996). A recent publication, based on contributions at the Antarctic Treaty Summit (celebrating the fiftieth anniversary of the Antarctic Treaty), is Paul Arthur Berkman, Michael A. Lang, David W.H. Walton, and Oran R. Young, *Science Diplomacy: Antarctica, Science, and the Government of International Spaces* (Washington, DC: Smithsonian Institution Scholarly Press, 2011).

17 A specific focus on environmental issues may be found in L.M. Elliott, *International Environmental Politics: Protecting the Antarctic* (London: Macmillan, 1994), 50ff; F. Francioni and T. Scovazzi, eds., *International Law for Antarctica* (The Hague: Kluwer Law International, 1996), 261ff; C.C. Juyner, *Governing the Frozen Commons: The Antarctic Regime and Environmental Protection* (Colombia: University of South Carolina Press, 1998), 147ff.

18 K.-H. Kock, *Antarctic Fish and Fisheries* (Cambridge: Cambridge University Press, 1992); D.J. Agnew, *Fishing South: The History and Management of South Georgia Fisheries* (St. Albans: The Penna Press, 2004).

19 Agnew, *Fishing South*, 55.

20 CCAMLR, *Statistical Bulletin* 19 (1997–2006), Hobart, 2007, Table 2, p. 23; A. Dommasnes, S.A. Iversen, and T. Løbach, "Fiskerier i Antarktis," in *Havets Ressurser*, ed. K. Michalsen (Bergen: Institute of Marine Research, 2004), 160–64.

21 CCAMLR, 33rd Annual Meeting, Hobart, 31 October 2014, at www.ccamlr.org (Convention for the Conservation of Antarctic Marine Living Resources website).

22 A "restraint in the pursuit of national interests" has obviously been important in explaining the historical performance of the Antarctic Treaty system, and it also gives some hope for its future performance. See O. Orheim, "Managing the Frozen Commons," in *Antarctica: Global Science from a Frozen Continent*, ed. D.W.H. Walton (Cambridge: Cambridge University Press, 2013), 273ff.

23 CCAMLR, 35th Annual Meeting, Hobart, 21 October 2016, at www.ccamlr.org.

24 See M.J. De Wit, *Minerals and Mining in Antarctica: Science and Technology, Economics and Politics* (Oxford: Clarendon Press, 1985); D. Shapley, *The Seventh Continent: Antarctica in the Resource Age* (Washington, DC: Resources for the Future, 1985); R.H. Rutford, ed., *Reports of the SCAR Group of Specialists on Antarctic Environmental Implications of Possible Mineral Exploration and Exploitation* (Cambridge: Scientific Committee on Antarctic Research, 1986). A thorough discussion of the challenges connected to resource management in Antarctica is found in Jørgensen-Dahl and Østereng, *Antarctic Treaty System in World Politics*.

25 R.T. Andersen, "Resource Management and Protection of the Environment," in Winther, ed., *Norway in the Antarctic: From Conquest to Modern Science* (Oslo: Schibsted, 2008), 109ff.

26 Two recent publications that both review the history of Antarctic tourism and discuss its environmental and management aspects are B. Stonehouse and J.M. Snyder, *Polar Tourism: An Environmental Analysis* (Bristol: Channel View 2010); and M. Lück, P.T. Maher, and E.J. Stewart, eds., *Cruise Tourism in Polar Regions: Promoting Environmental and Social Sustainability?* (London: Earthscan, 2010).

27 G. Sletmo and S. Holste, "Shipping and Competitive Advantage of Nations: The Role of International Ship Registers," *Maritime Policy and Management* 20, 3 (1993): 243–55.

28 A.D. Hemmings and R. Rogan-Finnemore, eds., *Antarctic Bioprospecting* (Christchurch: Gateway Antarctica Special Publication, 2005). See also a detailed discussion of the many management-related challenges in B.P. Herber, "Bioprospecting in Antarctica: The Search for a Policy Regime," *Polar Record* 42 (2006): 139–46.

29 S. Chaturvedi, "Biological Prospecting in the Southern Polar Region: Science-Geopolitics Interface," in *Legacies and Change in Polar Sciences*, ed. J.M. Shadian and M. Tennberg (Farnham, UK: Ashgate, 2009), 187.

12

The Rights of Indigenous Peoples to Land and Natural Resources

The Sami in Norway

HANNE HAGTVEDT VIK

In the winter of 1981 six hundred Norwegian police officers were dispatched from across Norway to the sparsely populated county of Finnmark, in the Arctic north. The police action was a response to ongoing civil disobedience by Sami and environmental activists who had blocked construction of a hydroelectric dam designed to supply electric power to Norway's northernmost region, with adverse effects for areas used to support reindeer herds. The dam was eventually constructed, but the dramatic event served to further alert the political establishment in the south to the grievances of the Sami population and reinforced the question of whether the Norwegian government could – legally and legitimately – make such decisions in what many considered the Sami heartland.

Norway's decade-long Alta River conflict was not unique. Many states were at the time experiencing conflicts between population groups and the government over land and natural resources. The international and transnational dimensions of such conflicts, however, were rapidly changing, especially for groups identifying as "indigenous populations/peoples,"[1] and gaining government recognition as such. The International Labour Organization (ILO) passed conventions in 1957 and 1989; the UN General Assembly adopted a declaration on the rights of Indigenous peoples in 2007. Through these international diplomatic processes, states developed overarching principles governing the rights of such populations, with land and natural resources at their heart.

Governments balance a range of concerns and interests when regulating natural resources, and the rights of some are almost invariably at the expense of the rights of others. Compensation for loss of historical or contemporary rights are possible in some cases, impracticable or insufficient in others and, as such, constitute a "hard case" for the power of international norms when it comes to shaping national policy. This chapter details the development of an international normative regime pertaining to the rights of Indigenous peoples and its impact on the Sami in Norway. When and how were these norms formulated? How did international-level developments affect successive Norwegian governments' policies on Sami rights and, in particular, their rights to land and natural resources? I argue that internationalization was crucial to Norway's recognition of the Sami as collective rights holders and players in resource distribution and management. International-level developments were of little significance before the post-1945 period. Norway's Sami policies evolved in the 1940s and 1950s, at a time when human rights norms were being formulated on European and, indeed, global levels. International networks and ideas grew in importance from the 1960s and gained momentum during the 1980s when the UN and the ILO developed modern norms for the rights of Indigenous peoples. Since then, international norms have directly affected the negotiation of conflicts of interest pertaining to Sami rights to land and natural resources.

International Developments prior to the 1960s

The early twentieth-century concept of "Indigenous population" was inextricably linked to the historical experience of colonialism and was used primarily as a term for the original populations of dependent countries. Occasionally, the term was used for the original populations of independent countries subjected to European overseas colonization in the past and was interchangeable with "Aboriginal" and "Indian." The Paris Peace Conference of 1919 saw the further development of three sets of international norms relevant to groups we today recognize as Indigenous. The first was the principle that peoples have the right to self-determination; the second concerned minority rights; and the third concerned what we may broadly call humanitarian rights. The ILO and the League of Nations in the 1920s and 1930s developed international norms pertaining to the treatment of Indigenous populations of colonial and mandated territories, including the League's mandate system and the ILO's efforts to combat slavery and forced labour. In this context, "Indigenous" was a generic term referring to the original populations of subjected territories.

Rights of Indigenous Peoples to Land and Natural Resources   279

From the mid-1930s the ILO engaged in initiatives to better conditions for original populations of independent countries when supporting regional initiatives in Latin America.[2] With the establishment of the United Nations in 1945, international emphasis shifted to universal rights, with only limited focus on minority rights. The following decades saw international consensus on the desirability of large-scale programs for societal and economic modernization, including efforts by various states and intergovernmental organizations in the 1950s and 1960s aimed at original populations of independent states – populations considered as "backward" and as having generally lower living standards and more social problems than the dominant populations. It was from these international efforts that the modern concept of "Indigenous peoples" evolved.

In the early 1950s, through the combined efforts of the ILO Secretariat and its Committee of Experts (mainly anthropologists), the ILO, UNICEF, and a few other intergovernmental organizations surveyed the working and living conditions of Indigenous populations and their place in the economies of independent states.[3] A joint report issued by the ILO in 1953 pointed out that white settlers in Latin America had used "every means both legal and illegal to encroach on aboriginal land and to dislodge the Indian."[4] Similar processes were described in the United States, India, Australia, and New Zealand, where the ILO reported that, in the century after 1840 (the year of the founding document of New Zealand, the Waitangi Treaty between the British Crown and Maori chiefs), the Maoris had "lost through sale or confiscation all but four million acres of the 66 million comprising the total area of New Zealand."[5] During the nineteenth century, land title was individualized and the institution of communal land holdings was abolished in many countries. Land ownership varied greatly between (and even within) states, with complex systems and rules and uncertainties regarding the land titles of Indigenous populations. The report noted that, by the 1920s, systems of cooperatively owned Indigenous territories had become common. Indigenous populations were often under the legal protection of the states, with restricted civil and political rights. The ILO paid less attention to the civil and political, focusing instead on social problems, land tenancy, harsh working conditions in agriculture and industry, and the prevalence of a subsistence economy in many Indigenous communities.[5]

The 1953 report signalled a broadened ILO interest in the concept of Indigenous populations and honed it to refer to marginalized, original populations of independent states, reflecting expansion from Latin America to a more global context. Keeping to its modus operandi, the ILO prepared a convention to guide states in how they should better the conditions of Indigenous populations. The ILO secretariat acknowledged the difficulty in defining "Indigenous" due to the great variation in legal and administrative criteria used by governments and the theoretical criteria used by anthropologists and sociologists. Instead, it suggested a pragmatic definition: "descendants of the peoples who inhabited the country at the time of conquest or colonisation, who lead a tribal or semi-tribal existence more in conformity with the social, economic and cultural institutions of the period before conquest or colonisation than with the institutions of the nation to which they belong, or who are governed by special legislation."[7] Emphasizing its aim of integrating marginalized groups living under similarly difficult economic and social conditions, the Secretariat also proposed to include groups that were not Indigenous in the historical sense but that had "a tribal or semi-tribal structure whose social and economic conditions are similar" to those covered by the definition above.[8] It estimated that between 50 and 70 million in the Americas, Asia, Africa, the Near and Middle East, and Oceania were Indigenous peoples of independent countries.[9]

On the basis of the Secretariat's proposal and replies from its member states, in 1957 the ILO International Labour Conference adopted the Convention Concerning the Protection and Integration of Indigenous and Other Tribal and Semi-Tribal Populations in Independent Countries (C107), which contained a set of protective rights covering the period it would take for these populations to become integrated into modern social and economic life. At the heart of these were collective land rights. Article 11 proclaimed: "The right of ownership, collective or individual, of the members of the populations concerned over the lands which these populations traditionally occupy shall be recognized." The next three articles obligated states to avoid non-consensual removal of populations from such territories and to secure compensation in exceptional cases; emphasized that customary transmission of ownership was to be respected; and recommended national agrarian programs to secure and develop sufficient land for the Indigenous populations.[10] The UN Food and Agricultural Organization expressed its approval of the land rights provision, emphasizing that the "primary rights of these populations to land should be firmly protected during the period of transition preceding that of development."[11] The assumption underlying C107 was the perceived need of these populations for modernization and development.

Rights of Indigenous Peoples to Land and Natural Resources 281

International Norms and the Sami in Norway before the mid-1960s

The Sami were historically nomadic hunter-gatherer population groups with languages differing from the Nordic (*norrøn*). Since time immemorial, they have lived in the extreme northwest corner of the European continent, now part of the territories of Norway, Sweden, Finland, and Russia. The interior far north of Norway – the arctic land plateau now known as *Finnmarksvidda* – was populated exclusively by Sami, entering the power sphere of the Scandinavian states only in the fourteenth century. The northern coastline and parts of the inland southern interior had Sami communities living side by side with Nordic agricultural or fishing communities, permanent Nordic settlements along the northern coastline most likely appearing in the 1300s.[12]

The border between Sweden and Denmark-Norway was drawn in 1751, with a specific annex known as *Lappecodicilen* pertaining to the rights of the Sami to cross borders. Norway entered a union with Sweden in 1814 (dissolved in 1905), and the border between Sweden-Norway and Russia was agreed in 1826. The result was Sami populations in the modern-day nation-states of Norway, Sweden, Finland, and Russia. In the mid-seventeenth century, on what is today Norwegian territory, the inland Sami began the large-scale domestication of reindeer.[13] The need for summer pastures in coastal areas led to recurring conflicts over land use in the north, among Sami communities and with other populations.[14] The nineteenth century saw fundamental changes within Sami communities: permanent housing for the coastal Sami, and for inland Sami housing at both their winter and summer pasture lands. Cross-cultural marriages became more common among Sami, Norwegian, and Kven populations (the latter emigrating from northern Finland/Sweden during the 1700s and 1800s). The jurist Sverre Tønnesen, writing in 1978, held that this made it more difficult to define "Sami" as well as historical "Sami areas."[15]

In the nineteenth century, the Norwegian state increasingly exercised its regulatory powers, including in the north, with new state laws and regulations relevant to the Sami. This included mining (1842), reindeer husbandry (1854, 1888), land sale (1864), gold (1869), fishing in the Tana River (1887), peat cutting (1897), and hunting (1899).[16] Notably, the state considered itself the rightful owner of all unregistered land in Finnmark, the northernmost regional administrative county of Norway.[17] This was a large area, the size of

Denmark. The Sami enjoyed full citizens' rights in Norway, but a "Norwegianization" policy targeting Kven and Sami language and religious practices was implemented from the middle of the nineteenth century and escalated through the second part of it and extended until the interwar years.[18]

International protective norms seem to have had little resonance in Norway. Historian Einar Niemi has pointed out how Norway, a strong supporter of minority issues in the League of Nations, "was acting quite differently on its home ground."[19] Some international influences were nevertheless traceable in discussions that occurred in the 1920s relating to the use of Sami as a supportive language in schools.[20] Statistics Norway applied the terminological change from "Lapps" or "Finns" to "Sami" in the 1930 census, revealing a degree of cultural sensitivity by using the in-group name for the Sami minority.[21] And in 1936 the Norwegian Parliament – the *Storting* – decided to allow the use of Sami as a supportive language in schools in north Norway, with one parliamentarian arguing that this was "the right of the Sami" as a "national minority."[22] Despite this, the international and the national were largely disconnected in Norwegian minority policies. This was true for both the Norwegian and Sami political realm, and historian Henry Minde has found that, during the interwar years, the Sami had "neither the knowledge nor the expertise in international law and the rights of minorities that was necessary if they were to see their own predicament within an international perspective, nor any idea that they could raise an issue in an international forum."[23]

The formal policies of Norwegianization were dismantled after the war, but the social and cultural process of assimilation continued.[24] The continued reduction in use of Sami language and other cultural expressions was connected to the experiences of the war and the modernization ideology of the postwar years. The German occupiers' forced evacuation of Finnmark at the end of the war included the burning of houses, barns, industrial buildings, churches, hospitals, and other structures, resulting in the destruction of material evidence of ethnicity.[25] Reconstruction was supported by government schemes that made available building materials for modern houses. The national culture of unity, born from the experience of foreign occupation, also furthered assimilation. Being Sami was a social stigma, associated with backwardness and a low standard of living.[26] It was not uncommon for Sami and Kven parents to see the Norwegian language as a prerequisite for a successful future for their children.[27] In the early 1960s, the disappearance of the Sami culture was noted with concern in some government quarters,

Rights of Indigenous Peoples to Land and Natural Resources 283

and the Ministry of Church and Education noted in 1962 that the Sami-speaking population was fast diminishing due not to normal demographic changes but, rather, because small, rural communities had succumbed to pressure from surrounding Norwegian-speaking communities "in Norwegianizing the social identities of the Sami and thereby their language."[28]

The Norwegian government and local administrators had pursued a policy of integration in the years after the Second World War, and some had expressed the view that the Sami would eventually become Norwegians.[29] This reflected modernization ideology shared by intergovernmental organizations and other governments in this period. However, in direct contrast to societal changes stemming from the birth of the welfare state, modernization ideology, and the rebuilding of northern Norway, the late 1940s and 1950s saw a gradual movement by the Norwegian government and local authorities towards recognition of Sami cultural rights, reflecting and possibly contributing to an emerging consciousness among the Sami that they were one people regardless of their livelihoods. The authorities had registered that the Sami shared allegiance with the Norwegian population during the war. On this basis and probably also reflecting international sensitivities towards racial discrimination, the high-ranking government official Einar Boyesen launched a reconsideration of Sami education policies.[30] As a result, the late 1940s saw the increased use of bilingual schoolbooks; Sami courses were given as part of the education of teachers in Tromsø (northern Norway's largest city); and economic support was provided to students wanting to learn Sami.[31]

During the late 1950s and 1960s, reindeer husbandry underwent modernization, with automation and market integration, in what was a "de facto self-governing society, under a limited civil servant rule."[32] The Reindeer Herd Management Act, 1933 (in force until 1979), protected inherited rights in vast areas.[33] Sami agricultural production changed from small subsistence production with two to three cows, a few sheep, and occasionally goats to farms that were growing modestly larger and were increasingly geared to production through public dairies and cooperatives (*Nord-Norges Salgslag*).[34] Developments in local farming in the north (Norwegian, Sami, and Kven alike) and reindeer pastoralism practices increased competition for pasture in outlying areas – *utmark* – as well as for wood for fuel and building materials. The same was true for fishing, hunting, and the collecting of eggs, feathers, berries, and various plants.[35] New roads made the Finnmark interior more accessible. The demand for hunting/fishing cabins coming from people who were permanent residents elsewhere but who came on a transient basis put greater pressure on limited resources.[36] According to Tønnessen, this combined pressure created a need for rules pertaining to the exclusive rights of the local population regarding hunting and fishing in waterways. The legal and judicial changes that occurred in 1951 and that were applied to hunting and natural resources policy were responses to demands from the local population.[37]

Early postwar ethno-politics did not herald a re-evaluation of the doctrine of the state as owner of all unregistered land in Finnmark. The decade of the 1950s saw Sami claims to land and natural resources reinforced, including the securing of usage rights and the right of ownership. The Finnmark Sami Council (established in 1953), led by teacher and politician Per Fokstad, himself of Sami background, claimed in 1956 that the Sami "live in the secure conviction that the inland mountains and hills and islands by the coast, which they have used since time immemorial has not been a land with no owner but has belonged to the Sami."[38] In March 1957, the council demanded that the government clarify the rights of the Sami to land and natural resources in their traditional areas.[39] The notion that the Sami had claims as valid as any written law or document was controversial. Court decisions had favoured agricultural over nomadic interests, but change was in the wind. In a 1957 minority view, Supreme Court Chief Justice Terje Wold argued that "neither convention nor law can limit the old rights of nomadic Sami as these rights have been practised since time immemorial [*alders tids bruk*]."[40]

Neither international organizations, nor the Norwegian state, nor Sami representatives seem to have considered international efforts to support Indigenous populations as relevant to a Norwegian context. None of the states with Sami populations had been scrutinized in the 1953 ILO document or mentioned in the report that preceded C107. Norway, like Sweden, had informed the ILO several times that it had "no population group which according to the definition in Article 1 of the proposed convention can be described as tribal or semi-tribal."[41] Internal papers reveal that the Norwegian Ministries of Agriculture and Social Affairs concluded that the draft convention was not relevant to the Norwegian Sami because they were "integrated into Norwegian society"; the issue had been discussed with the chair of the Sami Committee (appointed in 1956 by the government to examine Sami issues), who had concurred.[42] Finding the convention not relevant to its domestic situation, the Norwegian ILO delegation did not allocate a representative to the negotiations but merely observed in the plenary and

Rights of Indigenous Peoples to Land and Natural Resources 285

voted in support of the convention with no real engagement with its content.[43] The government forwarded C107 to Parliament with the recommendation that it not be ratified.[44] The responsible parliamentary committee had nothing to add, no parliamentarian took the floor during the plenary session, and Norway did not ratify C107.[45]

Parallel to the discussions within the ILO, the Sami Committee worked to outline cultural and economic measures to enable the Sami to develop skills and make the most of what society had to offer.[46] Sami activists and non-Sami intellectuals promoting Sami identity and interests dominated the Sami Committee.[47] The process saw the arrival of policies of special rights built on the dual expectations of further integration of the Sami population and preservation of the distinct Sami culture.[48] The Sami Committee's 1959 report underscored the significance of supporting the entire Sami minority, not only those working with reindeer (less than 10 percent of the population).[49] Its ethnically based policy reforms produced tense debate in Finnmark, however. Negative reactions included charges of "reservation politics" and arguments that Sami children learn Norwegian in order to benefit from economic development. Municipalities along the coast reacted more negatively to the committee's proposals than did those inland.[50]

Taking a supportive view, clearly sensitive to international developments, the Nordic Sami Council, established in 1956 by Sami groups, recommended that the Sami be recognized as an "Indigenous population" with attendant collective rights to natural resources.[51] This stemmed from a conference of lawyers with a specific interest in Sami rights to natural resources and organized by the Nordic Sami Council in the Swedish Parliament the same year the Sami Committee finalized its report.[52] Its subsequent initiative, in 1959, to the Nordic Council (consisting of parliamentarians from all Nordic countries) resulted in a recommendation that the governments "investigate the problems of the Sami population in order to identify strategies to develop the culture of this population and improve its standards of living."[53]

The international discrediting of racial policies after the war and attention to human rights have been highlighted as factors contributing to the rise of cultural sensitivity in Norwegian Sami policies after the war.[54] It wasn't until the late 1950s, however, that Sami activists argued that it was a *human right* to be educated in their mother tongue.[55] On the Norwegian Constitution Day, 17 May 1958, Norwegian prime minister Einar Gerhardsen proclaimed on *Sameradioen*, the Sami-language radio program of the Norwegian Broadcasting Company, that the democracy rested not only on the

Constitution but also on the UN Universal Declaration of Human Rights: these human rights "had their full validity also for the Sami in this country."[56] International focus on human rights exposed Norway's Sami policies as an Achilles' heel: in the 1960 UN General Assembly the South African foreign minister was affronted by Norwegian attacks on the apartheid system and lashed out.[57] Terje Wold, who served as a judge (1959–71) in the European Court of Human Rights, reinforced the view of the Sami as an Indigenous population in a 1962 speech to the Congress of the Nordic Sami Council. Although not addressing the Sami situation in detail, he emphasized that a familiarity with international law and minority rights norms might be helpful for "the Sami and for everyone who works with Sami problems." Wold distinguished between "minorities" and "Indigenous populations," arguing that, while UN and European human rights instruments did not mention the latter explicitly, international consensus held that populations like the Sami, as an original population of a territory with no allegiance to another state and that retained its cultural traits, was entitled to protection by Norwegian society.[58] This view would not become official state policy for another fifteen to twenty years.

The 1962 government white paper was based on the Sami Committee report and discussed its many proposals – and it also referred to the position of the Nordic Sami Council, which was that the Sami should enjoy particular rights as an Indigenous population – but it heralded no significant changes to accommodate the concerns of the committee regarding land rights and natural resources.[59] Unlike natural resources, cultural rights were less problematic, and the white paper approved, among other proposals, the more extensive use of the Sami language in education and public administration. One committee member later wryly termed the white paper "porridge made with water [not milk]."[60] The *Storting* Committee on Church and Education was more sympathetic to some of the proposals, and in the subsequent debate a few Norwegian parliamentarians suggested that the government consider recognizing special Sami rights to land and natural recourses, including fishing in certain inland waters. Three representatives cited the need to secure particular rights because these were the "human rights" of the Sami.[61]

Despite the international framing of the issue of Sami rights by the Nordic Sami Council and some Norwegian lawyers and politicians, international law had limited impact on government thinking on rights to land and natural resources. The Sami and other local populations were treated equally, *pace* some concessions to reindeer owners. Along the coast, after

Rights of Indigenous Peoples to Land and Natural Resources 287

the Second World War the local Sami population had not kept up with rapid technological developments in fishing, and the 1959 Sami Committee report proposed regulations pertaining to fishing in the fjords.[62] Coastal fishing, however, was considered a "national common property resource" and was regulated by the state with no safeguarding of Sami interests.[63] The Norwegian government and the *Storting* confirmed through a 1965 law that the title to all unregistered land in Finnmark County belonged to the state.[64] The interests of reindeer herders regularly conflicted with agricultural interests and industrial development. A much debated decision was the Bieddjovagge copper mines expansion, which was supported by government grants (*Distriktenes utbyggingsfond*) in Kautokeino after the 1966 rise in global copper prices. No rent was paid to the Sami, but economic compensation for loss of herding territories was given to individual families.[65]

International Framing of Sami Rights

The anthropologist Harald Eidheim wrote in 1969 that to be Sami was still a social stigma.[66] Sami politician Per Fokstad reflected that, during his childhood, "we did not know our history. We did not know that the Norwegians were colonizers up here, and that we were the Indigenous people."[67] Fokstad had been educated in Norway and then in Denmark and England and had also visited France, and he reflected on how questions of identity and racism resembled his own experience in Norway: "The Jews were not just French ... they were Jews, a distinct race. They were despised, like us. They were longing for their own country."[68] The loss of Sami culture weighed heavily on Fokstad: he felt it was on the brink of extinction.[69]

As elsewhere, in the late 1960s a new generation of Sami activists was making itself heard, partly through the special-interest organization Norske Samers Riksforbund (NSR), founded in 1968.[70] The objective of the NSR was to voice the interests of the Sami population to the Norwegian government and work to improve Sami social and economic conditions.[71] The organization demanded adherence to the Supreme Court's 1968 *Altevann* judgment recognizing Sami rights to land and natural resources, including granting rights of use equal status with rights of ownership, and that the government identify territories constituting a "Sami rights area." It also demanded that, in government discussions, the term "Sami" apply to *all* Sami, not just reindeer-owning Sami.[72]

Controversies over Sami land rights in the late 1950s and especially from the late 1970s turned on historical patterns of usage and the contemporary relevance of such knowledge. The emerging understanding of the Sami as a colonized people reflected how international events and debates defined Sami identity and shaped national academic and political debates. Several academic books published from the late 1960s to the mid-1970s pointed out similarities between the Sami situation and that of other groups, arguing that they constituted a nation colonized by Nordic peoples.[73] Some held that this colonization process was ongoing – the sociologist Per Otnes termed the expansion of the Bieddjovagge copper mines the "anti-Christ of new-colonialism," which "slowly but surely would empty Nordkalotten [the Arctic High North] of resources."[74] Scholars and Sami activists argued that the 1751 *Lappecodicilen* was a binding treaty with contemporary significance for the rights of the Sami people.[75] Ole Henrik Magga, the first president of the Sami Parliament in 1989, has recalled that his own thinking on this problem was greatly influenced by the lawyer Tomas Cramér, ombudsman (1962–82) for the National Sami Association of Sweden.[76] Cramér had been a principal in successful legal strategies to secure Sami rights to land and natural resources in Sweden in the 1960s (with markedly less favourable results when Sami reindeer interests conflicted with hydroelectric or mining industries) and contributed a chapter on *Lappecodicilen* and Sami rights to land and water to the 1969 book *Nordisk nykolonialisme* (Nordic new colonialism).[77]

In the late 1960s a massive hydroelectric project in northern Norway brought to a boil the simmering Sami activism of previous decades. The source of controversy was the river that flows 160 kilometres from near inland Kautokeino to coastal Alta, through sparsely populated inner Finnmark. Plans were first presented in 1968, supported by the government, local and national energy authorities, and the Finnmark County Council, prompting increasingly fierce opposition on the part of Sami organizations and environmental groups. After intense conflict, the proposal to submerge the predominantly Sami village of Masi was shelved in 1973; the scheme, however, was not, and it became a running battle over the next decade, including the event described in the opening of this chapter.

The historian Henry Minde has pointed to the "mutual lack of trust and respect between the government and Sami organizations during the 1970s."[78] Notwithstanding, in this period the government supported many cultural and educational initiatives. There was also some government sensitivity to Sami claims. Referring to the Alta River, the Norwegian government concluded in 1973–74 that "a coherent plan for the protection and use of natural resources in Sami areas" was needed,[79] and in 1975 it created the body known as the Resource Commission, led by the botanist and Social

Rights of Indigenous Peoples to Land and Natural Resources

Democrat Olav Gjærevoll. Its objective was to identify and assess local, district, and national interests related to the Finnmark plateau and to consider plans for major development and infrastructure projects. The mandate stipulated that this be done with an eye to preserving large natural areas for maintaining the patterns of life for the local population and to protect Sami culture. The commission was also instructed to prepare proposals for future use of the area, including mitigating the adverse effects of tourism.[80] In its 1978 report, the commission did not use the term "Indigenous population"; in more than three hundred pages it never once referred to international law or human rights. Strictly a national framing of the Sami rights issue, the report nevertheless described the Finnmark plateau as a "Sami heartland with a distinct way of life and culture" and a "Sami cultural landscape and not a wilderness area."[81] Some branches of the government were less responsive to Sami demands: the 1978 reindeer-herding act did not take into account what have since been recognized as unprecedented Supreme Court decisions of the late 1960s based on the principle of long-term use.[82]

Some government ministries and parliamentarians were becoming comfortable with an international framing of Sami issues, including the notion of "Indigenous population." Sami activists had rediscovered the ILO C107 through involvement with the nascent international Indigenous peoples movement in the mid- and late 1970s. Challenged by Sami representatives in 1977 to confirm that Norway had not ratified the convention, the Ministry of Social Affairs launched a review on the basis of the stated Sami desire to be considered an Indigenous population.[83] The following year, State Secretary of the Ministry of Foreign Affairs Thorvald Stoltenberg spoke, at the UN Conference on Racism, of the "threat against the indigenous peoples' existence" and pointed out that much remained to be done to make right the "long history of discrimination and forced assimilation of the Sami."[84] The Norwegian delegation furthermore drafted concern for Indigenous peoples into the conference's final document.[85] Johan J. Jakobsen, a member of the committee for foreign policy and president of the Centre Party (agrarian party) found that "the unclear legal situation [regarding land rights] has been a constant barrier between the Sami people and the rest of the Norwegian society," and he underscored Norway's international role in promoting Indigenous issues.[86]

The 1980 green paper on Norway's ratification of C107, penned by lawyer and officer of the Ministry of Justice's legal department Einar Høgetveit, concluded that the Sami were without doubt an Indigenous population as defined in C107. Høgetveit amended the official translation into Norwegian of the convention's key concept of "Indigenous populations": where the 1958 translation had *innfødte befolkningsgrupper*, which incorporates the historical experience of colonization, Høgetveit, in line with international developments, used *urbefolkninger*, which invokes the sense of habitation since time immemorial.[87] Høgetveit concluded, however, that both the integrationist framework of the convention and the Norwegian non-compliance with its land rights provisions argued against ratification.

Norway did not overturn its decision of non-ratification of C107, the sole international convention specifically dealing with Indigenous populations; however, from the mid-1980s the Norwegian government found itself simultaneously negotiating Indigenous rights on both domestic and international fronts.

The Rise of the Indigenous Collective as an Economic Actor

In direct response to the firestorm over the Alta River, the Norwegian government appointed a Sami cultural commission and a Sami rights commission in 1980 to reconsider the fundamental basis for Norwegian Sami politics,[88] including political representation and Sami rights to land and water in Finnmark.[89] A few years later, the UN and the ILO started work on instruments on the rights of Indigenous peoples. This decade saw the rise of the Indigenous collective as an economic actor in many nations, eventually also in Norway.

Dealing with Indigenous rights issues at local, national, regional, and international levels simultaneously was not unique to Norway. In New Zealand in 1985, the mandate of the 1975 Waitangi Tribunal was extended to historical claims dating back to 1840.[90] The Australian government declared the end to the policy of assimilation in 1972, following a decade of Aboriginal activism that included protests over transfer of land to large mining companies. The 1980s saw transfer of land title to Aboriginal owners in the Commonwealth-controlled Northern Territory and in northwest South Australia, and also controversies over proposed national land rights legislation that failed after having met "stern resistance from Aboriginal leaders, Labour party members and states" and was followed by path-breaking court litigation in the early 1990s.[91] In the United States, Native American claims for sovereignty over mineral resources on their reservations led to changes in federal laws in the 1980s and 1990s.[92] Similar developments took place in Canada, which, in 1971, declared itself a multicultural state.[93] In 1982, the government introduced a constitutional amendment specifically recogniz-

Rights of Indigenous Peoples to Land and Natural Resources

ing existing treaty rights, and the rise of Indigenous co-management in northern Canada as "an intellectual tradition and policy tool" from the 1980s was so rapid as to seem "like a revolution to some."[94] In Chapter 3 (this volume), Robin S. Gendron and Andreas R.D. Sanders similarly point to the increasing role of First Nations in the 1980s as a major development in Canadian natural resource management. These developments meant that, while discussions ran high at home, states were simultaneously formulating statements on Indigenous peoples' rights in the ILO and the UN.

What Sidney Tarrow has called "global framing" became critical in the reshaping of Norwegian Sami policies,[95] even though the international and national processes were not fully integrated at a personal or an institutional level. The mandate of the Norwegian Sami Rights Commission referred explicitly to international law and, in particular, to the minority clause of the 1966 UN human rights covenant on civil and political rights since Norway was a party to this convention. The commission was instructed to give priority to political rights – in particular, the question of a constitutional amendment and the establishment of a representative body for the Sami population.[96] Four years later, it nevertheless made some highly important assertions about economic rights in its first report, penned by its chairman, law professor and later supreme justice, Carsten Smith. The UN covenant on civil and political rights, the commission argued, obligated Norway to protect the material foundation of Sami culture, with the proposed constitutional provision on Sami rights interpreted accordingly.[97] The Department of Justice and the government concurred, and the *Storting* followed.[98]

On the international level, Norway's buoyant image as a promulgator of peace and human rights made its politicians particularly eager to contribute in a positive manner, especially after the Alta controversy, which had shaken the political establishment in Oslo. Rights to land and natural resources were at the heart of both UN and ILO deliberations. It was unproblematic for Norway to support political rights – including the right to be consulted – in the 1988–89 draft of what became ILO C169. Land rights, and the situation in Finnmark in particular, turned out to be particularly challenging. Strong legal protection of usage rights (the principle known as *alders tids bruk*) was unfamiliar in many states, and Indigenous activists worked hard to prevent any proposals that might undermine Indigenous land rights. At the eleventh hour, the conference agreed to a deal on land rights that diverged from Norway's preferred position of placing usage rights on a par with rights to ownership. Supported by a unanimous vote in Parliament,

Norway nevertheless ratified the convention a year after it was adopted – the first state to do so.[99]

After 1984, parallel to the international standard-setting processes, the Sami Rights Commission tackled the issue of economic rights. It was 1997 before the commission submitted its final report, titled *On the Foundation in Nature of the Sami Culture*,[100] and it was 2005 before Parliament adopted the path-breaking Finnmark Act on issues of Sami land rights. As noted by political scientist Anne Julie Semb, it is possible to trace the effects of international norms on the national developments that led to the Finnmark Act. The commission's 1997 report was informed by perceptions of Norway's international obligations and reflections on the practices of other states. Moreover, public debate revealed significant differences in opinion over the precise legal obligations stemming from C169, which reached a flashpoint after the Norwegian government tabled its draft law on unregistered land in Finnmark in 2003. Where the commission had recommended transfer of ownership through a semi-private agency of unregistered land in Finnmark to the local population as a collective, the government counter-proposed some state control over this agency.[101] The Sami Parliament (established in 1989) and several Sami organizations protested vociferously, finding support in a supplementary 1997 green paper on post-1984 international legal developments pertaining to Indigenous rights.[102] The Sami Parliament appealed to the UN and the ILO and succeeded in bringing international pressure to bear on the Norwegian government.[103]

Responding to its critics, the government commissioned expert opinion on the international legal aspects of the proposed act, which highlighted its problematic aspects.[104] Furthermore, the right to be consulted, embedded in C169, gave rise to formal consultations between the Norwegian Parliament and the Sami Parliament on the draft act. This resulted in strengthened local and Sami control over the new semi-private agency and the establishment of a commission to identify and settle individual rights claims in this area.[105] Thus we find a clear footprint of international norms on the political process that preceded the new law on unregistered land in Finnmark and the management and ownership system it established. Furthermore, political sensitivity to Sami rights was mirrored by the courts.[106] Questions of land rights are being negotiated to this day. Individual rights to land and natural resources, for Sami and other stakeholders, are currently being adjudicated by the Finnmark Commission. Issues of Sami land rights south of Finnmark are under consideration by the government.[107]

Rights of Indigenous Peoples to Land and Natural Resources

Delineating the precise effects of international norms on Sami rights to saltwater fishing is more complicated. In 1983, a New Zealand court interpreted for the first time its Fisheries Act, which stated "Nothing in this Act shall affect any Maori fishing right," and established a separate domain of customary rights that could not be taken away without the consent of the rights holders. This domain built on traditional rights but, at the same time, recognized the right of Indigenous peoples to participate in modern commercial activities.[108] There was no similar law or legal precedent in Norway. Sami rights to saltwater fishing became an increasingly contentious political issue. Inspired by the Alta River conflict, fishers had "made [their] Sami background relevant in the fisheries political arena" in the mid-1980s, which brought what had previously been an internal fisheries issue "into an ethno-political arena."[109] A quota system was set in place, in response to calls for stronger regulation to prevent overfishing, which the Sami Parliament charged neglected both Sami interests and Norwegian international legal obligations.[110]

Attention to the rights of Sami as an Indigenous people informed the Ministry of Fisheries appointment of a Sami fisheries commission in 1993, which concluded four years later that Norway, in lieu of any constitutional and international law, was obliged to use positive discrimination to secure Sami rights to saltwater fishing. In an earlier report, Smith predicted that this might appear unreasonable to local Norwegian fishers who would not be given similar protection and could see their fishing quotas reduced.[111] The commission proposed, mirroring Smith's suggestion, that the measures be structured as a collective, local right of the population in areas with a significant Sami presence.[112] The Sami Parliament, on the other hand, preferred a Sami fisheries zone.[113] As of 2015, key issues of Sami rights to fishing are still under debate.[114]

Extraction of subsurface resources in Sami traditional areas similarly became increasingly controversial. Since the mid-1980s, successive Norwegian governments sought to modernize national law on subsurface resources, merging provisions on non-claimable and claimable minerals. While Sami rights received only passing mention in the first green paper, by the mid-1990s it was of prime concern.[115] The Sami Parliament, deeply divided on this issue, emphasized Sami rights to traditional activities, including compensation for lost pastures or other rights and their rights to ownership, including rights to mineral rent (*urfolksvederlag*/Indigenous rents). The government engaged in a series of consultations with the Sami Parliament in

2009 but failed to achieve consensus.[116] The new law came into force the following year without the consent of the Sami Parliament, leaving issues of extraction of mineral resources in Sami traditional areas still unresolved.[117]

Conclusion

With roots in the 1930s, international norms on the rights of Indigenous populations from the 1950s limited the freedom of states to regulate natural resources as they saw fit. States that ratified the ILO conventions of 1957 and 1989 pledged to uphold their provisions on land rights, and these and other international instruments became part of local and national dynamics that undermined the legitimacy of long-held legal doctrines in many national settings related to ownership to land and water and the renewable and non-renewable resources therein. From the mid-1970s, these dynamics included increasingly vocal claims-making in international contexts by groups identifying as Indigenous peoples. This internationalized ongoing local and national struggles and formed a central context for how states in the 1980s and later implemented new systems of Indigenous co- and self-management over land and natural resources.

For Norway, international and national political initiatives on human rights and minority policies became intertwined after the Second World War, eventually leading to a reconsideration of the status of the Sami. International developments did not play a significant role for Sami rights to natural resources in the 1950s and 1960s but became a major factor in the late 1970s and the 1980s as lawyers and the government increasingly saw the Sami as an Indigenous people with distinct inherited rights. The years since 1989 have seen an ambitious and vocal Sami Parliament representing the Sami as a collective economic actor in interactions with the national government and private players, its position unique in the Norwegian political and administrative system.

However, while international and national political processes became increasingly enmeshed, the national framework remained dominant. The Sami gained traction from international instruments with regard to demands to land rights, which had gained explicit protection, in contrast to natural resources, which were not explicitly addressed. The latter included claims for rights to saltwater fishing and subsurface natural resources that conflicted with powerful national, private-sector, and public interests. Generally, there was little support for proposals based on positive ethnic discrimination in the economic sphere. Most economic concessions made to the Sami as an Indigenous population were designed as collective solutions for all

Rights of Indigenous Peoples to Land and Natural Resources 295

who live in regions designated as particular Sami administrative areas – those with a significant contemporary and historical Sami population. Many issues pertaining to Sami rights to land and natural resources, however, remain contested and are still in the process of being resolved. But the international framing of these issues has come to stay.

Notes

1 The uses of these terms have changed over time and are politically controversial. I use "populations" for the period up to 1989 and "peoples" thereafter, keeping to the change in terminology in the ILO treaties.
2 Luis Rodríguez-Piñero, *Indigenous Peoples, Postcolonialism and International Law: The ILO Regime, 1919–1989* (Oxford: Oxford University Press, 2006), 17–66.
3 Ibid., 89–98, 116–21.
4 International Labour Office, *Indigenous Peoples: Living and Working Conditions of Aboriginal Populations in Independent Countries* (Geneva: ILO, 1953), 295.
5 Ibid., 286.
6 Ibid., 302–54.
7 International Labour Conference, "Eight Item [sic] on the Agenda: Living and Working Conditions of Indigenous Populations in Independent Countries," in *39th Session, Report 8 (1)* (Geneva: International Labour Office, 1955), 48.
8 Ibid.
9 Ibid., 49.
10 Convention Concerning the Protection and Integration of Indigenous and Other Tribal and Semi-Tribal Populations in Independent Countries (C107), Articles 11–14.
11 ILO, Proceedings of the 39th Session of the Conference, 7.
12 Official Norwegian Report (hereafter NOU), 1978:18B, 145, 155–56; NOU 1994:21, 11–12, 16. NOU reports come out of an investigation by a government-appointed committee or commission. These reports often form the basis for major policy documents and proposals that the government presents to the *Storting* (the Norwegian Parliament) in the form of a white paper (St. Meld, which is an orientation or a policy statement about a particular field) or a proposition (St. Prp/Ot.Prp, such as a bill or budget). These were discussed and decided upon by the Parliament (St. Forh) on the basis of the recommendations of a parliamentary committee (Innst. O. or S.). See also Øyvind Ravna, "Samerett og samiske rettigheter i Norge," in *Juss i Nord: Hav, fisk og urfolk*, ed. Tore Henriksen and Øyvind Ravna (Oslo: Gyldendal, 2012), 150–52.
13 NOU 1978:18B, 156. Some have argued that this happened earlier. See Kirsti Strøm Bull in NOU 2001:34, part 4. See also NOU 1994:21, 63–65.
14 NOU 1978:18B, 158; NOU 1994:21, 57–58. The Danish king tended to decide in favour of the inland Sami in order to consolidate his tax base and thus strengthen Danish territorial claims in the event of border issues with Sweden. On other forms of resource competition/conflicts, see NOU 1994:21, 36–39, 53–56, 71–75.
15 Sverre Tønnesen in NOU 1978:18B, 195. Tønnesen had written his ground-breaking doctoral dissertation on Sami land rights in Finnmark a few years earlier. See Sverre Tønnesen, "Retten til jorden i Finnmark" (PhD diss., Universitetsforlaget, 1972). For

296   *Hanne Hagtvedt Vik*

more recent historically informed and detailed legal expositions of the question of Sami rights to land and natural resources, see NOU 1994:21; and Otto Jebens, *Om eiendomsretten til grunnen i Indre Finnmark* (Oslo: Cappelen Akademisk Forlag, 1999).

16 Tønnesen in NOU 1978:18B, 195–96; Strøm Bull in NOU 2001:34, part 4.

17 Ravna, "Samerett og samiske rettigheter i Norge," 152–53; Jebens, *Om eiendomsretten til grunnen i Indre Finnmark*. On the British Empire and land rights, see Louis A. Knafla, "'This Is Our Land': Aboriginal Title at Customary and Common Law in Comparative Contexts," in *Aboriginal Title and Indigenous Peoples: Canada, Australia, and New Zealand*, ed. Louis A. Knafla and Haijo Westra (Vancouver: UBC Press, 2010), 1–15; Paul McHugh, *Aboriginal Societies and the Common Law: A History of Sovereignty, Status and Self-Determination* (New York: Oxford University Press, 2004).

18 Knut Einar Eriksen and Einar Niemi, *Den finske fare: Sikkerhetsproblemer og minoritetspolitikk i Nord 1860–1940* (Oslo: Universitetsforlaget, 1981). See also Henry Minde, "Fornorskinga av samene – hvorfor, hvordan og hvilke følger?," *Gáldu čála, Tidsskrift for urfolks rettigheter* 3 (2005): 6–30.

19 Einar Niemi, "The Finns in Northern Scandinavia and Minority Policy," in *Ethnicity and Nation Building in the Nordic World*, ed. Sven Tägil (London: Hurst and Company, 1994), 167.

20 One of the central actors working for the Sami language in schools, Per Fokstad, himself stated that his influence was international, stemming from his experiencing similar peoples' struggles in other countries. See Eivind Bråstad Jensen, "Per Pavelsen Fokstad – en stridsmann for samisk utdanning, språk og kultur," in *Pedagogiske profiler: Norsk utdanningstenkning fra Holberg til Hernes*, ed. Harald Thuen and Sveinung Vaage (Oslo: Abstrakt Forlag, 2004), 199–224; Regnor Jernsletten, *Samebevegelsen i Norge: idé og strategi 1900–1940* (Tromsø: Senter for samiske studier, Universitetet i Tromsø, 1998).

21 "Fjerde hefte: Samer og Kvener. Andre lands statsborgere. Blinde, døvstumme, åndssvake og sinnsyke," in *Folketellingen i Norge 1 Desember 1930* (Oslo: Statistics Norway, 1930), 2–17.

22 Intervention by Labour party representative Kristian Berg, *Storting* debate of 7 July 1936, St. Forh. 8 (1936), 744. For a discussion of this incident and the decision not to allow the use of the Kven language in a similar way, see Eriksen and Niemi, *Den finske fare*, 298–99.

23 Henry Minde, "The Making of an International Movement of Indigenous Peoples," *Scandinavian Journal of History* 21, 3 (1996): 229.

24 Robert Paine, *Coast Lapp Situation* (Tromsø: Tromsø Museum, 1957), xiii; Ivar Bjørklund, *Fjordfolket i Kvænangen: Fra samisk samfunn til norsk utkant 1550–1980* (Tromsø: Universitetsforlaget, 1985), 365–404.

25 Bjørklund, *Fjordfolket i Kvænangen: Fra samisk samfunn til norsk utkant 1550–1980*, 380–81.

26 Harald Eidheim, *Aspects of the Lappish Situation* (Oslo: Scandinavia University Books, 1971), esp. 10; Camilla Bakken Larsen, "Om oppgjøret som forsvant? Norsk samepolitikk 1945–1963" (Master's thesis, University of Tromsø, 2012), 25.

27 Larsen, "Om oppgjøret som forsvant?," 25.

Rights of Indigenous Peoples to Land and Natural Resources 297

28 Ministry of Church and Education, St. Meld. 21 (1962–63), 4. Dividing the population along racial lines had lost its legitimacy during the war, and the minority categories were removed from the Norwegian census. Only information on language and self-identification was kept, see Einar Lie, "Numbering the Nationalities: Ethnic Minorities in Norwegian Population Censuses, 1845–1930," *Ethnic and Racial Studies* 25, 5 (2002): 819.

29 See, for example, report on the meeting in Karasjok, April 10, 1970, in Tor Edvin Dahl, *Samene i dag og i morgen: En rapport* (Oslo: Gyldendal norsk forlag, 1970), 205–9.

30 Larsen, "Om oppgjøret som forsvant?," 31, 33–39.

31 Eriksen and Niemi, *Den finske fare*, 349. For an exposition of the early use of Sami and bilingual books in schools, see Helge Dahl, *Språkpolitikk og skolestell i Finnmark 1814–1905* (Oslo: Universitetsforlaget, 1951). The 1951 book *ABC for folkeskolen* by Margrete Wiig was the most important book developed in the early postwar years and was funded by the Norwegian Ministry for Church and Education, see http://skuvla.info/sambok-n.htm (viewed 31 July 2016).

32 Jan Åge Riseth, "Sami Reindeer Management in Norway: Modernization Challenges and Conflicting Strategies," in *Indigenous Peoples: Resource Management and Global Rights*, ed. Svein Jentoft, Henry Minde, and Ragnar Nilsen (Chicago: University of Chicago Press, 2003), 230–31; Bård A. Berg, *Mot en korporativ reindrift: Samisk reindrift i Norge i det 20. århundre: eksemplifisert gjennom studier av reindriften på Helgeland* (Guovdageaidnu: Sámi instituhtta, 2000), 222–44.

33 For the historical background and legislative history of the act, see Bård A. Berg, *Reindriftsloven av 1933: om den første reindriftsloven som omfattet hele Norge: bakgrunn, forhistorie og innhold* (Guovdageaidnu: Sámi Instituhtta, 1994).

34 NOU 1978:18B, 168.

35 NOU 1978:18 B, 168–70, 177.

36 See, for example, discussion in Ot. Prp. 48 (1963–64), 11–14.

37 Tønnesen in NOU 1978:18B, 196.

38 Finnmark Sami Council, meeting, 27–29 March 1956, in Larsen, "Om oppgjøret som forsvant?," 70. The council was established on the initiative of acting county governor Dag Tønder. See Larsen, "Om oppgjøret som forsvant?," 43.

39 NOU 1984:18, 42.

40 Norsk Retstidende 1957 s. 867 in Kirsti Strøm Bull, "Om rettsanvendelse og etikk," in *Samisk forskning og forskningsetikk* (Oslo: Forskningsetiske komiteer, Nr. 2, 2002), 96.

41 Observations from the government of Norway on the proposed text concerning protection and integration of Indigenous and other tribal and semi-tribal populations in independent countries, Oslo, November 1956, Norwegian National Archives (hereafter RA), RA/S-3267/D/L0119/0002.

42 Draft Norwegian reply to the ILO, 22 October 1956, RA/S-3267/D/L0119/0002. My translation of the term "Det norske sameråd" in the document.

43 Minister for Social Affairs Gudmund Harlem to the Norwegian Government, draft report to the *Storting* on the 1955 ILO Labour Conference, 42, RA/S-3267/D/L0119/0002.

44 Ministry of Social Affairs, St.Prp. 36 (1958).

45 *Stortinget*, Committee on Social Affairs, Innst. S. 68 (1958); Parliamentary debate of 7 March 1958, St. Forh. 7a (1958), 451–52.
46 Ministry of Church and Education, St. Meld. 21 (1962–63), 1.
47 Eidheim, *Aspects of the Lappish Situation*, 10.
48 Larsen, "Om oppgjøret som forsvant?," 74–75.
49 Report by the Sami Committee, Annex to the Ministry of Church and Education, St. Meld. 21 (1962–63).
50 Ministry of Church and Education, St. Meld. 21 (1962–63), 32–37, 50; Larsen, "Om oppgjøret som forsvant?," 2, 79–95.
51 Nordic Sami Council cited in Ministry of Church and Education, St. Meld. 21 (1962–63), 9.
52 Per Otnes, *Den samiske nasjon* (Oslo: Pax Forlag, 1970), 186–88. See also Aksel Helmer Wigdehl, "Nordisk Sameråd: En oversikt over det nordisk-samiske organisasjonsarbeidets historie" (Master's thesis, University of Bergen, 1972).
53 Nordic Council recommendation 5/59 in Nordisk Råds forhandlinger, 7 session 1959, 2020, in Otnes, *Den samiske nasjon*, 187.
54 Reidar Hirsti, *En samisk utfordring* (Oslo: Pax, 1967), 33; Einar Niemi, *Kategorienes etikk og minoritetene i nord: Et historisk perspektiv' in Samisk forskning og forskningsetikk* (Oslo: Forskningsetiske komiteer, Nr. 2, 2002), 33.
55 Larsen, "Om oppgjøret som forsvant?," 46–47.
56 Einar Gerhardsen, speech printed in *Reindriftsbladet* for July 1958, cited in Berg, *Mot en korporativ reindrift*, 239–40.
57 *Dagbladet*, 17 October 1960, in Larsen, "Om oppgjøret som forsvant?," 84.
58 Terje Wold, "Minoritets- og menneskerettighetsspørsmålets folkerettslige stilling," lecture given at the Nordic Sami Congress in Kiruna, Sweden, August 1962, in Annex 2 to St. Meld. 21 (1962–63), 51. Wold defined Indigenous populations as those who did not have allegiance to another state but belonged to "a different race than the majority, spoke a different language and had not been assimilated into the rest of the population" (56) of the state in which they lived.
59 Ministry of Church and Education, St. Meld. 21 (1962–63).
60 Gutorm Gjessing, *Norge i Sameland* (Oslo: Gyldendal norsk forlag, 1973), 111.
61 *Storting* Committee on Church and Education, Innst. S. 196 (1962–63). Parliamentary debate of 27 May 1963, St. Forh. 413 (1963), 3428–61, esp. 3438 and 3455 (rights reserved for the Sami), 3449 (rights reserved to the local population). Three representatives, clearly inspired by international human rights norms, referred to "human rights" (see 3440, 3449, and 3451).
62 Ministry of Church and Education, St. Meld. 21 (1962–63), 22.
63 A. Davies and Svein Jentoft, "The Challenge and the Promise of Indigenous Peoples' Fishing Rights: From Dependency to Agency," in *Indigenous Peoples: Resource Management and Global Rights*, ed. Svein Jentoft, Henry Minde, and Ragnar Nilsen (Chicago: University of Chicago Press, 2003), 200.
64 Legal act of 1965, "Om statens umatrikulerte grunn i Finnmark fylke," Ministry of Justice, Ot. prp. 48 (1963–64) and parliamentary committee on agricultural issues, Innst. O. VI (1963–64).
65 Gjessing, *Norge i Sameland*, 117.

Rights of Indigenous Peoples to Land and Natural Resources 299

66 Harald Eidheim, "When Ethnic Identity Is a Social Stigma," in *Ethnic Groups and Boundaries*, ed. Fredrik Barth (Oslo: Universitetsforlaget, 1969), 39–58.

67 Per Fokstad, cited in Dahl, *Samene i dag og i morgen*, 10.

68 Ibid., 12.

69 Ibid., 14.

70 On international developments, see Hanne Hagtvedt Vik, "Indigenous Internationalism," in *Internationalisms: A Twentieth-Century History*, ed. Glenda Sluga and Patricia Clavin (Cambridge: Cambridge University Press, 2017), 315–39; and Jonathan Crossen, "Another Wave of Anti-Colonialism: The Origins of Indigenous Internationalism," *Canadian Journal of History* 52, 3 (2017): 533–59. On the rise of Indigenous activism since the 1960s within Canada, Australia, the United States, and New Zealand, see, for example, McHugh, *Aboriginal Societies and the Common Law*, 316ff.

71 *Ságat*, 4 July 1969, in Otnes, *Den samiske nasjon*, 207.

72 Ibid.

73 Ibid.; Per Otnes, "Nykolonialisme i sameland," in *Nordisk nykolonialisme: Samiske problem i dag*, ed. Linda R. Homme (Oslo: Samlaget, 1969); Gjessing, *Norge i Sameland*.

74 Otnes, *Den samiske nasjon*, 210, 15.

75 See, for example, Gjessing, *Norge i Sameland*, esp. 113. For "Lappecodicilen," see note 13.

76 RA, oral history collection, interview with Ole Henrik Magga, 6 November 2013, by Hanne Hagtvedt Vik, Anne Julie Semb, and Helge Pharo, University of Oslo, 14, 24–25.

77 Otnes, *Den samiske nasjon*, 205; Tomas Cramér, "Retten til land og vatn," in *Nordisk nykolonialisme: Samiske problem i dag*, ed. Linda R. Homme (Oslo: Samlaget, 1969), 117–48.

78 Henry Minde, "The Challenge of Indigenism: The Struggle for Sami Land Rights and Self-Government in Norway, 1960–1990," in *Indigenous Peoples: Resource Management and Global Rights*, ed. Svein Jentoft, Henry Minde, and Ragnar Nilsen (Chicago: University of Chicago Press, 2003), 78.

79 St. Meld. 33 (1973–74), 33.

80 NOU 1978:18A, 1.

81 NOU 1978:18A, 14.

82 Bull, "Om rettsanvendelse og etikk," 97.

83 Memorandum, Fifth Social Office, Ministry of Social Affairs, 9 September 1977, RA/S-3267/D/L0119/0002.

84 Speech by Thorvald Stoltenberg to the UN Conference on Racism, 15 August 1978, 5, Norwegian Ministry of Foreign Affairs (MFA), series 26.8/73, fol. 1. The Norwegian report to the conference was A/Conf.92/Nr.11.

85 Henry Minde, "The Destination and the Journey: Indigenous Peoples and the United Nations from the 1960s through 1985," in *Indigenous Peoples: Self-Determination, Knowledge, Indigeneity*, ed. Henry Minde (Eburon: Delft, 2008), 66.

86 Annual debate in Parliament on the state of affairs in Norway, 23 October 1979, St. Forh. 7a (1979–80), 141–42.

87 NOU 1980:53, 7.

88 NOU 1985:18; NOU 1985:24; and NOU 1987:34.

89 NOU 1984:18, chap. 2.

90 McHugh, *Aboriginal Societies and the Common Law*, 349–51.

91 Ibid., 339–41.

92 James Robert Allison, *Sovereignty for Survival: American Energy Development and Indian Self-Determination* (New Haven: Yale University Press, 2015).

93 Government of Canada, multiculturalism policy, statement to House of Commons, November 1971, cited in Berkman et al., *Science Diplomacy*, 664. See also McHugh, *Aboriginal Societies and the Common Law*, 331–33.

94 P. Jull, "The Politics of Sustainable Development," in *Indigenous Peoples: Resource Management and Global Rights*, ed. Svein Jentoft, Henry Minde, and Ragnar Nilsen (Chicago: University of Chicago Press, 2003), 29.

95 Sidney Tarrow, *The New Transnational Activism* (Cambridge: Cambridge University Press, 2005), 32.

96 NOU 1984:18, 44–45. This was the first NOU drafted by the Sami Rights Commission.

97 Article 27 of the convention, NOU 1984:18, 272 ff., 343.

98 Ot. Prp. 33 (1986–87), 37; Innst. O. 79 (1986–87), 5; Debate in the Parliament, St. forh. (1987–88), 3021–33, esp. 3026.

99 For an in-depth study of the Norwegian contributions to ILO C169 and the process that led to Norwegian ratification of the convention, see Hanne Hagtvedt Vik and A.J. Semb, "Who Owns the Land? Norway, the Sami and the ILO Indigenous and Tribal Peoples Convention," *International Journal on Minority and Group Rights* 20 (2013): 517–50.

100 NOU 1997:4. Author's translation. Original title: *Naturgrunnlaget for samisk kultur.*

101 NOU 1997:4; Ministry of Justice, Ot.prp. 53 (2002–03); Anne Julie Semb, "Internasjonal rett og nasjonal politikk: Finnmarksloven," in *Samepolitikkens utvikling*, ed. Bjørn Bjerkli and Per Selle (Oslo: Gyldendal Akademisk, 2015), 40–63.

102 NOU 1997:5, esp. 36–47.

103 UN Commission on Racial Discrimination, CERD/C/63/CO/810, December 2003; ILO, CEACR: individual observations concerning Convention No. 169, Indigenous and tribal peoples, 1989, Norway, 2004. Both discussed in Semb, "Internasjonal rett og nasjonal politikk," 51, 54–55.

104 Report by Hans Petter Graver and Geir Ulfstein (2003) in Semb, "Internasjonal rett og nasjonal politikk," 53. See also Hans Petter Graver and Geir Ulfstein, "The Sami People's Right to Land in Norway," *International Journal on Minority and Group Rights* 11 (2004): 337–77.

105 Innst. O. 80 (2004–05) and the Finnmark act of 17 June 2005.

106 Gunnar Eriksen, "Samiske sedvaner og bruk av naturressurser før og etter Selbu- og Svartskogdommene fra 2001," *Kritisk juss* (2004): 289–304.

107 NOU 2007:13.

108 Bjørn Hersoug, "Maori Fishing Rights," in *Indigenous Peoples: Resource Management and Global Rights*, ed. Svein Jentoft, Henry Minde, and Ragnar Nilsen (Chicago: University of Chicago Press, 2003), 125.

109 E. Eythórsson, "The Costal Sami: A 'Pariah Caste' of Norwegian Fisheries? A Reflection on Ethnicity and Power in Norwegian Resource Management," in *Indigenous*

Rights of Indigenous Peoples to Land and Natural Resources   301

Peoples: Resource Management and Global Rights, ed. Svein Jentoft, Henry Minde, and Ragnar Nilsen (Chicago: University of Chicago Press, 2003), 158; R. Nilsen, "From Norwegianization to Coastal Sami Uprising," in *Indigenous Peoples: Resource Management and Global Rights,* ed. Svein Jentoft, Henry Minde, and Ragnar Nilsen (Chicago: University of Chicago Press, 2003), 173–76.

110 Nilsen, "From Norwegianization to Coastal Sami Uprising," 177; NOU 1997:4, 308–10.

111 Carsten Smith, "Om samenes rett til naturressurser – særlig ved fiskerireguleringer," *Norsk juridisk tidsskrift* 9 (1990): 507–34.

112 Rapport fra Samisk fiskeriutvalg til Fiskeridepartementet, Tromsø, 10 April 1997, esp. chap. 4. https://urn.nb.no/URN:NBN:no-nb_digibok_2011081108233.

113 Ibid., 167.

114 See NOU 1997:4, chap. 5.6.3; NOU 2005:10, esp. chap. 3; NOU 2008:5. Discussion in *Storting* on 29 May 2008.

115 Compare NOU 1984: 8 with NOU 1996:11, esp. chap. 6. See also NOU 1997:4.

116 *National Broadcasting Company's Sámi Radio,* 24 April 2009, "Presidenten gruer seg"; "Stortinget overhørte Sametingets krav," *Ságat,* 9 June 2009; "Håper på FNs støtte," *Ságat,* 9 June 2009; "Sametingets krav til mineralselskapene," *Ságat,* 12 June 2009; "Sametinget opptrer svært uklokt," *Ságat,* 13 June 2009.

117 Susann Funderud Skogvang, "Ny minerallov og samiske rettigheter," *Lov og rett* 49, no. 1–2 (2010): 47–67.

13

"Europe Cannot Engage in Autarchical Policies"

European Raw Materials Strategy
from 1945 to the Present

HANS OTTO FRØLAND and MATS INGULSTAD

A spectre is apparently haunting Europe – the threat of losing access to the natural resources that feed its industries. In 2008, the European Union (EU) launched the Raw Materials Initiative (RMI), an ambitious program to deal with the critical dependence of the EU on raw materials considered crucial to the functioning of its economy.[1] The RMI was presented at the community level as the first integrated strategy to secure and improve the access to raw materials through three separate measures: ensuring a fair and sustainable supply of raw materials from global markets, fostering sustainable supply within the EU, and promoting resource efficiency and recycling.[2] The first of these measures was embodied in the EU's new-fangled Raw Materials Diplomacy, an effort to counter the spread of protectionist "resource nationalism" in the marketplace and to mitigate the price effects of an ongoing commodity boom.[3] The EU has especially targeted developing countries, suggesting that "many developing countries – especially in Africa – have not been able to translate their resource wealth into sustainable and inclusive growth, often because of governance issues related to regulatory frameworks or taxation ... The EU, through its development policies and in partnership with developing countries, can play a crucial role in creating win-win situations."[4]

While the RMI was presented as a new departure for the EU in 2008, designed to counter a specific challenge related to an ongoing commodity boom, these are hardly new concerns for the modern industrialized states in

Europe. Since 1945, there has been a long history of collective European action to deal with challenges to the supply of raw materials, particularly during periods of scarcity, rising prices, and high supply risks. After two world wars had unravelled the politico-economic networks that directed the flows of labour and raw materials from distant regions to the industrial workshops of the continent, Europe had effectively been decentred.[5] The sun set on the European empires, precisely at the time they most needed raw materials to feed their industries and enhance their prosperity. Consequently, a new set of relationships had to be forged to keep the raw materials flowing in a world no longer overwhelmingly dominated by European capital, firms, or colonial administrators. This challenge was beyond the ability of any single state to take up on its own: it required collective action. We investigate how the shifting constellations of European states have attempted to deal with these problems, through what organizational forms, and with what strategies.

By investigating Europe's raw materials policies we address the interests of the demander of natural resources. In general terms, our question concerns how a dependent political entity behaves in order to secure supplies over which it has no legal influence. Potentially, however, successful strategies might affect, directly and indirectly, the level and character of the national regulations used by resource-abundant countries. This might occur through bilateral relations, regional preferential arrangements, or wider multilateral agreements, all of which might constrain the potentially supplying countries' regulatory capacity when pursuing resource nationalism. In this exploratory chapter we do not attempt to pinpoint the de facto influence on the national level; rather, our aim is to elaborate upon how overall strategy at the European level derives from internal perceptions.

Collective crisis solution in Europe is often equated with institutional integration under the auspices of the EU and its predecessors: "L'Europe se fera dans les crises et elle sera la somme des solutions apportées à ces crises," in the words of Jean Monnet.[6] There has also been a gradual shift from protectionism, which has long been associated with the EU, particularly its agricultural sector, to an embrace of a free trade agenda.[7] The problem of ensuring sufficient supply of raw materials for European industries cuts to the very heart of the rationality informing the early stages of the integration process, in which economic integration was a means not only to rebuild the shattered industries but also to achieve political ends.[8] However, the history that emerges is hardly a unilinear progression towards ever-higher levels of institutional integration and multilateral trade orientation. A succession of

TABLE 13.1

The development of an integrated community-level trade policy for vital raw materials

	Intraregionalism 1945–57	Interregionalism, 1957–2000	Global multilateralism, 2000–15
Vital commodities targeted by the ECSC, EEC, EC, EU	Coal, steel	Soft commodities, oil, iron, copper, bauxite	Rare earth minerals
Main target	Western Europe	Former dependencies in Africa, Caribbean, and Pacific	China, Russia, Congo
Instruments	ECSC Treaty	Yaoundé, Lomé I–IV	Cotonou, RMI, WTO, EPA
Commodity boom years	1951–53	1972–74	2003–08

European organizations has attempted to develop a framework for managing resource dependency, from the Organisation for European Economic Co-operation (OEEC), the European Coal and Steel Community (ECSC), the European Economic Community (EEC)/European Community (EC), and finally the EU. Furthermore, the approach to trade policy has been riven by competing ideas and interests, particularly between regional and multi-lateral approaches to the liberalization of the raw materials trade. After the sidelining of the OEEC, the Western European states embraced resource intraregionalism through the formation of the ECSC, then entered a long phase of resource interregionalism embedded within the EEC/EC's relations with former colonies before transitioning to a post-Uruguay strategy of resource multilateralism to ensure that European industries receive access to necessary input factors from around the world. These approaches and their corresponding institutions, whose features are displayed in Table 13.1, are only partly overlapping. However, there were several failures to implement new strategies and institutional innovations along the way.

Intraregionalism by Default

During the first half of the Second World War the question of the reorganization of European trade and its need for raw materials for reconstruction and development loomed large. Some projects predated the war, such as intergovernmental commodity agreements and buffer stock schemes, but new ideas (like an international essential raw material development corporation to complement the World Bank and the International Monetary Fund) were also considered as means to secure the necessary quantities of raw materials at stable prices.[9] Since adequate solutions failed to materialize, the organizers of the first postwar European framework for economic cooperation faced a situation in which both the short-term and the long-term supply of raw materials were an acute concern. Particularly distressing at the time was the shortfall in production and transportation of coal, Europe's chief source of energy and a key input in its metallurgical industries.[10] The shortfall was largely covered by imports, which exacerbated the European balance-of-payments deficits.[11] These problems raised the question not only of how the immediate crisis was to be overcome but also of the direction of the postwar development of the European economy and its relationship with world markets.

Whereas the UN Economic Commission for Europe, established in 1947, was expected to tackle Europe's pressing resource shortages from a collective point of view,[12] it was the US offer of Marshall Aid that enabled European governments to make plans and build institutions for closer cooperation in postwar trade relations and raw materials supply. Initial discussions in the Committee of European Economic Co-operation (CEEC, later transformed into the OEEC) revealed widely diverging preferences for the postwar trade regime. Great Britain argued for freer international trade and multilateral tariff reductions: "We must never forget the enormous dependence of Europe on imports from the rest of the world. With increased prosperity our needs of foodstuffs and raw materials from the outside world will increase." The alternative on the table was a regional customs union to promote intra-European trade and better utilization and distribution of the resources on the continent, along the lines of the BeNeLux customs union. The British opposed this approach, warning that it was doubtful "whether a customs union in the modern world can be envisaged except as leading to a currency or even a full economic union."[13]

Once the European Recovery Program (ERP) got into full swing, the Western Europeans faced US pressure for further economic integration and trade liberalization through the OEEC. The OEEC's objective was to make Western Europe independent of outside aid (e.g., large shipments of commodities and machinery from the US), but this required a regional reorganization of both external and internal trade relations. The OEEC Council decided in 1949 that the participating countries should take the necessary steps to liberalize intra-European trade as far as possible by 1951. It adopted the Code of Liberalization as a step towards the elimination of quantitative restrictions and "the establishment of a single system of multilateral trade in the world." The Code required participants to free 60 percent of imports in manufactures, raw materials, and foodstuffs from restrictions. This was subsequently raised to 75 percent in October 1950.[14] As the OEEC noted in early 1950, freeing up intra-European trade alone would not do: "Western Europe is a small area which cannot possibly produce all the food and raw materials required by its large population."[15] Europe needed to sell its goods in international markets to pay for necessary raw materials imports, and therefore it also required a commensurate strategy for the multilateralization of commodity trade. Neither the failed International Trade Organization (ITO) nor the continued existence of the General Agreement on Tariffs and Trade (GATT) could fulfill this objective. While the US tirelessly pushed the Europeans to make the OEEC the first step towards a United States of Europe, the Europeans resisted vigorously for two years. In the process they developed their own ideas about a permanent organization to deal with the realities of international economic interdependence.[16]

In May 1950, the French foreign minister Robert Schuman proposed the pooling of French and German coal and steel under a "High Authority." This allowed Germany's productive potential to be safely harnessed for European growth, while France got access to coal and coke for its own steel industry.[17] Schuman invited other countries to join the European Coal and Steel Community, underlining that instead of reducing production to raise prices, the ECSC would rather merge the markets and "provide for the more rational distribution of production at the highest level of productivity."[18] ECSC membership required a commitment to abolish all import and export duties, quota restrictions, and other impediments to competition in the internal coal and steel markets. These would, however, remain as barriers to third countries. This was a violation of the OEEC Code of Liberalization, which required countries joining the European Payments Union (EPU) to eliminate discrimination against all other OEEC members. In 1953, the OEEC allowed the ECSC to abolish these restrictions within the borders of its six member countries without extending these concessions to all EPU members.[19] As this compromise reveals, intraregional trade liberalization took precedence over a full-fledged commitment to a global system of multilateral trade.

The ECSC only had a mandate to deal with two major industrial input factors, even though the Economic Commission for Europe warned that the sector would depend on external sources of other raw materials.[20] Western

"Europe Cannot Engage in Autarchical Policies"

European countries depended on imports of many raw materials from outside the area. The eruption of the Korean War in June 1950 amply demonstrated the risks this entailed. As the new superpowers clashed in the Far East, sharply rising commodity prices (excluding oil) caused substantial balance of payments difficulties for the European countries with raw materials producers in the Global South. As the French government complained, prices and shortages were reducing living standards, causing payment difficulties in the EPU, making rearmament more costly, and "interfering with integration."[21] Trilateral talks between the UK, the US, and France commenced in an attempt to find a remedy, whether resource allocation through NATO or some other mechanism. A proposed Anglo-French-American triumvirate ran afoul of the other Western Europeans, with Dutch foreign minister Dirk Stikker insisting that, without a multilateral approach, not only the OEEC but even the very notion of the "European spirit" was at stake.[22] To overcome the problems facing Western Europe by early 1951, the OEEC members needed a way not only to increase the production of materials both within Europe and in the overseas territories but also to ensure the best use of scarce materials as well as to ensure the equitable distribution of scarce materials between countries.[23]

The solution came in the form of the International Materials Conference (IMC), established in the spring of 1951. The IMC brought producers and consumers of fourteen different commodities together to balance supply and demand through exchange of information and allocation of scarce resources. As leading industrial nations, the ECSC's six members (Luxembourg, the Netherlands, Belgium, France, West Germany, and Italy) were broadly represented in the commodity committees.[24] It was, however, the OEEC rather than the ECSC that served as the main link between the six member countries of the latter and the IMC. The OEEC had a regional representative on the Central Committee and provided the IMC with staff as well. Through the OEEC representative even members not party to the IMC could be informed of its actions as well as have their views presented.[25] The IMC enjoyed no supranational powers, relying on its participants to bargain for resources and adhere to its allocations. As such it was an experiment with collective intervention in the global marketplace, and it was one the Western Europeans considered to have been beneficial.[26] The IMC was, however, disbanded soon after the commodity boom had passed, even though some OEEC members – notably Britain, Italy, the Netherlands, and France – wanted to retain it on stand-by in case similar problems arose in the future. After all, the "supply situation always required a certain amount of supervision," whether it was the European supply or an individual country's supply that caused concern.[27] Western European discussions on raw materials shortages continued in the functional expert committees of the OEEC (e.g., the Non-Ferrous Metal Committee). However, these were more about US-European exchange and about internal allocations than about developing a collective global approach to secure stable raw materials supply. Hence we conclude that the Korean price boom did not bring institutional innovation in terms of European resource security.

Another field in which the lack of institutional innovation, multilateralization, and collective action became apparent was in the policies for the European colonies and overseas territories. From the outset, all involved parties saw the ERP as premised on continued access to the natural resources of Africa. In 1948, the US State Department's Policy Planning Staff noted that the only way to make Western Europe strong and economically viable was through "some form of political, military and economic union" and that the exploitation of Africa would not only provide the necessary resources but "would [also] lend to the idea of Western European union that tangible objective for which everyone has been rather unsuccessfully groping."[28] Particularly in France the notion of Eurafrique had lingered, which only underlined the importance of external relations for the maintenance of European raw materials supply. The Schuman declaration proclaimed the development of Africa as one of Europe's most essential tasks, and, in 1951, the OEEC called for Europe's African colonies to increase their production of "scarce material."[29] There was nevertheless little cooperation on colonial development through the OEEC or the ECSC.[30] The European countries struggled to find common ground for an export policy for capital goods to raw materials producers. Should they provide the producers with capital goods and equipment to increase their output or did this run the risk of creating competition, prompting the producers to keep their resources for themselves?[31] Consequently, while the OEEC was flustered and the IMC was disbanded, the ECSC and its intraregionalism prevailed.

Interregionalism: Combining Trade and Development

The late 1950s and early 1960s brought new challenges, but it also brought opportunities for the six member countries of the ECSC. The strategic importance of coal and steel declined as changes in technology, transportation, and geopolitics led to an influx of plentiful American coal, cheap Middle Eastern oil, and steel from producers outside the continent.[32] The establishment of the European Economic Community coincided not only with a transition from a seller's to a buyer's market in commodities but also with the opening stages of decolonization in Africa.[33] For the European countries the issue of external raw materials trade became urgent when France insisted on including its dependent territories in the 1957 Treaty of Rome. France hoped in part to secure markets and access to raw materials, but it also hoped to shift the burdens of maintaining French Africa onto its European partners.[34] The Treaty of Rome not only charged the member states with providing investments for the development of their dependent territories but also specified that the customs duties of the dependencies were to be abolished in conformity with the establishment of the inner market.[35] Immediately afterwards the colonial empires of the EEC members started disintegrating, and they largely disappeared between 1958 and 1962. Despite the toxic legacies of colonialism the newly sovereign states and the EEC had a mutual interest in maintaining trade. In 1960, the French commissioner for overseas development, Robert Lemaignen, pointed to the EEC being the world's leading importer of raw materials – accounting for one-third of world trade – and suggested that this was the basis for reconciling European requirements with the "explosions of African nationalism."[36] The understanding was mutual, according to the Senegalese minister of justice Gabriel d'Arboussier: "L'Europe a besoin aujourd'hui de trois éléments: l'espace, l'énergie et les matières premières. L'Afrique attend les hommes, les techniciens et les capitaux. C'est dans un échange de dons que se trouve l'intérêt mutuel des deux continents et l'approfondissement de leur destinée."[37]

The "exchange of gifts," as d'Arboussier phrased it, required a new foundation for the trade relations between Europe and the former dependent territories in Africa. The solution was the 1963 Yaoundé Convention, which gave eighteen African states associated status with the EEC.[38] This created a new economic area covering parts of Europe and Africa, with Article 29 establishing that all nationals and companies of every member state should be placed on an equal footing.[39] Like the Treaty of Rome, the Yaoundé Convention gave the associated states free access to the EEC market while permitting them to impose restrictions on goods from the EEC in order to protect their own infant industries, as long as these were uniformly implemented for all of the six member countries. The Yaoundé Convention included tariff preferences for key commodity exports intended to divert trade from the non-associated to the associated states, but with limited effect. The associated states were outcompeted by Latin American exporters and also faced falling prices: the 65 percent rise in volume of EEC imports from the associated states between 1963 and 1965 was equivalent only to a 17 percent increase in value. The African and Malagasy Organization (OCAM) warned the EEC Commission in 1966 that the Yaoundé arrangements were proving highly unsatisfactory. OCAM demanded stable commodity prices, "tantamount to ensuring political stability in our states," and somewhat ominously suggested that this was also critical for protecting European investments.[40]

In the 1960s, the EEC embraced the trade and development agenda and linked it to freeing up trade in commodities through trade regulations tilted in favour of developing countries. In 1964, it floated a proposal in the UN system for several measures to remove obstacles to trade, including a ban on new tariff and quota restrictions on basic commodities originating mainly in the developing countries. It also suggested that the developed countries should increase import quotas and reduce customs duties on products originating in developing countries and eventually abolish both.[41] The EEC Directorate-General VIII (Development) broached the idea of creating a single free trade area consisting of all associated states and the EEC, but the idea was eventually rejected.[42] Another proposal by the EEC Commission was to make the associated states give up their special preferences so as to enable them and the EEC to participate in the planned UN Conference on Trade and Development (UNCTAD) scheme for a system of general preferences to be given to all developing countries.[43] It thereby would have replaced the system of interregional preferences with a more multilateral approach. This proposal, which would erode the comparative advantage conferred to the associated states by Yaoundé, went nowhere. Instead, the Second Yaoundé Convention (1969) required the full elimination of duties and quantitative restrictions between the associated states and the EEC, but not between the associated states themselves.[44] Interregionalism remained the order of the day.

The Abortive Attempt at Community-Level Resource Multilateralism

As the developing countries grew increasingly dissatisfied, their demands could not be met merely through new measures between the EEC and the associated states to stabilize commodity prices. The voices of the new states echoed in the halls of the UN General Assembly as they demanded a new international economic order, including better terms of trade and acknowledgment of their permanent sovereignty over their own reserves of raw materials. Fortified by dependency theories and resource nationalist sentiments, they were not mollified by the introduction of a new section on trade and development in the GATT protocols during the Kennedy Round.[45] From the 1960s to the mid-1970s a wave of nationalizations – of mines, smelters, and foundries – swept the Global South. Mining companies were nationalized in Chile, Peru, Venezuela, Zaire, and Zambia, while the threat of gradual nationalization through buy-outs or outright expropriation hung like the sword of Damocles over mining enterprises elsewhere. The political challenge was compounded by economic forces. From 1971 to 1972, commodity prices started rising, driven by the convergence of economic expansionary phases in the US, Japan, and Western Europe. Many metals peaked in 1973 or 1974 at twenty-year, or in some cases historic, highs. Afterwards they fell dramatically, depressed by large sales from the US stockpile and of Japanese excess industrial stocks.[46]

Concerns over supply grew in European capitals. The UK government, early in 1971, initiated a planning process that would subsequently establish a direct nexus between British development aid and its procurement of raw materials from abroad.[47] After OPEC successfully used the "oil weapon" in 1973, governments assessed "the likelihood of producer countries forming effective OPEC-type organisations for other materials."[48] Whereas the UK conclusion was negative, the cumulative concerns led France to set up a stockpile for non-ferrous metals in 1975. The general notion took hold that Europe had to devise a means to respond to the systemic challenges posed by the political demands from the developing countries, the high commodity prices, and fears that the finite supply of raw materials could run out.[49] In 1975, the OECD established the High Level Group on Commodities to consider the possibilities of concerted action.

EEC politicians perceived this as the last stage in an ongoing process of marginalization, in which European resources had been exhausted by centuries of economic activity and, particularly, industrialization. It was only a question of time before many manufacturing activities would shift from Europe to the point of origins of the raw materials. Consequently, the crisis had two dimensions: the most immediate causes of their woes were the violent price fluctuations, but they also had to face up to challenges of maintaining the long-term supply of European industries, as the EEC was dependent on external sources for roughly 75 percent of its raw materials. This rendered it vulnerable to a whole host of different political and economic risks associated with production being concentrated in a few countries (e.g., chromium, manganese, and platinum were produced in South Africa and the Soviet Union, tungsten in China, and copper in the CIPEC countries).[50]

In 1975, to cope with these challenges, the EEC Commission (from 1967 a joint commission with the ECSC and Euratom) developed a package of proposals strikingly similar to the current RMI. Industry commissioner Altiero Spinelli, a life-long federalist, called for a "fulcrum" to coordinate EEC action in the vast areas that were affected: "The enormity of the problem transcends the national frontiers of all the Member States."[51] The commission also called for industry to extend product lifetimes and to increase substitution, recycling, and the use of new technology to mine the seabed as well as low-grade deposits within the EEC. Furthermore, the expansion of the EEC in 1973 provided new mining opportunities, particularly in Ireland and Greenland, although prospectors would not necessarily find a warm welcome there.[52] Overall, the commission concluded that, due to geological factors, the EEC could never be self-sufficient in minerals, and it aptly formulated the policy implications: "Europe cannot engage in autarchical policies."[53]

The narrow European resource base, particularly in metallic minerals, induced the EEC Commission to strive for access to external resources through the strategy of resource multilateralization rather than through the strategy of interregional trade and development. After all, many of the materials giving the most cause for concern could not be secured through interregional cooperation with the associated states. Facing falling raw materials costs and increasing risks, European firms had sought refuge from decolonization in other developed countries. In 1966–67, the share of European mining investment going to other developed countries averaged 60 percent, while by a decade later it had risen to 85 percent. Meanwhile the share of European investments and mining exploration targeting Africa dropped from 4.4 percent in 1966 to 0.2 percent in 1977.[54] To reduce the clamour for nationalization and make the environment more hospitable for European firms, the commission proposed that developing countries should gradually increase their involvement and stake in the processing of their own raw materials. This system of cross-ownership along the entire value chain was supposed to create a "solidarity between the less developed countries and Europe, which to date has only been too lacking."[55] In return for opening the European markets for cross-ownership, and to enable European firms to engage more actively abroad, the commission wanted a concerted effort through the OECD and GATT to combat restrictive business practices, particularly in the form of quantitative export restrictions (particularly GATT Article 11).[56]

Hence, although the member states were more reluctant than the EEC Commission – clearly indicated by their reluctance towards the Integrated

"Europe Cannot Engage in Autarchical Policies" 313

Program for Commodities (IPC) adopted by UNCTAD IV in 1976 (which would cover price stabilization of eighteen raw materials)[57] – we suggest that the EEC was more active in seeking substantial solutions to the commodity crises of the 1970s than is usually assumed, testing ideas that foreshadowed the measures later adopted through the RMI and the implementation of Raw Materials Diplomacy. However, an ambitious expansion of the EEC Commission's competencies proved untenable, particularly with the EEC still in the throes of economic and political "eurosclerosis."[58]

Return to Interregionalism

While the EEC did not implement a concerted community-level policy of resource multilateralization as envisioned by the Commission in the mid-1970s, it expanded the scope of its interregional raw materials diplomacy. The enlargement in 1973, particularly the accession of Great Britain, entailed that the Yaoundé agreements had to be supplemented by a more comprehensive arrangement that could include the "associable" Commonwealth countries. The first Lomé Convention of 1975 created a framework for cooperation in trade, aid, and distribution of raw materials between the nine EEC members and forty-six states in Africa, the Caribbean, and the Pacific (ACP). Lomé entailed that the EEC would allow most of the ACP agricultural and mineral exports duty-free access. Recognizing the centrality of raw materials prices for the developing countries, the convention also introduced a mechanism (Stabex) to provide compensation from the European Development Fund if export earnings from commodities on the part of ACP states were to be eroded by falling prices.[59]

The contentions over commodities with concerns over supply security, dwindling reserves, and low investment rates in the 1970s left their mark on the second Lomé Convention, which saw a high priority placed on non-fuel minerals.[60] Lomé II, from 1979, like its predecessor, was based on the principle of duty-free access to the EEC without restrictions for ACP manufactures and raw materials that did not compete with production in Europe. This gave duty-free entry for 99.5 percent of exports from the ACP countries, but 75 percent of ACP exports were in the form of raw materials that would enter the EEC duty-free even without the convention.[61] In addition to providing for technical assistance and the use of EEC funds for exploration and the launching of mineral and energy projects, Lomé II also introduced a support mechanism for ACP mining industries (Sysmin).[62] Its main objective was to ensure that production capacity was maintained even in the face of falling prices. The determination to release funds was at the discretion of the European Commission, usually when capacity fell by more than 10 percent or income by more than 15 percent. As such, it was more concerned with EEC imports of copper, cobalt, phosphates, manganese, bauxite, aluminum, tin, and iron ore than making up for a shortfall in ACP earnings. This was widely seen as the result of the EEC's desire to strengthen the trade links with the ACP countries, as opposed to more powerful mineral producers like Australia, Canada, South Africa, the US, or members of the Eastern Bloc.[63] The EEC was, however, unsuccessful in securing guarantees for investment against political risk, which continued to act as a deterrent to mining companies in Africa.[64]

After the turbulent decade of the 1970s, the EEC could hope for smoother sailing in the 1980s as the internal integration process again started moving forward, and the commodity markets eventually calmed down. Some apprehensions lingered, as commission vice-president Wilhelm Haferkamp remarked in 1981: "The age when raw materials were in abundant supply and when we could indulge in large-scale waste, definitely belongs to the past." He further argued that the EEC needed to embrace this fact and promote the circulation of raw materials by showing its "attachment to the principles of free trade."[65] To an extent, the early 1980s seemed an opportune moment to do so. The notion of a new international economic order had hit a dead end, and a return to the free market seemed imminent as, in turn, the cartel-like International Commodity Agreements were suspended, lapsed, or collapsed spectacularly.[66] The fears of supply disruptions of strategic minerals also abated, even if they did not disappear entirely as commodity prices declined.[67]

By the mid-1980s, EEC members were still dependent on ACP states for a large proportion of their minerals imports, but the concerns had changed from securing a sufficient supply in the face of ever-growing shortages to meeting a slowly growing demand for minerals and the maintenance of geographically dispersed sources. EC-based firms owned little mining capacity in less-developed countries. As indicated in Table 13.2, which reveals the ACP share of EEC imports of selected commodities, the Lomé Conventions did not make ACP as a group a more significant supplier for the EEC. Unsurprisingly, the EEC also tried to use other avenues to diversify its supply sources; for example, it used ECSC funds to finance production of iron in Brazil.[68] With commodity prices generally in decline, and the importance of the ACP states as suppliers diminishing, the EEC refrained from engaging in long-range planning in raw materials supply.

The end of the Cold War led to the Western governments' further loss of interest in the management of their raw materials supply. Generally low

TABLE 13.2
ACP share (%) of EC imports of selected non-fuel minerals, 1973–84

Commodity	Pre-Lomé (1974)	Last year of Lomé I (1979)	Last year of Lomé II (1984)	ACP share of EC imports, 1980–84
Refined copper	44.4	32.7	29.9	3.5
Iron ore	21.1	16.9	17.9	2.4
Uranium and compounds	–	9.5	19.7	1.7
Blister copper	45.0	43.4	28,8	1,1
Aluminum oxide	70.0	79.3	65.3	1.0
Aluminum ore	39.0	54.5	63.3	0.9
Copper ore	31.4	45.0	49.2	0.73

Source: Compiled from data provided in Joanna Moss and John Ravenhill, "The Evolution of Trade under the Lomé Conventions: The First Ten Years," in Christopher Stevens and Joan van Themaat, eds., *Europe and the International Division of Labour: New Patterns of Trade and Investment with Developing Countries* (London: Hodder and Stoughton, 1987), 24.

commodity prices, along with the establishment of the World Trade Organization (WTO) as a continuation of GATT after the Uruguay Round, ensured that international markets acquired a degree of legitimacy they had not previously enjoyed.[69] The EEC did not see the need for strategic intervention, although its dependency on imported raw materials increased. Extraction of raw materials within the EU remained more or less constant over the 1980 to 2000 period, whereas net imports of all raw materials increased by 19 percent, leaving the EU dependent on imports to cover 61 percent of its requirements of industrial materials and ores.[70]

As the EEC was replaced by the European Community (EC) under the wider competencies of the European Union in 1993, the organization acquired more members that did not have strong historical links to the ACP states. In 1996, the European Commission concluded that the colonial and postcolonial periods were now past, and with them the rationale for the ACP group, which existed only for the sake of relations with the EU. While the Commission increasingly cast itself as a key player in framing and enforcing multilateral rules promoting free trade, it still had to contend with the discrepancies between the EU's special preferences and the generalized system of preferences admissible under GATT/WTO rules.[71] The Lomé Conventions were subsequently replaced by the Cotonou Agreement between the EU and the ACP states in 2000, facilitated by a WTO waiver that allowed the EU to provide preferential access for imports originating in the

ACP without extending them to third countries through 2007.[72] The EU pledged that this would be the last ACP waiver and that its future arrangements would be WTO compatible.[73] This period allowed for developing new forms of regional trade agreements, moving away from preferential access towards reciprocal free trade.

Global Multilateralism

From the early 2000s, commodity prices rose again, driven by demand from China and India as they deliberately engaged in minerals-intensive economic development.[74] At the same time, trade in raw materials became a more important part of world trade, its share of the total rising from 12 percent in 2000 to 28 percent in 2008.[75] While this new raw materials boom was less volatile than its predecessor in the 1970s, it lasted far longer and had a more appreciable impact on metals and minerals prices.[76] The EU faced significant challenges with raw materials prices as both energy and mineral prices rose sharply.[77] Dependency rates for the most important metallic minerals ranged from 48 percent for copper to 100 percent for cobalt, platinum, titanium, and vanadium. In this context, concern about resource supply security lingered in Europe as resource nationalism spread among resource-abundant countries. Exporting countries such as Russia, China, India, and Vietnam introduced an array of export restrictions, including quotas, duties, licensing, and negative incentives to retain the commodities for their own manufacturing industries.[78] Spreading to less powerful states, the European Commission identified over 450 restrictive regulations on more than four hundred different raw materials.[79] In 2010, the EU identified fourteen minerals or metals whose supply was classified as "critical" due to political risk and concentration of extraction in countries like a neo-mercantilist China, a politically unpredictable Russia, and an unstable Democratic Republic of Congo, in addition to Brazil and South Africa.[80] In 2014, the EU extended the criticality list by six materials, of which some were non-metallic.[81]

Anticipating increasing tension in the global markets for raw materials, metallic minerals in particular, and stating that "fundamental changes in global markets are threatening the competitiveness of European industry," the EU responded to these challenges by adopting the Raw Materials Initiative in 2008.[82] Ordered along three pillars, the RMI consisted of various measures to enhance the security of raw materials supply. In addition to reducing distortions and encouraging transparency in international trade to increase foreign supply (first pillar), it would also improve mining conditions within Europe (second pillar), and promote recycling and a more parsimonious use of resources in European industry (third pillar). Designed to increase intra-EU production while simultaneously reducing consumption of imported minerals, the two latter pillars would reduce import dependency. So far, however, the EU has spent most of its energy on the first pillar, which is a quite elaborate caryatid in comparison to the other two.

The goals set for the first pillar were, first, to "work towards the elimination of trade distorting measures taken by third countries in all areas relevant to raw materials." This meant that the EU would labour to remove export duties, export quotas, and non-automatic export licences. The second goal was to establish "a level playing field between companies and countries wanting to access raw materials." This translates into an effort to enhance foreign companies' accessibility to raw materials extraction in resource-abundant countries by removing restrictive investment rules.[83] To reach these two goals, the RMI called for increased and concerted Raw Materials Diplomacy in the EU's foreign affairs by linking together its various trade, investment, and development policies. This was referred to as "an integrated approach," and the RMI explicitly stated that the EU should employ various trade policy instruments, such as preferential trade agreements and the EU Market Access Partnership, to bring about "open and well-functioning raw material markets, in particular by ensuring coherence between the opening up of the EU market (e.g., tariffs) and restrictive measures taken by third countries."[84] Further, as many important raw materials were located in developing countries, there was "an obvious case for coherence between development policy and the EU's need for undistorted access to raw materials."[85] As far as possible, the pursuit of objectives would take place within adequate multilateral frameworks such as existing Free Trade Areas and the WTO. Bilateral free trade agreements would be applied if necessary. To achieve its goals, the European Commission might provide targeted incentives to its various development aid packages (e.g., investment credits from the European Investment Bank), but its repertoire also contained defensive trade instruments. To increase its bargaining leverage, the commission might threaten to sustain or reintroduce EU import barriers.[86]

Because the RMI was a so-called communication, not a legal document, it simply formulated policy objectives. Even so, the European Commission enjoyed sufficient supranational powers to implement "the integrated approach."[87] The four reports published so far on implementation allow us to draw a picture of its raw materials diplomacy.[88] As for using development policy to further the RMI, the commission put much effort into negotiations with ACP states under the European Partnership Agreements (EPAs), which, under the framework of the Cotonou Agreement, provide for non-reciprocal trade agreements between the EU and each individual state. Such bilateral negotiations had started in 2002 but were pursued in conformity with the RMI. In 2010, through the Joint Africa-EU Strategy, the European Commission met the African Union Commission to agree on a joint development strategy in the minerals sector. It deliberately linked aid investments to infrastructure close to raw materials deposits. Policy for the tenth European Development Fund was modified to include mineral developments among its priorities.[89] Also under the Cotonou Agreement, funds from the European Investment Bank were transferred into the mining sector through the ACP Investment Facility.

The EU enshrined its commitment to binding international agreements in the Treaty of Lisbon from 2009. In order to shape an advantageous international economic order the EU has made the WTO a core target of its raw materials diplomacy. An important premise was the fact that WTO rules do not prohibit export restrictions. The EU was therefore a driving force in filing complaints in which the WTO twice, in July 2011 and March 2014, has ruled against China for restricting exports of raw materials.[90] A new complaint against China on rare earths was filed in March 2014. The WTO has meanwhile struck down the use of GATT Article 20 on general exemptions (it claims some restrictions were temporary in nature, their purpose being to relieve critical shortages). China needed to bring its export duty and export quotas into conformity with its WTO obligations.[91] The EU has further sought to frame the international raw materials agenda and discourse in international political forums such as the OECD, G20, and UNCTAD, and it deliberately used the Transatlantic Trade and Investment Partnership (TTIP) negotiations with the US to establish regulations that reach beyond WTO rules on trade and investments. Thereby, the TTIP might indirectly set an agenda for liberal trade and non-discriminatory access to raw materials in equivalent negotiations with other countries.[92]

The European Commission has demanded "investment protection," limitations on export restrictions, and a ban on export duties of raw materials when negotiating new trade agreements, whether these concerned Partnership and Cooperation Agreements (PCAs), FTAs, or WTO membership. The agreement with Mongolia in 2010 was the first PCA to take account of the RMI diplomacy as trade provisions restrained the level of Mongolian export duties. Entering into force in 2011, the first FTA after the announcement of the RMI was with South Korea, which easily agreed to the removal of export

"Europe Cannot Engage in Autarchical Policies"

restrictions. Subsequently, the commission has negotiated equivalent FTAs with a multitude of countries. When Russia joined the WTO in 2011, the commission was a driving force behind having constraints on existing and future export duties written into the accession treaty. From 2011 to 2012, the commission also initiated bilateral policy dialogues about raw materials extraction and trade with a large group of resource-rich countries, including countries enjoying the status of Strategic Partnerships with the EU.[93]

Conclusion

It has been almost forty years since the EC Commission noted that Europe's raw materials problem was a "vast but long-term one which does not lend itself to spectacular, instant solutions," and asked whether the EEC would be able to take advantage of the absence of immediate pressure to set up systems needed to map out a long-term policy. The answer to this question must be a qualified yes. The adoption, and subsequent development, of the RMI after 2008 goes some way towards addressing many of these issues. Particularly in what might be the so-called first pillar measures, the EU is directly engaging raw materials-producing countries through a wide variety of means, ranging from the pursuit of more accommodating conditions for trade in raw materials through FTAs or the TTIP to direct challenges in the use of export restrictions to the WTO.

The RMI was an innovation. In contrast to the confused postwar period of intraregionalism it introduced a global strategy: multilateralism. The RMI coherently responded to a wide set of external challenges, whereas policies during the period of interregionalism were more ambiguous. We suggest that this at least partly reflects the fact that the EU was a more cohesive political entity than the EC, but it also reflects the fact that the external environment had changed.

In comparing the aborted policy proposals of the 1970s with the strategies adopted forty years later, one finds many similarities. The rejection of stockpiling as a viable alternative is one recurrent feature, as is the attempt to reach out to producers of raw materials in the Third World through the Yaoundé, Lomé, and Cotonou Agreements. One notable departure is that, while the North-South dimension remains a key element in current raw materials diplomacy, the East-West dimension has seen several important developments. First of all, the main supply risk, both in terms of sourcing and political disagreement, is no longer seen to be Moscow but, rather, Beijing. This is a natural consequence of the fact that China is a source of eighteen of the twenty raw materials now defined as critical by the EU, of which it provides almost exactly half the global supply (49 percent).[94] But as long as the Chinese appetite for imported minerals is strong enough to drive price movements across the board, it is difficult to envision Beijing spearheading a global movement for increasing export restrictions, resulting in a potential reduction of the trade in the very raw materials China is purchasing abroad.[95]

It is still an open question whether the US-dominated international system for free trade in raw materials, as embodied by the WTO, will survive what the mining economist David Humphreys has described as the resurgence of "resource nationalism" in the minerals-producing countries.[96] If this surmise is correct, the EU may again be forced to deal with the consequences of a decentring of the established trade system for raw materials, and its Raw Materials Diplomacy will surely be put to the test. In view of the rather limited EU effort to grapple with export restrictions, rather than protectionism on a larger scale, there is currently little reason for the European Commission to engage in tough talk about a global effort to "keep markets open" and to "help trade flow as freely as possible."[97] In that regard, it may be pertinent to remind EU officials of a Chinese saying that, in the 1970s, commission vice-president Christopher Soames used to describe the lack of appropriate community-level policy response to the challenge of raw materials: "Don't make a noise like a hen unless you intend to lay an egg."[98]

Notes

1 European Commission, "The Raw Materials Initiative – Meeting Our Critical Needs for Growth and Jobs in Europe," COM (2008) 699 final, 4 November 2008.

2 European Commission, "European Commission Proposes New Strategy to Address EU Critical Needs for Raw Materials," 4 November 2008, IP/08/1628; European Commission, "The Commission Calls for Action on Commodities and Raw Materials," 2 February 2011, IP/11/122.

3 Peter Mandelson, "The Challenge of Raw Materials," speech delivered at Trade and Material Conference, Brussels, 29 September 2009.

4 European Commission, "Tackling the Challenges in Commodity Markets and on Raw Materials," COM (2011) 25 final, 2 February 2011.

5 Nora Fisher Onar and Kalypso Nicolaïdis, "The Decentring Agenda: Europe as a Post-Colonial Power," *Cooperation and Conflict* 48, 2 (2013): 283–330.

6 Jean Monnet, *Mémoires* (Paris: Fayard, 1976), 488.

7 Peter Debaere, *EU Coordination in International Institutions: Policy and Process in Gx Forums* (London: Palgrave, 2016), 95–96.

8 Frank McDonald and Stephen Dearden, *European Economic Integration* (Harlow: Pearson, 2005).

9 Harry Dexter White, preliminary draft, "United Nations Stabilization Fund and a Bank for Reconstruction and Development of the United and Associated Nations," 17 March 1942, Mudd Library, Princeton, Harry Dexter White Papers, box 6, United

"Europe Cannot Engage in Autarchical Policies"

Nations Stabilization Fund and a Bank for Reconstruction and Development of the United and Associated Nations; André Istel, "'Equal Access' to Raw Materials," *Foreign Affairs* 20, 3 (1942): 450–65; Helen O'Neill, *A Common Interest in a Common Fund* (New York: United Nations, 1977).

10 James Keen to Assistant Secretary General for Economic Affairs, 28 December 1946, UN Archives and Records Management Section (hereafter UNARMS), New York, S-0472-0060-5; European Central Inland Transport Organisation, Present Position with Regard to the Transport of Coal in Europe, ECITO/C/156, 18 November 1946, UNARMS, New York, S-0472-0060-5.

11 Alan S. Milward, *The Reconstruction of Western Europe, 1945–51* (London: Routledge, 1992), 35.

12 Economic Commission for Europe, Raw Materials, 1950, The National Archives (hereafter TNA), Kew, BT 64/1308.

13 The CEEC and its report on 22 September 1947, Historical Archives of the European Union (hereafter HAEU), Traver's Archive, Organisation for European Economic Co-operation (hereafter OEEC), 274.

14 OEEC, Steering Board for Trade, Liberalization of Intra-European Trade, C (49) 83 Final, 4 July 1949, HAEU, OEEC-0480; Otto Hieronymi, *Economic Discrimination against the United States in Western Europe, 1945–1958* (Geneva: Libraire Droz, 1973), 99, 105.

15 OEEC, *European Recovery Programme: Second Report of the OEEC* (Paris: OEEC, 1950), 160.

16 Milward, *Reconstruction of Western Europe,* 170–72.

17 John Gillingham, *Coal, Steel, and the Rebirth of Europe, 1945–1955* (Cambridge: Cambridge University Press, 1991).

18 Trevor Salmon and William Nicoll, eds., *Building European Union: A Documentary History and Analysis* (Manchester: Manchester University Press, 1997), 44–46.

19 OEEC Council, Decision of the Council Concerning the Member States of the European Coal and Steel Community, C (53) 9 Final, 10 February 1953, HAEU, OEEC-0481.

20 United Nations Economic Commission for Europe, "The Coal and Steel Industries of Western Europe," *Economic Bulletin for Europe* 2, 2 (1950): 16–52.

21 Spofford to Acheson, 26 February 1951, *Foreign Relations of the United States, 1951,* vol. 3, *European Security and the German Question Pt. I* (Washington: Government Printing Office), 66–67.

22 Council Deputies, Raw Materials Problems, 16 September 1950, NATO Archives (hereafter NA), Council Deputies, D-D/106; North Atlantic Council, Summary Record of the Second Meeting, Brussels, 19 December 1950, NA, North Atlantic Council, C6-R/2.

23 Organization for European Economic Cooperation, *International Organization* 5, 3 (1951): 632–36. See also OEEC, *Economic Progress and Problems of Western Europe* (Paris: Organisation for European Economic Co-operation, 1951).

24 Luxembourg 0, the Netherlands 1, Belgium 6, France 8, West Germany 7, Italy 6. Sara Nocentini, "Le Materie Prime nelle Relazioni Internazionali: l'International Materials Conference, 1950–1953" (PhD diss., Università degli Studi di Firenze, 2005).

25 CE/M (51) 10 (Prov.), 16 March 1951, HAEU, OEEC 130.

26 C/M (52) 57 (1st Rev.), 15 March 1952, HAEU, OEEC 030.
27 C/M (52) 18 (Prov.), 13 June 1952, Annex, Recent Developments Concerning the International Materials Conference, HAEU, OEEC 32; C/M (53) 33, Council Minutes, 9 December 1953, HAEU, OEEC 44; C/M (53) 31 (Prov.) Council Minutes, 13 November 1953, HAEU, OEEC 44.
28 Policy Planning Staff, PPS-23, Review of Current Trends, US Foreign Policy, 22 January 1948, NARA/RG 59, General Records of the Department of State, Records of the Policy Planning Staff 1947–1953, box 1, PPS–23.
29 OEEC, *Investments in Overseas Territories in Africa South of Sahara* (Paris: OEEC, 1951), 20.
30 Rik Shreurs, "A Marshall Plan for Africa? The Overseas Territories Committee and the Origins of European Cooperation in Africa," in *Explorations in OEEC History*, ed. Richard Griffiths (Paris: OECD, 1997), 87–98.
31 C/M (51) 9 (Prov.) 17 March 1951, HAEU, OEEC 22.
32 Gillingham, *Coal, Steel, and the Rebirth of Europe*, 24.
33 John Wilkinson Foster Rowe, *Primary Commodities in International Trade* (Cambridge: Cambridge University Press, 1965).
34 Frances Lynch, *France and the International Economy: From Vichy to the Treaty of Rome* (New York: Routledge, 1997); Yves Montarsolo, *L'Eurafrique, centrepoint de l'idée d'Europe – Le cas francais de la fin de la deuxiemmme guerre mondiale aux négotiations des Traités de Rome* (Aix en Provence: Publications de l'Université de Provence, 2010).
35 Treaty of Rome, Part 4, Article 131; Rapport: Du groupe de travail de l'Association des territoires d'Outre-mer à la Communauté économique européenne et études sur et études sur le commerce des produits, Genève, 1958, BAC 56/1980, nr. 194.
36 Robert Lemaignen, "L'association des pays d'outre-mer à la Communauté économique Européenne," *Annuaire Européen, Publié Sous les Auspices du Conseil de L'Europe* 8 (1960): 36–51.
37 Georges Elgozy, *L'Europe des européens* (Paris: Flammarion, 1961), 241.
38 Adrian Flint, "The End of a 'Special Relationship'? The New EU-ACP Economic Partnership Agreements," *Review of African Political Economy* 36, 119 (2007): 79–92.
39 European Community Information Service, *Partnership in Africa: The Yaondé Association*, Community Topics (Yeovil: Edwin Snell and Sons, 1966).
40 Europe "Common Market," no. 2557, 18 November 1966, UNARMS, S-0552-0048-1.
41 Proposals by the six countries [that are] members of the European Economic Community, 22 May 1964, Annexes A & B, UNARMS, S-0552-0049-11.
42 Papanicolaou to Imru, 2 November 1967, UNARMS, S-0552-0048-1.
43 Imru to Prebisch, Trade Policy Developments in the EEC, 3 November 1967, UNARMS, S-0552-0048-1.
44 Lorand Bartels, "The Trade and Development Policy of the European Union," *European Journal of International Law* 18, 4 (2007): 715–56.
45 GATT Agreement, Part 4, Trade and Development (Articles 36–38).
46 Richard Cooper and Robert Lawrence, "The 1972–75 Commodity Boom," *Brookings Papers on Economic Activity* 3 (1975): 671–723.
47 Minutes of a meeting held in the prime minister's room, House of Commons SW1, on Tuesday 2 February 1971 at 4:45 p.m., 3 February 1971, TNA, Kew, FCO 67/451.

48 "Working Party on Raw Materials Procurement and Overseas Aid Policy: Raw Materials – The OPEC Example," paper by the Department of Trade and Industry, n.d., TNA, Kew, FCO 69/481.

49 Donella H. Meadows, Dennis L. Meadows, Jørgen Randers, and William W. Behrens III, *Limits to Growth* (New York: New American Library, 1972).

50 The Intergovernmental Council of Copper Exporting Countries (CIPEC) was formed in 1967 by Chile, Peru, Zaire, and Zambia. Australia, Indonesia, Papua New Guinea, and Yugoslavia joined as full or associate members in 1975, bringing CIPEC's share of world primary copper exports to 65 percent. See John Soussan, *Primary Resources and Energy in the Third World* (London: Routledge, 1988), 39.

51 Altiero Spinelli, "Community Raw Materials Supplies," statement by Mr. Spinelli at his press conference of 7 February 1975, IP (75) 25.

52 In Greenland, the call for home rule was strengthened by the desire to leave the EEC and was partly inspired by the UN declaration on the right of peoples to freely dispose of their natural resources. See Axel Kjær Sørensen, *Denmark-Greenland in the Twentieth Century* (Viborg: The Committee for Scientific Research in Greenland, 2006), 150.

53 European Commission, "The Community's Supplies of Raw Materials," communication from the *Commission to the Council,* COM (75) 50 final, 5 February 1975.

54 European Commission, "The Raw Materials Challenge," *European File* 1 (1981).

55 European Commission, "Community's Supplies of Raw Materials." See also H. Schwörer, interim report drawn up on behalf of the Committee on Economic Affairs on the community's supplies of raw materials, working documents 1976–77, document 585/76, 7 March 1977.

56 Communication from the Commission to the Council on raw materials in relations with the developing countries that export raw materials, COM (75) 226 final, 21 May 1975.

57 Jan Isaksen, "Western European Reactions to Four NIEO Issues," in *Western Europe and the New International Economic Order*, ed. Ervin Laszlo and Joel Kurtzman (New York: Pergamon Press, 1980), 12–13. Driven by the UK and Germany the EC preferred a commodity-by-commodity approach.

58 Giuliano Garavini, "The Conference for International Economic Cooperation: A Diplomatic Reaction to the Oil Shock, 1975–1977," in *The Road to a United Europe: Interpretations of the Process of European Integration*, ed. Morten Rasmussen and Ann-Christina L. Knudsen (New York: Peter Lang, 2009), 153–68.

59 "Stabex" is an acronym for Système de Stabilisation des Recettes d'Exportation. See Berchi Mohammed, "Stabilisation des recettes d'exportations et taux de change des pays en voie de développement," *Tiers-Monde* 20, 80 (1979): 747–71.

60 Phillip Daniel, "Interpreting Mutual Interest: Non-Fuel Minerals in EEC-ACP Relations," in *Renegotiating Lomé*, ed. Christopher Stevens (London: Hodder and Stoughton, 1984), 63–88.

61 Overseas Development Institute, *Lomé II: Briefing Paper No 1 1980* (London: Overseas Development Institute, 1980).

62 "Sysmin" is an acronym for System of Stabilization of Export Earnings from Mining Products. See Wolfgang Maenning, "SYSMIN: An Evaluation," in *Intereconomics*, January/February 1988, 35–38.

63 Cristopher Dent, *The European Economy: The Global Context* (London: Routledge, 1997), 203; William Brown, *The European Union and Africa: The Restructuring of North-South Relations* (London: I.B. Tauris, 2002), 66.

64 John Ravenhill, *Collective Clientelism. The Lomé Conventions and North-South Relations* (New York: Columbia University Press, 1985), 145.

65 Wilhelm Haferkamp, "The European Community in the World Economy," address by Mr. Wilhelm Haferkamp, vice-president of the Commission of the European Communities, in charge of external relations, at the EEC-China Business Week, Brussels, 30 March 1981.

66 Christopher Gilbert, "International Commodity Agreements: An Obituary Notice," *World Development* 24, 1 (1996): 1–19.

67 Rocco Paone, *Strategic Nonfuel Minerals and Western Security* (Lanham: United States Naval Academy, 1992); Alfred Maizels, *Commodities in Crisis: The Commodity Crisis of the 1980s and the Political Economy of International Commodity Policies* (Oxford: Clarendon Press, 1992).

68 Daniel, "Interpreting Mutual Interest," 67–69.

69 David Humphreys, "Whatever Happened to Security of Supply? Minerals Policy in the Post-Cold War World," *Resources Policy* 21, 2 (1995): 91–97.

70 Eurostat, *Material Use in the European Union, 1980–2000: Indicators and Analysis* (Luxembourg: European Communities, 2002), 17.

71 European Commission, *Green Paper on Relations between the European Union and ACP Countries on the Eve of the 21st Century* (Luxembourg: Office for Official Publications of the European Communities, 1996).

72 European Communities: The ACP-EC Partnership Agreement, WT/MIN (01)/15, 14 November 2001.

73 James Gathii, *African Regional Trade Agreements as Legal Regimes* (Cambridge: Cambridge University Press, 2011), 133–34.

74 David Humphreys, "The Great Metals Boom: A Retrospective," *Resources Policy* 35, 1 (2010): 1–13.

75 World Trade Organization, *World Trade Report, 2010. Trade in Natural Resources* (Geneva: World Trade Organization, 2010).

76 Marian Radetzki, "The Anatomy of Three Commodity Booms," *Resources Policy* 31 (2006): 56–64.

77 European Commission, analysis of the non-energy extractive industry in the EU, commission staff working document SEC (2007) 771, 4 June 2007.

78 Organisation for Economic Co-operation and Development, *OECD Trade Policy Studies: The Economic Impact of Export Restrictions on Raw Materials* (Paris: OECD, 2010), 162–67.

79 European Commission, "European Commission proposes new strategy to address EU critical needs for raw materials," 4 November 2008, IP/08/1628.

80 European Commission, Critical raw materials for the EU, report of the Ad Hoc Working Group on defining critical raw materials, version of 30 July 2010.

81 European Commission, Report on critical raw materials for the EU, report of the Ad Hoc Working Group on defining critical raw materials, May 2014, COM (2014) 297 final, on the review of the list of critical raw materials for the EU and the implementation of the Raw Materials Initiative.

82 The RMI was revised in 2011 without profound changes.

83 Quotes from COM (2008) 699 final, "The Raw Materials Initiative: Meeting Our Critical Needs for Growth and Jobs in Europe," 7.

84 Ibid.

85 Ibid., 8.

86 European Commission, "Trade, Growth and World Affairs: Trade Policy as a Core Component of the EU's 2020 Strategy," 2010; "Trade as a Driver of Prosperity," commission staff working document accompanying the commission's communication on "Trade, Growth and World Affairs," 2010.

87 According to the Treaty on the Functioning of the European Union 2007, common commercial policy and competition policy are union competences, whereas development policy is a shared competence between the union and the member states.

88 European Commission, Directorate-General for Trade, *Raw Materials Policy, 2009 Annual Report* (European Commission, 2009); European Commission, Directorate-General for Trade, *EU Trade Policy for Raw Materials, Second Activity Report* (European Commission, 2012); COM (2013) 442 final, On the implementation of the Raw Materials Initiative, 24 June 2013; SWD (2014) 171 final, On the implementation of the Raw Materials Initiative, 26 May 2014.

89 SWD (2014) 171 final, on the implementation of the Raw Materials Initiative, 26 May 2014.

90 Chien-Huei Wu, "Access to Raw Materials: The EU's Pursuit of Trade Disciplines on Export Control," in *The EU's Role in Global Governance: The Legal Dimension*, ed. Bart Van Vooren, Steven Blockmans, and Jan Wouters (Oxford: Oxford University Press, 2013), 178–92; Krüger Tilman, "The EU as a Strategic Litigant in the WTO," in *The European Union's Shaping of the International Legal Order*, ed. Dimitry Kochenov and Fabian Amtenbrink (Cambridge: Cambridge University Press, 2014), 169–90.

91 Markus Wagner, "WTO Law and the Right to Regulate: China – Rare Earths," *American Society of International Law Insights* 18, 10 (2014), at https://www.asil. org/insights/volume/18/issue/10/wto-law-and-right-regulate-china-%E2%80%93 -rare-earths.

92 SWD (2014) 171 final, On the implementation of the Raw Materials Initiative, 26 May 2014. See also the European Commission's initial position paper on raw materials and energy for the TTIP at http://trade.ec.europa.eu/doclib/docs/2013/july/ tradoc_151624.pdf (European Commission trade website).

93 COM (2013) 442 final, on the implementation of the Raw Materials Initiative, 24 June 2013; SWD (2014) 171 final, On the implementation of the Raw Materials Initiative, 26 May 2014.

94 The US is a distant second with 9 percent, followed by Brazil and South Africa tied for third place with 6 percent. See European Commission, Report on critical raw materials for the EU, report of the Ad Hoc Working Group on defining critical raw materials, May 2014, COM (2014) 297 final.

95 Masuma Farooki and Raphael Kaplinsky, *The Impact of China on Global Commodity Prices: The Global Reshaping of the Resource Sector* (Abingdon, UK: Routledge, 2012).

96 David Humphreys, *The Remaking of the Mining Industry* (London: Palgrave, 2015), 205.

97 Caroline Boeshertz, Market Access, Industry, Energy and Raw Materials Unit, Directorate General Trade, European Commission: "The EU Trade policy and raw materials" EU-Latin America 10-11 March 2014, at http://ec.europa.eu/DocsRoom/documents/4910/attachments/1/translations/en/renditions/pdf (European Commission website).

98 Christopher Soames, "The World Economy: Toward a new Consensus," speech before the Oil Industries Club, 1 July 1975, at http://aei.pitt.edu/8493/1/8493.pdf (archive of European Integration website).

14

Mitigating Import Dependency

Japan's Energy and Mining Policies

TAKEO KIKKAWA

All modern economies need access to natural resources in order to prosper. While no major countries are self-sufficient with regard to natural resources, few – if any – are as dependent on imports as Japan. It has no important onshore natural resources bar hydropower, coal, and some minerals. The country is therefore very vulnerable to supply shocks. A stable supply of a wide range of natural resources is a critical requirement for maintaining the national livelihood and economic activity.

Most of the contributions in this book deal with how resource-abundant countries have regulated their natural resources. This chapter changes the perspective: it discusses how a country has tried to mitigate its import dependency through a set of policy measures. These policies include conservation, stockpiling, development of alternative types of energy, and exploration for new resources as well as foreign policy initiatives in the form of state support for Japanese investments in overseas resource industries. Japan's attempts at reducing import dependency have thus had both a domestic and an international impact. Japan's need for supply security has influenced not only the demand for natural resources but also how resource-abundant countries have developed their resource endowments.

This chapter explores how Japan's mining and energy policies have developed in the postwar era. Under American tutelage, Japan adopted a liberal mining law in 1950. In the 1970s, a decade that experienced repeated turmoil in commodity markets, supply security became a more pressing issue. The chapter discusses the evolution of Japanese resource policies from the 1970s onwards,[1] and it discusses why Japan revised its mining law in 2011. A key issue is exploration for and regulation of natural resources in the vast ocean areas surrounding Japan.

Japan's High Dependence on Imports of Natural Resources

As one of the world's most industrialized countries Japan consumes vast amounts of natural resources, most of which are imported. This dependency raises serious questions pertaining to import security – questions that have led to a set of differing policy responses, ranging from stockpiling to conservation efforts, recycling, diversifying import sources, and foreign policy initiatives. Japan's three main aims have been to reduce its dependency on imports, to stockpile in order to reduce vulnerability, and to import vital commodities from politically stable and/or friendly countries. In the following discussion I focus on two cases of import dependency – namely, energy and rare earths.

According to a 2011 report from the Japanese Agency for Natural Resources and Energy, Japan was more dependent on imported energy than most other major countries.[2] In 1960, 60 percent of Japan's energy requirements were covered by domestic sources, primarily coal and hydroelectric power. In the following years, the self-sufficiency ratio decreased. Energy consumption increased rapidly at the same time as domestic coal was replaced by cheap imported oil. Almost all natural gas and uranium used in nuclear power generation was imported from overseas. By 2007, only 4 percent of Japan's energy consumption came from domestic sources. However, nuclear power may be regarded as quasi-domestic since uranium can be stored for a long time after it is imported. If nuclear power is counted as a domestic energy source, Japan's energy self-sufficiency ratio in 2007 rises to 18 percent (Table 14.1).

After the two oil crises in the 1970s, Japan initiated energy conservation measures and promoted the diversification of energy sources.[3] Despite these efforts, however, the nation still depends on oil for about 50 percent of its total energy supply. Japan also made efforts to diversify its sources of oil to avoid overdependence on any specific country or region, a policy that temporarily helped reduce its energy dependence on the Middle East. However, as the main alternative sources (China and Indonesia) have more or less dried up, Japan has again become dependent on the Middle East. Japan's government has therefore tried to increase the country's cooperation with oil-producing nations, and it has encouraged conservation and exploration

Mitigating Import Dependency 329

TABLE 14.1
Energy self-sufficiency ratio (%) for eleven countries, 2007

Country	Ratio not including nuclear power	Ratio including nuclear power
Italy	15	15
Japan	4	18
Republic of Korea	2	19
Germany	30	41
France	8	51
United States	62	71
India	75	76
United Kingdom	76	83
China	91	92
Canada	144	153
Russia	177	183

Note: The portion exceeding 100 percent represents export.
Source: Ministry of Economy, Trade and Industry, Agency for Natural Resources and Energy, *Energy in Japan 2010* (Tokyo: Ministry of Economy, Trade and Industry, 2010), 11.

for petroleum in Japan's territorial waters. The authorities have also supported Japanese companies exploring and/or developing oilfields abroad. As a result, the ratio of crude oil imported from Japanese-owned or Japanese-operated reserves abroad increased from 8 percent in 1973 to 16 percent in 2008. However, this ratio is still far lower than those in many other developed countries.

In case of unanticipated suspension of imports, oil is being stockpiled, both by the government and by private companies. At the end of 2009, a total of 83.64 million kiloliters, covering almost two hundred days' consumption, was stockpiled. This stockpile has functioned effectively in emergencies after the oil crises of the 1970s. Oil was discharged to the market during the Gulf Crisis in August 1990 and following a major hurricane that disrupted the United States in August 2005.

Japan also depends on imports of liquefied petroleum gas (LPG), which is a relatively clean energy source. Around 28 percent of imported LPG comes from Saudi Arabia, and about 86 percent comes from the Middle East as a whole. As in the case of oil, Japan's dependency on the Middle East is perceived as a potential problem.[4] To help ensure a stable supply, Japanese importers are currently required by law to stockpile enough LPG to equal fifty days' consumption. In addition, a national stockpiling system is being promoted.

Japanese authorities have promoted natural gas as an alternative to oil, partly because of energy security, partly because it is a clean type of energy.[5] By 2008, natural gas accounted for 17 percent of Japan's primary energy consumption. The authorities were less concerned with the supply security of natural gas than with that of oil and LPG. Whereas most of the oil and LPG comes from the Middle East, natural gas is imported from multiple regions, such as Southeast Asia, Oceania, and the Middle East.

Japanese authorities aim to convert thermal power plants from using oil and coal to using natural gas. They also promote the use of vehicles fuelled by natural gas as well as more fuel-efficient equipment. Another plan under consideration is to modify gas and use it as a liquid fuel. These new fuels, called GTL (Gas-to-Liquid) and DME (Dimethyl Ether), are expected to provide fuel for transport and industry in the future. The realization of these plans will require substantial research as well as investments in the domestic pipeline network.

Japanese authorities also hope to develop new technology to utilize the methane hydrate resources in the country's territorial waters. Methane hydrate is an ice-like material in which methane gas and water are crystallized under low-temperature and high-pressure conditions. Production of methane hydrate might therefore increase Japanese energy self-sufficiency.

There are abundant coal deposits in the Pacific area, and Japan imports coal from politically stable countries such as Australia.[6] Supply risks are thus small. Coal is also cheap per thermal unit. It is, however, a larger pollutant than other types of fossil fuels. Japanese authorities have therefore endeavoured to, and succeeded in, increasing the efficiency of coal-fired power generation in Japan.

Japan also depends on imports of rare metals and rare earths.[7] These minerals are essential for a number of industrial purposes. Supply security is a main issue. A large part of the world's deposits of rare metals and earths are located in a limited number of countries: 97 percent of rare earth originates in China, as does 75 percent of tungsten; 77 percent of the supply of platinum comes from South Africa. Japanese authorities have therefore followed a number of different policies in order to mitigate potential supply problems. These include offering support to several export countries in order to foster friendly relations. The authorities have assisted private Japanese enterprises in their endeavours to secure supplies of rare metals from abroad. "Urban mining" has been promoted in order to increase recycling. In addition, Japan has sought to develop new materials that may replace or reduce the need for rare metals. Last, but not least, as in the case of energy, rare metals have been stockpiled in order to withstand short-term supply shocks.

The Fukushima nuclear accident of March 2011 aggravated the Japanese energy and resource situation. The *Strategic Energy Plan* of April 2014,[8] endorsed by the Japanese Cabinet, showed that, after the nuclear power plants were shut down, the energy self-sufficiency rate declined to 6 percent in 2012. Japan's dependency on fossil fuels as a power source increased from 60 percent before the earthquake to 90 percent after it. The country thus became even more vulnerable to supply shocks. Due to increased imports of fossil fuels, for the first time in more than thirty years, from 2011 to 2013, Japan had a negative trade balance. The extra fuel imports after the nuclear shutdown cost about $3.6 trillion in 2013.

The increased imports of fossil fuels also aggravated Japan's dependency on the Middle East for energy imports. In 2013, 83 percent of its oil imports and 30 percent of its imports of natural gas came from this area. This became all the more challenging due to the increased political instability in the Middle East. However, Japan's extensive stockpiles of oil offer protection in case of disruptions. Natural gas is imported from several different countries. Japan is also continuing its endeavours to diversify its supply, including imports of natural gas from North America. The supply risks of natural gas are thus smaller than are those for oil.

Historical Overview of Japan's Mining Policy
The postwar Allied occupation authorities sought to restructure Japanese society. One of their goals was to "democratize the mining industry of Japan."[9] The prewar and wartime mining industry had been under heavy governmental control and had aimed for self-sufficiency. The Americans intended to establish a more market-based mining sector, wanting to reduce both government control and the role played by Japanese big business. After four years of deliberations between American occupiers and Japanese officials and business interests, a new mining law was enacted in 1950. As was the case with so many of the American objectives in postwar Japan, the aims were somewhat watered down and compromises were made with Japanese elites. Foreign investment in Japanese mining remained out of the question, and large Japanese mining corporations maintained their control of the industry, but the autarkic bent of the old legislation was scrapped.[10]

In the Pax Americana of the 1950s and 1960s, supply security was not seriously threatened. However, due to the rapid pace of Japanese industrialization, and the resulting growth of its requirements for energy and

TABLE 14.2
Basic directions for Japanese mining policy, 1972

Theme	Policy
Domestic mining	Promotion of exploration for minerals. Stable supply a priority
Domestic smelters	Improvement of profitability through independent efforts
Overseas development	Exploration, economic cooperation / development projects
Imports and stockpiling	Cooperation with resource exporting countries

Source: Japan Oil, Gas and Metals National Corporation (JOGMEC), *Base Metals: International Conditions and Changes in Japan's Mining Resources Policy* (Kawasaki: JOGMEC, 2007).

minerals, security of supply became a major issue in the 1970s. This was especially the case for oil.[11] The growing turmoil in the commodity markets only added to this.

In June 1972, the Mining Industry Council Mine Subcommittee published the report *Fundamental Direction for Future Mining Policy*. This became a key document for the Japanese government's mining resources policy. The report mapped out the basic directions with regard to the four themes depicted in Table 14.2: approach to domestic mines, approach to domestic smelters, approach to overseas development, and approach to overseas ore transactions and stockpiling.

In May 1973, new regulations on pollution from the mining industry were introduced. Pollution had become a serious environmental and social problem. In order to implement the new regulations the government reorganized and expanded the existing Metallic Minerals Exploration Promotion Agency of Japan, renaming it the Metal Mining Agency of Japan (MMAJ). The revamped agency was entrusted with responsibility for all mining resources policies.

In 1974, MMAJ started an overseas exploration financing and investment policy. It also subsidized joint geological structure surveys overseas. In 1976, the agency began an import stabilization and stockpiling system, and in 1983 it started up a rare metal stockpiling system. Thus MMAJ came to serve as the main actor with regard to all Japan's mining resources policies.

Based on the points described above, the following four key programs have existed as part of Japan's mining resources policy from the 1970s:

Mitigating Import Dependency 333

(1) promotion of domestic mineral exploration in order to secure stable domestic mineral supply; (2) support of overseas resource development activities, and technical cooperation with countries in which development is taking place, in order to secure stable overseas mining resources; (3) creation of a rare metals stockpiling system; and (4) prevention of mine pollution from suspended or abandoned domestic mines.

In 2004, the Japan Oil, Gas and Metals National Corporation (JOGMEC) was created through the merger of Japan National Oil Corporation and MMAJ.[12] It took over the four aforementioned programs from MMAJ. The following paragraphs look back on the development of mining resources policy in Japan by exploring each of these main programs, with the exception of the fourth (prevention of mine pollution).

In 1964, MMAJ's predecessor, the Metallic Minerals Exploration Promotion Agency of Japan, began undertaking precise geological structure surveys. It did so partly because of the above-mentioned concerns over supply security, but it also did so in the hope of discovering high-grade commercially viable mineral deposits. In 1966, the government consigned wide-area geological structure survey activities to the Metallic Minerals Exploration Financing Agency of Japan.

The Mining Industry Council prepared the *First Domestic Exploration Long-Term Plan* in 1966. The plan covered six metals – copper, lead, zinc, manganese, gold, and tungsten – and selected twenty-eight regions as survey sites. The *Second Domestic Exploration Long-Term Plan*, initiated in 1973, included twenty-five additional regions as survey sites. The domestic mine surveys and exploration were implemented through a three-stage process, beginning with wide-area geological structure surveys and then proceeding to precise geological structure surveys and corporate exploration.

The Mining Industry Council implemented revisions to the *Domestic Exploration Long-Term Plan* in 1988. Nineteen regions were selected for exploration. The domestic mine survey and exploration activities were based on the three-stage process, and the plan was a success. It led to nine projects that either reached the stage of mine development or the expansion of existing mines. However, the exploration program was terminated in 2003–06.

The cost of these domestic mine surveys was approximately ¥42.6 billion. When calculated using metal prices in September 2007, the value of the resources extracted by domestic mining companies based on this survey and exploration activity exceeded ¥450.0 billion.[13]

Japan followed a three-pronged strategy in order to secure a stable supply from overseas mineral resources. First, state authorities encouraged overseas exploration and investment in mineral resources. In 1968, Japan started helping companies finance overseas exploration and issued guarantees for liabilities. Six years later a state-supported system of raising equity capital for overseas exploration was introduced. By 2006, the Japanese state had granted ¥7.9 billion plus $960,000 to eighty exploration projects overseas. It had also provided ¥6.2 billion (three projects) as equity capital for such exploration projects as well as liability guarantees for twelve projects, totalling ¥34.0 billion plus $26.48 million.

The second prong of the strategy involved the Metallic Minerals Exploration Financing Agency of Japan, MMAJ, and JOGMEC commencing overseas geological structure surveys in 1968 and an overseas joint geological structure survey subsidy system in 1974. The latter system covered joint ventures between Japanese and host country companies. These surveys were implemented in regions in which Japanese companies or other entities held exploration rights (and regions in which they were reliably expected to acquire such rights) and had operations. The overseas joint geological structure survey subsidy system funded up to 50 percent of Japanese corporations' overseas exploration costs. By 2005, seventy-one overseas geological structure survey projects had been conducted, and forty-two projects were implemented under the overseas joint geological structure survey subsidy system.

The third prong of the strategy involved Japan seeking to foster cooperation with mineral-rich countries. As the private sector was underdeveloped in many mineral-rich countries, Japan often had to cooperate with government institutions. Resource development cooperation base surveys were begun in 1970. The aim was to promote exploration and development in partner countries by dispatching survey teams based on requests from their respective governments. This included preliminary surveys as well as precise surveys of mining resources in cooperation with the partner countries. By 2006, resource development cooperation base surveys had been implemented in 180 regions in forty-six countries.

From the 1970s onwards, Japanese authorities perceived deep seafloor mining as vital for future stable access to mineral resources. The deep seafloor resources include manganese nodules, cobalt-rich crust, and seafloor hydrothermal deposits. The advanced survey vessel *Hakurei Maru No. 2* was launched in May 1980.

MMAJ and JOGMEC have carried out surveys of deep seafloor mining resources since 1975. Exploration for manganese nodules were carried out in waters southeast of the Hawaiian Islands from 1975 to 1996. The results contributed to Deep Ocean Resources Development Co. Ltd. acquiring a Japanese concession covering seventy-five thousand square kilometres in 1987. Cobalt-rich crust surveys in the Chubu Pacific Ocean region were begun in 1987. Deep seafloor hydrothermal deposit surveys were conducted along the East Pacific Rise off the coast of Mexico (1985–94), in the Okinawa Trough (1995–99), and in the ocean areas around Izu and Ogasawara (2000–05), which led to the discovery of the "Hakurei Deposit," a new deposit located in the Bayonnaise Knoll in the Izu-Ogasawara ocean area in 2003.

A survey concerning the extension of Japan's continental shelf was begun in 1998. This survey aims at documenting the resource potential in the ocean areas off Japan, where continental shelf extension might be a possibility.

Japan is very dependent on imports of so-called rare metals. "Rare metals" is a generic term for metallic elements that exist only in scant quantities in the earth's crust or that are difficult to extract. They are very important in a number of alloys with iron, aluminum, and copper. They are also used in superconducting materials, semiconductors, in metal alloys for hydrogen storage, in shape-memory alloys, and in electronic materials such as ceramic capacitors, permanent magnets, and environmental impact load mitigation catalysts. The rare metals originate in a limited number of countries, among them Russia, China, and South Africa. Consequently, there is a significant risk of product shortages and sudden price jumps due to political or economic instability in the producing countries. In 1983, Japan's government set up a rare metals stockpiling system and consigned national stockpiling activities to MMAJ. This activity was later continued by JOGMEC.

MMAJ and JOGMEC have sold stockpiled rare metals, as appropriate, in response to market fluctuations. Triggers of rare metals sales include increases in demand as well as sudden jumps in rare metals prices caused by mine closures, mine accidents, mine strikes, and other incidents.

In December 1984, the Rare Metal Comprehensive Policy Special Subcommittee of the Mining Industry Council's Mine Subcommittee drafted a report entitled *Comprehensive Rare Metals Countermeasures: Toward Technical Innovation, Industrial Revitalization and Economic Security*. The report focused on three main issues: (1) promotion of exploration and development, (2) promotion of technological development, and (3) expansion of the stockpiling system. Points (1) and (2) included measures such as a survey of the domestically available rare metals mining resources, support for independent rare metals exploration overseas, development of rare metals resource exploration technologies, research cooperation concerning the effective utilization of unused rare metals, and development of advanced rare metals separation and refinement technologies.

Although the need to ensure rare metals supplies had been recognized in the mid-1980s, the awareness was heightened in the 2000s when rare metals demand soared and prices skyrocketed. In July 2009, the Ministry of Economy, Trade and Industry prepared and released a report entitled *Strategy for Ensuring Stable Supplies of Rare Metals*, which was based on the results of a study conducted by the Mineral Resources Subcommittee, Advisory Committee for Natural Resources and Energy. This strategy identified various factors as the "issues surrounding rare metals," including scarcity; uneven distribution; the expansion of consumption on a global scale; growth of demand in the new energy, energy conservation, and environmental protection sectors; the emergence of resource nationalism; and the intensifying competition to acquire resources.

The report recommended four policy measures: securing overseas resources, increased recycling, development of alternative materials, and stockpiling. It recommended building strategic, mutually beneficial relationships with resource-producing countries. This included Official Development Assistance (ODA) tools for the construction of infrastructure around mines, cooperation through programs such as those dealing with technology transfers, and collaboration on environmental preservation – all of which should demonstrate Japan's strengths. The report also emphasized the need for investments in rare metals resources and the development of seafloor hydrothermal deposits and other resources in the oceans around Japan.

Background to the 2011 Revision of the Mining Act

Japan possesses the world's sixth largest ocean area in terms of the size of its territorial waters, exclusive economic zone (EEZ), and continental shelf. In addition to oil and natural gas, there are confirmed deposits of energy and mining resources such as methane hydrate and seafloor hydrothermal deposits. However, several problems remain to be solved before these resources can be commercially exploited. These include understanding the amount of available resources and the status of its availability, the development of production techniques, and dealing with environmental issues.

The government has so far conducted only limited geophysical surveys in this ocean area. By 2009, two-dimensional geophysical surveys covered only about 120,000 square kilometres, while three-dimensional geophysical surveys about six thousand square kilometres. The three-dimensional geophysical surveys sharply improve the accuracy of exploration site selection.

Mitigating Import Dependency 337

TABLE 14.3

Comparison of resource exploration regulations by country (as of 31 March 2010)

	Type of resource exploration regulation	Regulated exploration	Administration of exploration data
United States	Permit system	Geological surveys (exploration, etc.) and geophysical surveys (seismic surveys, etc.)	Submission in response to government request
United Kingdom	Permit system	Geological surveys based on physical and chemical methods and shallow drilling not accompanied by acquisition of resources	Submission in response to government request
Australia	Permit system	Seismic surveys etc., and surveys implemented with the intent to use data and information from said surveys to acquire samples and discover oil	Submission in response to government request
Norway	Permit system	Geological surveys or rock physical surveys, geophysical surveys, geochemical surveys, geoengineering surveys, shallow drilling	Submission in response to government request
Japan	No regulation	–	No regulation

Source: Advisory Committee for Energy, Mining Subcommittee and Oil Subcommittee Combined Legislation Working Group, reference materials from *Approach to Japan's Future Mining Legislation System*, 1 January 2011, Tokyo.

However, no Japanese firms at the time were able to conduct such surveys. In February 2008, the Japanese Agency for Natural Resources and Energy introduced the survey vessel named *Resources*. The aim was to create domestic three-dimensional geophysical exploration capacity in order to discover oil and natural gas resources in Japan's ocean area.

In contrast to many other developed countries with large ocean areas, Japan lacks a regulatory framework for resource exploration (see Table 14.3). Japan does not have a systematic framework for dealing with the submission of survey data. As a result, its resource exploration activities were

TABLE 14.4
Comparison of each country's method for allocating permissions for resource development (as of 31 March 2010)

	Method for deciding development entities	Confirmed points
United States	Selection of applicants based on tenders etc., not first-to-file	The highest bidder is selected. The bidder must demonstrate that it is financially capable of conducting operations.
United Kingdom	Selection of applicants based on tenders etc., not first-to-file	The most appropriate applicant is selected after confirming that it has the sufficient technical and financial capabilities.
Australia	Selection of applicants based on tenders etc., not first-to-file	The selection is based on the contents of the applicant's business plan or tender. It must confirm that it has the sufficient technical and financial capabilities.
Norway	Selection of applicants based on tenders etc., not first-to-file	The applicants' technical capabilities, financial base and the contents of its business plan are evaluated.
Japan	First-to-file principle	Checks only non-approval requirements such as adverse effects on other industries and elimination of redundant concessions.

Source: Advisory Committee for Energy, Mining Subcommittee and Oil Subcommittee Combined Legislation Working Group, reference materials from *Approach to Japan's Future Mining Legislation System*, 1 January 2011, Tokyo.

disorganized. The de facto resource exploration activity conducted by foreign vessels in ocean areas took advantage of this systematic deficiency.

Japan adopted a first-to-file principle for allocating resource development permits. This had harmful effects. The applicants' technical and financial capabilities were not investigated. In several cases entities acquired permits without having the necessary capabilities to develop the resources. As of the end of March 2010, the state had allocated 8,179 mining rights. Only 1,558 of these were in production, while 5,562 had not yet begun operations and 1,059 were dormant. Table 14.4 compares how different countries allocate resource development permits.

In order to resolve the above-mentioned problems, the Diet revised the Mining Act during its 2011 session.[14] This was the first revision since the law was enacted in 1950. Four major changes are worth noting: (1) the first-to-file principle for allocating mining rights was abolished, and provisions covering the applicants' financial and technological capabilities as well as the public interest were included; (2) the revision introduced a specified area system for the creation of mining rights, and this enabled the government to solicit and select development entities in specified areas designated by the government for "Specified Minerals" (oil, natural gas, etc.) that are especially important for the national economy and for supply security; (3) a permission system for exploration for mineral resources was introduced, with the result that entities wishing to engage in mineral resource exploration were henceforth required to apply for permission; and (4) the government could require reports on exploration results. With this first full-fledged revision of the Mining Act in sixty-one years, the two problems concerning mining resources development in Japan identified earlier have begun moving towards a resolution.

Japan's Efforts at Producing Methane Hydrate

As discussed previously, Japan has the possibility of becoming the world's preeminent source of marine resources. One example of such a resource is methane hydrate. This is an ice-like substance formed from the crystallization of methane gas and water under low-temperature, high-pressure conditions. If it can be produced and used, methane hydrate will greatly improve Japan's energy situation.

The *Ocean Energy and Mineral Resource Development Plan* formulated by the Ministry of Economy, Trade and Industry in March 2009 discusses how methane hydrate – often called "flammable ice" – is separated into water molecules and methane gas molecules when subjected to changes such as increased temperature or lower pressure. The separated methane molecules possess the same principal components as conventional natural gas, and methane hydrate is being anticipated as a non-conventional hydrocarbon resource.

Provided that methane hydrate production technology is established and the practical application and commercialization of methane hydrate are realized, it will give Japan – a country that depends on imports from other countries for more than 80 percent of its primary energy supply – a secure domestic supply of energy. This will have an extremely significant impact because Japan is well endowed with large quantities of methane hydrate in its territorial waters, in its exclusive economic zone, and within its continental shelf. Supply risks would thus be mitigated. For that reason, the development of methane hydrate production technology is extremely important with regard to Japan's ability to secure a stable energy supply.

Large quantities of methane hydrate are thought to lie in the ocean area around Japan, centred on the eastern portion of the Nankai Trough ocean area (Tokai coast-Kumano open sea). Because methane hydrate is found within strata as a solid, however, it cannot, like conventional oil and natural gas resources, be made to flow simply by sinking wells. To produce natural gas (methane) stably and economically from methane hydrate strata, it will be necessary to develop new production technologies, including methods to decompose the substance by lowering pressure.

Japan has been the world leader in undertaking R&D on methane hydrate, mainly through JOGMEC. In 2007, JOGMEC established a procedure to evaluate the quantity of in-place methane hydrate. It published the quantity of in-place resources in the eastern Nankai Trough ocean area (about fourteen years' worth of Japan's natural gas consumption). In the following year, a joint Canadian and Japanese team achieved a major breakthrough – namely, the world's first successful continuous collection of methane gas obtained using the "depressurization method." This was done in onshore production tests using methane hydrate layers in the permafrost region of the Canadian Arctic. JOGMEC has also pioneered the testing of offshore methane hydrate production. These tests commenced in 2009.

Conclusion

Japan has been one of the world's largest importers and consumers of natural resources. Its resource policies, therefore, have a substantial impact both on export countries and on international commodity markets. One of Japan's key aims has been to mitigate its dependency on imports of natural resources and to limit the risk of supply shocks. This has involved both domestic and foreign policy initiatives. Japanese authorities attempted to reduce consumption through different conservation measures, limiting vulnerability through stockpiling and securing imports of vital commodities from politically stable and/or friendly countries.

In recent years, Japan has also pushed for increased state control and development of the natural resources in Japan's ocean areas. For a long time, becoming a "major ocean resources country" was nothing more than a dream for Japan. The revision of the Mining Act in 2011 and the new system of allocating exploration and production rights may become the first step towards actually achieving that dream.

Mitigating Import Dependency

Notes

1 Japan's mining resources policy has been consistently in pursuit of both mining promotion and mining regulation. See Noboru Honda, *Japan's Policy for Sustainable Development of Mining Resources and Policy of Environment* (Tokyo: Ministry of Economy, Trade and Industry, 2014), 2.

2 Ministry of Economy, Trade and Industry, Agency for Natural Resources and Energy, *Energy in Japan 2010* (Tokyo: Ministry of Economy, Trade and Industry, 2010).

3 Ibid., 12, 31–32.

4 Ibid., 34.

5 Ibid., 33.

6 Ibid., 35.

7 Ibid., 36.

8 Japanese Cabinet Decision, *Strategic Energy Plan* (Tokyo: Ministry of Economy, Trade and Industry, 2014), 9–10.

9 Albert H. Solomon, "Revision of the Japanese Mining Law under the Occupation," *Washington Law Review and State Bar Journal* 26, 3 (1951): 232.

10 Ibid., 232–46.

11 Raymond Vernon, *Two Hungry Giants: The United States and Japan in the Quest for Oil and Ores* (Cambridge, MA: Harvard University Press, 1983), 82.

12 Hirotoshi Kunimoto, "Japan's Metal Mining Policy and the Role of JOGMEC" (Kawasaki: Japan Oil, Gas and Metals National Corporation, 2004).

13 The data in the following sections are taken mainly from *Base Metals: International Conditions and Changes in Japan's Mining Resources Policy* (Kawasaki: Japan Oil, Gas and Metals National Corporation, 2007).

14 Ministry of Economy, Trade and Industry, *The Amended Mining Act of Japan*, 22 July 2011.

Conclusion

ANDREAS R.D. SANDERS, PÅL T. SANDVIK,
and ESPEN STORLI

In his *Politics*, Aristotle offers one of the earliest descriptions of the uneasy relationship between private control of natural resources and state power. Around 400 BC a wealthy man in Sicily acquired "all the iron from the iron mines" and thus became the only seller of iron. The operation became very profitable. According to Aristotle, "without much increasing the price, he gained 200 per cent." However, he soon ran into political trouble. The highly intelligent yet oftentimes cruel, suspicious, and vindictive tyrant Dionysius in Syracuse in eastern Sicily found the iron monopoly "injurious to his own interests." Fortunately, the tyrant acted with some restraint. The speculator cum investor was allowed to keep his head and even profits, but he was expelled from Syracuse.[1]

While Aristotle does not provide any more detail on the political economy of iron ore in ancient Sicily, the case contains many of the elements that we can find much later in modern conflicts over natural resources, such as control over strategic raw materials, allocation of resource rent, monopolization, investor security, and the effects of confiscation. Aristotle's book on politics was intended to guide rulers and statesmen and to give them practical knowledge about politics. It was based on a comprehensive approach to the subject, and in order to properly understand political phenomena, the author had his students collect information on the political organization and history of 158 different cities. Based on this data, Aristotle created a

Conclusion   343

typology of six different kinds of political regimes and ranked them according to how beneficial they were. Tyranny, as practised by Dionysius, was ranked as the most flawed regime. Democracy was also characterized as a flawed regime, albeit the best of the bad.

Like Aristotle's work, this book is also based on historical case studies. It consists of fourteen chapters, each offering a case study that examines different aspects of resource regulation in sovereign countries, colonies, or dependencies as well as the growing internationalization of resource policy through international organizations, treaties, and other forms of international cooperation. Countries or colonies from all continents are included, and the chapters span the nineteenth, twentieth, and early twenty-first centuries and cover a variety of resources.

The difference in resource bases, different domestic institutional set-ups, political traditions, power structures, and so forth naturally make each historical case unique. However, put together, this wide variety of cases makes it possible for us to discern an outline of some broad trends in the global history of resource regulations since the mid-nineteenth century. The most marked trend during this period is the rise and transformation of regulations aimed at claiming a greater share of strategic benefits (or economic rents) from natural resources for the states in which those resources are located. We group the policies that comprise this phenomenon under the umbrella term "resource nationalist." The rise and transformation of resource nationalism can be grouped into four distinct periods. This periodization follows many of the wider developments of the international economy, but it also has elements that are largely unique to the regulation of natural resources.

This volume begins in the middle of the nineteenth century, when international economic liberalism was arguably at its height in the Western world, and European imperialism forced liberalism on large parts of the non-Western world. Restrictions on foreign ownership and exports of natural resources were fairly rare. However, the first liberal period gradually began to give way to more state intervention towards the end of the nineteenth century.

The emergence (or at times re-emergence) of regulating ownership or capturing rents and downstream production from domestic natural resources can be seen in Canada and the Nordic countries around the turn of the twentieth century, and this was brought to new heights during the First World War. As is the return of protectionism in general, the Great War is often viewed as a watershed moment in the first wave of globalization, yet the reaction against economic globalization had begun to manifest itself in many Western countries before this time. This can be seen as the beginning of the second transitory period, during which state intervention in natural resources became more widespread. As is seen in Chapter 10, the League of Nations' attempts to re-establish a more liberal world order during the interwar era were ultimately unsuccessful. However, outside the Soviet Union, outright nationalizations were rare. This began to change just before the Second World War, when the oil industry was nationalized in countries such as Mexico and Bolivia, and oil resources were reserved for the state in Brazil.

These were precursors of things to come, as ownership of natural resources became more controversial than ever during the decolonization period following the Second World War. In this third period, stretching roughly from the Second World War to the 1980s, resource nationalism reached new heights. Key mineral resources were nationalized in a number of countries in the developing world, in former colonies, as well as in states that had considerable Western economic influence, exemplified in this volume by countries such as Venezuela and Iran (see Chapters 4 and 8, respectively). As shown in Hove and Osei-Tutu's chapter on the Gold Coast and Nigeria (Chapter 7), the shift in social licence also affected colonial administrators prior to decolonization, at a time when they were keen to ensure at least a minimum of local spillover in order to reduce local opposition.

The nationalizations following the Second World War were thus the culmination of a long period of increased state intervention in natural resources. However, these resource nationalist initiatives often failed to provide the results for which its proponents had hoped. Beginning in the 1980s, a reliberalization took place, and many state-owned companies were privatized or otherwise reformed. Even though multinationals would once again play a greater role, there was no return to the low-regulation, low-tax regime of the First World War era. Public rights to rents generated from natural resources is widely acknowledged, and flexible concessions and contract renegotiations are much more accepted than they were a century before. Moreover, resource nationalism reasserted itself in some states following a boom in raw materials prices in the 2000s, as may be seen in countries such as Brazil and Russia.

Also in this same time period, concerns other than those of the classical resource nationalist increasingly come to the forefront. One of these is the environmental impact of resource extraction and exploitation. The other,

Conclusion 345

and at times related, concern is the consequences of resource exploitation for Indigenous peoples and their right to influence, gain from, or veto the exploitation of natural resources in their traditional areas.

This prompts the question: What factors drove this long change in resource regulations? A central tenet of all resource nationalist initiatives is the idea that, without targeted policies and regulations, an unfair amount of rents and other economic and strategic benefits provided by the exploitation of a resource is likely to be taken from the country in which that resource is located. In other words, resource nationalism is closely tied to changing ideas regarding how best to achieve long-term economic development. This ties the spread of resource nationalism to the wider spread of protectionism in the latter part of the nineteenth century in that it assumes that a fully liberal system of trade and investments is mainly beneficial to the richer states. Indeed, as is seen in the Canadian case (see Chapter 3), resource nationalism was to a large extent a reaction to the protectionist policies of the United States, which had created a disadvantage for downstream production in Canada.

These resource nationalist ideas were, however, often linked to the wider notion that the natural resources of a state were separate from other economic resources and that members of the public at large had a moral right to the fruits of the resources located in their own state. A recurring topic in many of the chapters concerns the fact that the private ownership of natural resources has tended to be more contested than have many other types of private property. In resource-rich countries there was often a widespread notion that tribal, local, and/or national communities have some kind of moral ownership of natural resources. The political economy of natural resources is thus also a moral economy.

It is thus perhaps not surprising that resource nationalist initiatives were introduced in resource-rich countries that were also among the more democratic at the time, such as Canada and the Nordic countries. Another example of this can be seen in Marcelo Bucheli's chapter on Venezuela and Colombia (Chapter 4). Here, it was easiest for the regimes that rested on a narrow elite base to support liberal policies on natural resources. However, as the size of the political coalitions increased, so did the demand for a more hands-on statist policy towards the country's key natural resources. As Bucheli shows, how this shaped the mandate of the national oil companies differed depending on the type of "winning coalition" that happened to be in place. The variety of ways of implementing resource nationalist policies is also evident in the history of the Nordic countries. Even if their overall objectives were often the same, Sweden granted more freedom to its domestic-owned companies; Norway opted for more hands-on government regulation of all companies wanting to acquire natural resources; and Finland placed a greater emphasis on direct state ownership.

It should be noted that widening popular influence did not always lead to increased state control. As is evident in Zdravka Brunkova and Martin Shanahan's case study of Australia (Chapter 1), popular demand did not strengthen the pre-existing government rights to "royal metals" when gold was discovered; rather, it promoted a regulatory system that favoured the large number of smaller pan-and-shovel prospectors. In the Australian case the specific resource in question, alluvial gold, did not have great barriers to entry, and the colonial administration did not have the resources to prevent illegal panning. Initially, the regulation of natural resources in Australia lacked a clear resource nationalist dimension. This dimension was only established as foreign ownership of minerals became regulated during the First World War.[2]

The global changes in regulatory policy were, however, not driven solely by internal trends towards rising state power and democratization: they were also influenced by transnational and international ideas. During the last couple of decades, legal scholars have increasingly paid special attention to what happens when one legal order, system, or tradition influences another in some significant way.[3] Although many different terms have been used to describe this phenomenon (e.g., "reception," "transplants," "spread," "expansion," "transfer," "exports and imports," "imposition," "circulation," "transmigration," "transposition," and "transfrontier mobility of law"), "diffusion of law" has now become the most common. Inspired by this concept and supported by what is argued in the chapters in this volume, it is possible to identify three main categories of transnational influence on the historical development of natural resource regulation: (1) comparative law, (2) those regulated, and (3) international law.

The first category, comparative law, concerns the instances in which new regulation is inspired from existing regulation in other states. This category also covers instances in which what is perceived to be a lack of regulation (or failed regulation) abroad serves as an inspiration for the development of new regulation. As Chapter 2 on the Nordic states illustrates, when the new Norwegian concession law was first implemented in 1906 it was inspired both by existing laws in Switzerland and by what politicians perceived as the excesses of big business in other states. The new law was established as an

Conclusion

attempt to avoid problematic corporate behaviour such as that witnessed on the part of the mining company Rio Tinto in Spain and the big American trusts that were willing to exploit their market power.

The second category – the regulated (i.e., the economic actors themselves) – at times also transmitted and disseminated principles of natural resource regulations. Chapter 1 shows how the regulation of the goldfields in the different colonies on the Australian continent was influenced by the gold miners, who arrived having had prior experiences in other gold rushes. When the colonial authorities tried to regulate matters connected to access to and ownership of potentially gold-bearing areas, their ideas about what regulation should look like was challenged by the perceptions of regulatory regimes that the gold rush veterans brought with them. A similar development can be found in Jon Olav Hove and John Kwadwo Osei-Tutu's chapter on the regulation of oil concessions in British West Africa. When, in the 1930s, the global oil companies took an interest in exploring for oil in Nigeria and the Gold Coast colony, the colonial governments were forced to consider developing regulatory measures to manage the exploration, prospecting, and mining activities of these companies. These measures were influenced by the expectations of the large oil companies, which brought with them the experience of having operated in a number of different states and which, therefore, had clear ideas about what were fair regulatory measures and what were not.

Finally, national regulations influenced and were shaped by international law (the third category) and the policies of resource-importing countries. Besides the fact that most independent countries followed a fairly liberal policy on natural resource regulations, pre-First World War international law was clear about what was and was not permissible with regard to the expropriation of private property, including natural resources. Resource nationalist initiatives could trigger counter-measures such as punitive tariffs, as is seen in both US reaction to Canadian manufacturing and German responses to the Swedish proposal to put export tariffs on iron.

Liberal orthodoxy was put under severe strain by the outbreak and aftermath of the First World War. As seen in Chapter 10, written by Mats Ingulstad, challenges to the effort to re-establish a liberal order came not only from resource-rich states seeking to claim a greater share of their natural wealth (such as Canada and the Nordic countries) but also from the European empires seeking to maintain the option to deny potential rivals access to raw materials. Efforts to establish new international accords pertaining to the extraction and trade of raw materials, most notably by the

League of Nations, failed due to international rivalries and the diverging interests of the "haves" and the "have-nots."

The postwar era would see the establishment of radical new international legal principles in favour of resource-rich states. In 1962, instead of adopting a new liberal order pertaining to natural resources, the UN General Assembly adopted a resolution on the "Permanent Sovereignty over Natural Resources" that enshrined the principle that any state could freely dispose of the natural resources found on its territory. As decolonization was picking up speed, this resolution helped legitimize the wave of nationalizations that had already begun and that would continue.

These changes to the international order did not affect resource regulation only in resource-rich states. For example, as seen in Chapter 13 on the European Union and Chapter 14 on Japan, increased supply risk also prompted import-dependant countries to introduce efforts to mitigate these changes. As hard power responses to supply security became increasingly unacceptable in the post-Second World War world, Japan as well as the European Union instead tried to promote and subsidize domestic production or to seek strategic long-term partnerships with more resource-abundant states. However, the success and impact of these initiatives have been variable at best, and both ultimate rely on the continued international trade of raw materials under the US-dominated economic order.

The postwar international institutions have, however, not just strengthened the right of states over resources on their territories but also, in some cases, constrained their freedom with regard to resource policy. This was particularly the case with regard to Indigenous rights. In the postwar era it was increasingly accepted that Indigenous peoples had moral rights to both land and natural resources. The International Labour Organization passed conventions regarding the rights of Indigenous groups in 1957 and 1989, and the UN General Assembly adopted a declaration on the rights of Indigenous peoples in 2007. With regard to Canada, Gendron and Sanders state that "the need to secure the agreement of Aboriginal peoples vis-à-vis resource development ... has become a defining element of resource projects" (see Chapter 3). This has particularly been the case since 1982, when reforms entrenched respect for Aboriginal treaty rights within Canada's Constitution. For Norway, international and national political initiatives on human rights and minority policies became intertwined after the Second World War, eventually leading to an improvement of the status of the Sami people, who live in the northern parts of the country (see Chapter 12). Hanne Hagtvedt Vik shows that international developments did not play a

Conclusion

significant role for Sami rights to natural resources in the 1950s and 1960s but became a major factor by 1980.

Also, efforts to establish shared international principles on the regulation of natural resources have not been limited to regulations within or between states. There were also attempts to establish regulatory frameworks for and protection of what could be called the global "commons." In his contribution to this volume, Bjørn Basberg gives an overview of resource regulation in the Antarctic (Chapter 11). It started with British attempts to regulate whaling before the First World War, but successful multilateral regulation was only achieved in 1959 with the Antarctic Treaty. This success was no doubt helped by the fact that regulation came before the commercial extraction of resources (except whaling) and that the resource rents were perceived to be low or even negative. The moral importance of protecting endangered species and unspoiled nature also became increasingly important.

However, while there is a clear pattern to the general historical development of the regulation of natural resources, the chapters in this book also illustrate the fact that such regulation is contingent upon the specificities of the particular resource in question. The economic logic of resource regulation varies according to, for instance, the barriers to entry, negative externalities, resource rents, and/or market power. The regulatory room that a state has for any given natural resource is therefore not only decided by the regulatory capacity that the state possesses as such but also, to a large extent, by the power structures within the international resource economy.

More than any other resource-based industry, oil has embodied market power. Until the 1970s, the seven largest companies controlled most international trade in petroleum as well as significant shares of extraction, transport, refining, and marketing. Extraction and consumption of oil took place in very distant locations, requiring both costly and complex logistics, creating high barriers to entry. Large companies were therefore able to control significant parts of the resource rents. However, by the early twentieth century, the oil companies' market power was curtailed in the United States as a result of anti-trust legislation and other types of regulation. Most significantly, the behemoth Standard Oil was broken up into thirty-four companies. In the US, monopoly prices were not politically accepted. In the rest of the world, however, most host countries' regulatory powers remained weak and the oil companies retained most if not all their market power for several decades.

This volume includes case studies of various aspects of oil policy in Venezuela, Colombia, Brazil, the Gold Coast, Nigeria, Iran, India, and Russia, spanning most of the twentieth century and the first decade of the twenty-first century. In Venezuela and Colombia regulation and taxation of the oil industry was initially light. While the government take was gradually increased, the companies managed to retain a large part of the resource rents throughout their concession periods. Developments took a more dramatic turn in Iran. When Iran nationalized its oil industry the country proved unable to sell its oil production. The market power of the major companies proved to be too strong.

However, politicians throughout the world, both in the so-called First World and in the so-called Third World, had long noted the market power and the monopoly profits of the oil companies. As Neveen Abdelrehim and Shraddha Verma show, in newly independent India the government took care to avoid clashes with the established oil companies at the same time as it endeavoured to limit their market power (Chapter 8). Gail Triner records a broadly similar development in Brazil (Chapter 6). While domestic oil production was negligible in the 1950s, a national oil company, Petrobras, was established and foreign oil companies were not allowed to explore for or produce oil. By the end of that decade, Petrobras's monopoly was extended to the transport, refining, and marketing of oil products. Other countries also tried to limit the market power of the international oil companies. This was aided by developments in international law, which gave nation-states a stronger legal basis for regulating their natural resources. The confrontation with the leading oil companies reached an apex in the 1970s as a number of countries, most notably in the Middle East, nationalized their oil industries.

Oil was special because of the industry's rapid growth, strategic importance, barriers to entry, high rents, and powerful companies. Regulation of oil was therefore highly resource specific. The chapter on the Nordic countries analyzes to what extent the regulation of other types of natural resources has been contingent upon the specificity of those resources. In the decades around 1900, Norway, Sweden, and Finland introduced comprehensive regulation of their resource endowments. They all had a broad spectrum of natural resources. For resources to which the barriers to entry were low, such as forestry or fishing, the countries tried to protect small-scale producers. In the case of hydro power, in which the technical and capital requirements were higher, the governments tried to ensure that the benefits were spread to as much of the population as possible. Both Sweden and Finland opted for extensive state ownership of power production and distribution. In Norway, which had far more hydro power than its neighbours

Conclusion

combined, state ownership was less prevalent before 1945. Foreign enterprises were therefore needed in order to utilize the country's hydro-power potential. However, foreign investors had to accept comprehensive regulation from Norwegian authorities.

Mining also offers an example of how regulation was not only resource specific but also dependent on the national and international economic context. Mining was somewhat similar to petroleum as many mining companies were vertically integrated, had transnational value chains, and wielded considerable market power. Sweden, which had a competitive mining and metal industry, chose a statist and resource-nationalistic approach, keeping foreign owners at bay. Rents and spillover effects were to be kept inside the country. Both Finland and Norway had weaker and less advanced industrial sectors than Sweden. They therefore accepted comprehensive foreign ownership in the mining industry, believing that some investments and some rents were better than no investments and no rents.

Economic development that is based heavily on raw materials has often been perceived as especially challenging. Indeed, many of the resource nationalist policies covered in this volume were intended to mitigate the perceived disadvantages of resource-based development. However, as – paradoxically – many resource-rich countries have consistently underperformed economically since the latter half of the twentieth century, a number of scholars have theorized that large resource rent incomes can be detrimental to economic and political development. Some have also suggested that a key part of the problem lies in resource nationalist initiatives themselves, pointing to, for example, forced contract renegotiations or how expropriation increases political risk in the economy as a whole.[4]

From the case studies covered in this volume, it is not obvious that resource nationalism in all its forms is corrosive to a state's liberal institutions. As has been pointed out many times before, countries such as Canada and the Nordic countries, which, over the past century, have introduced many resource nationalist regulations, generally score high when ranking transparency and low corruption. However, as perhaps is best exemplified in Gail Triner's chapter on Brazil, resource nationalism does come at a price. The value of natural resources is not constant as supply and demand change over time, and states can easily overreach when negotiating concessions or creating regulatory frameworks. This added risk and uncertainty might drive off investors who have the technology and capital needed to utilize the resource at all.

Moreover, it should be underlined that the resource nationalist policies introduced in countries such as Canada and the Nordic countries rarely involved outright nationalization or forced contract negotiations. In most cases, the legislation introduced in these countries only affected future developments, which made it easier for investors to trust that their investments would remain safe. This more gradual approach was of course not available to many other states in the now developing world, where regulations and concessions were granted when the state's independence was severely curtailed or when the future state was currently a direct colony of a European state.

Furthermore, public demands for a greater share of natural resource exploitations might not necessarily be equally shared geographically within a state. As is seen in Chapter 3 on Canada, the provinces in which a valuable resource is located might advocate a more liberal policy with regard to exports and ownership in order to increase extraction and investments locally and thus undermine the more wide-reaching resource nationalist ambitions of the metropole. This phenomenon is even more prevalent when the local population is of a different ethnicity to that of the metropole, as exemplified in Chapter 9 on New Caledonia, where New Caledonian nationalists championed foreign investments as a counter-balance to French resource nationalist schemes.

Local demands are, however, not only a question of how to share the spoils. As seen in Chapter 3 on Canada and Chapter 12 on the Sami in Norway, in some cases local protests or protests from Indigenous groups are arguing not for a greater amount of the rents generated but, rather, against any kind of development at all. This is especially the case if the development has considerable detrimental environmental effects that can risk pre-existing economic activities. These conflicts are difficult to resolve through a simple redistribution of rents and will likely require new forms of compromise.

Yet, as this volume also shows, the moral economy of natural resources has not just been a source of conflict. The presence of alluvial gold in Australian colonies and the prospectors' demands that it should be available to the settlers at large proved to be a catalyst for greater democratization among the European-descended population. In a somewhat similar vein, popular demands for a more equally shared natural bounty functioned to curtail the hold of some of the old elites over key parts of the economy in the Nordic countries. The presence of rich resources has at times sown

Conclusion 353

discord, but it has also at times functioned as a focal point for populations hoping to gain more influence over their own destinies.

What all these case studies illustrate is that, in order to understand the development of resource regulation, on must take into account any given state's moral economy. However, as the cases also show, morals or social and political norms differ considerably between cultures, geographical settings, and over time. One can, however, note some main development patterns. Since the gold diggers in Australia forced their way into the continent's goldfields it has gradually become harder to prevent Indigenous peoples, local inhabitants, or other stakeholders from having influence over resource management. While the degree of inclusion varies considerably, the tendency towards increasing participation is clearly discernible. Resource regulation has thus been influenced and/or shaped by the global trends towards democratization and decolonization.

Notes

1 Aristotle, *Politics*, trans. Stephen Everson (Cambridge: Cambridge University Press, 1988).
2 Statutory Rules 1916, no. 323, War Precautions (Mining) Regulations 1916; War Precautions Act Repeal, no. 54 of 1920.
3 For a good overview of the concept of diffusion of law, see William Twining, "Diffusion of Law: A Global Perspective," *Journal of Legal Pluralism* 49 (2004): 1–45.
4 See, especially, Nathan M. Jensen and Noel P. Johnston, "Political Risk, Reputation, and the Resource Curse," *Comparative Political Sudies* 44, 6 (2011): 662–88.

Contributors

Neveen Abdelrehim is a senior lecturer in accounting and finance at Newcastle University Business School, and in the Faculty of Commerce at Portsaid University

Bjørn L. Basberg is a professor of economic history at the Norwegian School of Economics (NHH)

Zdravka Brunkova is a researcher and independent scholar in Adelaide, South Australia

Marcelo Bucheli is an associate professor of business administration at the University of Illinois

Stephen Fortescue is an honorary associate professor in Russian politics at the University of New South Wales and a visiting fellow at the Centre for European Studies, Australian National University

Hans Otto Frøland is a professor of contemporary European history at the Norwegian University of Science and Technology (NTNU)

Robin S. Gendron is an associate professor of history at Nipissing University

Jon Olav Hove is an associate professor at the Department of Historical Studies, Norwegian University of Science and Technology (NTNU)

Mats Ingulstad is a research fellow at the Department of Historical Studies, Norwegian University of Science and Technology (NTNU)

Contributors

Takeo Kikkawa is a professor of management at Tokyo University of Science

John Kwadwo Osei-Tutu is an associate professor at the Department of Historical Studies, Norwegian University of Science and Technology (NTNU)

Andreas R.D. Sanders is a postdoctoral researcher at the Department of Historical Studies, Norwegian University of Science and Technology (NTNU)

Pål Thonstad Sandvik is a professor of economic history at the Norwegian University of Science and Technology (NTNU)

Martin Shanahan is a professor of economic and business history at the University of South Australia

Espen Storli is a professor of modern Norwegian history at the Norwegian University of Science and Technology (NTNU)

Gail D. Triner is a professor of history at Rutgers University

Shraddha Verma is a senior lecturer of accounting at The Open University

Hanne Hagtvedt Vik is an associate professor of international history at the University of Oslo

Index

Abbreviations

AIOC	Anglo-Iranian Oil Company
BOC	Burmah Oil Company (India)
EU	European Union
ILO	International Labour Organization
INCO	International Nickel Company (of Canada)
SLN	Société Le Nickel (France)

Notes: (f) after a page number indicates a figure; (t) after a page number indicates a table

Abadan oil refinery (Iran), 189, 190, 194, 198, 203

AbitibiBowater Inc., 85

Aboriginal peoples. *See* Indigenous peoples, *and entry following*

Acción Democrática (Venezuela), 105–7, 112–13

African and Malagasy Organization (OCAM), 310

Alberta, 69, 78–79, 81, 88; and National Energy Program, 83–85, 89

Allardyce, William Lamond, 262–65

Allied Maritime Transport Council (1917), 233

Alta River (Norway), hydroelectric dam on, 277, 288–89

Amax Nickel Inc., 215

Angell, Norman, 244–45

Anglo-Iranian Oil Company (AIOC), 14, 186–94, 204–5; Abadan refinery of, 189, 190, 194, 198, 203; African explorations by, 169–70, 171; and BOC, 190, 196, 197, 198, 202; British control of/dependence on, 190–92; compared to BOC, 201–4; and consortium ownership, 193–94; early history of, 189–90; and nationalization crisis/British oil boycott, 192,

Index

203–4, 350; in political/economic context, 188–89; and US involvement, 192–93. *See also* Burmah Oil Company; Iran, oil regulation in

Anglo-Persian Oil Company (later AIOC), 190

Anglo-Saxon Petroleum Company, 169–70

Antarctic Convergence (Polar Front), 259, 260(f), 270

Antarctic Treaty (1959), 268–70, 271, 273, 349

Antarctica, 15, 259–73, 349; boundaries/ map of, 259, 260(f); categories/ chronology of industry in, 260–62, 261(t); countries claiming territory/ waters in, 268; "heroic age" of exploration in, 259, 261; krill industry in, 269–70; maritime industries/ activities in, 261(t), 271–73. *See also entry below*

Antarctica, industries/activities in: bio-prospecting, 272–73; fisheries, 259, 260–61, 269–71, 273; maritime transport/shipping, 272; mineral extraction, 260–61, 269, 271, 273; philately, 272; scientific research, 261, 268–69, 272; sealing, 259, 260–62, 263, 273; ship registration, 272; tourism, 259, 261, 271–72, 273; whaling, 259, 260–67, 269, 273, 349. *See also specific industries*

Arab-Israeli War (1973), 82

Arboussier, Gabriel d', 309

Aristotle: *Politics*, 342–43

Armstrong, A.C.F., 178

Assam Oil Company (India), 187, 197, 199

Associated Tin Mines of Nigeria Limited, 168

Attolico, Bernardo, 239

Australia, 9, 85, 236, 268, 314, 330, 337(t), 338(t); Aboriginal land title issues in, 279, 290; convict settlement in, 24–25, 29, 32, 36, 39;

federation of colonies in, 24, 35–36; wool industry in, 26–27(t), 28, 30, 31, 34–35, 36, 39, 40. *See also entry below*

Australia, gold rushes in (1850–1900), 12, 23–42, 346, 347, 352–53; and democratic milestones/political institutions, 37(t), 42; and economy/ standard of living, 23, 24, 42; vs pastoralism, as obstacle to mining rights/democratic governance, 24, 28, 30, 31–32, 33–34, 36, 38–39, 41, 42; population explosion caused by, 23, 24–25, 25(f), 42; and resource exports/legislation, 26–27(t); and universal male suffrage, 23, 29–30, 32, 33–34, 35, 37(t), 38, 40, 41, 42. *See also entries for specific Australian colonies*

Australian Colonies Government Act (UK, 1850), 29

Avenol, Joseph, 247, 249

Azikiwe, Nnamdi, 174, 175

Baldesi, Gino, 237

Beck, Adam, 76

Bieddjovagge copper mines (Norway), 287, 288

Billotte Laws (New Caledonia), 218, 223, 228n34

Biological Investigation of Marine Antarctic Systems and Stocks (BIOMASS), 269

bio-prospecting, in Antarctica, 272–73

Boundary Waters Treaty (Canada-US, 1909), 69

Boyesen, Einar, 283

BP. *See* British Petroleum Company (BP)

Brazil, petroleum in, 13–14, 139–55, 345; early history of, 140–41; and formation/regulation of Petrobras, 141–42, 144–47, 350, 351; imports of, and world prices (1960–2011), 142, 142(f); and industry corruption scandal, 154, 155n1, 160n65, 160n68, 161n74; offshore deposits of, 142–44, 143(f), 146–47, 149, 150, 153; offshore production of, as percentage of total production, 143, 144(f); in open market environment, 147–50, 158n35; pre-salt deposits of, 143–44, 145(t), 150–54; reserves of, compared to those of top global producers (2009), 144, 145(t). *See also* Petrobras

BRGM (French geological agency), 222, 223

Bridges, Harold, 178

British Burmah Petroleum Company, 168

British Columbia, 71, 79, 80, 84, 90n7; and pipeline issue, 87–88

British North America Act (1867), 68–69

British Petroleum Company (BP), 169; in Brazil, 147, 152, 161n74

British West Africa, oil exploration in, 14, 165–81; in Gold Coast, 14, 165–68, 171–73, 180–81; in Nigeria, 14, 165–71, 173–81; before Second World War, 167–71; during Second World War, 171–73. *See also* Gold Coast; Nigeria

Burmah Oil Company (BOC, India), 168, 186–88, 190, 194–205; and AIOC, 190, 196, 197, 198, 202; compared to AIOC, 201–4; and Assam Oil, 187, 197, 199; early history of, 195–96; before Indian independence, 195–99, 204; after Indian independence, 199–201, 204; in political/economic context, 194–95. *See also* Anglo-Iranian Oil Company; India, oil regulation in

Burmah Shell (BS), 197

Burns, Alan, 172–73

Cameroon(s), 167, 171, 173, 174, 177

Campos Basin (Brazil), 143(f), 147

Canada, 9, 97, 314, 329(t), 347; nickel industry in, 211, 212, 215–16, 224, 226n13. *See also entries below*

Canada, resource regulation in, 12–13, 67–89, 343, 351–52; foreign investment and, 69, 74, 78, 80–85; Indigenous land claims and, 68, 69, 87, 89n2, 90n7, 290–91, 348, 352; jurisdictional framework for, 68–70; in nationalist era, 67–68, 78–84, 88–89; in neoliberal era, 68, 84–88; provincial nationalism and, 67, 70–80, 88; staple thesis and, 17n10, 67; US as factor in, 68, 69, 70–72, 73, 74, 75–78, 79, 81–85, 94n62, 345, 348

Canada, resources regulated by (specific): hydroelectric power, 75–78, 78(f), 79, 86; mining, 72–73, 74(f), 75(f), 78; oil and gas, 68, 78, 79, 81–85, 89; timber/pulp and paper, 71–72, 74, 78, 85, 94n62

Canada Development Corporation, 82

Canada Forestry Act (1949), 80

Canada-US Free Trade Agreement (FTA), 68, 84–85

Caron, Roland, 224

cartels, commodity, in League of Nations era, 232, 240–42, 243–44, 246, 248; EEC agreements as types of, 314

Central Intelligence Agency (CIA), 192

Chamberlain, Neville, 249

Chávez, Hugo, 97, 107

Chevron Corporation, 147, 161n74

China, 261, 327, 328(t); as rare metal/rare earth exporter, 303(t), 311, 315–16, 318, 319, 330, 335

China National Offshore Oil Corporation (CNOOC), 152, 154

China National Petroleum Corporation (CNPC), 152, 154

Churchill, Winston, 190

Citgo Petroleum Corporation, 147

Clark, Christy, 87–88

Clarke, Andrew, 40

Clémentel, Étienne, 233–34

coalitions, studies of. *See* Colombia, oil industry in; Russia, resource rent

Index

management in; Venezuela, oil industry in

Coderre, Denis, 88

coffee industry (Colombia), 100, 107–8, 110, 111, 112

COFIMPAC (French mining company), 222–23, 228n34, 228n37

Colombia, oil industry in, 13, 96–100, 107–13, 345, 350; as analyzed using selectorate theory, 98–100, 112–13; and coffee industry, 100, 107–8, 110, 111, 112; under conservative coalition, 107–10; under Depression-era liberal coalition, 110–11; under postwar conservative/pro-oil coalition, 111–12; production/export statistics for, 100, 101(f), 102(f); and total exports as percentage of GDP, 100, 103(f); and transition to state ownership, 96–97, 111–12, 113

Columbia River Treaty (Canada-US), 79

Comité de Organización Política Electoral Independiente (COPEI, Venezuela), 106–7

Committee of European Economic Co-operation (CEEC), 305

Compagnie française des pétroles (CFP), 193

Companhia Petróleos do Brasil, 141

Comprehensive Economic and Trade Agreement (CETA), 85

Concession Laws (Norway), 54–56, 61, 62, 346–47

C107 (ILO convention on Indigenous rights). *See* Convention Concerning the Protection and Integration of Indigenous and Other Tribal and Semi-Tribal Populations in Independent Countries

conferences, economic: Geneva (1927), 241–42; London (1933), 243–44; Paris (1916), 233

Constitution Act (Canada, 1982), 69

continental shelf: Japan and, 335, 336, 339; Nigeria and, 177–80; Russia and, 127–28

Convention Concerning the Protection and Integration of Indigenous and Other Tribal and Semi-Tribal Populations in Independent Countries (ILO, 1957), 16, 277, 280; and land rights, 280; Norway's non-ratification of, 284–85, 289–90

Convention for the Abolition of Import and Export Prohibitions and Restrictions (League of Nations, 1927), 242, 248

Convention for the Conservation of Antarctic Marine Living Resources (CCAMLR), 269–71

Convention on the Regulation of Antarctic Mineral Resource Activities (CRAMRA), 271

Cotonou Agreement, 304, 315, 317, 319

Cramér, Tomas, 288

crofters: in Denmark, 48; in Finland, 53, 57–58, 59–60, 61; in Sweden, 51

Crown Lands Bill (Gold Coast, 1894), 167–68

D'Arcy, William, 189–90, 191

Deep Ocean Resources Development Co. Ltd., 335

Deepwater Horizon explosion/oil spill (Gulf of Mexico, 2010), 153

Denison, William, 34

Denmark, resource regulation in: of farmland/farm ownership, 46, 47–48, 49, 53, 58, 61; of forestry, 46, 48–49; of hydroelectric power, 60; important aspects of, 49

Dingley Act (US, 1897), 71

Dionysius I of Syracuse, 342–43

Disarmament Conference (League of Nations), 239

"Dutch disease," 9, 18n17; Russia and, 124, 133–34

Dvorkovich, Arkady, 129

ECOPETROL (Colombia), 96–97, 111–12, 113

Eden, Anthony, 246

Eidheim, Harald, 287
Electrical Development Company (EDC, Ontario), 76
Elf Aquitaine (French oil company), 147
Energy East pipeline (proposed), 87, 88
energy self-sufficiency: of Brazil, 142–44, 145, 147; of selected countries, 329(t). *See also* Japan, measures to mitigate energy dependency in
European Coal and Steel Community (ECSC), 304, 306–8, 314
European Community (EC), 304, 314, 315, 318–19
European Economic Community (EEC), 12, 304, 309–15, 318
European Partnership Agreements (EPAs), 304, 317
European Payments Union (EPU), 306–7
European raw materials strategies. *See* raw materials, international regulation of, after First World War; raw materials strategies, of postwar Europe
European Recovery Program (ERP), 305, 308
European Union (EU), 12, 302–4, 315–20, 348; Raw Materials Initiative of, 302, 304, 312, 313, 316–17, 319
externalities (impacts) of resource exploitation, 4, 348; in Brazil, 141–42

Falconbridge Limited, 215–16, 223
Falkland Islands and their Dependencies, 260(f); whaling in, 262–65, 263(t)
Federación Nacional de Cafeteros de Colombia (FNCC), 108, 110, 111
Finland, 57–60, 281; civil war/rural poverty alleviation in, 58; copper mining in, 59–60, 351; crofters' rights/land ownership in, 53, 57–58, 59–60, 61; foreign ownership issue in, 57, 58–60, 61, 346; forestry in, 46, 57, 58–59; hydroelectric power in, 59, 61, 350; nickel deposit of, 60, 61

fisheries, Antarctic, 259, 260–61, 273; and marine protected areas, 270–71; postwar expansion of, 269; regulation/management of, 269–71; species predominating in, 269, 270
Fitzgerald, Charles, 39
FitzRoy, Charles Augustus, 28
Foccart, Jacques, 219–20
Fokstad, Per, 284, 287, 296n20
Foreign Investment Review Agency (FIRA), 82, 84
foreign ownership issue, 5–8; in Australia, 345; in Brazil, 144–50, 155; in Canada, 74, 80–84, 343; in New Caledonia, 14–15, 210–11, 213–14, 216–25, 352; in Nordic countries, 12, 45–62, 343, 345–47, 351. *See also* resource nationalism
forests and forestry products: in Canada, 71–72, 74, 78, 85, 94n62; in Denmark, 46, 48–49; in Finland, 46, 58–59; in Norway, 53, 54, 55–56, 61; in Sweden, 46, 49, 51–52, 53, 61
Fosdick, Raymond, 237
France, 177, 287, 329(t); and Antarctica, 268, 272; and League of Nations, 233–34, 235, 245; and Nordic resources, 56, 59; in postwar Europe, 306, 307–9, 311. *See also* New Caledonia, nickel mining in
Freeport Minerals Company, 215
Frick, Wilhelm, 246
Fukushima nuclear plant (Japan), accident at (2011), 331

Gaitán, Eliécer, 111
Garnier, Jules, 211
Gaulle, Charles de, 219–20
Gazprom (Russian gas company), 121
General Agreement on Tariffs and Trade (GATT), 306, 310–11, 312, 315, 318
Gerhardsen, Einar, 285–86
Germany, 46, 47, 73, 243, 306, 307, 329(t); and colonial mandate system, 167, 171, 236; and League of Nations,

Index 361

233–34, 236, 243, 244–49, 250, 251; oil drilling technique developed in, 168; in Second World War, 191, 198, 213, 282; and Swedish mining companies, 51, 347; whaling by, 266, 269

Ghana, 14, 166, 180, 183*n*42. *See also* Gold Coast

Gini, Corrado, 238, 245–46

Gjærevoll, Olav, 289

Gold Coast (now Ghana), 14, 165–68, 180–81, 344, 347; formation of, 167; Indigenous opposition to resource appropriation in, 167–68, 170, 172, 176, 180; Shell-D'Arcy exploration in, 171–73

Gold Coast Petroleum Company, 172, 173

Goldfield Licensing Act (Western Australia, 1888), 40

Gómez, Juan Vicente, 104

Gómez, Laureano, 111

Gordon, Walter, 81–82

Goro nickel reserves (New Caledonia), 223, 224, 228*n*37

Gray, Herb, 82

Great Britain, 46, 220, 268, 279, 329(t), 337(t), 338(t); and Australia, 24, 28, 29–30, 39, 42; and Canadian resource regulation, 68–69, 70, 74; and League of Nations, 234–36, 238, 240–41, 244–45, 247, 249; and New Caledonia nickel industry, 211–12; in postwar Europe, 305, 307, 311, 313; and South American oil, 104, 105, 108–9, 110; Swedish resource ownership by, 49–50, 52, 58; whaling by, 15, 261, 262–67, 349. *See also* British West Africa, oil exploration in; India, oil regulation in; Iran, oil regulation in

Great Crash (stock market crash, 1929), 231, 242

Great Depression: in Colombia, 108, 110; in Iran, 191; raw materials regulation and, 242–44

Greenland, 312, 322*n*52

Grey, Ralph, 178–79

Gulf Oil, 193

Hakurei hydrothermal deposit (Japan), 335

Hanna mining company, 215

Harper, Stephen, government of, 86

Headland, Robert K., 260

Higginson, John, 211

Hirschman, Albert O., 8–9

Hitler, Adolf, 198; and League of Nations, 245, 248–49, 250

Hoare, Samuel, 245–46, 250

Hobsbawm, Eric, 5

Høgetveit, Einar, 289–90

Hoover, Herbert, 234–35

Humphreys, David, 319

Hurstfield, Joel, 239

hydrocarbons: in Antarctica, 271; in Brazil, 144–45; in Japan, 330, 339–40; in Russia, 120–22, 125, 130–31

Hydro-Electric Power Commission of Ontario. *See* Ontario Hydro

hydroelectric power: in Canada, 67, 75–78, 79, 86; in Denmark, 60; in Finland, 59, 61, 350; in Japan, 327, 328; in Norway, 53–55, 56, 62, 277, 288–89, 350–51; in Sweden, 52, 350

Imatra Falls (Finland), 59

imperialism, 11, 342; in Gold Coast, 14, 165–68, 170, 171–73, 176, 180–81, 344, 347; in India, 14, 186–88, 190, 194–205, 350; in Iran, 14, 186–94, 204–5, 344, 350; in New Caledonia, 14–15, 210–25, 352; in Nigeria, 14, 165–71, 173–81, 344, 347

India, 279, 315–16, 329(t); independence of, 187, 195, 198–99, 202–3, 204. *See also entry below*

India, oil regulation in, 14, 186–88, 190, 194–205, 350; before independence, 195–99, 204; after independence, 199–201, 204; political/economic context of, 194–95. *See also* Burmah Oil Company

Indian National Congress, 203
Indigenous peoples: absence of, in Antarctica, 259; collectives of, as economic actors, 290–94; early treatment of, 252, 278–80; ILO recognition of/convention on rights of, 16, 277–80, 284–85; postwar concerns of, 344–45; UN Declaration on Rights of, 7, 277, 348. *See also entry below;* Sami (Nordic Indigenous people)
Indigenous peoples (specific): of Australia, 279, 290, 353; of Canada, 68, 69, 87, 89n2, 90n7, 290–91, 348, 352; of Gold Coast, 167–68, 170, 172, 176, 180; of New Zealand, 279, 290, 293; of Nigeria, 167, 170, 173–74, 176, 177, 180–81; of Norway, 15–16, 277–95, 348–49, 352
Intergovernmental Council of Copper Exporting Countries (CIPEC), 311, 322n50
International Association of Antarctic Tour Operators (IAATO), 271–72
International Covenant on Civil and Political Rights (UN, 1966), 291
International Geophysical Year (1957–58), 268
International Labour Organization (ILO): early Indigenous rights work by, 16, 277–80; Indigenous rights convention of, 277, 280, 284–85, 289–90; and regulation of raw materials, 237, 247, 249, 289, 290–92, 294, 348
International Materials Conference (IMC), 307–8
International Miners Congress, 237–38
International Monetary Fund, 158n35, 305
International Nickel Company (INCO): in Finland, 60, 61; and First World War production controversy, 73; in New Caledonia, 210, 212–13, 215–16, 219–20, 221, 222–24, 226n6, 228n37; Sudbury operations of, 86, 224

International Petroleum Company, 107–8
International Whaling Commission (IWC), 266–68
Iran, oil regulation in, 14, 186–94, 204–5, 344, 350; Britain and, 189–94, 203–4; and consortium ownership, 193–94; early history of, 189–90; and nationalization crisis/British oil boycott, 192, 203–4, 350; political/economic context of, 188–89; under Reza Shah, 190–91; US involvement in, 192–93. *See also* Anglo-Iranian Oil Company
Ireland, 48, 312
Italy, 307, 328(t); and League of Nations, 234–35, 237–38, 239–40, 244–46, 250

Jakobesen, Johan J., 289
Japan, 85, 198, 311; and Antarctica, 268, 269; dependence on resource imports by, 12, 16, 327–40, 348; energy policies/measures in, 327, 328–30, 339–40; energy self-sufficiency of, 328–31, 329(t); Fukushima nuclear accident in, 331; mining policy/legislation in, 331–39; nickel industry of, 212, 215, 225n5; and raw materials regulation, 244, 246, 247, 248, 249; supply of rare metals in, 330–31, 332, 333, 335–36; territorial ocean area of, 336–39; whaling by, 266, 267. *See also entries below*
Japan, measures to mitigate energy dependency in, 16, 327, 328–30; conservation, 16, 327, 328, 336, 340; diversification of sources, 328–30, 331; increased use of natural gas, 329–30; methane hydrate production, 330, 339–40; more efficient use of coal, 330; overseas oilfield development, 329; regulated exploration/development of territorial ocean area, 336–39, 337(t), 338(t); stockpiling of oil, 16, 327, 328, 329, 331, 340

Japan, mining industry of, 331–39, 348; deep seafloor surveys by, 334–35; and domestic exploration/production, 332, 333, 335; new postwar law governing, 331; and overseas exploration/development, 333–34; and regulated exploration/development of territorial ocean area, 336–39, 337(t), 338(t); regulation/prevention of pollution in, 332, 333; report on future of, 332, 332(t); revision to law governing, 338–39; and supply/stockpiling of rare metals, 330–31, 332, 333, 335–36; US postwar "democratization" of, 331
Japan Oil, Gas and Metals National Corporation (JOGMEC), 333, 334–35, 340

Kaiser Aluminum, 215
Kanak nationalist movement (New Caledonia), 223–24
Kellogg, Remington, 266
Keynes, John Maynard, 237
Keystone XL pipeline (proposed), 87
Khanty-Mansiisk Autonomous Region (KhMAO), 129–30
Khodorkovsky, Mikhail, 121
Kinder Morgan/Trans Mountain pipeline extension (proposed), 87, 88, 94n71
Knudsen, Gunnar, 54
Korean War, 215, 307
krill, Antarctic, 269–70
Kven (Nordic people), 281, 282, 283

Lafleur, Henri, 214, 225n5
Lamont, Thomas, 234
Land and Native Rights Ordinance (Gold Coast, 1931), 168
La Trobe, Charles, 31
League of Nations, 15, 231–52, 266, 282, 343, 346–47; and colonial mandate system, 167, 169, 171, 173, 235–36, 239–40, 244–45, 246, 248–49, 250, 252, 278; Covenant of, 235–36, 240,

245; disarmament conference of, 239; economic conferences of, 241–44; as economic overseer/regulator, 231–32, 234–35; and "have-not" states' demands/territorial aggression, 244–49, 250; initial involvement with raw materials by, 237–38; and rationalization of trade, 238–41; raw materials inquiry of, 246–49; ultimate failure of economic efforts by, 249–50; US as non-member of, 241, 250. *See also* raw materials, international regulation of, after First World War
Leaseholder's Act (Finland, 1918), 58
Leith, Charles Kenneth, 240
Leith-Ross, Frederick, 247
Lemaignen, Robert, 309
Lenormand, Maurice, 214, 218, 225n5
liquefied petroleum gas (LPG), 328–29
loi-cadre (French system of colonial autonomy reforms, 1956), 217–18, 226n9
Lomé Conventions, 304, 313–14, 315, 319
London Monetary and Economic Conference (League of Nations, 1933), 243–44
López Contreras, Eleázar, 104–5
López Pumarejo, Alfonso, 110
Lougheed, Peter, 83, 84
Lukoil (Russian oil company), 128

Mackenzie Valley pipeline (proposed), 87
Macpherson, John, 175
Maduro, Nicolás, 97,
Maersk Energy, 152
Magga, Ole Henrik, 288
mandate system (League of Nations/United Nations), 236; in Africa, 167, 169, 171, 173, 236; and regulation/control of raw materials, 235–36, 239–40, 244–45, 246, 250, 252, 278; and treatment of Indigenous peoples, 278

Maori, 279, 290, 293
Marathon Oil Company, 147
maritime transport/shipping, in Antarctica, 272
Marks, Seaborn, 168–70
Marshall Plan, 305
Marx, Karl, 235
Matignon Accord (New Caledonia, 1988), 223
Medina, Isaías, 105
Medvedev, Dmitry, 129–30
Metal Mining Agency of Japan (MMAJ), 332–33, 334–35. *See also* Japan Oil, Gas and Metals National Corporation (JOGMEC)
Metallic Minerals Exploration Financing Agency of Japan, 332, 334
Metallic Minerals Exploration Promotion Agency of Japan, 332, 333
methane hydrate production, in Japan, 330, 339–40
mineral extraction, in Antarctica, 260–61, 269, 271, 273
Mining Code (Brazil), 144
Mining Industry Council (Japan), 331, 333, 335–36
Ministry of Economy, Trade and Industry (Japan), 336, 339
Ministry of Mining and Energy (Brazil), 146, 149
Mitrany, David, 239
Mohammad Ali Shah, Shah of Iran, 189
Mohammad Reza Pahlavi, Shah of Iran, 191, 192
Mond Nickel Company, 215
Monnet, Jean, 239, 303
Montalvo, José Antonio, 109–10
Mulroney, Brian, government of, 84
Musaddiq, Mohammad, 192, 203
Mussolini, Benito, 245, 250

National Council for Energy Policy (CNPE, Brazil), 149
National Energy Council (Brazil), 146
National Energy Program (NEP, Canada), 68, 83–85, 89

National Iranian Oil Company (NIOC), 193–94
national oil companies: ECOPETROL (Colombia), 96–97, 111–12, 113; NIOC (Iran), 193–94; PDVSA (Venezuela), 96–97, 106–7, 113; Petro Canada, 83, 84; Petrobras (Brazil), 141–42, 144–55; Rosneft (Russia), 83, 84; 121, 128. *See also* Petrobras; resource nationalism
national oil companies, creation of, 97–100; by dictatorial regimes, 98, 99; neo-institutional theory of, 98; neo-Marxist theory of, 98; and "obsolescing bargaining power," 97–98; and selectorate theory of political survival, 98–100, 112–13. *See also* Colombia, oil industry in; Venezuela, oil industry in
National Petroleum Agency (ANP, Brazil), 149, 151–52
National Policy (Canada), 70
National Sami Association of Sweden, 288
nationalization of resources. *See* national oil companies, *and entry following*; resource nationalism
natural resources, exploitation of, 3–5; negative impacts (externalities) of, 4, 141–42, 349; return on (resource rent), 4. *See also* resource regulation; resource rent(s)
Nauru, 236
Nehru, Jawaharlal, 203
New Caledonia, nickel mining in, 14–15, 210–25; background/history of, 211–13; and foreign investment debate, 14–15, 210–11, 213–14, 216–25, 352; and France's reassertion of political control, 216–22; INCO's involvement in, 210, 212–13, 215–16, 219–20, 221, 222–24, 226n6, 228n37; and internationalization of nickel industry, 215–16; later environmental/safety problems of, 224; by *petits mineurs*, 212, 216, 217, 221, 225n5,

226n8; and political autonomy issue, 210, 217–18, 223–24, 225; post-1968 developments affecting, 222–24. *See also* Société Le Nickel (SLN)

New South Wales (Australia), 25, 26(t), 28–30, 32, 34, 42; democracy/political institutions in, 29–30, 32, 34, 41; gold discovery in, 24, 27–28; mining licences/regulations in, 28–29, 30–31, 42; mining vs pastoralism in, 28, 30; "un-locking" of land access in, 30

New Zealand, 210, 236, 268; Maori rights in, 279, 290, 293

Niagara Falls, 75–76, 77

nickel industry: in Ontario, 72–73, 86, 224; postwar internationalization of, 215–16. *See also* International Nickel Company (INCO); New Caledonia, nickel mining in; Société Le Nickel (SLN)

Nigeria, 14, 165–71, 173–81, 344, 347; British/Dutch oil conglomerates in, 169–71; Indigenous peoples of, 167, 170, 173–74, 176, 177, 180–81; early exploration/mining in, 167–68; formation of, 167; government-industry negotiations in, 173–77, 180–81; imperial entrepreneurs in, 168–70; and implications of continental shelf exploration, 177–80; Owerri opposition to oil industry in, 173–74, 176, 180–81; US oil companies in, 177, 179–80

Nigeria Bitumen Corporation, 168

Nigerian Electricity Supply Corporation, 168

Nordic countries, resource regulation in (1880–1940), 12, 45–62, 343, 345–47, 350–53; and crofters' rights, 48, 51, 53, 57–58, 59–60, 61; and economic development/GDP, 47; social engineering as factor in, 47–48, 49, 51–52, 53, 57–58. *See also* Denmark, resource regulation in; Finland; Norway, resources

regulated in; Sweden, resource regulation in

Nordic Sami Council, 284–86

Norske Samers Riksforbund (Sami organization), 287

North American Free Trade Agreement (NAFTA), 68, 69, 85

Northern Gateway pipeline (proposed), 87–88, 94n71

Norway, 9, 47, 122(t), 216, 268; Finnish resource ownership by, 58, 59; whaling by, 264, 265–66, 267. *See also entries below*

Norway, Indigenous rights to land/resources in. *See* Sami (Nordic Indigenous people)

Norway, resources regulated in, 53–57, 337(t), 338(t); electrochemical, 53–54, 55, 56; forestry, 53, 54, 55–56, 61; hydroelectric power, 53–55, 56, 62, 349–50; mining, 53, 54, 55, 56, 62; by repatriation, 56; by right of reversion, 54; by use of Concession Laws, 54–56, 61, 62, 346–47

Nouméa Accord (New Caledonia, 1988), 223

Novak, Alexander, 129

offshore exploration: Arctic, 271; in Brazil, 142–44, 143(f), 144(f), 146–47, 149, 150, 153, 161n72; in Japan, 340; in Nigeria, 177–80

oil and gas industry, Canadian, 68, 78, 79, 81–85, 89; and foreign ownership issue, 81–83; and National Energy Program, 68, 82–84, 85, 89; pipeline projects of, 68, 79, 81, 83, 86, 87–88

Olaya, Enrique, 110

Ontario, 69, 70; hydroelectric power in, 75–77, 79, 86; mining/minerals in, 72–73, 74(f), 78, 87, 89n2; timber/pulp and paper in, 71–72, 78. *See also* International Nickel Company (INCO)

Ontario Hydro, 76–77, 92n41

Ontario Power Company (OPC), 76

Ontario Water Resources Commission, 80

Organisation for European Economic Co-operation (OEEC), 304, 305–8

Organization of the Petroleum Exporting Countries (OPEC), 82, 106, 311

Ospina, Mariano, 111

Otnes, Per, 288

Outokumpu Company (Finland), 59–60

Owerri region (Nigeria), 173–74, 176, 180–81

Paddon, James, 211

Pan American International Oil Company, 179

Paris Peace Conference (1919), 278; and Treaty of Versailles, 249

Partnership and Cooperation Agreements (PCAs), 318

Pearson and Son (British oil company), 108–9

Pérez Jiménez, Marcos, 106

Persia. *See* Iran, oil regulation in

Petro Canada, 83, 84

Petrobras (Petróleo Brasileiro S.A.): formation/functioning of, as state-owned enterprise, 141–42, 144–50, 154–55, 158n37, 344, 350, 351; and industry corruption scandal, 154, 155n1, 160n65, 160n68, 161n74; international partners of, 147, 152, 154; offshore accidents of, 153, 161n72; offshore/pre-salt deposits extracted by, 142–44, 143(f), 146–47, 149, 150, 153; regulation of, 144–47; regulation of, in open market environment, 147–50, 159n50; and regulation of pre-salt extraction, 150–54

Petróleos de Venezuela (PDVSA), 96–97, 106–7, 113

Petroleum Law (Brazil): (1953), 141; (1997), 148–49, 160n64

Petsamo nickel deposit (Finland), 60

philately, in Antarctica, 272

pipelines: in Brazil, 148–49; in Canada, 68, 79, 81, 83, 86, 87–88; in Colombia, 109; in Iran,190, 194; in Japan, 329; in Russia, 129

Pollution Control Act (BC, 1967), 80

Pompidou, Georges, 219, 220

Potash Corporation (Saskatchewan), 79, 90n6

Poynton, Hilton, 179

Prebisch, Raúl, 9

Pré-Sal Petróleo S.A. (PPSA, Brazil), 151–53, 154

pre-salt petroleum deposits, in Brazil, 150–54

Putin, Vladimir, 13, 119, 121–34, 134n1; and cronyism, 122, 123, 133; vs oil oligarchs, 121; tax system of, 124–32. *See also* Russia, oil tax system of, *and entry following*

Quebec, 70, 71, 78, 79, 83, 88; hydroelectric industry in, 77, 79

Queensland (Australia), 25, 26(t), 32–34; democracy/political institutions in, 33–34, 37(t), 41; dominance of pastoralism in, 32–34, 39; gold discovery in, 24, 33; labour radicalization in, 34

rare metals/rare earth minerals: Antarctic search for, 271; countries as sources of, 303(t), 311, 314, 315–16, 318, 319, 330, 335; European trade policy on, 304, 318; Japan's need to import, 330–31, 332, 333, 335–36; recycling as source of, 330, 336

Rathenau, Walther, 233, 251

raw materials, international regulation of, after First World War, 15, 231–52, 344, 347–48; and colonial mandate system, 235–36, 239–40, 244–45, 246, 248–49, 250, 252; commercial policy disagreements over, 235–36; commodity cartels as barrier to, 232, 240–42, 243–44, 246, 248; effect of stock market crash/Great Depression

Index

on, 242–44; European and American views on, 233–35; failure of, 249–50; and "have-not" states' economic demands/territorial aggression, 244–49, 250; initial League of Nations involvement in, 237–38; League-appointed inquiry into, 246–49; opposition to restrictive nature of, 241–42; rationalization approach to, 238–42, 243, 251; wartime models for, 232–33

Raw Materials Initiative (RMI), of EU, 302, 304, 312, 313, 316–17, 319

raw materials strategies, of postwar Europe, 16, 302–20; early default intraregionalism, 304–8; inter-regionalism (1950s–60s), 308–10; community-level multilateralism (1960s–70s), 310–13; return to interregionalism (mid-1970s–early 2000s), 313–15; global multilateralism (early 2000s on), 315–18; table summarizing, 304(t)

Rees-Williams, David, 176

Repsol (Spanish energy company), 152

"resource curse," 9–10, 23, 123–24, 166

resource nationalism, 5–8, 10–11, 342–45, 346, 350–51; in Canada, 13, 67–68, 70–84, 88–89; EU and, 302–3, 316, 319–20; in Russia, 118–19, 133. *See also* foreign ownership issue; national oil companies, *and entry following*; Petrobras

resource regulation, 3–16, 341–52; in domestic settings, 11, 12–14; history of, 5–8; imperialism and, 11, 14–15; internationalization of, 12, 15–16; and "resource curse," 9–10, 23, 123–24, 166; theories of, 8–11 ; UN resolution on, 7

resource rent(s), 8, 9–10, 61, 348–49, 350; definition of, 4; good management of, 76–77, 119–20; small vs big coalitions and, 122–23. *See also* Russia, resource rent management in

Restriction Act (Sweden, 1916), 51, 55

Reza Shah Pahlavi, Shah of Iran, 190–91

"Ring of Fire" (Ontario), mineral/chromite deposits in, 87, 89n2

Rio Tinto (Spanish mining company), 346

Robe, Frederick, 38

Rojas Pinilla, Gustavo, 111

Roosevelt, Franklin D., 220, 245, 250

Rose, Duncan, 182n12

Rosneft (Russian energy company), 121, 128

Rothschild family, of Paris, 212, 214, 219, 221

Royal Dutch Shell, 104, 145, 152, 154, 166, 169, 171, 193. *See also* Shell-BP; Shell D'Arcy

Russia, 329(t), 344; and Nordic countries, 50, 57–58, 59, 61; as rare metal/rare earth exporter, 303(t), 311, 316, 318, 335; Sami in, 281. *See also entries below*; Soviet Union

Russia, oil and gas regions in: continental shelf/Arctic, 127–29; East Siberia, 128, 136n31; Khanty-Mansiisk region, 129–30; West Siberia, 120–21, 127–28, 132

Russia, oil tax system in, 124–32; and brownfield vs "frontier" oil output, 127–29, 131–32, 136n31; and energy/finance ministries' competing tax proposals, 129–32; and producers' tax concession demands, 127–29, 131–32; Putin's interventions in, 130–31

Russia, resource rent management in, 13, 118–34, 345; and absence of democracy, 118–19, 122–23, 133–34; administrative/technical capacity for, 119–22, 124–25; and cronyism, 122, 123, 133; and crude oil output (2000–13), 126, 127(f); and "Dutch disease," 124, 133–34; and minerals extraction tax, 126, 128–29; and oil rents, as percentage of GDP (2013), 121, 122(f); and oil tax system, 124–32; by small vs big coalitions, 122–23, 124–25, 133–34; success or failure of, 123–24. *See also* Putin, Vladimir; Soviet Union

Sachs, Jeffrey, and Andrew Warner, 9
Salter, Arthur, 231, 239
Sami (Nordic Indigenous people), 12, 15–16, 277–95, 348–49, 351; and Alta River hydro dam, 277, 288–89; background/early history of, 281; Council of, 284–86; and early international norms, 281–87; and early UN/ILO Indigenous rights work, 277–80; and ILO convention, as not ratified by Norway, 16, 277, 280, 284–85, 289–90; and international framing of rights, 287–90; language of, 281, 282–83, 285, 286; Norway's early governance/assimilation of, 281–83; Parliament of, 288, 292–94; reindeer husbandry by, 277, 281, 283, 285, 286–88, 289; as residents of Finnmark plateau, 277, 281–92; and rise of Indigenous economic activism, 290–94; saltwater fishing by, 293
Sami Rights Commission (Norway), 291–92
Santos, Juan Manuel, 97
Schacht, Hjalmar, 246
Schuman, Robert, 306, 308
scientific research, in Antarctica, 261, 268–69, 272
sealing, in Antarctica, 259, 260–62, 263, 273
selectorate theory of political survival, 98–100, 112–13. *See also* Colombia, oil industry in; Venezuela, oil industry in
Shell-BP (Nigeria), 177–80
Shell D'Arcy (Nigeria), 171–73, 177
Sherritt Gordon Mines Limited, 215
ship registration, in Antarctica, 272
Siberia, oil and gas production in, 120–21, 127–28, 132, 136n31

Siluanov, Anton, 130
Singer, Hans, 9
Sinochem (Chinese oil company), 152
Smith, Adam, 235
Smith, Carsten, 291
Smuts, Jan, 234
Soames, Christopher, 320
Société Caledonia, 212
Société Le Nickel (SLN), 14–15, 211–22; establishment/early years of, 211–13; French support of, 216–22, 224; and INCO, 210, 212–13, 215–16, 219–20, 221, 226n6; and Kaiser Aluminum, 222; New Caledonians' hostility/opposition to, 213–14, 217, 220–21, 224–25
Socony Mobil Oil Company. *See entry below*
Socony-Vacuum Oil Company: in Iran, 193; in Nigeria, 177, 179
softwood lumber dispute, Canada-US, 85, 94n62
South Africa, 268, 286; as rare metal/rare earth exporter, 311, 314, 316, 330, 335
South Australia, 25, 27(t), 36–39; copper discovered in, 36, 38–39; democracy/political institutions in, 29, 36, 37(t), 38–39, 42; minerals as private resource in, 38; pastoralists in, 36, 38–39
Soviet Union, 61, 135n11, 311; and Antarctica, 268, 270; and Iranian oil, 188–89, 190, 191; nationalizations in, 7, 343; resource economy in, 7, 120–21, 122–23, 124, 125, 127, 132–33, 134n1. *See also* Russia, *and entries following*
Special (later Scientific) Committee on Antarctic Research (SCAR), 268
Spinelli, Altiero, 312
St. Laurent, Louis, 79
St. Lawrence Seaway, 79, 86
Stalin, Joseph, 120
Standard Oil Company, 196, 197–98; breakup of, 349

Index

Standard Oil Company of California (Socal), 179, 193

Standard Oil Company of New Jersey: in Brazil, 145; in Colombia, 107–8, 110, 111; in Iran, 193; in Nigeria, 179

Standard Oil Company of New York. *See* Socony-Vacuum Oil Company

Statoil (Norwegian energy company), 152

Stevenson Restriction Scheme (British plan to stabilize rubber prices), 240–41

Stikker, Dirk, 307

stock market crash (1929), 231, 242

Stoltenberg, Thorvald, 289

Strangways Act (South Australia, 1869), 36, 38

Sudbury, ON: nickel deposits/mining in, 72, 73, 86, 211, 224

Suez Crisis, 179

Sweden, resource regulation in, 49–53, 345; of forestry, 46, 49, 51–52, 53, 61; of hydroelectric power, 52, 350; of iron ore, 46, 49–53, 347, 351; Sami and, 281, 284, 288; of water, 52

Tarrow, Sidney, 291

Tasmania, 26(t), 34–36; as convict settlement, 25, 34; democracy/ political institutions in, 29, 35–36, 37(t); gold rush exodus from, 34; pastoralism in, 34, 36; tin and copper in, 34–35

Távora, Juarez, 145

Texas Company (Texaco), 193

Tiebaghi nickel mine (New Caledonia): INCO's operation of, 224, 228*n*37

timber/pulp and paper industries: in Canada, 71–72, 74, 78, 85, 94*n*62; in Sweden, 46, 49, 51–52, 53, 61. *See also* forests and forestry products

Tønnesen, Sverre, 281

Total (French energy company), 154

tourism, in Antarctica, 259, 261, 273; regulation of, 271–72

Transatlantic Trade and Investment Partnership (TTIP), 318, 319

TransCanada Corporation, Energy East project of, 87, 88

TransCanada Pipeline, 79, 81

Trans-Iranian Railway, 191

Trans-Pacific Partnership (TPP), 85

Treaty of Rome (1957), 309

Treaty of Versailles (1919), 249

Tropical Oil Company, 107–8, 109

Trudeau, Justin, government of, 86, 94*n*71

Trudeau, Pierre Elliott, government of, 82–84

Trump, Donald, 85

Tsilhqot'in First Nation, 87, 90*n*7

Union Calédonienne, 214, 217–18, 227*n*17, 227*n*19, 228*n*34

Union Oil Company, 147

United Africa Company, 172

United Kingdom. *See* Great Britain

United Nations, Indigenous rights provisions of, 7, 277, 279, 280, 290–92, 348; and First Nations of Canada, 290–91; and Sami of Norway, 285–86, 289, 291–92

United Nations Conference on Trade and Development (UNCTAD), 232, 252, 310, 312–13, 318

United Nations Convention on the Law of the Sea, 69

United Nations Declaration on the Rights of Indigenous Peoples, 7, 277, 348

United Nations Economic Commission for Europe, 305, 306–7

United Nations Food and Agricultural Organization, 280

United States: and Antarctica, 261, 266, 268; anti-trust laws in, 193, 198, 215, 348; and Canada, 68, 69, 70–72, 73, 74, 75–78, 79, 81–85, 94*n*62, 337(t), 338(t), 345, 347; and Colombia, 107–9, 110; energy self-sufficiency of, 329(t); and Indian oil industry, 198,

203; Indigenous peoples in, 279, 290; and Iranian nationalization crisis, 192–93, 203; and Japanese mining industry, 331; and League of Nations, 233–36, 241, 250; nickel industry in, 216, 220, 221, 222; and oil exploration in Nigeria, 177, 179–80; and postwar Europe, 305–6, 307, 308, 318, 319, 348

Universal Declaration of Human Rights, 286

Universal Postal Union, 240

Uribe, Alvaro, 97

USSR. *See* Soviet Union

Vargas, Getúlio, 141

Venezuela, oil industry in, 13, 96–100, 100–7, 109, 112–13, 344, 345, 350; as analyzed using selectorate theory, 98–100, 112–13; under authoritarian (small coalition) regimes, 104–5, 112; under civilian (large coalition) governments, 105–7, 112–13; nationalization of, 96–97, 106–7, 113; production/export statistics for, 100, 101(f), 102(f); and total exports as percentage of GDP, 100, 103(f)

Victoria (Australia), 25, 26(t), 30–32, 42; democracy/political institutions in, 29, 31, 32, 34, 41; dominance of pastoralism in, 31, 32, 34, 39; gold discovery in, 24, 30–31, 36; mining licences/regulations in, 31–32; mining vs pastoralism in, 31–32, 33

Waitangi Treaty (New Zealand), 279, 290

West African Oil and Fuel Company, 168

Western Australia, 25, 39–41; democracy/political institutions in, 34, 35, 37(t), 39, 40–41; gold discovery in, 24, 39–40; pastoralism in, 39, 40; resource exports/legislation of, 27(t), 40

whaling, in Antarctica, 259, 260–67, 269, 273, 349; Allardyce's management of, 262–65; British/Norwegian quotas on, 265–66; conventions on, 266; and "full utilization" of carcass requirement, 263, 264, 266; and International Whaling Commission, 266–68; "scientific," by Japan, 267

Wheat Executive (1916), 233

Wilson, Woodrow, 234–35

Wold, Terje, 284, 286, 298n58

wool industry, in Australia, 26–27(t), 28, 30, 31, 34–35, 36, 39, 40

World Bank, 158n35, 305

World Conference Against Racism (UN, 1978), 289

World Economic Conference (League of Nations, 1927), 241–42

World Trade Organization (WTO), 304, 315, 317–19

Yaoundé Convention, 304, 309–10, 313, 319

Yukos (Russian oil and gas company), 121

Zeeland, Paul van, 250

Zimmern, Alfred, 235